CALIFORNIA

Life

elevate science

Pearson

Boston, Massachusetts   **Chandler, Arizona**
Glenview, Illinois   **New York, New York**

AUTHORS

You're an author!

As you write in this science book, your answers and personal discoveries will be recorded for you to keep, making this book unique to you. That is why you are one of the primary authors of this book.

✎ **In the space below, print your name, school, town, and state. Then write a short autobiography that includes your interests and accomplishments.**

YOUR NAME ....

SCHOOL ....

TOWN, STATE ....

AUTOBIOGRAPHY ....

....

....

....

....

Your Photo

Pearson Education, Inc. 330 Hudson Street, New York, NY 10013

 **Pearson**

ISBN-13:   978-1-418-27481-8
ISBN-10:   1-418-27481-X
4   19

Program Authors

ZIPPORAH MILLER, Ed.D.

Coordinator for K-12 Science Programs, Anne Arundel County Public Schools
Dr. Zipporah Miller currently serves as the Senior Manager for Organizational Learning with the Anne Arundel County Public School System. Prior to that she served as the K-12 Coordinator for science in Anne Arundel County. She conducts national training to science stakeholders on the Next Generation Science Standards. Dr. Miller also served as the Associate Executive Director for Professional Development Programs and conferences at the National Science Teachers Association (NSTA) and served as a reviewer during the development of Next Generation Science Standards. Dr. Miller holds a doctoral degree from the University of Maryland College Park, a master's degree in school administration and supervision from Bowie State University and a bachelor's degree from Chadron State College.

MICHAEL J. PADILLA, Ph.D.

Professor Emeritus, Eugene P. Moore School of Education, Clemson University, Clemson, South Carolina
Michael J. Padilla taught science in middle and secondary schools, has more than 30 years of experience educating middle-school science teachers, and served as one of the writers of the 1996 U.S. National Science Education Standards. In recent years Mike has focused on teaching science to English Language Learners. His extensive experience as Principal Investigator on numerous National Science Foundation and U.S. Department of Education grants resulted in more than $35 million in funding to improve science education. He served as president of the National Science Teachers Association, the world's largest science teaching organization, in 2005–6.

MICHAEL E. WYSESSION, Ph.D

Professor of Earth and Planetary Sciences, Washington University, St. Louis, Missouri
Author of more than 100 science and science education publications, Dr. Wysession was awarded the prestigious National Science Foundation Presidential Faculty Fellowship and Packard Foundation Fellowship for his research in geophysics, primarily focused on using seismic tomography to determine the forces driving plate tectonics. Dr. Wysession is also a leader in geoscience literacy and education; he is the chair of the Earth Science Literacy Initiative, the author of several popular video lectures on geology in the *Great Courses* series, and a lead writer of the *Next Generation Science Standards**.

REVIEWERS

Program Consultants

Carol Baker
Science Curriculum

Dr. Carol K. Baker is superintendent for Lyons Elementary K-8 School District in Lyons, Illinois. Prior to this, she was Director of Curriculum for Science and Music in Oak Lawn, Illinois. Before this she taught Physics and Earth Science for 18 years. In the recent past, Dr. Baker also wrote assessment questions for ACT (EXPLORE and PLAN), was elected president of the Illinois Science Teachers Association from 2011–2013, and served as a member of the Museum of Science and Industry (Chicago) advisory board. She is a writer of the Next Generation Science Standards. Dr. Baker received her B.S. in Physics and a science teaching certification. She completed her master's of Educational Administration (K-12) and earned her doctorate in Educational Leadership.

Jim Cummins
ELL

Dr. Cummins's research focuses on literacy development in multilingual schools and the role technology plays in learning across the curriculum. *Elevate Science* incorporates research-based principles for integrating language with the teaching of academic content based on Dr. Cummins's work.

Elfrieda Hiebert
Literacy

Dr. Hiebert, a former primary-school teacher, is President and CEO of TextProject, a non-profit aimed at providing open-access resources for instruction of beginning and struggling readers, She is also a research associate at the University of California Santa Cruz. Her research addresses how fluency, vocabulary, and knowledge can be fostered through appropriate texts, and her contributions have been recognized through awards such as the Oscar Causey Award for Outstanding Contributions to Reading Research (Literacy Research Association, 2015), Research to Practice award (American Educational Research Association, 2013), and the William S. Gray Citation of Merit Award for Outstanding Contributions to Reading Research (International Reading Association, 2008).

Content Reviewers

Alex Blom, Ph.D.
Associate Professor
Department Of Physical Sciences
Alverno College
Milwaukee, Wisconsin

Joy Branlund, Ph.D.
Department of Physical Science
Southwestern Illinois College
Granite City, Illinois

Judy Calhoun
Associate Professor
Physical Sciences
Alverno College
Milwaukee, Wisconsin

Stefan Debbert
Associate Professor of Chemistry
Lawrence University
Appleton, Wisconsin

Diane Doser
Professor
Department of Geological Sciences
University of Texas at El Paso
El Paso, Texas

Rick Duhrkopf, Ph.D.
Department of Biology
Baylor University
Waco, Texas

Jennifer Liang
University of Minnesota Duluth
Duluth, Minnesota

Heather Mernitz, Ph.D.
Associate Professor of Physical Sciences
Alverno College
Milwaukee, Wisconsin

Joseph McCullough, Ph.D.
Cabrillo College
Aptos, California

Katie M. Nemeth, Ph.D.
Assistant Professor
College of Science and Engineering
University of Minnesota Duluth
Duluth, Minnesota

Maik Pertermann
Department of Geology
Western Wyoming Community College
Rock Springs, Wyoming

Scott Rochette
Department of the Earth Sciences
The College at Brockport
State University of New York
Brockport, New York

David Schuster
Washington University in St Louis
St. Louis, Missouri

Shannon Stevenson
Department of Biology
University of Minnesota Duluth
Duluth, Minnesota

Paul Stoddard, Ph.D.
Department of Geology and Environmental Geosciences
Northern Illinois University
DeKalb, Illinois

Nancy Taylor
American Public University
Charles Town, West Virginia

Teacher Reviewers

Rita Armstrong
Los Cerritos Middle School
Thousand Oaks, California

Tyler C. Britt, Ed.S.
Curriculum & Instructional
Practice Coordinator
Raytown Quality Schools
Raytown, Missouri

Holly Bowser
Barstow High School
Barstow, California

David Budai
Coachella Valley Unified School District
Coachella, California

A. Colleen Campos
Grandview High School
Aurora, Colorado

Jodi DeRoos
Mojave River Academy
Colton, California

Colleen Duncan
Moore Middle School
Redlands, California

Nicole Hawke
Westside Elementary
Thermal, California

Margaret Henry
Lebanon Junior High School
Lebanon, Ohio

Ashley Humphrey
Riverside Preparatory Elementary
Oro Grande, California

Adrianne Kilzer
Riverside Preparatory Elementary
Oro Grande, California

Danielle King
Barstow Unified School District
Barstow, California

Kathryn Kooyman
Riverside Preparatory Elementary
Oro Grande, California

Esther Leonard M.Ed. and L.M.T.
Gifted and Talented Implementation Specialist
San Antonio Independent School District
San Antonio, Texas

Diana M. Maiorca, M.Ed.
Los Cerritos Middle School
Thousand Oaks, California

Kevin J. Maser, Ed.D.
H. Frank Carey Jr/Sr High School
Franklin Square, New York

Corey Mayle
Brogden Middle School
Durham, North Carolina

Keith McCarthy
George Washington Middle School
Wayne, New Jersey

Rudolph Patterson
Cobalt Institute of Math and Science
Victorville, California

Yolanda O. Peña
John F. Kennedy Junior High School
West Valley City, Utah

Stacey Phelps
Mojave River Academy
Oro Grande, California

Susan Pierce
Bryn Mawr Elementary
Redlands Unified School District
Redlands, California

Cristina Ramos
Mentone Elementary School
Redlands Unified School District
Mentone, California

Mary Regis
Franklin Elementary School
Redlands, California

Bryna Selig
Gaithersburg Middle School
Gaithersburg, Maryland

Pat (Patricia) Shane, Ph.D.
STEM & ELA Education Consultant
Chapel Hill, North Carolina

Elena Valencia
Coral Mountain Academy
Coachella, California

Janelle Vecchio
Mission Elementary School
Redlands, California

Brittney Wells
Riverside Preparatory Elementary
Oro Grande, California

Kristina Williams
Sequoia Middle School
Newbury Park, California

Safety Reviewers

Douglas Mandt, M.S.
Science Education Consultant
Edgewood, Washington

Juliana Textley, Ph.D.
Author, NSTA books on school science safety
Adjunct Professor
Lesley University
Cambridge, Massachusetts

Go to PearsonRealize.com to access your digital course.

VIDEO
- Public Health Advisor

INTERACTIVITY
- What All Living Things Have in Common
- Mom's Car Must Be Alive
- Classify It
- Life as a Single Cell
- Viruses by the Numbers
- Vaccines and Populations
- There's Something Going Around
- Modifying a Virus
- Different Cells, Different Jobs
- Identifying an Organism
- Organization of Organisms

VIRTUAL LAB

ASSESSMENT

eTEXT

APP

HANDS-ON LABS

uConnect Is It an Animal?

uInvestigate
- Cheek Cells
- Living Mysteries
- A Mystery Organism No More!
- Life In a Drop of Pond Water
- Algae and Other Plants

uDemonstrate
It's Alive!

Go to PearsonRealize.com to access your digital course.

▶ **VIDEO**
• Environmental Engineer

👆 **INTERACTIVITY**
• There's No Place Like Home
• An Ecological Mystery
• Factors Affecting Growth
• Energy Roles and Flows
• Living Things in an Ecosystem
• A Changing Ecosystem
• Cleaning an Oil Spill
• Cycles of Matter
• Earth's Recyclables

📱 **VIRTUAL LAB**
• Chesapeake Bay Ecosystem Crisis

☑ **ASSESSMENT**

📖 **eTEXT**

📱 **APP**

HANDS-ON LABS

uConnect Every Breath You Take

uInvestigate
• Elbow Room
• Observing Decomposition
• Following Water

uDemonstrate
Last Remains

TOPIC 3

Populations, Communities, and Ecosystems 104

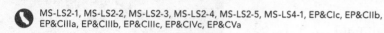

Essential Question How do living and nonliving things affect one another?

Quest KICKOFF To Cross or Not to Cross 106

MS-LS2-1, MS-LS2-2, MS-LS2-3, MS-LS2-4, MS-LS2-5, MS-LS4-1, EP&CIc, EP&CIIb, EP&CIIIa, EP&CIIIb, EP&CIIIc, EP&CIVc, EP&CVa

California Spotlight

California Floristic Province

Go to PearsonRealize.com to access your digital course.

▶ VIDEO
- Field Biologist

INTERACTIVITY
- Symbiotic Relationships
- Life on a Reef
- Shared Interactions
- Succession in an Ecosystem
- A Butterfly Mystery
- Biodiversity in the Amazon
- Human Impacts on Biodiversity
- Maintaining Healthy Ecosystems
- Preventing Soil Erosion
- Walk This Way

VIRTUAL LAB

ASSESSMENT

eTEXT

APP

HANDS-ON LABS

uConnect How Communities Change

uInvestigate
- Competition and Predation
- Primary or Secondary
- Modeling Keystone Species
- Ecosystem Impacts

uDemonstrate
Changes in Ecosystems

Go to PearsonRealize.com to access your digital course.

▶ VIDEO
• Illustrator

👆 INTERACTIVITY
• Through a Microscope • Functions of All Cells • A Strange Specimen • Structure Function Junction • Build a Cell • Specialized Cells • Cell Transport • Entering and Leaving the Cell • A Cell Divides • How Does a Broken Bone Heal? • The Cell Cycle • Making Food for Cells • From Sunlight to Sugar • Making Energy for Cells

📱 VIRTUAL LAB

☑ ASSESSMENT

📖 eTEXT

📱 APP

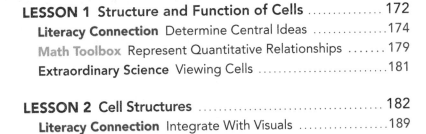

HANDS-ON LABS

uConnect What Can You See?

uInvestigate
• Observing Cells
• Comparing Cells
• Egg-speriment with a Cell
• Modeling Mitosis
• Energy From the Sun
• Exhaling Carbon Dioxide

uDemonstrate
Design and Build a Microscope

Go to PearconRealize.com to access your digital course.

▶ **VIDEO**
• Nutritionist

👆 **INTERACTIVITY**
• Human Body Systems • Interacting Systems • Balancing Act
• Communication and Homeostasis
• Joints • A Variety of Symptoms
• Bits and Pieces • Investigating Cells and Homeostasis • A Day in the Life of a Cell • Body Highways and Byways
• Testing a Training Plan • Circulatory System • Body Systems Revisited
• Humans vs. Computers • Flex Your Reflexes

📱 **VIRTUAL LAB**

☑ **ASSESSMENT**

📖 **eTEXT**

📱 **APP**

HANDS-ON LABS

иConnect How is Your Body Organized?

иInvestigate
• Observing Cells and Tissues
• Parts Working Together
• Measuring Calories
• Body Systems Working Together
• Parts of the Nervous System

иDemonstrate
Reaction Research

 MS-LS1-4, MS-LS1-5, MS-LS3-2, EP&CIIc, EP&CIVb

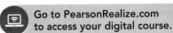

Go to PearsonRealize.com to access your digital course.

VIDEO
- Zookeeper

INTERACTIVITY
- Inheritance of Traits
- Animal Reproduction
- Twin Studies
- Designer Flowers
- Plants and Pollinators
- They're Acting Like Animals
- Fireflies
- See How They Grow
- Breeding Bigger Bovines
- Growing Crops

VIRTUAL LAB

ASSESSMENT

eTEXT

APP

HANDS-ON LABS

Connect To Care or Not to Care

Investigate
- Is It All in the Genes?
- Modeling Flowers
- Behavior Cycles
- Watching Roots Grow

Demonstrate
Clean and Green

xi

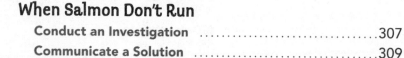

Go to PearsonRealize.com to access your digital course.

▶ **VIDEO**
• Genetic Counselor

👆 **INTERACTIVITY**
• Making Copies
• Offspring Season
• Look Inside
• Colorful Chromosome
• The Role of DNA
• Making Proteins
• Sex-Linked Traits and Disorders
• Track Your Traits
• DNA Fingerprinting
• Solving Problems with Genetics

📱 **VIRTUAL LAB**

☑ **ASSESSMENT**

📖 **eTEXT**

📱 **APP**

HANDS-ON LABS

иConnect Making More

иInvestigate
• Observing Pistils and Stamens
• Chromosomes and Inheritance
• Modeling Protein Synthesis
• Observing Traits
• Extraction in Action

иDemonstrate
Make the Right Call!

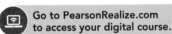
Go to PearsonRealize.com to access your digital course.

 VIDEO
• Evolutionary Biologist

 **INTERACTIVITY**
• Mystery on the Galapagos Islands
• Animal Feeding Adaptations
• Adaptations and Variations • Mice Selection on the Prairie • Species Adaptations • Lessons from the Potato Famine • Mutations Aren't All that Bad • Separated Species • Along the Canyon Wall • Legs, Arms, Wings, Flippers • Tiny Clues • Fossils Around the World • Tree of Life • Long Necks and Hoofed Feet

VIRTUAL LAB

ASSESSMENT

eTEXT

APP

HANDS-ON LABS

Connect Fins and Limbs!

Investigate
• How Do Species Change Over Time?
• Variation in a Population
• Adaptations of Birds
• Finding Proof
• Evidence of Evolution

Demonstrate
A Bony Puzzle

Elevate your thinking!

California Elevate Science takes science to a whole new level and lets you take ownership of your learning. Explore science in the world around you. Investigate how things work. Think critically and solve problems! *California Elevate Science* helps you think like a scientist, so you're ready for a world of discoveries.

Exploring California

California spotlights explore California phenomena. Topic Quests help connect lesson concepts together and reflect 3-dimensional learning.

- Science concepts organized around phenomena
- Topics weave together 3-D learning
- Engineering focused on solving problems and improving designs

California Spotlight
Instructional Segment 2

Before the Topics
Identify the Problem

California Flood Management

Phenomenon In February of 2017, workers at the Orov...

Quest KICKOFF

How can you use solids, liquids, and gases to lift a car?

STEM Phenomenon Auto mechanics often need to go under cars to repair the parts in the under-carriage, such as the shocks and exhaust ...

Student Discourse

California Elevate Science promotes active discussion, higher order thinking and analysis and prepares you for high school through:

- High-level write-in prompts
- Evidence-based arguments
- Practice in speaking and writing

Model It !

Crystalline and Amorphous Solids
Figure 5 ✏ A pat of butter is an amorphous solid. The particles that make up the butter are not arranged in a regular pattern. The sapphire gem stones are crystalline solids. Draw what you think the particles look like in a crystalline solid.

☑ **READING CHECK** Explain In your own words, explain the main differences between crystalline solids and amorphous solids.

Quest CHECK-IN

In this lesson, you learned what happens to the particles of substances during melting, freezing, evaporation, boiling, condensation, and sublimation. You also thought about how thermal energy plays a role in these changes of state.

Predict Why do you need to take the temperature of the surroundings into consideration when designing a system with materials that can change state?

Academic Vocabulary

In orange juice, bits of pulp are suspended in liquid. Explain what you think *suspended* means.

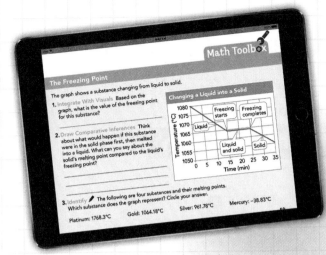

Build Literacy Skills

By connecting science to other disciplines like:

- Mathematics
- Reading and Writing
- STEM/Engineering

Focus on Inquiry

Case studies put you in the shoes of a scientist to solve real-world mysteries using real data. You will be able to:

- Analyze data
- Formulate claims
- Build evidence-based arguments

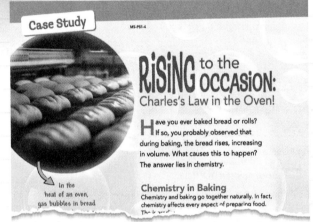

Case Study

MS-PS1-4

RISING to the OCCASION:
Charles's Law in the Oven!

Have you ever baked bread or rolls? If so, you probably observed that during baking, the bread rises, increasing in volume. What causes this to happen? The answer lies in chemistry.

Chemistry in Baking

Chemistry and baking go together naturally. In fact, chemistry affects every aspect of preparing food.

In the heat of an oven, gas bubbles in bread

Enter the Digital Classroom

Virtual labs, 3-D expeditions, and dynamic videos take science beyond the classroom.

- Open-ended virtual labs
- Google Expeditions and field trips
- NBC Learn videos

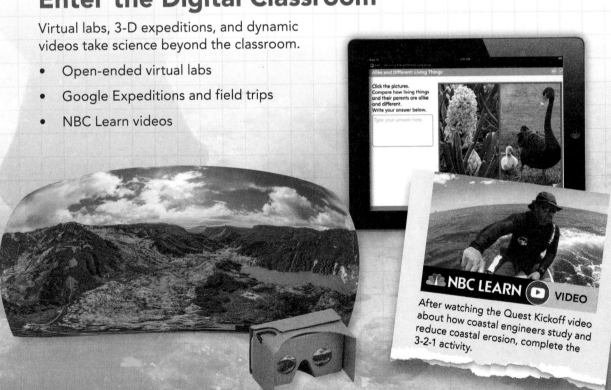

NBC LEARN VIDEO

After watching the Quest Kickoff video about how coastal engineers study and reduce coastal erosion, complete the 3-2-1 activity.

MS-LS1-1, MS-LS1-2, MS-LS1-3,
MS-LS2-1, MS-LS2-2, MS-LS2-3,
MS-LS2-4 MS-LS2-5, EP&CIb, EP&CIc,
EP&CIIa, EP&CIIb, EP&CIIc, EP&CIIIc,
EP&CIVc, EP&CVa

Guiding Questions

- How do parts of an ecosystem interact?
- How does natural selection relate to ecosystem changes?
- How do people affect ecosystems? Which activities have a positive impact and which negative?

Topics

1 Living Things in the Biosphere
2 Ecosystems
3 Populations, Communities and Ecosystems

Before the Topics
Identify the Problem

California Floristic Province

Phenomenon California is one of the most biologically diverse places in the world! The state is home to an amazing number of different plant and animal species.

However, the needs of an increasing human population can make it difficult to protect California's biodiversity.

View of the California coastline from the Bixby Bridge in Big Sur

Biodiversity Hotspots

Scientists have identified several areas on Earth as being *biodiversity hotspots*. A biodiversity hotspot is an area that supports an especially high number of endemic species that do not exist anywhere else, and is also rapidly losing biodiversity. Hotspots are critical to global biodiversity. Only two biodiversity hotspots exist in North America; the California Floristic Province is one of them.

The California Floristic Province is characterized by hot, dry summers and cool, wet winters. It is considered to be a Mediterranean climate. The California Floristic Province is made up of many different habitats and ecosystems such as mountains, volcanoes, deserts, forests, salt marshes, and vernal pools. These diverse ecosystems are home to 3,488 species of plants, of which 2,124 are endemic, or native.

A variety of organisms interact with one another in the California Floristic Providence. The table below shows the number of diverse and endemic species that have been identified.

The California Floristic Province begins in southwestern Oregon, covers a majority of California, and ends in northwest Baja California, Mexico.

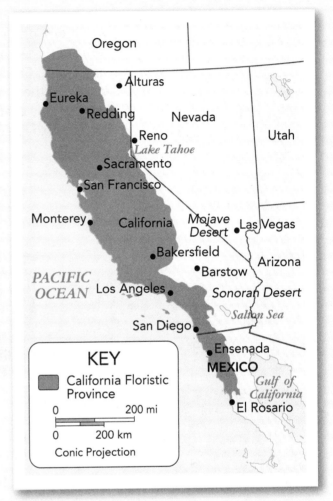

KEY

California Floristic Province

0   200 mi

0   200 km

Conic Projection

SEP Use Mathematics 🖊

Complete the table by calculating the percentage of each category of endemic species.

Types of Organism	Species	Endemic Species	Percent Endemic
Plants	3,488	2,124	
Mammals	157	18	
Birds	340	8	
Reptiles	69	4	
Amphibians	46	25	
Freshwater Fishes	73	15	

Physical Diversity of California

The landscape of California is due in large part to geological and other natural processes. As tectonic plates have moved, shifted, and collided with one another, landforms and geographic features have formed. Earthquake fault lines, volcanoes, and mountains are some examples. Over time, some of these landforms eroded and contributed to the soil. As a result, California is known to have the greatest diversity of soils in the U.S. Soil provides a resource that has allowed such diverse and endemic plant life to thrive in the California Floristic Province.

California's landscape is due to the movement of Earth's plates, which has resulted in volcanoes, mountains, and earthquakes.

San Andreas fault, near Santa Margarita, California

Mt. Lassen, an active volcano in the northeastern part of the state, near Mineral, California

Mt. Whitney, the tallest mountain in the contiguous United States, near Lone Pine, California

Threats to the Province

As California's human population increases, so does the demand for basic needs such as housing, food, and energy. Each of these needs is an example of an ecosystem service—a benefit that humans receive from ecosystems. To meet the demands of a growing human population, habitats are often destroyed to make room for new homes, roads, agriculture, and the extraction of energy sources such as oil. When we destroy habitats, the natural cycling that occurs between living organisms and non-living things is disrupted. These actions can also cause different types of pollution and erosion.

Commercial agriculture and farming are not only important to the residents of California, but also to the rest of the country. The rich soils in the California Floristic Province allow for plant diversity, and they help to generate many of the agricultural products consumed in the U.S. Scientists estimate that 75% of the vegetation that was originally found in the California Floristic Province has been damaged or lost.

About 43 million acres of California's land are used for agriculture. Grazing land takes up 16 million acres, while there are 27 million acres of cropland.

SEP Construct Explanations How do natural processes and human activities impact biodiversity and ecosystem services in the California Floristic Province?

....

....

....

Protecting the Province

Throughout this segment, you will learn about the common characteristics of all living things, how energy and matter flow through ecosystems, and the factors that affect populations and communities of organisms. Scientists need to understand the relationships between Earth's natural processes, ecosystems, and the role of humans in order to protect the California Floristic Province.

California is often thought to be a forerunner in establishing conservation efforts and environmental policies. For example, the California Biodiversity Council was established in 1991 to help improve cooperation between environmental preservation and conservation groups at the federal, state, and local levels. Members of the council exchange ideas, solve problems, and discuss and develop strategies to conserve California's biodiversity. While steps have been taken to preserve the biodiversity of the California Floristic Province hotspot, more still needs to be done. Currently, only 37 percent of the total land area of the California Floristic Province is officially protected.

Establishing national parks and breeding programs are just some examples of how biodiversity has been protected in California.

The largest trees in the world grow in the protected lands of Sequoia National Park, near Visalia, California.

The California condor, the largest bird in North America, is found within the California Floristic Province.

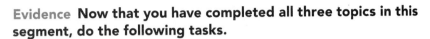

After the Topics
Conduct an Investigation

Evidence **Now that you have completed all three topics in this segment, do the following tasks.**

Collaborative Conversations ✎ With a partner, discuss what you have learned in this segment and how it relates to the California Floristic Province. Then, develop and expand the graphic organizer below to include evidence from this segment that helps to explain how natural processes and human activities impact biodiversity and ecosystem services in the province.

Natural Processess

California Floristic Province

Human Activities

Research an Endemic Species

Case Study Now that you have identified evidence that helps to explain how natural processes and human activities impact biodiversity and ecosystem services in the California Floristic Province, you will take a closer look at how those factors affect a specific species. There are many species that exist only in California and nowhere else in the world. These endemic species are often the focus of conservation efforts within the California Floristic Province.

To learn more about the endemics species found in the California Floristic Province and what actions are being taken to preserve them, identify a specific species you want to learn more about. It could be a plant, mammal, bird, reptile, amphibian, or freshwater fish.

Now research your chosen species to learn more about it. You will want to identify and learn about the ecosystem the species lives in. You will need to understand how the species interacts with other organisms within the ecosystem. You will also need to consider how environmental changes could impact the ecosystem and how that might affect the species over time. It will also be important to investigate how human activities have impacted the ecosystem and the species. Use your completed graphic organizer as a guide for your research regarding the impact of natural processes and human activities on your species. Finally, identify any actions that have been put in place to protect your species.

These organisms are examples of endemic organisms found within the California Floristic Province.

San Francisco garter snake

San Joaquin kit fox

Communicate a Solution

Based on your research, answer the following questions.

1. **SEP Communicate Information** Describe the species you researched, the ecosystem it lives in, and how it interacts with other organisms.

....

....

....

....

....

2. **CCC Stability and Change** What sort of environmental changes impact this ecosystem? Explain how your species is affected.

....

....

....

....

....

....

3. **CCC Cause and Effect** What human activities affect this ecosystem? Explain how your species is affected.

....

....

....

4. **SEP Construct Explanations** At the beginning of this segment, you made a claim about the impact of natural processes and human activity on biodiversity and ecosystem services in the California Floristic Province. Using evidence from the segment and your research, explain how the evidence supports your claim.

....

....

....

....

Living Things in the Biosphere

How can this tree be organized into a group?

MS-LS1-1 Conduct an investigation to provide evidence that living things are made of cells; either one cell or many different numbers and types of cells.

MS-LS1-2 Develop and use a model to describe the function of a cell as a whole and ways parts of cells contribute to the function

MS-LS1-3 Use argument supported by evidence for how the body is a system of interacting subsystems composed of groups of cells.

MS-LS4-2 Apply scientific ideas to construct an explanation for the anatomical similarities and differences among modern organisms and between modern and fossil organisms to infer evolutionary relationships.

MS-ETS1-1 Define the criteria and constraints of a design problem with sufficient precision to ensure a successful solution, taking into account relevant scientific principles and potential impacts on people and the natural environment that may limit possible solutions.

MS-ETS1-2 Evaluate competing design solutions using a systematic process to determine how well they meet the criteria and constraints of the problem.

MS-ETS1-3 Analyze data from tests to determine similarities and differences among several design solutions to identify the best characteristics of each that can be combined into a new solution to better meet the criteria for success.

MS-ETS1-4 Develop a model to generate data for iterative testing and modification of a proposed object, tool, or process such that an optimal design can be achieved.

- ▶ VIDEO
- 👆 INTERACTIVITY
- 📱 VIRTUAL LAB
- ☑ ASSESSMENT
- 📖 eTEXT
- ⚗ HANDS-ON LABS

HANDS-ON LAB

uConnect Expand your knowledge of what might be an animal.

The Essential Question

How do scientists define and organize living things?

CCC Patterns Many redwood trees, like these Coastal Redwood trees located in Prairie Creek State Park, California, are resistant to wildfires. The center of a mature Coastal Redwood tree is often burned, leaving a hollowed-out fire cave. Coastal Redwood trees can live for several years with the center of the tree missing. For many other trees, a wildfire like the one these trees experienced would kill them. How could scientists organize types of trees?

....

....

....

....

Quest KICKOFF

How can you design a field guide to organize living things?

Phenomenon A 2011 scientific study estimates that there are around 8.7 million species on our planet (give or take 1.3 million). Guess how many species have actually been identified! About two million. To identify these new organisms, taxonomists look at characteristics. Taxonomy is the branch of science that classifies organisms. In this problem-based Quest activity, you will be a taxonomist! You will design a field guide to help people identify the organisms they may see at a nature center. By applying what you learn in each lesson, digital activity, or hands-on lab, you will gather key Quest information. With this information, you will develop your field guide in the Findings activity.

👆 **INTERACTIVITY**

Sort Out Those Organisms

 MS-LS4-2

NBC LEARN ▶ VIDEO

After watching the Quest Kickoff video about discovering and categorizing organisms, choose two organisms that you observe in your daily life. Complete the Venn diagram by describing what makes them similar and different.

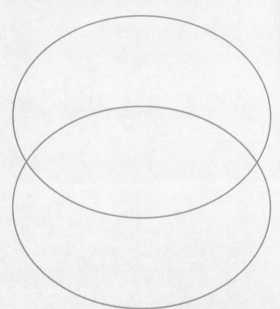

Quest CHECK-IN

IN LESSON 1

What do all living things have in common? Analyze specimens to determine whether they are living or nonliving.

👆 **INTERACTIVITY**

Under the Microscope

Quest CHECK-IN

IN LESSON 2

What characteristics do taxonomists consider when grouping organisms? Model a scientific classification system using seeds.

HANDS-ON LAB

Classifying Seeds

Quest CHECK-IN

IN LESSON 3

What distinguishes unicellular and multicellular organisms? Classify organisms based on their characteristics as unicellular or multicellular.

👆 **INTERACTIVITY**

Discovering Rainforest Organisms

This plant can be identified by making detailed observations about its characteristics and comparing those observations to descriptions in a field guide.

Quest CHECK-IN

IN LESSON 4

How are plants and animals different from other organisms and from each other? Discover more rainforest organisms.

INTERACTIVITY

Multicellular Rainforest Organisms

Quest FINDINGS

Complete the Quest!

Identify the criteria and constraints for your field guide. Then create a field guide that will help people identify different organisms in a local nature center.

INTERACTIVITY

Create Your Field Guide

① Living Things

Guiding Questions

- What evidence is there that all living things are made of cells?
- Where do living things come from?
- What do living things need to stay alive, grow, and reproduce?

Connection

Literacy Conduct Research Projects

 MS-LS1-1 Conduct an investigation to provide evidence that living things are made of cells; either one cell or many different numbers and types of cells.

HANDS-ON LAB

u**Investigate** Identify structures found in the cells of living things.

Vocabulary

organism
cell
unicellular
multicellular
stimulus
response
spontaneous
  generation
homeostasis

Academic Vocabulary

characteristics

Connect It !

✎ **Circle the things in the image that appear to be living.**

SEP Conduct an Investigation Suppose you scraped off some of the pale green stuff from the tree bark. How would you know whether it was alive or not? What observations would you note? What tests could you do to see whether it's alive?

....

....

....

Characteristics of Living Things

An **organism** is any living thing. It could be a horse, a tree, a mushroom, strep bacteria, or the lichens (LIE kins) in **Figure 1**. Some organisms are familiar and obviously alive. No one wonders whether a dog is an organism. Other organisms are a little harder to distinguish from nonliving things. Lichens, for example, can be very hard and gray. They don't seem to grow much from year to year. How can we separate living from non-living things? The answer is that all organisms share several important **characteristics**:

- All organisms are made of cells.
- All organisms contain similar chemicals and use energy.
- All organisms respond to their surroundings.
- All organisms grow, develop, and reproduce.

HANDS-ON LAB

Explore what makes a living thing alive.

Academic Vocabulary

A *characteristic* is a feature that helps to identify something. How would you describe the characteristics of a good movie or book?

....

....

....

....

....

Still Life with Lichens

Figure 1 Lichens blend in with the trees.

Characteristics of Living Things

Figure 2 All living things share certain characteristics.

SEP Determine Similarities What is the one characteristic that all living things and only living things have in common?

....

....

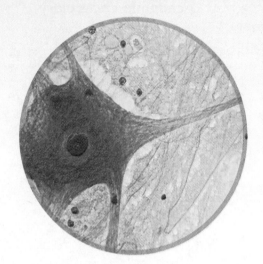

Cellular Organization All living things are made of smaller living units called cells. **Cells** are the basic unit of structure and function in living things. In a single-celled or **unicellular** organism, one cell carries out the functions necessary to stay alive. Organisms consisting of many cells are **multicellular**. You are a multicellular organism with trillions of cells specialized to do certain tasks. The nerve cell shown here sends electrical signals throughout your body. It may signal you to let go of something hot or to take a step. In a multicellular organism, all cells work together to keep the organism alive.

The Chemicals of Life All substances, including living cells, are made of chemicals. The most common chemical in cells is water, which is essential for life. Other chemicals, called carbohydrates (kahr boh HY drayts) provide the cell with energy. Proteins and lipids are chemicals used in building cells, much as wood and bricks are used to build schools. Finally, nucleic (noo KLEE ik) acids provide chemical instructions that tell cells how to carry out the functions of life. You've probably heard of DNA, deoxyribonucleic acid, but did you know what it looks like? You can see it at the right. The nucleic acid DNA directs the actions of every cell in your body.

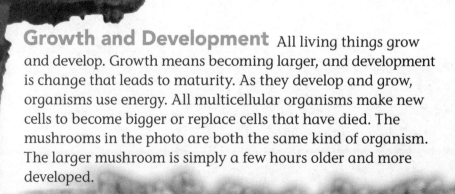

Growth and Development All living things grow and develop. Growth means becoming larger, and development is change that leads to maturity. As they develop and grow, organisms use energy. All multicellular organisms make new cells to become bigger or replace cells that have died. The mushrooms in the photo are both the same kind of organism. The larger mushroom is simply a few hours older and more developed.

Response to Surroundings Have you ever touched the palm of a baby's hand? If so, you may have observed the baby's fingers curl to grip your fingertip. The baby's grip is a natural reflex. Like a baby's curling fingers, all organisms react to changes in their surroundings. Any change or signal in the environment that can make an organism react in some way is called a **stimulus** (plural *stimuli*). Stimuli include changes in light, sound, flavors, or odors. An organism reacts to a stimulus with a **response**—an action or a change in behavior. Responding to stimuli helps the baby and all other organisms to survive and function.

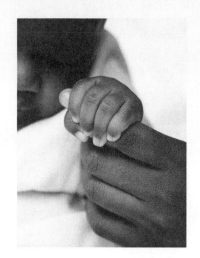

Reproduction Organisms reproduce to create offspring that are similar to the parent or parents. Some organisms reproduce asexually, creating an identical offspring with only one parent. One example is the young hydra (HY druh) budding off the parent hydra in the image. Mammals, birds, and most plants reproduce sexually. In sexual reproduction, two parents combine their DNA to create an offspring with a mix of both parents' characteristics.

Energy Use All organisms need energy to power their cells. Within an organism's cells, chemical reactions break down materials to get energy. Some organisms, called producers, can get energy from sunlight in a process known as photosynthesis, while other producers use different chemicals in their environment to make energy. Other organisms, called consumers, get energy by eating other living things. The shrew pictured here must eat more than its own weight in food every day. A shrew can starve to death if it goes five hours without eating!

HANDS-ON LAB

☐**Investigate** Identify structures found in the cells of living things.

Life Produces More Life

Every spring, wildflowers seem to pop up out of the ground from nowhere. Do the plants sprout directly from rocks and soil? No, we know that the new plants are reproduced from older plants. Four hundred years ago, however, people believed that life could appear from nonliving material. For example, when people saw flies swarming around spoiled meat, they concluded that the meat produced the flies. The mistaken idea that living things arise from nonliving sources is called **spontaneous generation**. It took hundreds of years and many experiments to convince people that spontaneous generation does not occur.

Redi's Experiment In the 1600s, an Italian doctor named Francesco Redi helped to prove spontaneous generation wrong. Redi investigated the source of the maggots that develop into adult flies on rotting meat. Redi performed a controlled experiment so he was certain about the cause of the results. In a controlled experiment, a scientist carries out two or more tests that are identical in every way except one. As shown in **Figure 3**, Redi set up two jars in the same location with meat in them. Then Redi changed just one variable in his experiment and watched to see what would happen.

Redi's Experiment
Figure 3 Redi showed that meat did not cause the spontaneous generation of flies.

Relate Text to Visuals
✏ Read the steps below. Then sketch steps 2 and 3.

Step 1 Redi placed meat in two identical jars. He covered one jar with a cloth that let in air, the control in the experiment.

Step 2 After a few days, Redi saw maggots (young flies) on the decaying meat in the open jar.

Step 3 Redi reasoned that flies had laid eggs on the meat in the open jar. The eggs hatched into maggots.

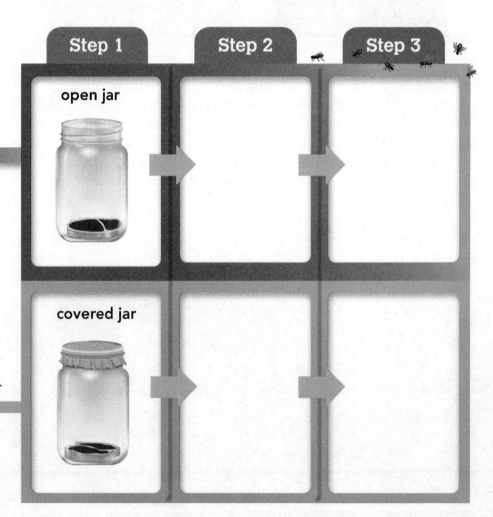

Pasteur's Experiment Even after Redi's experiment, many people continued to believe in spontaneous generation. Almost 200 years after Redi's experiment, French chemist Louis Pasteur (pah STUHR) decided to put spontaneous generation to the test. In his experiment, Pasteur used a control group. A control group is exposed to the same factors as the experimental group, except that it is not exposed to the variable being tested. **Figure 4** shows the experiment that convinced the scientific community that spontaneous generation was just a myth.

☑ CHECK POINT **Gather Information** How did both the Redi and Pasteur experiments prove there was no such thing as spontaneous generation?

....

....

....

Pasteur's Experiment
Figure 4 Pasteur carefully controlled his experiment.

1. Relate Text to Visuals
   ✎ Draw and label the flasks in steps 2 and 3. Label the control and experimental flasks.

2. Draw Conclusions
   What did the bacterial growth in Step 3 confirm for Pasteur?

....

....

....

Step 1	Step 2	Step 3
Pasteur put clear broth into flasks with curved necks. The necks let in air but kept out bacteria. He boiled the broth in the flasks to kill all bacteria present.	The boiled broth remained clear. Pasteur then set some of the flasks aside, just as they were.	The broth in these flasks remained clear. Pasteur concluded that bacteria could not arise from the broth.
	Pasteur broke the curved necks off the other flasks. Bacteria from the outside air were able to enter these flasks.	The broth in the broken flasks became cloudy, showing bacterial growth.

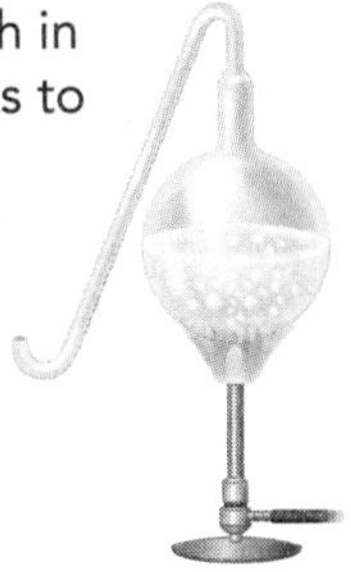

Literacy Connection

Conduct Research Projects

Use multiple print and online sources to gather information about the special properties of water. Can you find a good substitute for water?

Autotrophs and Heterotrophs

Figure 5 Every organism has to eat!

CCC Apply Concepts

✏ Write whether each organism is an autotroph or a heterotroph in the space provided.

Needs of Living Things

Though it may seem surprising, pine trees, worms, and all other organisms have the same basic needs as you do. All living things must satisfy their basic needs for water, food, living space, and homeostasis.

Water All living things depend on water for their survival. In fact, some organisms can live only for a few minutes without water. All cells need water to carry out their daily functions. Many substances dissolve easily in water. Once food or other chemicals are dissolved, they are easily transported around the body of an organism. About half of human blood is made of water. Our blood carries dissolved food, waste, and other chemicals to and from cells. Also, many chemical reactions that take place in cells require water.

Food All living things require food for energy. Some organisms, such as plants, capture the sun's energy and use it to make food through the process of photosynthesis. Producers are organisms that make their own food. Producers are also called autotrophs (AW toh trohfs). *Auto-* means "self" and *-troph* means "feeder." Autotrophs use the sun's energy to convert water and a gas into food.

Every organism that can't make its own food must eat other organisms. Consumers are organisms that cannot make their own food. Consumers are also called heterotrophs (HET uh roh trohfs). *Hetero-* means "other," so combined with *-troph* it means "one that feeds on others." A heterotroph may eat autotrophs, other heterotrophs, or break down dead organisms to get energy. **Figure 5** shows an interaction between autotrophs and heterotrophs.

Crocodile

Plan It

Can a Person Be an Autotroph?

Shelby and Michaela are learning about organisms. Shelby says she is sometimes an autotroph because she makes her own food after school, a bowl of cut fruit.

SEP Explain Phenomena How can Michaela prove to Shelby that she is not an autotroph? What could she do to help Shelby investigate how an autotroph makes their own food?

....

....

....

Space All organisms need a place to live—a place to get food and water and find shelter. Whether an organism lives in the savanna, as shown in **Figure 5**, or the desert, its surroundings must provide what it needs to survive. Because there is a limited amount of space on Earth, some organisms compete for space. Trees in a forest, for example, compete with other trees for sunlight. Below ground, their roots compete for water and minerals. If an organism loses its living space, it must move to a new place or it may die.

☑ **CHECK POINT** **Cite Textual Evidence** Why do living things need water, food, and space to live?

....

....

....

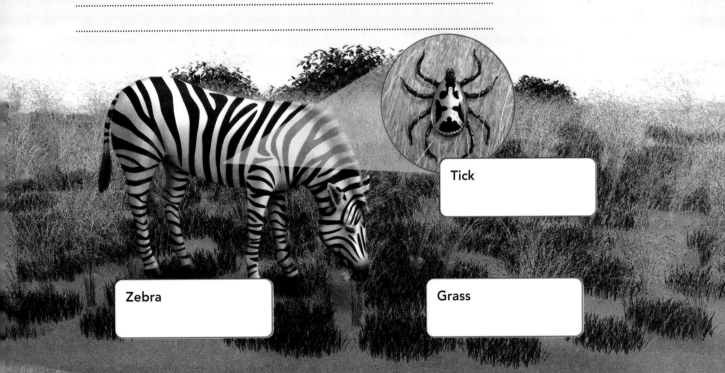

Tick

Zebra

Grass

INTERACTIVITY

Examine why an object that
has only a few characteristics
of living things is not living.

Salty Sneezes

Figure 6 Laysan albatrosses
are a common sight in
southern California. After
they dive to catch fish,
these albatrosses maintain
homeostasis by releasing
salty liquid through their bills.

CCC Apply Concepts
Which basic need is an
albatross meeting by
feeding on fish?

....

....

Homeostasis

Homeostasis When you go outside on a freezing cold
day, does your body temperature fall below freezing as well? Of
course not! Your body is able to keep the temperature of your
insides steady even when outside conditions change. Shivering
is one of many responses your body completes to help you stay
warm. The maintenance of stable internal conditions is called
homeostasis (hoh mee oh STAY sis). All organisms maintain
homeostasis to stay alive.

Organisms have many different methods for maintaining
homeostasis. The methods depend on the challenges faced
by the organism. Consider the Laysan albatross pictured in
Figure 6, which fishes around California's coasts. Albatrosses
swallow a lot of salty water when they dive to catch fish.
To maintain homeostasis, albatrosses need a way to get rid
of the extra salt. In a human, extra salt would be removed
in sweat, tears, or urine. The albatross has a different way of
maintaining homeostasis. They produce very salty liquid that
comes out of holes above their bills. A sort of sneezing clears
the salty liquid away. Homeostasis is maintained!

☑ **CHECK POINT** **Determine Central Ideas** The paws of
the Arctic fox are covered in thick fur. How does this help the fox
maintain homeostasis?

....

....

....

....

1. **SEP Stability and Change** Why is it necessary for organisms to maintain stable internal conditions?

....

....

2. **SEP Use Models** ✏ Draw a diagram showing all the things that an organism needs to survive. Label the drawing to show how the organism can meet its needs right where it lives.

3. **SEP Plan an Investigation** A student is designing a controlled experiment to test whether the amount of water that a plant receives affects its growth. Which factors should the student hold constant and which variable should the student change?

....

....

....

....

4. **SEP Construct Explanations** What sort of evidence can you use to show that all living things grow and develop?

....

....

....

....

....

....

....

....

....

....

Quest CHECK-IN

In this lesson, you learned about the characteristics of living things and where living things come from. You also learned about what living things need to grow, stay alive, and reproduce.

SEP Evaluate Your Plan What are your plans for your field guide? How will you use the characteristics of living things to identify and categorize different organisms?

....

....

....

....

INTERACTIVITY

Under the Microscope

Go online to observe different objects and determine whether they are living or nonliving.

2 Classification Systems

Guiding Questions

- How are living things classified into groups?
- How does the theory of evolution support the classification of organisms?

Connections

Literacy Assess Sources

Math Write an Expression

 MS-LS4-2 Apply scientific ideas to construct an explanation for the anatomical similarities and differences among modern organisms and between modern and fossil organisms to infer evolutionary relationships.

HANDS-ON LAB

uInvestigate Create a taxonomic key to classify different tree leaves.

Vocabulary

species
classification
genus
binomial
  nomenclature
taxonomy
domain
evolution
convergent
  evolution

Academic Vocabulary

determine

Connect It!

✏️ **Draw arrows and label parts of the organism that help you to identify it.**

SEP Make Observations What kind of living thing do you think this is? Explain.

....

....

....

Classifying Organisms

It is estimated that there are approximately 8.7 million species of organisms on the planet, with thousands more discovered each day. A **species** is a group of similar organisms that can mate with each other and produce offspring that can also mate and reproduce. Biologists place similar organisms into groups based on characteristics they have in common. **Classification** is the process of grouping things based on their similarities. To classify the organism in **Figure 1**, you'd first need to know about its characteristics. Then you could figure out which group it belonged to.

Linnaean Naming System

In the 1730s, biologist Carolus Linnaeus arranged organisms in groups based on their observable features. Then he gave each organism a two-part scientific name. The first word in the name is the organism's **genus**, a group of similar, closely-related organisms. The second word is the species and might describe where the organism lives or its appearance. This system in which each organism is given a unique, two-part scientific name that indicates its genus and species is known as **binomial nomenclature**. Today, scientists still use this naming system that classifies organisms according to their shared characteristics.

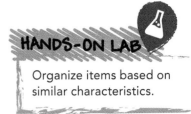

HANDS-ON LAB

Organize items based on similar characteristics.

Write About It Pick a favorite animal or plant. What is it that you find most interesting? In your science notebook, describe its characteristics.

Animal, Vegetable, or Mineral?
Figure 1 Some organisms are much harder to classify than others!

Literacy Connection

Assess Sources Books become outdated and the Internet is full of incorrect information. If you need an accurate answer to a scientific question, where would you look? Whom could you ask for help?

....

....

....

....

....

....

....

Taxonomy The scientific study of how organisms are classified is called **taxonomy** (tak SAHN uh mee). Scientists use taxonomy to identify the name of an unknown organism or to name a newly discovered organism. For example, if you look closely at the characteristics of the organism in **Figure 1**, you might classify it as a sea slug. It would then be simple to look up sea slugs and find out that they are animals related to slugs and snails. All sea slugs have sensitive tentacles that they use to smell, taste, and feel their way around. They eat other animals by scraping away their flesh. Sea slugs can even gain the ability to sting by eating stinging animals!

Domains In classification of organisms, the broadest level of organization is the **domain**. There are three domains: Eukarya, Archaea, and Bacteria. Eukarya (yoo KA ree uh) includes the familiar kingdoms of plants, animals, and fungi, and a less familiar kingdom, Protista, which has much simpler organisms. Members of Domain Eukarya are called eukaryotes. Eukaryotes have nuclei containing DNA. Domain Archaea (ahr KEE uh) contains a group of one-celled organisms with no nuclei in their cells. Members of Domain Bacteria, like Archaea, have only one cell and no nucleus, but bacteria have different structures and chemical processes from those of Archaea. **Figure 2** shows the levels of classification for Domain Eukarya.

✓ CHECK POINT **Determine Central Ideas** What do scientists use to determine how organisms are classified in each level? Explain your answer.

....

....

....

Model It !

So Many Levels of Classification!

There are ways to memorize a long list of terms so that you can remember them months or even years later. A mnemonic (nee MON ic) can help you memorize a list of terms in order. To create one type of mnemonic, you compose a sentence from words that start with the first letter of each term in the list. One popular mnemonic for levels of classification is: "Dear King Philip Come Over For Good Spaghetti." In the space, devise your own mnemonic to help you remember the levels of classification.

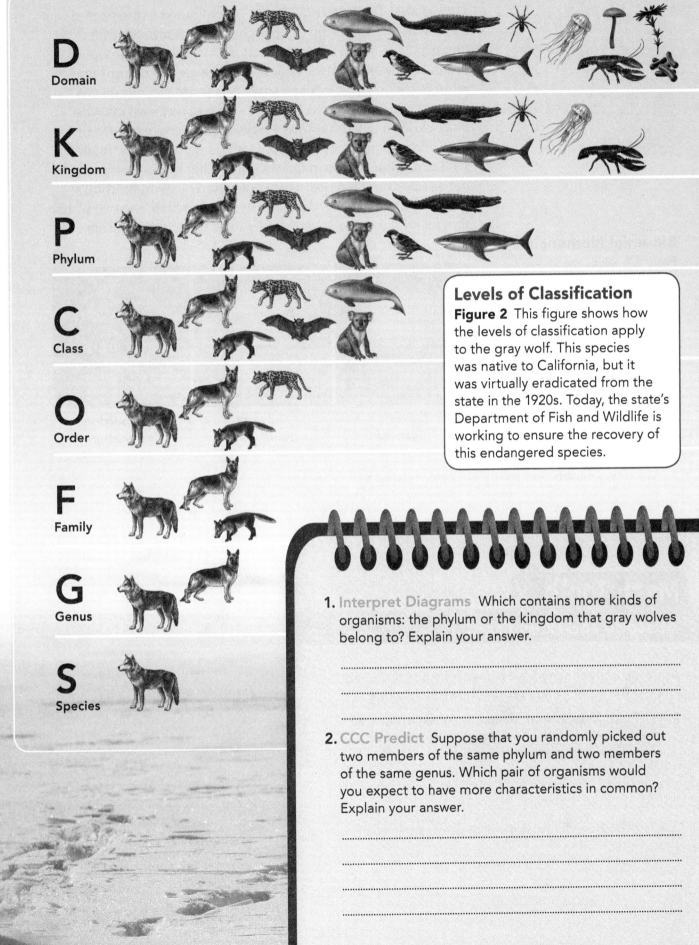

D Domain	
K Kingdom	
P Phylum	
C Class	
O Order	
F Family	
G Genus	
S Species	

Levels of Classification

Figure 2 This figure shows how the levels of classification apply to the gray wolf. This species was native to California, but it was virtually eradicated from the state in the 1920s. Today, the state's Department of Fish and Wildlife is working to ensure the recovery of this endangered species.

1. **Interpret Diagrams** Which contains more kinds of organisms: the phylum or the kingdom that gray wolves belong to? Explain your answer.

....

....

....

2. **CCC Predict** Suppose that you randomly picked out two members of the same phylum and two members of the same genus. Which pair of organisms would you expect to have more characteristics in common? Explain your answer.

....

....

....

....

Binomial Nomenclature As explained at the start of this lesson, the first word in an organism's scientific name is its genus. The genus (plural *genera*) is a classification grouping of similar, closely related organisms. Each genus contains one or more species. The more classification levels two organisms share, the more characteristics they have in common and the more closely related they are. **Figure 3** shows a giant puffball mushroom found in the genus *Calvatia*. Another closely related kind of puffball is also in *Calvatia*. Still other puffballs that are not as closely related are in other genera. The giant puffball's species name, *gigantea*, describes its size. Together, the two words that identify the genus and species form the scientific name.

Binomial Nomenclature

Figure 3 All of these mushrooms are commonly called puffballs.

1. SEP Make Observations List some characteristics that all three mushrooms share.

....

....

....

Calvatia gigantea   **Calvatia craniiformis**   **Lycoperdon echinatum**

2. SEP Determine Similarities Which two mushrooms are most closely related to one another? Explain.

....

....

Math Toolbox

Aristotle and Classification

Aristotle, a Greek scholar who lived from 384 to 322 BCE, created the classification system shown in the table.

1. Write an Expression ✏ Use variables to write an expression to find the percentage of animals that swim. Then, complete the table.

....

....

2. Classify How did Aristotle organize the animals?

....

....

Animals with blood that...	Percentage of animals
fly 	22%
walk, run, or hop 	46%
swim	

Scientific Names

Scientific Names A complete scientific name is written in italics. The first letter in the first word is capitalized. You will notice that most scientific names use Latin. Linnaeus used Latin in his naming system because it was the common language used by all scientists. **Figure 4** shows how using different common names for the same organism can cause confusion. Scientists also use taxonomic keys, as shown in **Figure 5**, to help name and identify organisms.

✓CHECK POINT **Determine Meaning** How are scientific names written?

....

....

Using a Taxonomic Key

Figure 5 While on a hike, you find an organism with eight legs, two body regions, claw-like pincers, and no tail. Use the key.

1. Interpret Diagrams How many different organisms can be identified using this key?

....

2. CCC Patterns Use the taxonomic key to identify the organism you observed on your hike.

....

Confusing Common Names

Figure 4 This Pacific fisher cat is not a cat that fishes for food. It is actually related to weasels, not cats. It lives inland, and can be found in the forests of northern California. So, instead of eating fish from the marsh, it prefers porcupine!

Predict What do you think might have caused people to call this animal a "cat"?

....

....

....

....

HANDS-ON LAB

Use a taxonomic key to identify an unknown pest.

Taxonomic Key

Step		Characteristics	Organism
1	1a.	Has 8 legs	Go to Step 2.
	1b.	Has more than 8 legs	Go to Step 3.
2	2a.	Has one oval-shaped body region	Go to Step 4.
	2b.	Has two body regions	Go to Step 5.
3	3a.	Has one pair of legs on each body segment	Centipede
	3b.	Has two pairs of legs on each body segment	Millipede
4	4a.	Is less than 1 millimeter long	Mite
	4b.	Is more than 1 millimeter long	Tick
5	5a.	Has clawlike pincers	Go to Step 6.
	5b.	Has no clawlike pincers	Spider
6	6a.	Has a long tail with a stinger	Scorpion
	6b.	Has no tail or stinger	Pseudoscorpion

Evolution and Classification

When Linnaeus was alive, people thought that species never changed. This point of view changed when Charles Darwin developed a new idea in the 1830s. Darwin was an Englishman. He sailed around the world for five years observing nature and collecting samples of fossils and animals. During the voyage, he was fascinated by the relationships between modern species and ancient types, as shown in **Figure 6**. Darwin was one of the first scientists to understand **evolution**, or the process of change over time. He concluded that all modern species developed from earlier kinds of life through natural selection. Natural selection is the idea that some individuals are better adapted to their environment than others. The better-adapted individuals are more likely to survive and reproduce than other members of the same species.

Common Ancestry Evolution by natural selection is the organizing principle of life science. Evidence from thousands of scientific investigations supports the idea of evolution. As understanding of evolution increased, biologists changed how they classify species. Scientists now understand that certain organisms may be similar because they share a common ancestor and an evolutionary history. The more similar the two groups are, in fact, the more recent their common ancestor.

1.75 million years ago (mya)

Pakicetus, land-dwelling, four-footed mammal

4.15 mya

Ambulocetus, "walking whale," mammal lived both on land and in water

4.5 mya

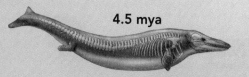

Dorudon, "spear tooth," water-dwelling mammal

Evolution of the Dolphin

Figure 6 Darwin compared ancient and modern species to develop his theory of evolution by natural selection. Skeletons of dolphin ancestors show how the species evolved.

Form a Hypothesis Why do you think the ancient ancestor of the dolphin became a water-dwelling animal?

....

....

....

2.2 mya

Odontocetus, modern "toothed whale"

2.2 mya

Stenella frontalis, Atlantic spotted dolphin

Convergent Evolution

Figure 7 These three organisms evolved a similar characteristic over time.

1. **Identify** ✏ Circle the characteristic that the three organisms share.

2. **Form a Hypothesis** From this common characteristic, can you determine how closely related the organisms are?

....

....

....

....

....

....

....

....

Evolutionary Relationships

Scientists **determine** the evolutionary history of a species by comparing the structures of organisms. Scientists also compare the genetic information contained in the DNA of organisms' cells. Sometimes, unrelated organisms that live in similar environments evolve similar characteristics, as shown in **Figure 7**. Sharing common characteristics, however, does not necessarily mean that organisms are closely related. The process by which unrelated organisms evolve similar characteristics is called **convergent evolution**. When scientists discovered convergent evolution, they had to change the placement of organisms within the classification system. Because scientific research leads to discovery and new knowledge, scientists sometimes reclassify organisms to account for new evidence. In this sense, the system of classification also evolves.

☑ **CHECK POINT** **Assess Sources** Suggest one reliable source of information about Charles Darwin. What makes this source reliable?

....

....

....

Academic Vocabulary

To determine is to find out an answer by doing research. When have you determined the answer to an important question?

....

....

....

....

☑ LESSON 2 Check

1. Draw Conclusions What can you conclude about two organisms that can mate and produce fertile offspring?

....

2. SEP Distinguish Relationships Use the chart. Which two species are most closely related? How do you know? Which species is the least related to the other three? Explain.

Some Types of Trees				
Common Name	Kingdom	Family	Genus	Species
Bird cherry	Plants	Rosaceae	*Prunus*	avium
Flowering cherry	Plants	Rosaceae	*Prunus*	serrula
Smooth-leaved elm	Plants	Ulmaceae	*Ultima*	minor
Whitebeam	Plants	Rosaceae	*Sorbus*	aria

....

....

....

....

....

3. SEP Determine Similarities How are evolution and classification related?

....

....

....

4. SEP Construct Explanations How did Darwin's discoveries change scientists' understanding of species?

....

....

....

....

....

5. SEP Evaluate Claims A friend claims her pet ferret is descended from the wild polecat. You want to learn more about this ferret ancestor. An online search shows several different kinds of polecats. How could you use scientific names to figure out which one is the ferret ancestor?

....

....

....

....

Quest CHECK-IN

In this lesson, you learned how scientists classify living things based on shared characteristics.

CCC Systems and System Models What are some limitations of using a classification system to categorize living things?

....

....

....

....

HANDS-ON LAB

Classifying Seeds

Go online for a downloadable worksheet of this lab. Model a scientific classification system using seeds. Then brainstorm ideas for how you might use classification in your field guide.

When Is a Species NOT a Species?

The following excerpt is from an article "Wolf Species Shake-Up" by Laurel Hamers. The article examines a 2016 study that concluded red wolves and eastern wolves are not distinct wolf species.

Red wolves and eastern wolves look similar to gray wolves but are often treated as different species. Eastern wolves live in the Great Lakes region, where gray wolves are now scarcer. Red wolves call the southeastern United States home. That's a region where gray wolves no longer exist.

The new study looked at the entire genetic makeup, or genome, of 23 wild canines from around North America. The researchers compared the genomes in these individuals to those from pure coyotes and Eurasian wolves. That let them figure out how much of each animal's genetic material came from wolves or coyotes.

Red wolves have about 75 percent coyote genes and just 25 percent wolf genes, they found. Eastern wolves have about 25 to 50 percent coyote ancestry. The international team of scientists reported its finding online July 27 in Science Advances.

The new data mean that both red and eastern wolves have mated with coyotes in the past. Gray wolves also have some coyote genes. And eastern wolves and red wolves are just as closely related to gray wolves as they are to other members of their species.

CONNECT TO YOU

Find out more about new research that changes the way scientists classify certain organisms. Use several sources of information. As you read, come up with more focused questions for later exploration. Discuss what you have learned with a classmate. How do you think advances in genetic testing and other technologies might impact the way that some organisms are currently classified?

LESSON
3 Viruses, Bacteria, Protists, and Fungi

Guiding Questions

- What are all living things made of?
- What are the characteristics of viruses, bacteria, protists, and fungi?
- How do viruses, bacteria, protists, and fungi interact with nature and people?

Connections

Literacy Conduct Research Projects

Math Analyze Relationships

 MS-LS1-1 Conduct an investigation to provide evidence that living things are made of cells; either one cell or many different numbers and types of cells.

HANDS-ON LAB

uInvestigate Discover unicellular and multicellular organisms in pond water.

Vocabulary

virus
host
vaccine
bacteria
protist
parasite

Academic Vocabulary

resistant

Connect It!

✎ **Write a checkmark on one individual of each kind of living thing you see.**

SEP Make Observations Describe the different types of organisms you see.

....

....

SEP Explain Phenomena Now that you've seen these magnified images, explain why it might be unwise to drink water from a pond.

....

....

....

Microorganisms

When people think of organisms, they picture plants or animals. Yet many of the organisms we come in contact with every day are so small that you need a microscope to see them. These microorganisms are vital for the survival of all plants and animals. **Figure 1** shows some amazing microbes living in a single drop of pond water.

Protists are classified in Domain Eukarya and are simpler than the plants, animals, and fungi they are grouped with. However, organisms in Domains Archaea and Bacteria are less complex than protists. Archaea and bacteria are unicellular microorganisms that do not have a nucleus. These microorganisms are classified in different domains because of their different characteristics.

Many archaea live in extreme conditions and make food from chemicals. You might find archaea in hot springs, very salty water, or deep underground.

Bacteria have different structures and chemical processes than archaea do. Some bacteria are autotrophs, meaning they can make their own food. Other bacteria are heterotrophs who must find their food. Still other types of bacteria are decomposers that absorb nutrients from decaying organisms. Bacteria are found in soil, water, and air. In fact, bacteria are found everywhere, even inside you.

✔ **CHECK POINT** **Determine Central Ideas** If you had a powerful microscope, how could you determine whether a cell was from a eukaryote?

....

....

....

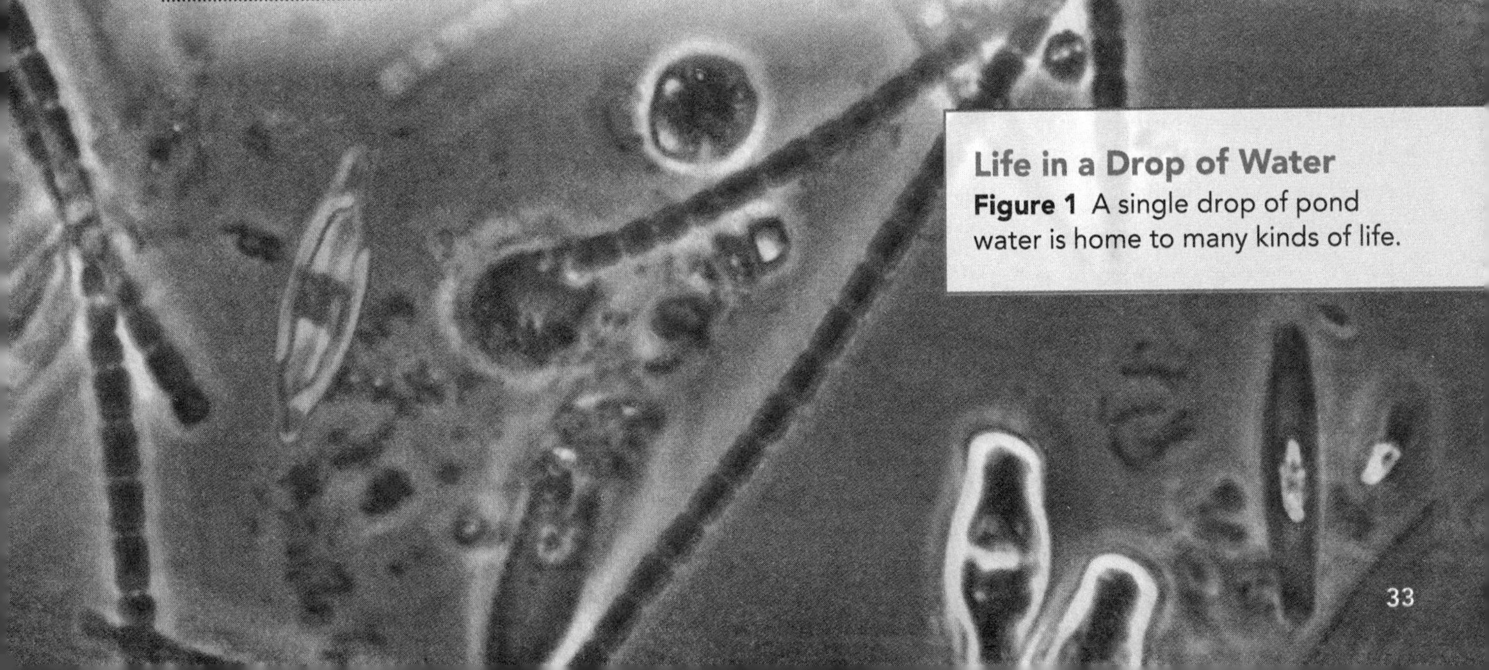

Student Discourse

In a small group, discuss the similarities and differences between the domains Archaea and Bacteria. Together, develop a Venn diagram to compare and contrast the two domains. Record your ideas in your science notebook.

Life in a Drop of Water
Figure 1 A single drop of pond water is home to many kinds of life.

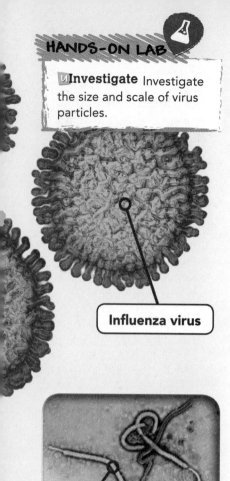

Influenza virus

Ebola virus

Bacteriophage

Viral Variety

Figure 2 Viruses come in many shapes. These images have been magnified and colorized to show details.

SEP Determine Similarities

Circle the virus that most closely resembles a cell. Explain your choice.

....

....

Viruses

You may have noticed that viruses were not included in the domains of living things. That's because viruses are not alive. A **virus** is a tiny, nonliving particle that enters and then reproduces inside a living cell. They lack most of the characteristics of living things. Some viruses may look like cells, but they are not cells. Viruses cannot reproduce on their own. Instead, they cause the cells they enter to reproduce more viruses. Viruses do not use food for energy or to grow. They also do not respond to their surroundings or produce wastes.

Shapes and Names Viruses can be round or shaped like bricks, threads, or bullets. Some viruses even have complex, robot-like shapes, as shown in **Figure 2**. Viruses are so small that they are measured in units called nanometers (nm), or one billionth of a meter. The common cold virus is 75 nm in diameter. The diameter of a red blood cell—7,500 nm—is much larger. Scientists name some viruses after the disease they cause or after the area where they were discovered.

Reproduction A virus is very small and simple. All viruses contain genetic material with a protein coating. The genetic material contains chemical instructions for making more copies of the virus. To reproduce, a virus attaches itself to a host cell, as shown in **Figure 3**. A **host** is an organism that provides a suitable environment for a virus to multiply. The virus either enters the cell or injects its genetic material into the host cell. Inside the host cell, the virus's genetic material takes over and forces the cell to make more copies of the virus! Finally, the host cell bursts open, releasing many new viruses which then infect other healthy cells, repeating the process.

Disease Many copies of a virus attacking your cells at once may cause a disease. Some viral diseases are mild, such as the common cold. Other viral diseases can produce serious illnesses. Viruses spread quickly and attack the cells of nearly every kind of organism. Fortunately, scientists have developed vaccines to prevent many dangerous viral diseases. A **vaccine** is a substance used in vaccinations that consists of pathogens, such as viruses, that have been modified to safely trigger the body to produce chemicals that destroy the pathogens. **Figure 4** shows the vaccination process.

☑ CHECK POINT **Distinguish Facts** What makes viruses so dangerous and vaccines so important?

....

....

Virus Invasion!

Figure 3 A cell invaded by a virus becomes a kind of zombie. All the cell's energy goes into making more viruses.

SEP Apply Scientific Reasoning Which evolved first: viruses or living organisms? Explain.

....

....

....

VIRUS

HOST CELL

Step 1 Virus injects genetic material into host cell.

Step 2 Cell makes copies of virus.

Step 3 Cell bursts, releasing many new copies of virus.

Vaccine Protection

Figure 4 Vaccinations can prevent measles and other viral diseases.

SEP Construct Explanations Why is it important to use a dead or weakened virus in a vaccine?

....

....

The virus that causes a disease is isolated. The virus is then damaged by heat, and a vaccine is prepared from it.

After being injected with a vaccine, the body prepares defenses against the virus.

The body can now resist infection by the disease-causing virus.

Math Toolbox

A Viral Epidemic

When a virus sickens many people at the same time within a limited geographic area, it is called an epidemic. In May 2014, during the Ebola epidemic in West Africa, people quickly became sick. There were about 375 new Ebola cases at the beginning of June and 750 in July.

1. **SEP Identify Variables** On the graph, circle the variable that depends on the other.

2. **Analyze Relationships** Explain the relationship between the number of cases reported and time.

....

3. **Write an Expression** ✏ Find the number of new cases expected by September. Use an expression to plot the number of new cases for September and October on the graph. Then finish drawing the line.

....

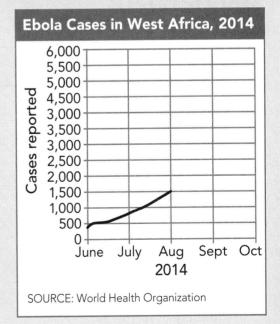

Ebola Cases in West Africa, 2014

Cases reported (y-axis): 0, 500, 1,000, 1,500, 2,000, 2,500, 3,000, 3,500, 4,000, 4,500, 5,000, 5,500, 6,000

2014 (x-axis): June, July, Aug, Sept, Oct

SOURCE: World Health Organization

Bacteria Shapes

Figure 5 The shape of a bacterium helps a scientist to identify it.

Apply Concepts

✎ Label the shape of the bacteria.

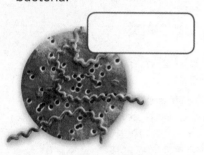

[ ]

[ ]

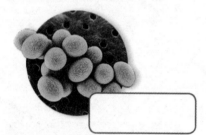

[ ]

Bacteria

If life were a movie, bacteria would be both villains and heroes. Bacteria would also make up most of the supporting cast. Bacteria make up the great majority of organisms on Earth. Bacteria are very small; millions can fit into the period at the end of this sentence. The smallest bacteria are about the size of the largest viruses. Most bacteria are one of three basic shapes: ball, rod, or spiral. You can see some of these shapes in **Figure 5**. The shape of the cell helps scientists identify the type of bacteria.

Infectious Bacteria You have probably heard of *E. coli*, *Streptococcus* ("strep throat"), and *Staphylococcus* ("staph"). They are types of infectious, or disease–causing, bacteria. Someone can become infected when the bacteria enter the person's body. The bacteria then grow and multiply quite quickly. Because these bacteria give off toxins (dangerous chemicals that damage surrounding cells and tissues), they can cause serious infections. Luckily, fewer than one percent of bacteria are actually infectious.

Bacterial Cell Structures Bacteria are single-celled organisms, also known as prokaryotes, that lack a nucleus. Each cell is a separate living organism that performs all the functions needed for life. **Figure 6** shows the structure of a typical bacterial cell. Bacteria have cell walls that protect them from attacks and keep them from drying out. Inside the cell wall is a cell membrane. The cell membrane controls what substances pass into and out of the cell. Some bacteria have structures attached to the cell wall that help them move around. Flagella whip around like propellers to drive some bacteria toward their food.

Model It ❗

Bacterial Cell Structures

Figure 6 Structures in a bacterial cell help them function and survive.

SEP Develop Models ✎ Use the descriptions below to label the structures.

cytoplasm gel-like substance inside the cell

genetic material string-like chemical instructions for cell

pili fibers that help cell move and reproduce

ribosomes round structures where proteins are made

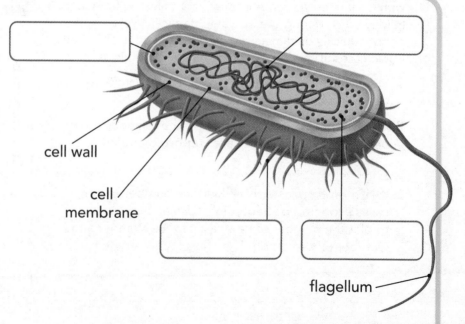

[ ]

[ ]

cell wall

cell membrane

[ ]

[ ]

flagellum

Obtaining Food Some bacteria make their own food from sunlight, like plants do. Other bacteria create food from chemicals. Chemicals from underwater volcanoes feed the bacteria in **Figure 7**. A third group of bacteria take in food through their cell walls. Food for these bacteria could be milk, sugar, meat, or dead cells. Your digestive system is a good home for bacteria! Some bacteria use the energy from food to make poisonous chemicals called toxins. Toxins cause the pain and sickness you feel when you get food poisoning.

Survival Bacteria cannot move fast. They cannot escape intense heat or hunt for food. In harsh conditions, some bacteria survive by sheltering in place. A thick-walled shell forms around the genetic material and cytoplasm, forming a tough endospore. The endospore can grow back into a full cell when conditions improve.

Bacterial Reproduction Bacteria also keep ahead of predators by reproducing rapidly. Even if predators eat some individual bacteria, there are always more. Bacterial reproduction is shown in **Figure 8**. Most bacteria reproduce asexually by growing and then dividing into two identical cells. Asexual reproduction in bacteria is called binary fission.

Bacteria can also pass genetic material to a neighboring bacteria through conjugation. Conjugation occurs when two bacteria cells come together and exchange genetic material. Conjugation does not produce more bacteria, but it does allow genetic information to spread. For example, one bacterial cell could be **resistant** to antibiotics. The antibiotic-resistant cell could pass the resistance on to other bacteria by conjugation. Soon, the whole bacteria population can become resistant and the antibiotic will stop working.

INTERACTIVITY

Observe and compare different unicellular organisms.

Undersea Mystery
Figure 7 These "rocks" are layers of bacteria that have grown up around the mouth of the seafloor volcano.

Academic Vocabulary

Resistant means able to work against or hold off an opposing force. When have you been resistant?

....

....

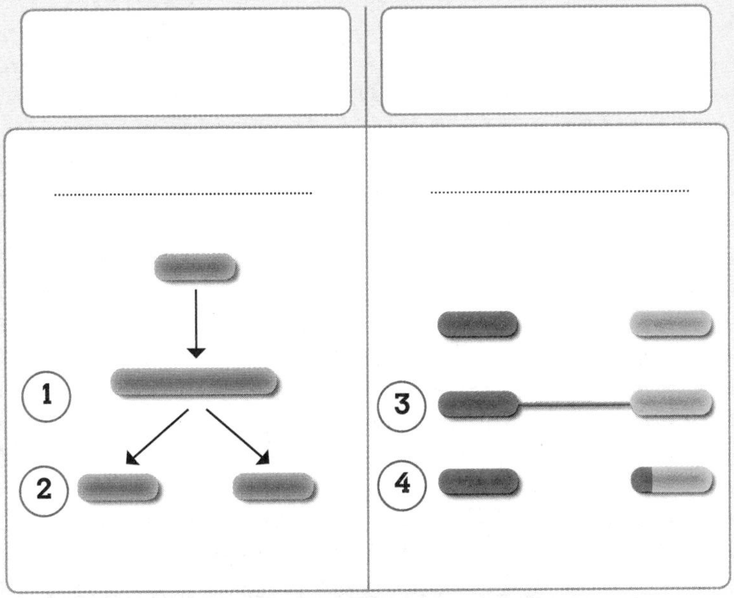

Bacterial Reproduction
Figure 8 🖊 Label the diagram with these terms: asexual reproduction, binary fission, conjugation, and transfer of genetic material. Then, match the number in the diagram to the step it describes below.

_____ Cells separate; one now has some genetic information from the other cell.

_____ Cell splits into two identical cells.

_____ Cell grows larger before dividing.

_____ One cell passes some of its genetic information to another cell.

① ② ③ ④

Conduct Research Projects
Use multiple print and online sources to gather information about the importance of bacteria. Would humans survive without bacteria? Discuss how your research supports your answer with a peer.

The Many Roles of Bacteria

Figure 9 🖉 Bacteria do other things besides make people sick. They have many important roles in nature and human life. There are many ways we interact with bacteria. Circle or highlight one or more examples of harmful bacteria.

✅ **CHECK POINT** **Cite Textual Evidence** According to what you have read, how do bacteria protect their genetic material and cytoplasm during harsh conditions?

....

....

....

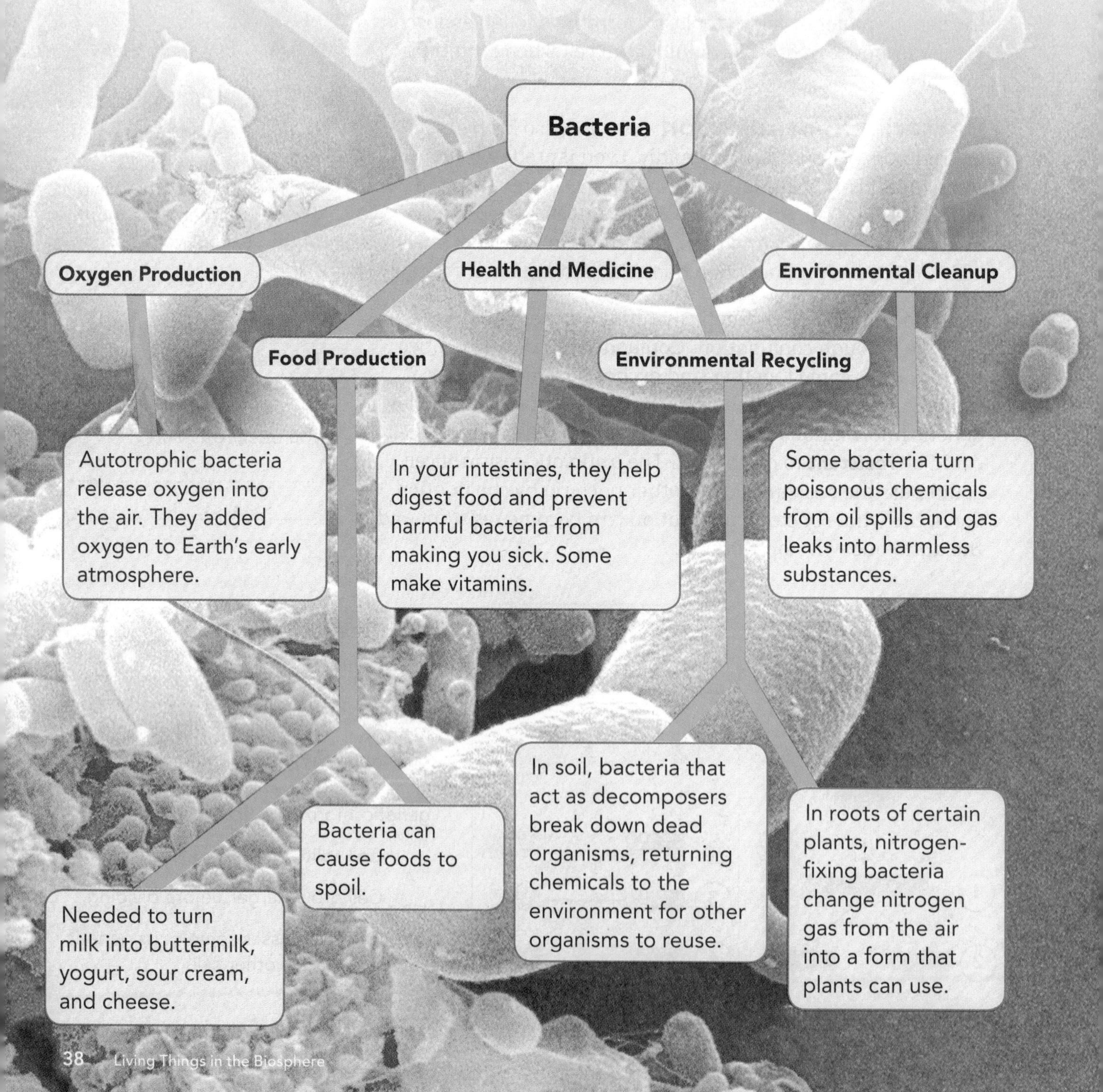

Bacteria

Oxygen Production

Health and Medicine

Environmental Cleanup

Food Production

Environmental Recycling

Autotrophic bacteria release oxygen into the air. They added oxygen to Earth's early atmosphere.

In your intestines, they help digest food and prevent harmful bacteria from making you sick. Some make vitamins.

Some bacteria turn poisonous chemicals from oil spills and gas leaks into harmless substances.

In soil, bacteria that act as decomposers break down dead organisms, returning chemicals to the environment for other organisms to reuse.

Bacteria can cause foods to spoil.

In roots of certain plants, nitrogen-fixing bacteria change nitrogen gas from the air into a form that plants can use.

Needed to turn milk into buttermilk, yogurt, sour cream, and cheese.

Protists

Protists are eukaryotic organisms that cannot be classified as animals, plants, or fungi. **Figure 10** shows that protists have a wide range of characteristics. All protists live in moist environments and are common where humans interact. Most protists are harmless, but some can cause illness or disease. Most harmful protists are **parasites**, organisms that benefit from living with, on, or in a host. Drinking water contaminated with these protists can cause fever, diarrhea, and abdominal pain. For example, a person can become ill after drinking water containing the protist *Giardia*. The protist attaches itself to the small intestine, where it takes in nutrients and prevents those nutrients from entering the human. The person gets ill from the disease giardiasis. Another parasitic protist travels with a mosquito. When a mosquito that is carrying the protist *Plasmodium* bites a human, the protist infects the red blood cells, causing malaria.

☑ **CHECK POINT** **Cite Textual Evidence** Tasha and Marco examine a cell through a microscope. Tasha suggests that the cell is a protist. Marco thinks it might be a bacterium. What evidence would prove Tasha right?

....

....

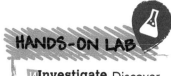

HANDS-ON LAB

Investigate Discover unicellular and multicellular organisms in pond water.

Diversity of Protists

Figure 10 Protists are classified in Domain Eukarya and Kingdom Protista. The three separate types are shown in the table below.

Identify Use information in the chart to identify the three photos of protists below. Write the name of each type of protist in the space provided.

	Protozoa: Animal-like Protists	Protophyta: Plant-like Protists	Slime Molds and Water Molds
Food	Heterotrophs	Autotrophs; some also heterotrophs	Heterotrophs
Features	Unicellular	Unicellular or multicellular	Unicellular, but often live in colonies
Movement	Free-swimming	Free-swimming or attached	Move during some part of life cycle
Reproduction	Asexual and sexual	Sexual and asexual	Asexual
Examples	Amoebas: surround and trap food particles Giardia: common parasite, has eight flagella	Red algae: seaweeds people eat, known as nori Dinoflagellates: glow in the dark	Slime molds: brightly colored, grow in garden beds Water molds: attack plants, such as crops

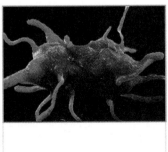

Reflect Find out more about the different ways that fungi are both helpful and harmful to people. Record your findings in your science notebook.

Fungi

What's the largest organism ever to exist on Earth? Good guesses would be a dinosaur, a blue whale, or a giant tree. These are wrong. The biggest living thing is a honey fungus colony growing under a forest in Oregon. The colony is larger than a thousand football fields! Like all other fungi, the honey fungus has eukaryotic cells with cell walls. Fungi are heterotrophs that feed by absorbing food through their cell walls. Most of the honey fungus is unseen underground. The cells of fungi are arranged into hyphae, or threadlike tubes. Hyphae, like those shown in **Figure 11**, give fungi structure and allow them to spread over large areas. Hyphae also grow into food sources and release chemicals. Food is broken down by the chemicals and then absorbed by the hyphae. Some fungi act as decomposers and consume dead organisms, while others are parasites that attack living hosts.

Fungal Reproduction
Fungi occasionally send up reproductive structures called fruiting bodies. Some fruiting bodies are the familiar mushrooms that you eat or see growing in damp environments. Fruiting bodies produce spores that are carried by wind or water to new locations. Each spore that lands in the right conditions can then start a new fungal colony. Fungi can also reproduce sexually when hyphae from two colonies grow close together and trade genetic information.

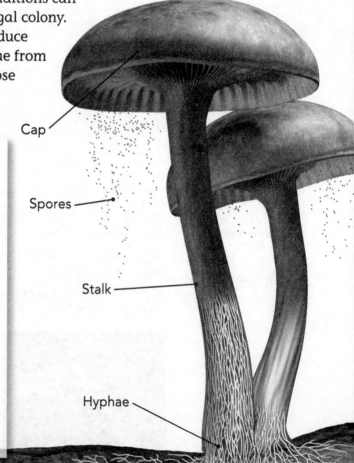

Cap

Spores

Stalk

Hyphae

Structure of a Honey Mushroom

Figure 11 The honey mushroom is native to California and found in the northern part of the state. The part of the mushroom you can see above ground is tiny compared to the network of hyphae underground.

Hypothesize What is a possible relationship between the fungus and the tree root?

....

....

☑ CHECK POINT Determine Central Ideas
What is the purpose of fungal spores?

....

....

Roles of Fungi

Fungi come in many forms and have varying life cycles. We depend on fungi for many services. **Figure 12** explores some of the ways that fungi are helpful and harmful. At the same time, fungi can destroy our property and food and make us sick. You've probably heard of *athlete's foot* and *ringworm*. These are both common rashes—mild skin infections caused by fungi in the environment. They are easily treated. Some fungi, however, can cause serious diseases. In fact, more people die each year from fungal infections than from malaria and certain common cancers. There are no vaccines to prevent fungal infections.

INTERACTIVITY

Use research to develop medicine needed for someone that is ill.

Fungi: Friend or Foe?

Figure 12 🖊 Circle evidence of harm in the image descriptions.

1. **CCC Energy and Matter** Why would a fungus growing on a rock need a partner to provide it food?

....

....

2. **SEP Construct Explanations** Why would fungi be better than seeds at absorbing water?

....

Mycorrhiza

Grows around plant seeds and roots.

Brings water to plant and eats plant sugars.

Helps plants grow.

Penicillium Mold

Grows on food products.

Spoils food.

Produces chemicals used in antibiotics.

Some produce poisons or cause allergic reactions.

Shiitake Mushroom

Grows on and consumes dead logs.

Provides tasty food.

Breaks down dead wood and makes nutrients available for living things.

Lichen

Forms partnership with autotrophic algae or bacteria.

Provides water, shelter, and minerals, while partner provides food.

Produces chemicals used in dyes, perfumes, and deodorant.

Provides food for animals in harsh environments.

Yeast

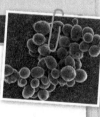

Eats carbohydrates, turning them into alcohols and carbon dioxide.

Helps to bake bread and make beverages.

Causes diaper rash and skin infections.

Destroys stored foods.

Fungi Files

41

☑ LESSON 3 Check

1. Apply Concepts What is unique about parasites?

....

....

....

2. Identify What are three ways that fungi interact with other kinds of living things?

....

....

....

3. SEP Construct Arguments Could you have two or more viral infections at the same time? Explain, using evidence to support your argument.

....

....

....

....

....

4. SEP Use Scientific Reasoning Which of these taxonomic groups are most closely related: Fungi, Archaea, Bacteria, Protista? Explain.

....

....

....

....

5. SEP Develop Models 🖊 Draw a Venn Diagram to compare and contrast two types of infectious agents.

Quest CHECK-IN

In this lesson, you learned about the characteristics of viruses, bacteria, protists, and fungi. You also discovered how some of these living and nonliving things interact with nature and people.

SEP Integrate Information When developing a classification system, do you think identifying similarities or identifying differences is more helpful? Explain.

....

....

....

👆 INTERACTIVITY

Discovering Rainforest Organisms

Go online to classify organisms as unicellular or multicellular.

MS-LS1-1

A Disease Becomes a Cure

Viruses make you sick when they work their way into healthy cells. But some scientists are taking advantage of a virus's ability to invade cells to make people better.

The Challenge: To use viruses to deliver targeted therapy to cells.

Phenomenon Cancer therapies battle cancer cells, but they often damage healthy cells in the process. This can lead to serious side effects, from severe nausea to hair loss. Scientists are seeking engineering advances that allow them to better target diseased cells.

Biologist James Swartz looked to nature for inspiration. Viruses are great at targeting specific cells. He and his team at Stanford University in California re-engineered a virus by removing the disease-causing properties, leaving a hollow shell that could carry medicine inside. Next, they altered the spiky surface of the virus and attached tiny "tags" to it. The tags send the engineered virus to sick cells to deliver medicine.

It's an important discovery. But Swartz and his team still have to do a lot of research and testing to see whether this delivery system works. If it does, they'll have engineered a virus that works in reverse—infecting you with medicine rather than disease.

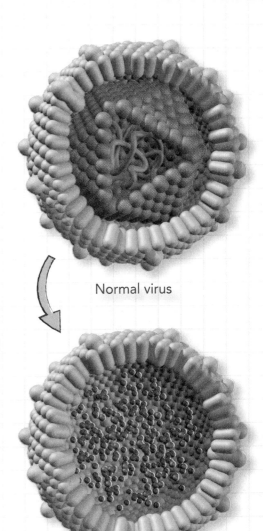

Normal virus

Re-engineered virus

The redesigned protein coat in the middle section of this virus removed the disease-causing properties, leaving the protein able to carry medicine. The spiky virus surface contains tags to direct the virus to the correct cells.

> **INTERACTIVITY**
>
> Explore how viruses are engineered to solve problems.

DESIGN CHALLENGE Can you engineer a virus to perform a specific function? Go to the Engineering Design Notebook to find out!

4 Plants and Animals

Guiding Questions

- What makes animals and plants different in form and function?
- Which special structures inside plant and animal cells determine an organism's characteristics?
- How do similar cells work together to help plants and animals function?
- Which traits are unique to animals?

Connection

Literacy Gather Information

 MS-LS1-1 Conduct an investigation to provide evidence that living things are made of cells; either one cell or many different numbers and types of cells.

MS-LS1-2 Develop and use a model to describe the function of a cell as a whole and ways parts of cells contribute to the function

MS-LS1-3 Use argument supported by evidence for how the body is a system of interacting subsystems composed of groups of cells.

HANDS-ON LAB

uInvestigate Discover where land plants come from.

Vocabulary

tissue
vascular plants
nonvascular
  plants
vertebrates
invertebrates
organ
mammals

Academic Vocabulary

symmetry

Connect It!

✏ **Circle a plant and place a square around an animal.**

SEP Determine Differences What characteristics of each organism helped you identify it as either a plant or an animal?

....

....

....

Form and Function

The plants and animals you see in **Figure 1**, along with protists and fungi, are all classified in Domain Eukarya. As eukaryotes, they share some characteristics. They are all made of one or more cells, and each cell contains a nucleus with DNA. However, they also have characteristics that set them apart, such as how they get energy and move around. These differences are what separate plants into Kingdom Plantae and animals into Kingdom Animalia.

All living things need water and food for energy. Plants are autotrophs, or producers. They use photosynthesis to make their own food. Plant cells have specialized structures that make food. Animals are heterotrophs, or consumers. They get food by eating other organisms. Animals have specialized body structures that break down food they consume.

Mobility, the ability to move around, also separates plants and animals. To get food, animals need to move around. Structures such as legs, fins, and wings allow movement from one place to another. Because most plants are anchored to the ground, they cannot move around.

✓ **CHECK POINT** **Summarize Text** Why are plants and animals placed in different kingdoms?

....

....

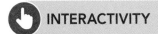

INTERACTIVITY

Explore the different types of cells that make up multicellular organisms.

Plants and Animals
Figure 1 Plants and animals are classified in the same domain, but their differences place them in two separate kingdoms.

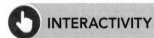

INTERACTIVITY

Explore the different roles of various cells.

HANDS-ON LAB

⊞Investigate Discover where land plants come from.

Plant Cell Features

Figure 2 🖊 Plants need specialized structures to carry out their life functions. Label the stoma, cell wall, chloroplast, and vacuole. Then list the function of each part. Finally, circle where the chlorophyll is located.

Characteristics of Plants

All land plants are multicellular. In addition, nearly all plants are autotrophs. DNA analysis has led some scientists to classify green algae as part of the Kingdom Plantae. Almost all algae are single-celled organisms and live in the water. All plants undergo photosynthesis to make food. Plants take in carbon dioxide, water, and sunlight to produce food (and oxygen as a by-product). Specialized structures, called stomata, are located on each leaf (**Figure 2**). Each stoma (plural: stomata) is a small opening on the underside of a leaf through which oxygen, water, and carbon dioxide can move. It also prevents water loss.

Plant cells have specialized structures that serve specific functions. Look at the plant cell in **Figure 2**. Surrounding the plant cell is a strong rigid cell wall, which is used for structural support and protection. The largest structure inside the cell is the vacuole. It stores water, wastes, and food. The chloroplasts, which look like green jellybeans, are the cell structures where food is made. Chloroplasts contain a green pigment called chlorophyll that absorbs sunlight, the energy that drives photosynthesis.

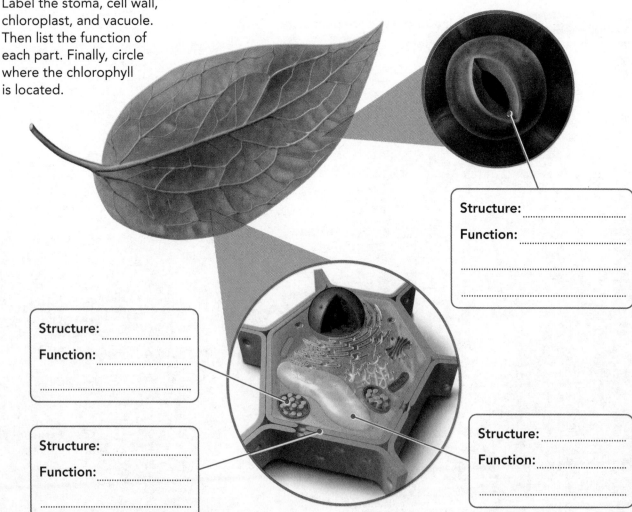

Structure: ....
Function: ....
....
....

Structure: ....
Function: ....
....

Structure: ....
Function: ....
....

Structure: ....
Function: ....
....

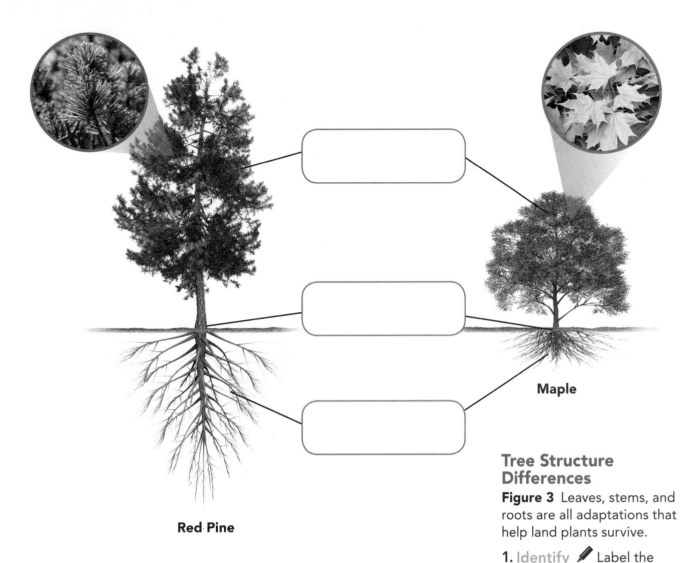

Red Pine

Maple

Tree Structure Differences

Figure 3 Leaves, stems, and roots are all adaptations that help land plants survive.

1. Identify ✏ Label the roots, stem, and leaves in the diagram.

2. CCC Structure and Function
   Explain any differences in the trees' structures.

....

....

....

....

....

....

....

....

....

....

Plant Structure Think about the aquatic plants you identified in **Figure 1**. To make food, they need water and sunlight. But land plants need special structures to get the water they need to make food. There are three main parts to a land plant: leaves, stem or branch, and roots. A leaf has two functions: to capture light energy and gas exchange. The stem provides support and stores food for the plant. The stem is where leaves, flowers, cones, and buds grow. Stems also connect roots to leaves, so that leaves can get the water they need to carry out photosynthesis. The roots of trees have three major functions. First, roots absorb water and nutrients from the ground. Second, roots anchor the plant to the ground. Third, roots store food and nutrients. See if you can identify the different tree structures in **Figure 3**.

✅ CHECK POINT **Cite Textual Evidence** What is the function of the stem on a plant?

....

....

Beech Trees are seed plants that produce beechnuts and can grow to a height of 35 m. All seed plants are vascular plants.

Moss are seedless, nonvascular plants that do not typically grow taller than 10 cm.

Ferns are seedless, vascular plants that range in height from less than 1 cm to 25 m.

Plants

Figure 4 Some plants have vascular tissue to transport water, food, and minerals.

1. **Claim** 🖊 Circle two different types of vascular plants in the picture.

2. **Evidence** What evidence supports your claim?

....

....

....

3. **Reasoning** Explain how the evidence supports your claim.

....

....

....

....

....

....

....

Vascular Plants Tall, short, large, or small, plants are made up of many cells. A group of similar cells that perform a specific function are called **tissues**. Some plants have vascular tissue. The cells that make up vascular tissue work together to transport water, food, and minerals through tube-like structures in the plant. Plants with true vascular tissue are **vascular plants**.

Characteristics of Vascular Plants Vascular plants have vascular tissue, true roots, and a cuticle on their leaves. Vascular tissue carries important materials like water and nutrients to all the parts of a plant. Because of the way cells are grouped together, vascular tissue also strengthens the body of the plant. This support gives plants stability and allows plants to have height. The roots of vascular plants anchor the plant to the ground, but they also draw up water and nutrients from the soil. Vascular plants have a waxy waterproof layer called a cuticle that covers the leaves and stems. Since leaves have stomata for gas exchange, the cuticle prevents water loss.

Vascular Tissue There are two types of vascular tissue that transport materials throughout vascular plants. Food moves through the vascular tissue called phloem (FLOH um). Once food is made in the leaves, it must travel through phloem to reach other parts of the plant that need food. Water and minerals, on the other hand, travel through the xylem (ZY lum). Roots absorb water and minerals from the soil and the xylem moves them up into the stem and leaves.

Nonvascular Plants The characteristics of nonvascular plants are different from those of vascular plants. The moss in **Figure 4** is a **nonvascular plant**, a low-growing plant that lacks vascular tissue for transporting materials. Most nonvascular plants live in moist areas and feel wet, because they obtain water and minerals from their surroundings. They are only a few cell layers thick, so water and minerals do not travel far or quickly. Nonvascular plants do not have true roots that take up water and nutrients from the soil. The function of their roots is to anchor them to the ground. Also, their cell walls are thin, which prevents them from gaining height.

☑ CHECK POINT **Determine Central Ideas** Name three characteristics of vascular plants that make them different from nonvascular plants.

....

....

Plan It

Plants need water, carbon dioxide, and sunlight to grow. You want to determine the impact of sunlight on plant growth. Consider how you could prove that sunlight is an important factor in plant growth.

SEP Plan an Investigation ✏ Design a procedure to investigate how sunlight affects the growth of a plant. Include a sketch of your investigation.

Procedure:

....

....

....

....

Sketch:

Gather Information

Use the Internet to conduct research on two different animals. What structures do they have that allow them to function differently? How are they classified? Explain and provide support.

Academic Vocabulary

In math class, how would you explain an object that had symmetry?

....

....

....

Characteristics of Animals

All organisms are classified according to how they are related to other organisms, by comparing DNA, body structure and development. All animals are classified based on whether or not they have a backbone. **Vertebrates** are animals with a backbone. Animals without a backbone are classified as **invertebrates**.

Structure of Animals

All animals are multicellular and most have several different types of tissue. Complex animals have organs and organ systems. An **organ** is a body structure composed of different kinds of tissues that work together. An organ performs a more complex task than each tissue could alone. For example, the eye is a specialized sense organ. It has about ten different tissues working together to enable sight. A group of different organs that work together to perform a task is called an organ system. The organization of cells, tissues, organs, and organ systems describes an animal's body structure.

Most organisms have a balance of body parts called **symmetry**. As you see in **Figure 5**, animals have different types of symmetry or no symmetry. Animals with no symmetry are asymmetrical and have simple body structures with specialized cells but no tissues.

Types of Symmetry

Figure 5 ✎ Symmetry occurs when the organism can be divided into two or more similar parts. Draw the lines of symmetry on the animals that have radial and bilateral symmetry.

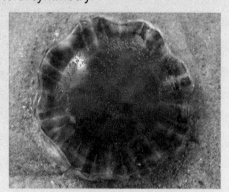

Asymmetrical Animals without symmetry, such as this sea sponge, are asymmetrical.

Radial Symetry Animals with radial symmetry, such as this jellyfish, live in water and have complex body plans with tissues and usually have organ systems. An animal has radial symmetry if many imaginary lines drawn through a central point divide the body into two mirror images.

Bilateral Symetry Most animals, such as this horseshoe crab, have bilateral symmetry. Only one line can be drawn to divide the body into halves that are mirror images.

Invertebrates

Most animals are invertebrates. Scientists separate invertebrates into six main groups. **Figure 6** shows the different characteristics defining each group. While invertebrates do not have backbones, many have structures that support their bodies in a similar way. For example, arthropods have an exoskeleton, a tough waterproof outer covering that protects, supports, and helps prevent evaporation of water from the body. In contrast, echinoderms have an endoskeleton, a structural support system that is found within the animal.

INTERACTIVITY

Determine how to use characteristics of an organism to identify it.

✓ **CHECK POINT** **Determine Meaning**
What is the difference between an exoskeleton and an endoskeleton?

....

....

....

Echinoderms have a system of tubes to move and obtain food and oxygen.

Mollusks have one or two hard shells to protect internal organs.

Worms are simple animals but have a brain and digestive system.

Arthropods have jointed appendages and shed their exoskeleton as they grow.

Cnidarians have stinging cells and take food into a central body cavity.

Invertebrates

Figure 6 This diagram shows how scientists believe invertebrates evolved, starting with sponges and ending with echinoderms. Consider other characteristics that separate invertebrates into different groups.

CCC Relate Structure and Function Starting at sponges and moving to echinoderms, what happens to the body structures of the invertebrates?

....

....

....

....

Sponges are made of specialized cells, adults are attached, and they take food into their bodies to get energy.

51

VIDEO

Explore the differences between plants and animals.

Vertebrates Most of the animals you see at an aquarium or zoo are members of the phylum Chordata and are called chordates. All chordates belong to Domain Eukaryota and Kingdom Anamalia and have a nerve cord. Most chordates, like you, have a backbone to protect the nerve cord. Some chordates, like sea squirts (**Figure 7**), do not have a backbone.

Common Structures All chordates have three structures in common: a notochord, a nerve cord, and pouches in the throat area. A notochord is a flexible rod that supports the chordate's back. The nerve cord runs down the back. It connects the brain to nerves. For most chordates, the throat pouches disappear before birth. In fish, they become gill slits.

Body Temperature Vertebrates must maintain their body temperature (**Figure 7**). Animals, such as amphibians and reptiles, that produce little internal body heat are ectotherms. Their body temperature changes with the environment. To stay warm, they go to a sunny spot and bask in sunlight. In contrast, endotherms control their internal heat and regulate their own temperature. Birds and mammals are endotherms. They have structures such as sweat glands, fur or feathers.

Vertebrate Groups **Figure 8** shows the five major groups of vertebrates: fish, amphibians, reptiles, birds, and mammals. Members of each group share unique characteristics. For example, a **mammal** is a vertebrate whose body temperature is regulated by its internal heat, and has skin covered with hair or fur and glands that produce milk to feed its young.

Animals Control Their Body Temperature

Figure 7 Animals control their body temperature one of two ways.

1. **SEP Apply Scientific Reasoning** Hypothesize whether each animal is an endotherm or ectotherm.

2. **SEP Construct Explanations** Would it be more difficult for the California desert cottontail to live in the Rocky Mountains or a frog to live in the Arctic? Explain.

....

....

....

sea squirts

Monotremes are the only egg-laying mammals. Examples include: duck-billed platypus and spiny echidnas.

Marsupials carry their young in a pouch. Examples include: kangaroo, koalas, possums, and opossums.

Placentals have live births. While developing in the mother, the embryo receives nourishment from an organ that surrounds the embryo called a placenta. Examples include: rodents, whales, cattle, dogs, and humans.

Mammals have mammary glands to feed their young milk. They are further grouped into three types: monotremes, marsupials, and placentals.

Birds have wings, lightweight bones, and a 4-chambered heart.

Reptiles have scales, thick skin, and lay their eggs on land.

Amphibians have permeable skin; they live their early life in water and adult life on land.

Fish live in water, have scales, and use gills to collect dissolved oxygen.

Vertebrates

Figure 8 This diagram shows how scientists believe vertebrates have evolved, from fish through mammals. Consider other differences among these five groups of vertebrates.

1. **CCC Patterns** What is one characteristic that amphibians, reptiles, birds, and mammals share?

....

2. **SEP Determine Differences** How are amphibians different from fish?

....

Movement Adaptations

Figure 9 Animals display a wide range of adaptations for movement. ✐ Rate each movement adaptation from 1 (fastest) to 5 (slowest) in the circles. Explain your highest rank.

....

....

....

Wings Birds and insects have wings that allow them to fly, hover, dive, and soar.

Fins Fish and whales have fins, and their bodies are streamlined to help them move through water.

Tube Feet Echinoderms have several tiny tube feet under their body. Water moves from their vascular system to the tube feet. This water movement expands each foot, causing it to move.

Muscular Foot Mollusks have a foot that is made of several thin muscles. This foot is used for digging or creeping along the surface.

Jet Propulsion Octopuses take water into a muscular sac and quickly expel it to move. They also expand and contract their arms to move.

CHECK POINT

Evaluate What adaptations does the octopus have that would help it open a jar?

....

....

....

....

👆 **INTERACTIVITY**

Explain the organization of different organisms.

Traits Unique to Animals

All animals have unique traits. Characteristics that organisms inherit to help them survive in their environment are called adaptations. These adaptations may be used to separate animals into more specific groups.

Adaptations for Movement Animals have a variety of adaptations for movement. Humans walk on two legs, while other animals use four. Animals are best adapted to the environment in which they live. As you see in **Figure 9**, adaptations vary greatly within the animal kingdom.

Adaptations for Conserving Water Obtaining fresh water from the salty ocean or dry desert is difficult for animals. Some animals, however, have adaptations that help them hold on to as much water as they can. A reptile's kidneys can remove solid material from its waste and then reabsorb the liquid material. Because they recycle the fluid part of their waste, reptiles do not need to take in as much water. Whales, seals, and dolphins also have specialized kidneys to conserve water. Their fresh water comes from the food they eat. Their waste first passes through a filter that removes the salt. It then passes through another tube that absorbs more water.

☑ LESSON 4 Check

MS-LS1-1, MS-LS1-2, MS-LS1-3

1. **SEP Determine Similarities** What are two characteristics that both plants and animals have in common?

....

....

2. **CCC Analyze Properties** How do some animals protect themselves against water loss?

....

....

....

3. **CCC Apply Concepts** What is the function of a backbone in vertebrates?

....

....

4. **CCC Relate Structure and Function** What are the three functions of roots?

....

....

....

....

....

5. **SEP Apply Scientific Reasoning** The tallest plants on Earth are redwood trees. They can grow to heights over 100 m. How are redwood trees able to transport water and nutrients from their roots to their leaves?

....

....

....

....

....

....

....

6. **SEP Construct Explanations** Why are organisms that have organs classified as more complex than organisms without organs?

....

....

....

....

....

....

Quest CHECK-IN

In this lesson, you learned that plants and animals are classified into different groups based on their cell structures, presence of different tissue types, traits, and adaptations.

SEP Determine Differences When you create your field guide, what physical characteristics would you use to separate plants and animals?

....

....

....

....

INTERACTIVITY

Multicellular Rainforest Organisms

Go online to to take a field trip to a rain forest. There, you will make observations and use them to classify various organisms.

1 Living Things

🕐 MS-LS1-1

1. What are the basic building blocks of all living things?
A. food
B. energy
C. cells
D. water

2. Which is an example of homeostasis?
A. reproduction
B. controlling an experiment
C. growth and development
D. maintaining a steady temperature

3. The kind of reproduction that requires two parents is called ....

4. CCC Analyze Systems An oasis is a place in a sandy desert where water rises to the surface. Trees and plants often grow by the water and animals make their homes there. What would happen to the organisms living in an oasis if the water dried up?

....

....

....

5. SEP Plan Your Investigation Design a controlled experiment to demonstrate that birds do not spontaneously generate on birdfeeders.

....

....

....

....

....

....

2 Classification Systems

🕐 MS-LS4-2

6. The mosquito *Aedes aegypti* is a carrier of the Zika virus. *Aedes* is the name of the mosquito's
A. order.
B. family.
C. genus.
D. species.

7. Which could happen through convergent evolution?
A. Two unrelated species could evolve into one species.
B. Two unrelated species could evolve similar features.
C. Two unrelated species could evolve very different features.
D. Two unrelated species could finish evolving.

8. Two organisms that share several classification levels will be ....
and have ....
in common.

9. SEP Develop Models 🖊 Develop a taxonomic key that a person could use to identify the following animals: hawk, alligator, duck, snake.

hawk   alligator   duck   snake

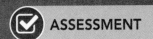
3 Viruses, Bacteria, Protists, and Fungi

MS-LS1-1

10. Which of the following groups is always heterotrophic?
   A. Domain Archaea
   B. Domain Bacteria
   C. Kingdom Fungi
   D. Kingdom Protista

11. Which statement is true about viruses?
   A. Viruses contain very small cells.
   B. Viruses never eat any food.
   C. Viruses can reproduce themselves quickly.
   D. Viruses have hyphae that help them take up water.

12. Two ways that bacteria help people are

.... and

....

13. SEP Defend Your Claim Why is *diverse* a good word to use to describe protists?

....

....

....

....

....

14. CCC Predict Describe three problems that could occur if all the fungi on Earth disappeared.

....

....

....

....

4 Plants and Animals

MS-LS1-1, MS-LS1-2, MS-LS1-3

15. CCC Cause and Effect Explain why vascular plants can gain height, but nonvascular plants only grow close to the ground.

....

....

....

....

....

....

....

....

....

....

....

....

16. SEP Distinguish Relationships Explain how vertebrates and invertebrates are similar and different.

....

....

....

....

....

....

....

....

....

....

MS-LS1-1, MS-LS1-2, MS-LS1-3

Evidence-Based Assessment

Naya is using a microscope to investigate the similarities and differences between two organisms. One is an animal called a rotifer and the other is a protist called a paramecium. She records her observations about both organisms in a table.

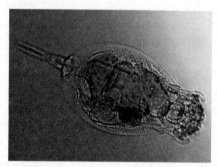

rotifer

paramecium

Observations	Organism A	Organism B
Organization is more complex	X	
Injury to one cell does not affect ability of the organism to stay alive	X	
Organism's lifespan is relatively short		X
Contains substances such as water, proteins, and lipids	X	X
Creates offspring through sexual reproduction	X	X
Gets energy by using hair-like structures to move food into its mouth		X
Requires energy in order to survive	X	X
Can only be observed with microscope	X	X
Responds to surroundings		
No cell differentiation		
One cell carries out necessary functions for life		

1. **SEP Make Observations** Refer to the images and existing observations to complete the table for the last three observations. Write an X in the appropriate column(s).

2. **SEP Analyze Data** Based on the data in the table, which statements are true?
   - [ ] Both organisms are unicellular.
   - [ ] Organism A is multicellular.
   - [ ] Organism B maintains homeostasis.
   - [ ] Both organisms respond to their surroundings.
   - [ ] Organism B has different types of cells.

3. **SEP Interpret Data** Naya adds another row for the following observation: Can only be produced from other living cells. For which organism is this statement true?
   - A. Organism A
   - B. Organism B
   - C. Both organisms
   - D. Neither organism

4. **SEP Use Scientific Reasoning** Complete the sentences by circling the correct words to properly classify Organism A and Organism B.

   Organism A is the rotifer/paramecium because it is multicellular/unicellular and has more/fewer structures in it.

   Organism B is the rotifer/paramecium because it is multicellular/unicellular and has more/fewer structures in it.

5. **CCC Apply Concepts** Suppose that Naya decides to observe a sample of quartz, a mineral found in Earth's crust. If Naya were to add quartz to the table, which observations could she check off for it? Explain.

   ....
   ....
   ....
   ....
   ....

6. **SEP Construct Arguments** Explain why both the paramecium and rotifer are considered living things. Which organism is more complex, and which may live longer?

   ....
   ....
   ....
   ....
   ....
   ....
   ....
   ....

Quest FINDINGS

Complete the Quest!

Phenomenon In a group, identify the criteria and constraints for your field guide. Then, create your guide for the nature center.

SEP Identify Limitations What are some of the difficulties of creating classification systems for your field guide? How else could you organize living things?

....
....
....
....
....
....

⬆ INTERACTIVITY

Create Your Field Guide

MS-LS1-1

It's Alive!

How can you **gather evidence** to **distinguish living** things from **nonliving** things?

Background

Phenomenon Before scientists could peer into microscopes, they had very different ideas about what living things were made of. It was a challenge to classify organisms when they couldn't even distinguish between living and nonliving things.

It may seem pretty obvious to you today that a flower is a living thing and a rock is a nonliving thing. But how could you explain this difference to a class of third-grade students in a way they would understand? In this investigation, you will observe samples of living and nonliving things. You will use the data you collect to develop an explanation of how living things can be distinguished from nonliving things.

Materials

(per group)

- hand lens
- samples of living and nonliving things
- prepared slides or microscope pictures of living and nonliving things
- microscope

Safety

Be sure to follow all safety guidelines provided by your teacher. The Safety Appendix of your textbook provides more details about the safety icons.

Dust mite

Procedure

HANDS-ON LAB

⬇**Demonstrate** Go online for a downloadable worksheet of this lab.

1. Work with a partner. At your workstation, you should have a hand lens, a microscope, and paper and pencils for drawing.

2. Discuss with your partner what you should be looking for to help you determine whether your samples are living or nonliving. Then, from the class supplies, choose one sample and the microscope slide or microscope photograph that goes with it. Take them to your station to examine.

3. On a separate paper, make detailed observations of your sample, label it, note whether it is living or nonliving, and describe any structures you observe.

4. Return your sample and select a new one. Continue until you have examined five different samples. You should include three different organisms and two nonliving things, and include at least one fungus and one autotroph.

5. Based on your observations, complete the data table that follows. There may be some spaces that you are not sure how to fill out. If you have time, take another look at the sample(s) in question to gather more evidence.

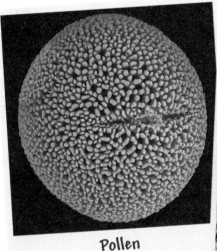

Pollen

Honey

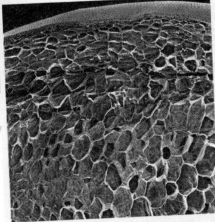

Cross-section of tomato

uDemonstrate Lab

Observations

Sample Name	Living or Nonliving?	Observations	Sketches

Analyze and Interpret Data

1. **CCC Evaluate Scale** Why is the microscope necessary for determining whether a sample is living or nonliving?

....

....

....

....

....

2. **CCC Analyze Properties** Compare the appearance of the living samples to the appearance of the nonliving samples. How do you explain the differences in structures?

....

....

....

....

....

....

3. **SEP Characterize Data** Based on what you observed, what are some ways that the living things in this lab could be grouped or organized?

....

....

....

....

....

4. **SEP Construct Explanations** How would you explain to third-graders the difference between living things and nonliving things? What examples could you give to support your claim?

....

....

....

....

....

....

TOPIC

2

Ecosystems

MS-LS2-1 Analyze and interpret data to provide evidence for the effects of resource availability on organisms and populations of organisms in an ecosystem.

MS-LS2-3 Develop a model to describe the cycling of matter and flow of energy among living and nonliving parts of an ecosystem.

EP&Clib Students should be developing an understanding that direct and indirect changes to natural systems due to the growth of human populations and their consumption rates influence the geographic extent, composition, biological diversity, and viability of natural systems.

EP&CIIIa Students should be developing an understanding that natural systems proceed through cycles and processes that are required for their functioning.

HOW are these manatees well suited to their environment?

HANDS-ON LAB

uConnect Explore how you are part of a cycle on Earth.

GO ONLINE
to access your
digital course

▶ VIDEO

👆 INTERACTIVITY

🧪 VIRTUAL LAB

☑ ASSESSMENT

📖 eTEXT

🧪 HANDS-ON LABS

The Essential Question

How are matter and energy cycled in an ecosystem?

CCC Energy and Matter Manatees are large aquatic mammals that travel along the coast of states in the Southeast. Their closest living relatives are elephants, and their ancestors lived on land. What are some things in a manatee's environment that it might need to survive? Record your ideas below.

....

....

....

....

....

Quest KICKOFF

What do you think is causing Pleasant Pond to turn green?

Phenomenon In 2016, algal blooms turned bodies of water green and slimy in California, Florida, Utah, and many other states. These blooms put people and ecosystems in danger. Scientists that study lakes and other inland bodies of water, known as limnologists, are working to predict and prevent future algal blooms. In this problem-based Quest activity, you will investigate an algal bloom at a lake and determine its cause. In labs and digital activities, you will apply what you learn in each lesson to help you gather evidence to solve the mystery. With enough evidence, you will be able to identify what you believe is the cause of the algal bloom and present a solution in the Findings activity.

 INTERACTIVITY

Mystery at Pleasant Pond

 MS-LS2-1, MS-LS2-3, EP&CIIb, EP&CIIIa

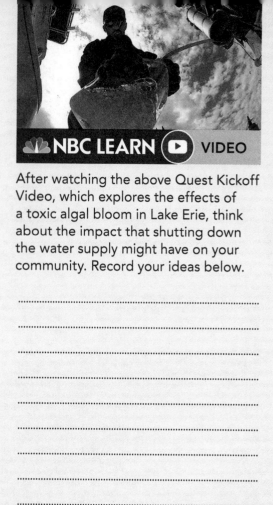

NBC LEARN ▶ VIDEO

After watching the above Quest Kickoff Video, which explores the effects of a toxic algal bloom in Lake Erie, think about the impact that shutting down the water supply might have on your community. Record your ideas below.

....
....
....
....
....
....
....
....

Quest CHECK-IN

IN LESSON 1

What are some possible causes of the algal bloom in the pond? Evaluate data to identify possible explanations for the problems at the pond.

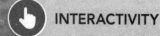 **INTERACTIVITY**

Suspicious Activities

Quest CHECK-IN

IN LESSON 2

How do nutrients affect organisms in an aquatic environment? Investigate how the nonliving factors can affect the organisms in a pond.

 INTERACTIVITY

Nutrients and Aquatic Organisms

An algal bloom can seriously disrupt an ecosystem by interfering with an organism's ability to find food or function properly.

Quest CHECK-IN

IN LESSON 3

How are cycles of matter and energy affected by environmental change? Explore the cycling of matter and the flow of energy among organisms in a pond.

👆 **INTERACTIVITY**

Matter and Energy in a Pond

Quest FINDINGS

Complete the Quest!

Write a news story explaining what you think is the cause of the algal bloom in the pond. Tell how it has impacted the ecosystem and include a proposal for restoring the pond.

👆 **INTERACTIVITY**

Reflections on a Pond

Living Things and the Environment

Guiding Questions

- How are populations affected by changes to the amount and availability of resources?
- How are population size and resource availability related?

Connections

Literacy Cite Textual Evidence

Math Represent Relationships

MS-LS2-1 Analyze and interpret data to provide evidence for the effects of resource availability on organisms and populations of organisms in an ecosystem. (Also **EP&CIIb**)

ʋ**Investigate** Model how space can be a limiting factor.

Vocabulary

organism
habitat
biotic factor
abiotic factor
population
community
ecosystem
limiting factor

Academic Vocabulary

resources
density

Connect It!

 Circle and label some of the nonliving things at the beach.

SEP Construct Explanations Why are these things considered nonliving, and why do organisms need them?

....

....

....

Organisms and Habitats

At the beach shown in **Figure 1**, animals such as California sea lions stop to molt, breed, and give birth. A sea lion is an **organism**, or living thing. Different types of organisms live in different types of surroundings, or environments. All organisms are dependent on their environmental interactions with both living things and nonliving factors. An organism interacts with its environment to get the **resources**—food, water, shelter, and other things—that it needs to live, grow, and reproduce. An environment that provides the things a specific organism needs to live, grow, and reproduce is called a **habitat**.

In nature, every organism you see in a particular habitat is there because that habitat meets the organism's needs. Some organisms have the ability to move from one habitat to another as conditions change or as different needs arise, but many organisms stay in the same habitat for their entire lives. The living and nonliving things in a particular environment and the interactions among them define the habitat and its conditions.

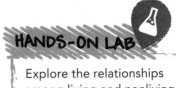

HANDS-ON LAB

Explore the relationships among living and nonliving things in a local area.

Academic Vocabulary

Have you heard the term *resources* in other contexts? List some examples.

....

....

....

....

A Hangout in the Habitat
Figure 1 In any environment, like La Jolla Beach located north of San Diego in California, living and nonliving things interact with each other.

69

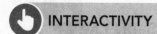

INTERACTIVITY

Explore the factors in a habitat.

VIDEO

Explore biotic and abiotic factors in everyday life.

Reflect What are some of the biotic and abiotic factors in the ecosystem in which you live?

Biotic Factors

Biotic Factors What types of living things are in the Pacific Gopher snake's forest habitat below (**Figure 2**)? The parts of a habitat that are or were once alive and that interact with an organism are called **biotic factors**. These biological components include the trees and plants. Animals that the gopher snake eats are biotic factors, as are the other snakes it encounters. Waste products made by these organisms and others are also considered biotic factors. Bacteria, mushrooms, and other small organisms are other types of biotic factors that play important roles in the habitat.

Abiotic Factors

Abiotic Factors Organisms also interact with nonliving things in the environment. **Abiotic factors** are the nonliving parts of an organism's habitat. These physical components include water, oxygen, space, rocks, light, temperature, and soil. The quality and condition of the abiotic factors can have a major effect on living things. For example, water in a habitat may contain pollutants. The poor quality of the water may result in sickness or death for the organisms that live there.

CHECK POINT **Cite Textual Evidence** Why do you think snakes do not live in the Arctic tundra? Use evidence from the text to support your answer.

....

....

Gopher Snake Habitat

Figure 2 This Pacific gopher snake, native to California, interacts with many biotic and abiotic factors in its habitat.

Design It!

There are different biotic and abiotic factors in a habitat.

SEP Develop Models Using common materials to model biotic and abiotic factors, draw a model of a local habitat. Include a key to identify what the different materials represent.

Organism Population Community Ecosystem

Ecosystem Organization

An organism rarely lives alone in its habitat. Instead, organisms live together in populations and communities that interact with abiotic factors in their ecosystems. Interactions can also occur among the various populations. **Figure 3** summarizes the levels of organization in an ecosystem.

Organisms All of the Sandhill cranes that live in Central California are members of one species. A species (SPEE sheez) is a group of organisms that can mate with each other and produce offspring that can also mate and reproduce.

Populations All the members of one species living in a particular area are referred to as a **population**. The Sandhill cranes that live in the San Joaquin Valley, for example, are one example of a population.

Communities A particular area usually contains more than one species of organism. The San Joaquin Valley is home to hundreds of bird species, as well as mammals, plants, and other varieties of organisms. All the different populations that live together in an area make up a **community**.

The community of organisms that lives in a particular area, along with the nonliving environment, make up an **ecosystem**. The study of how organisms interact with each other and with their environment is called ecology.

✓ CHECK POINT **Determine Meaning** What makes up a community in an ecosystem?

....

....

....

Levels of Organization
Figure 3 A single individual in an ecosystem is the organism, which forms a population with other members of its species. Different species form communities in a single ecosystem.

CCC Systems Make a prediction about how a lack of resources in an ecosystem might impact the levels of organization.

....

....

....

....

....

....

....

Literacy Connection

Cite Textual Evidence Suppose farmers in an area spray insecticides on their crops. A population of birds that feeds on insects begins to decline. Underline the text that supports the idea that the insecticide may be responsible for the decline in the bird population.

Populations

Remember from your reading that a population consists of all of the organisms of the same species living in the same area at the same time. For example, all of the gopher snakes living in the same forest would be a distinct population. There are several things that can change a population's size.

Births and Deaths New individuals generally join a population by being born into it. A population grows when more individuals are born into it than die in any period of time. So when the birth rate (the number of births per 1,000 individuals for a given time period) is greater than the death rate (the number of deaths per 1,000 individuals for a given time period) a population may increase. When the birth rate is the same as the death rate, then the population usually remains stable. In situations where the death rate is greater than the birth rate, the population will decrease.

Math Toolbox

Graphing Population Changes

Changes over time in a population, such as deer in California, can be displayed in a graph.

Deer Population Trends, 2000–2010

Year	Population (estimated)	Year	Population (estimated)
2000	509,000	2006	420,140
2001	674,500	2007	438,140
2002	554,000	2008	487,000
2003	525,230	2009	484,400
2004	475,800	2010	445,446
2005	602,650		

1. **Represent Relationship** ✏ Use the data table to complete a graph of the changes in the deer population. Then describe the trend in the graph.

....

....

....

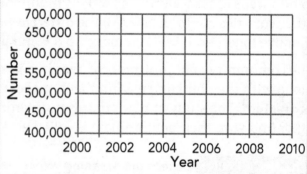

SOURCE: California Department of Fish and Wildlife

2. **SEP Interpret Data** What factors do you think might be responsible for spikes and drops in the deer population?

....

....

Immigration and Emigration A population's size also can increase or decrease when individuals move into or out of the population. Immigration (im ih GRAY shun) means moving into a population. Emigration (em ih GRAY shun) means leaving a population. For instance, if food is scarce, some members of the antelope herd in **Figure 4** may wander off in search of a better habitat. If they become permanently separated from the original herd, they will no longer be part of that population.

Population Density If you are a scientist studying an ecosystem or population, it can be helpful to know the population **density** —the number of individuals in an area of a specific size. Population density can be represented as an equation:

$$\text{Population density} = \frac{\text{Number of individuals}}{\text{Unit area}}$$

For example, suppose an ecologist estimates there are 800 beetles living in a park measuring 400 square meters. The population density would be 800 beetles per 400 square meters, or 2 beetles per square meter.

☑ CHECK POINT **Summarize Text** How do birth and death rates affect a population's size?

....

....

....

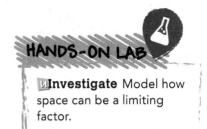

HANDS-ON LAB

☑**Investigate** Model how space can be a limiting factor.

Academic Vocabulary
Have you heard the term *density* before? What did it mean in that other context?

....

....

Emigration
Figure 4 Food scarcity is just one cause of emigration.
SEP Construct Explanations What factors might cause individuals in this antelope herd to emigrate?

....

....

....

....

....

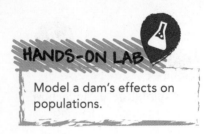
Factors That Limit Population Growth

In any ecosystem, organisms and populations with similar requirements for food, water, oxygen, or other resources may compete with each other for limited resources. Less access to these resources consequently constrains their growth and reproduction. An environmental factor that causes a population to stop growing or to decrease in size, such as a fatal disease infecting organisms, is a **limiting factor**.

Food and Water Food and water can be limiting factors for virtually any population. An adult elephant eats an average of around 180 kilograms of vegetation each day to survive. Suppose the trees in its habitat can provide 1000 kilograms of vegetation daily. In this habitat, not more than 5 adult elephants could survive. The largest population that an area can support is called its carrying capacity.

Climate and Weather Changes in climate can limit population growth. Warmer weather in the early winter, for example, can cause some plants to continue growing. Natural disasters such as hurricanes and floods can have immediate and long-term effects on populations.

Space and Shelter Other limiting factors for populations are space and shelter, as illustrated by the nesting site in **Figure 5**. When individual organisms must compete for space to live or raise young, the population can decrease. Competition for suitable shelter also can limit the growth of a population.

☑ CHECK POINT **Summarize Text** How do limiting factors affect a population of organisms?

....

....

Limited Space

Figure 5 🖉 In the image of the gannets, circle the available space in the environment for nesting and raising young.

CCC Cause and Effect How does the lack of space act as a limiting factor for these gannets?

....

....

....

....

....

☑LESSON 1 Check

1. **CCC Systems** Identify the levels of organization in an ecosystem from smallest to largest.

....

....

Use the graph to answer questions 2 and 3.

Changes in Mouse Population

2. **SEP Analyze Data** What trends do you observe in the mouse population for the four years?

....

....

....

3. **SEP Interpret Data** Does the data support the idea that this population is relatively stable? Give evidence to support your answer.

....

....

....

4. **SEP Construct Explanations** How can biotic and abiotic factors in an ecosystem affect populations? Give two examples of each.

....

....

....

....

....

....

....

5. **CCC Stability and Change** Why is climate considered to be a limiting factor for populations in an ecosystem?

....

....

....

Quest CHECK-IN

In this lesson, you learned how ecosystems are organized and how different factors affect populations.

CCC Cause and Effect What effect might an algal bloom in a pond have on populations of organisms that make their home there?

....

....

....

....

....

....

INTERACTIVITY

Suspicious Activities

Go online to research and explore explanations for the algal bloom. Then, using the information you have gathered, identify three possible causes for the bloom.

LESSON 2

Energy Flow in Ecosystems

Guiding Questions

- What are the energy roles in an ecosystem?
- How is energy transferred between living and nonliving parts of an ecosystem?
- How is energy conserved in an ecosystem?

Connections

Literacy Integrate with Visuals

Math Analyze Proportional Relationships

 MS-LS2-3 Develop a model to describe the cycling of matter and flow of energy among living and nonliving parts of an ecosystem. (Also **EP&CIIIa**)

HANDS-ON LAB

ʋInvestigate Observe how decomposers get energy.

Vocabulary

producer
consumer
decomposer
food chain
food web
energy pyramid

Academic Vocabulary

role

Connect It!

✏ **Shade in one of the arrows to indicate the direction in which energy flows between the tule elk and the grass.**

CCC Energy and Matter Where do you think the plants in the image get the energy they need to grow and survive?

....

....

....

Energy Roles in an Ecosystem

In gym class, have you ever been assigned to play a position like catcher or goalie for your class team? If so, you know what it's like to have a specific **role** in a system. Similar to positions in sports, every organism has a role in the movement of energy through its ecosystem.

Energy roles are based on the way organisms obtain food and interact with other organisms. In an ecosystem, organisms play the energy role of either a producer, consumer, or decomposer.

Producers Energy enters most ecosystems as sunlight. Some organisms, such as the terrestrial plants shown in **Figure 1** and some types of bacteria, use nonliving parts of the ecosystem to carry out life functions. For example, in a process called photosynthesis, these organisms use the sun's energy to recombine atoms from various elements and molecules of water and carbon dioxide into food molecules—all of which are nonliving.

An organism that can make its own food is a **producer**. Producers interact with the ecosystem when they become the source of food for other organisms. In terrestrial ecosystems, plants grow on the land and capture energy from sunlight. However, in an aquatic environment of the dark deep ocean, some bacteria convert chemical energy into food from hydrothermal vents in the ocean floor. They are the producers in these ecosystems that include worms, clams, and crabs.

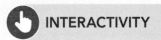

INTERACTIVITY

Identify the sources of your dinner.

Academic Vocabulary

Have you heard the term *role* in other contexts? List some examples.

....

....

....

Obtaining Energy

Figure 1 Tule elk are found only in the marshy areas and the grasslands of California's Central Valley. Their lush habitat provides them with their food of choice—tule sedge, a flowering plant that resembles grass.

INTERACTIVITY

Model energy roles and energy flow in ecosystems.

INTERACTIVITY

Explore the roles living things play in ecosystems.

✏️ **Write About It** What are some producers, consumers, scavengers, and decomposers you have seen in your neighborhood? Record your observations.

Life and Death in an Alaskan Stream

Figure 2 Salmon migrate upstream to this forest environment after spending most of their lives at sea. As they travel, many of them become food for the ecosystem's carnivores.

SEP Develop Models ✏️
Label the producers, consumers, decomposers, and scavengers in the image.

Consumers Organisms like the animals in **Figure 2** cannot produce their own food. Instead, one way these organisms interact with their ecosystem is by eating other organisms. A **consumer** obtains energy by feeding on other organisms.

To classify consumers according to what they eat, scientists make observations and look for patterns. As consumers eat, the food is broken down into nonliving molecules that help supply them with energy.

Consumers that eat only animals are carnivores. Great white sharks, owls, and tigers are examples of carnivores. Some carnivores are scavengers. A scavenger is a carnivore that feeds on the bodies of dead organisms. Scavengers include hagfish and condors. Some carnivores will scavenge if they cannot find live animals to prey upon.

Herbivores are consumers that eat only plants and other photosynthetic organisms. Grasshoppers, rabbits, and cows are herbivores.

Consumers that can eat both plants and animals are omnivores. Raccoons, pigs, and humans are omnivores.

Decomposers If the only roles in an ecosystem were producer and consumer, then some of the nonliving matter that is essential for life, such as carbon and nitrogen, would remain in the waste products and remains of dead organisms. However, decomposers have a role in ecosystems to prevent this from happening. **Decomposers** break down biotic wastes and dead organisms, returning the raw materials to the ecosystem. For example, after adult salmon swim upstream and reproduce, they die. Their carcasses litter the riverbeds and banks. Bacteria in the soil help break down the carcasses, releasing their nutrients to trees, grasses, shrubs, and other producers that depend on them.

In a sense, decomposers interact with their environment as nature's recyclers. While obtaining energy, decomposers also return nonliving matter in the form of simple molecules to the environment. These molecules can be used again by other organisms. Mushrooms, bacteria, and mold are common decomposers.

HANDS-ON LAB

☑**Investigate** Observe how decomposers get energy.

☑ CHECK POINT **Integrate with Visuals** In terms of their energy roles, what similarities do the bear, salmon, and coyote in **Figure 2** share?

....

....

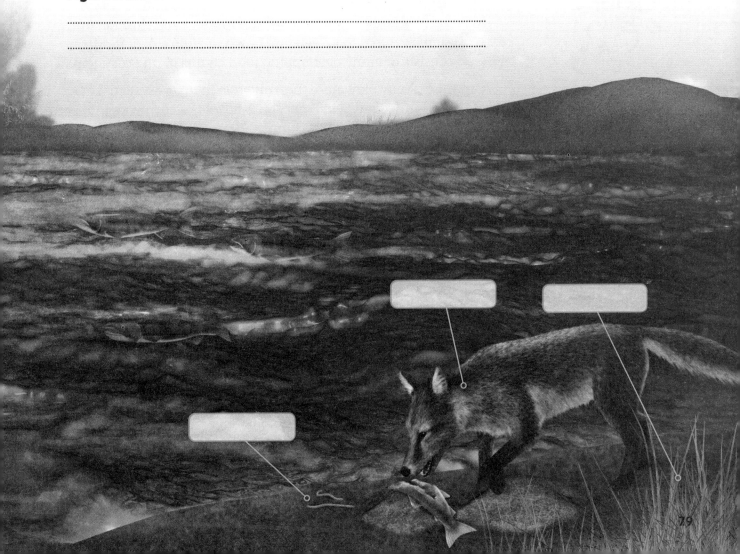

Food chain

Grizzly bear

Salmon

Crustaceans

Zooplankton

Phytoplankton

Energy and Matter Transfer

Energy in most ecosystems comes from sunlight, and producers convert this energy into food through photosynthesis. The transfer of energy can be tracked as energy flows through a natural system. The energy and matter are contained in atoms and molecules that are transferred to herbivores that eat the producers. Then they move on to carnivores feeding on the first, or primary, consumers. The energy and matter next move on through other meat-eating secondary consumers. This pattern of energy and matter movement can be described through different models: food chains, food webs, and energy pyramids.

Food Chains A food chain is one way to show how energy and matter move through an ecosystem. A **food chain** is a series of events in which one organism eats another and obtains energy and nutrients. **Figure 3** illustrates one example of a food chain. The arrows indicate the movement of energy and matter as organisms are consumed up the food chain.

Food Webs Energy and matter move in one direction through a food chain, but they can also take different paths through the ecosystem. However, most producers and consumers are part of many overlapping food chains. A more realistic way to show how energy and matter cycle through an ecosystem is with a food web. As shown in **Figure 4**, a **food web** consists of many overlapping food chains in an ecosystem.

Organisms may play more than one role in an ecosystem. Look at the red-tailed hawk in **Figure 4**. A hawk is a carnivore that eats mostly second-level consumers. However, when a hawk eats a kangaroo rat, it is a third-level consumer.

Humans also play a role on the natural cycling of food webs. We depend upon food webs for energy and financial gain. Yet, we can alter the natural system of a food web by destroying habitats and removing too much energy. When we do this, we interrupt the natural cycle needed for the food web to function.

Food Chain

Figure 3 The food chain tracing a path from the phytoplankton to the grizzly bear is a simple way of showing how energy and matter flow from one organism to the next in the Alaskan stream ecosystem shown in **Figure 2**.

CCC System Models What are some limitations of modeling the flow of energy and matter in an ecosystem with a food chain?

....

....

Model It !

Food Web

Figure 4 This food web depicts relationships among some of the organisms that live in the Mojave Desert in California.

SEP Develop Models ✎ Complete the food web by drawing and identifying the missing organisms listed below. Add arrows to the diagram to complete the web. Then, label the nonliving parts of the ecosystem.

| cactus | coyote | deer | rattlesnake |

Red-tailed Hawk

Third-level consumers eat the second-level conumers

Scorpion

Tarantula

Second-level consumers eat the first-level conumers

Jerusalem cricket

Kangaroo rat

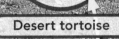
Desert tortoise

First-level consumers eat the producers

Joshua tree

Grass

Producers form the base of the food web

Literacy Connection

Integrate with Visuals

Why is an energy pyramid shaped like a triangle with the point on top?

....

....

....

....

Energy Pyramids A diagram called an **energy pyramid** shows the amount of energy that moves from one feeding level to another in a food web. Each step in a food chain or food web is represented by a level within an energy pyramid, as shown in **Figure 5**. Producers have the most available energy so they make up the first level, or base, of the pyramid. Energy moves up the pyramid from the producers, to the first-level consumers, to the second-level consumers and so on. There is no limit to the number of levels in a food web or energy pyramid. However, each level has less energy available than the level below. When more levels exist between a producer and a consumer, a smaller percentage of the producer's original energy is available to that consumer.

When an organism consumes food it obtains energy and matter used to carry out life activities. These activities produce heat, which is released and lost to the environment, reducing the amount of energy available to the next level.

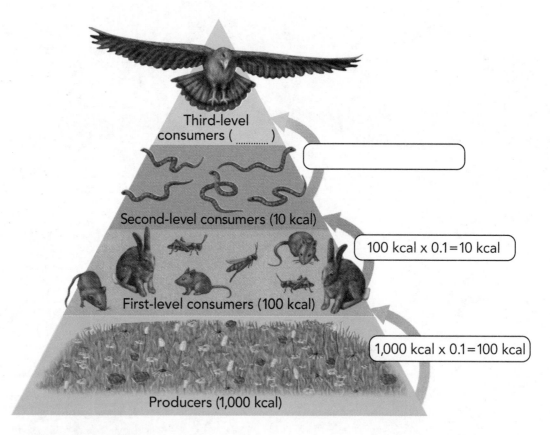

Energy Pyramid

Figure 5 This energy pyramid shows how the amount of available energy decreases as you move up an energy pyramid from the producers to the different levels of consumers. Only about 10 percent of the energy is transferred from level to level. Energy is measured in kilocalories, or kcal.

SEP Use Mathematics ✐ Write in the missing equation and fill in the energy that gets to the hawk at the top.

Energy Availability As you can see in **Figure 5**, only about 10 percent of the energy at one level of a food web is available to the next higher level. This greatly limits how many different levels a food chain can have, as well as the numbers of organisms that can be supported at higher levels. This is why it is typical for there to be fewer organisms as you move from one level of a pyramid or one "link" in a food chain up to the next level.

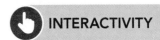

INTERACTIVITY

Model how altering a food web affects the flow of energy and matter in an ecosystem.

✓ **CHECK POINT** **Summarize Text** Why is energy reduced at each level of the energy pyramid?

....

....

....

Math Toolbox

Relationships in an Energy Pyramid

In the San Francisco Bay Area Delta ecosystem, shrimp eat algae. Chinook salmon eat the shrimp, and great blue herons eat the Chinook salmon. Suppose that the algae contain 550,000 kilocalories.

1. **SEP Calculate** 🖊 Complete the pyramid by calculating the energy available to each level.

2. **Analyze Proportional Relationships** How would the amount of energy in the pyramid change if the shrimp ate only half of the available algae?

....

....

....

....

....

....

....

Third-level consumers

Second-level consumers

First-level consumers

550,000 kcal

Producers

☑ LESSON 2 Check

MS-LS2-3, EP&CIIIa

1. CCC System Models Which model best illustrates the flow of energy and matter in an ecosystem—a food chain or a food web? Explain.

....

....

....

....

....

2. SEP Evaluate Information A student says an organism that is both a first-level and second-level consumer is an omnivore. Is that student correct? Explain.

....

....

3. CCC Energy and Matter Suppose a rancher wants to buy some grassland to raise cattle. What should she know about energy flow before she invests in the land or the cattle?

....

....

....

....

....

....

4. CCC Patterns In Massachusetts, a team of scientists studying great white sharks estimates that a population of 15,000 seals supports fewer than 100 sharks during the summer. Why are there so few top-level consumers in this system?

....

....

....

....

....

....

5. SEP Construct Explanations Human activity can affect ecosystems by removing producers, consumers, and decomposers. What limiting factors may result from human actions, and what effects might they have on the flow of energy and matter in an ecosystem?

....

....

....

....

....

....

....

Quest CHECK-IN

In this lesson, you learned about the general roles that organisms can play in an ecosystem, as well as how relationships among those roles can be modeled through food chains, food webs, and energy pyramids.

CCC Stability and Change How might knowing about energy roles help you understand what's happening in the pond?

....

....

 INTERACTIVITY

Nutrients and Aquatic Organisms

Go online to analyze what might happen to a pond ecosystem when nutrient levels are altered. Then discuss how the results of your analysis could help you solve the mystery.

MS-LS2-1, MS-LS2-3, EP&CIIb, EP&CIIIa

Eating Oil

Do you know how tiny organisms can clean up oil spills? You engineer it! Strategies used to deal with the Deepwater Horizon oil spill, the worst in U.S. history, show us how.

The Challenge: To clean up harmful oil from marine environments

Phenomenon On April 20, 2010, part of an oil rig in the Gulf of Mexico exploded. It leaked oil for 87 days. By the time the leak was fixed, about 200 million gallons of oil had spilled into the water. Oil destroys beaches, marshlands, and marine ecosystems. It coats birds, fish, and marine animals, such as dolphins and sea turtles. The oil makes it difficult for many animals to move and get food, and causes others to suffocate.

Ecologists engineered a solution that relied on nature to help with the cleanup. They poured chemicals into the water that helped break up the oil into smaller droplets. Then the bacteria and fungi in the water broke down the oil droplets.

Bioremediation uses natural living things to reduce contaminants in an environment. In the event of an oil spill, oil-eating populations of bacteria and fungi grow quickly. Now, scientists are working to engineer ways to increase the speed at which these decomposers work and to make sure the oceans can support optimal populations of these tiny oil eaters.

👆 **INTERACTIVITY**

Design your own method to clean up an oil spill.

The oil-eating bacteria helped in the cleanup after the Deepwater Horizon oil spill.

DESIGN CHALLENGE Can you put decomposers to work and build your own composter? Go to the Engineering Design Notebook to find out!

③ Cycles of Matter

Guiding Questions

- How is matter transferred between the living and nonliving parts of an ecosystem?
- How is matter conserved in an ecosystem?

Connections

Literacy Determine Central Ideas

Math Analyze Relationships

 MS-LS2-3 Develop a model to describe the cycling of matter and flow of energy among living and nonliving parts of an ecosystem. (Also **EP&CIIIa**)

HANDS-ON LAB

ᴜ**Investigate** Model the water cycle.

Vocabulary

Law of Conservation of Mass
Law of Conservation of Energy
evaporation
condensation
precipitation

Academic Vocabulary

system
components

Connect It !

✏ **Draw arrows on Figure 1 and label them to show how energy enters and leaves the terrarium.**

CCC Cause and Effect What would happen to the ecosystem in the terrarium if it were a closed system for energy?

....

....

SEP Explain Phenomena Why is this ecosystem considered a closed system and how could that system be changed?

....

....

....

Conservation of Matter and Energy

During photosynthesis and cellular respiration, matter and energy change form but the amounts stay the same. **The Law of Conservation of Mass** states that matter is neither created nor destroyed during any chemical or physical change. **The Law of Conservation of Energy** states that when one form of energy is transformed to another, no energy is lost in the process. Energy cannot be created or destroyed, but it can change from one form to another. The cycling of matter and energy can be observed in natural systems.

All over Earth, the transfer of matter and energy can be tracked as they flow through natural systems. For example, the terrarium in **Figure 1** is a closed **system** for matter. Matter cannot enter or exit. The plants, soil, air, rocks, water, microorganisms, and animals in the terrarium are all **components** of the system. As natural systems cycle, these components change form, but their total mass remains the same.

☑ CHECK POINT **Summarize Text** What would you tell a classmate who claims that food is destroyed when you eat it?

....

 INTERACTIVITY

Consider your role in the cycling of energy.

Academic Vocabulary

The schools in one area are often called a *school system*. What are some of the *components* of this system?

....

....

....

....

Ecosystem in a Jar
Figure 1 After it is sealed, a terrarium becomes a closed system for matter. But energy can still flow in and out through the glass.

Spring Water

Figure 2 The water at Yellow Springs is high in iron, which stains the rocks orange.

Water Cycle

Recall that matter is made up of tiny particles called atoms and two or more atoms can join to make a molecule. Two hydrogen atoms combined with one oxygen atom forms a molecule of water.

Water is essential for life. Water cycles in a continuous process from Earth's surface to the atmosphere and back. As energy is transferred through the water cycle, it can be tracked as it changes into various forms, or states. The water cycle involves the processes of evaporation, condensation, and precipitation. Follow along on **Figure 3** as you read about each process.

Evaporation Water molecules move from Earth's surface into the atmosphere by evaporation. **Evaporation** is the process by which molecules at the surface of liquid water absorb enough energy to change to a gas. This water vapor rises into the atmosphere as part of atmospheric convection. The energy needed for evaporation comes from sunlight. Water evaporates from oceans, lakes, fields, and other places. Smaller amounts of water also evaporate from living things. For example, plants release water vapor from their leaves. In addition, animals release liquid water in their wastes and water vapor when they exhale. You may recall that one of the products of cellular respiration is water.

Model It!

Where does your water come from?

Yellow Springs, Ohio, shown in **Figure 2**, has been a source of refreshing water for animals and people for centuries. Geologists studying the Yellow Spring have determined that the spring is fed by rain that falls only a few miles north. After the rain soaks into the ground, it travels underground for 12 to 18 months before flowing out of the spring.

SEP Develop Models ✏ Does your drinking water come from a central water supply, a well, or bottles? Identify the source of your water and trace its origin back as far as you can. Make a model of the path the water takes to get to your home.

Condensation

Rising water vapor reaches a point in the atmosphere where it cools. As it cools, it turns back into small droplets of water in a liquid state. The process of a gas changing to a liquid is **condensation.** The water droplets collect around dust particles and eventually form clouds. Dew is water that has condensed on plants or other objects on a cool morning.

Precipitation

Condensing water vapor collects as clouds, but as the drops continue to grow larger, they become heavier. Eventually the heavy drops fall in the form of **precipitation:** rain, snow, sleet, or hail. Precipitation can fall into oceans, lakes, or rivers. Precipitation falling on land may soak into the soil and become groundwater, or it may run off the land and flow into rivers or oceans.

HANDS-ON LAB

⎚**Investigate** Model the water cycle.

📓**Write About It** Think how you interacted with water today. Where did that water come from? Where did it go next? Write a story that traces the water molecule's trip.

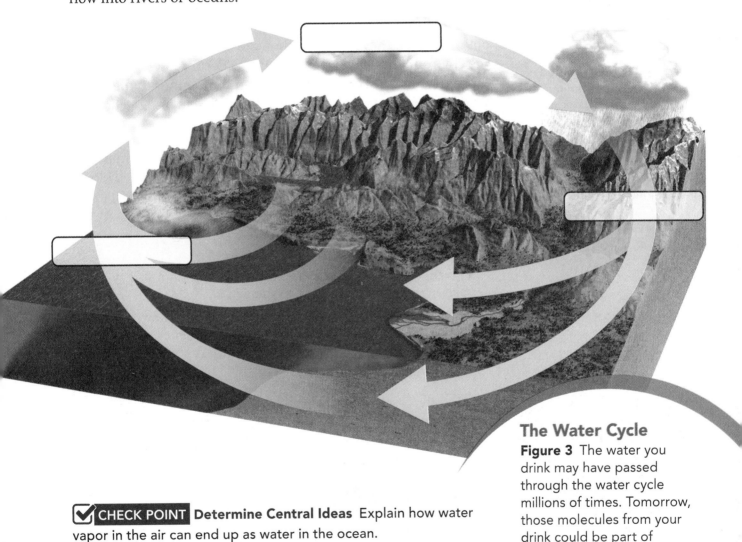

The Water Cycle

Figure 3 The water you drink may have passed through the water cycle millions of times. Tomorrow, those molecules from your drink could be part of a cloud, a drop of rain, a stream, or water vapor in the air.

CCC Systems ✏ Label the three processes of the water cycle.

☑**CHECK POINT** **Determine Central Ideas** Explain how water vapor in the air can end up as water in the ocean.

....

....

....

89

Carbon and Oxygen Cycles

Carbon and oxygen are essential for life. Carbon is the building block of living things. For example, carbon is a major component of bones and the proteins that build muscles. Most organisms also use oxygen for their life processes. **Figure 4** shows how carbon and oxygen cycles in ecosystems are linked. Producers, consumers, and decomposers all play roles in recycling carbon and oxygen.

Carbon Cycle

Most producers take in carbon dioxide gas from the air during photosynthesis. Producers use the carbon to make food—carbon-containing molecules, such as sugars and starches. Carbon is also converted by plants to compounds that help plants grow. Consumers eat other organisms and take in their carbon compounds. When producers and consumers then break down the food to obtain energy, they release carbon dioxide and water into the environment. When organisms die, decomposers break down the remains, and release carbon compounds to the soil where it is available for use. Some decomposers also release carbon dioxide into the air.

Oxygen Cycle

Oxygen also cycles through ecosystems. Producers release oxygen as a product of photosynthesis. Most organisms take in oxygen from the air or water and use it to carry out cellular respiration.

Literacy Connection

Determine Central Ideas
Work with a partner. Think about one food you have eaten recently. Where did the carbon in that food come from? Was the food made from plants, animals, fungi, or bacteria—or all of those sources? Where will the carbon go now that you have eaten the food? Share your response with another pair of students.

The Carbon and Oxygen Cycles

Figure 4 Producers, consumers, and decomposers all play roles in recycling carbon and oxygen.

SEP Develop Models ✏ Draw arrows to show how carbon and oxygen move through the ecosystem.

Oxygen (O_2) in the air

Carbon compounds in the soil

Law of Conservation On Earth, the atoms that make up the organisms in an ecosystem are cycled repeatedly between living and nonliving parts of the ecosystem. For example, the number of carbon and oxygen atoms remains constant when producers undergo photosynthesis. The Law of Conservation of Mass also supports that atoms may appear in different chemical compounds as they cycle through Earth's systems, but these atoms are never created or destroyed.

Human Impact Some human activities affect the levels of carbon and oxygen in the air. When humans burn gasoline, natural gas, and plant fuels, carbon dioxide is released into the atmosphere. Carbon dioxide levels also rise when humans clear forests to create farmland or to use the wood for fuel.

When trees are removed from an ecosystem, there are fewer producers to absorb carbon dioxide. If fallen trees are left on the ground, decomposers will break down their tissues through cellular respiration and release carbon dioxide into the air. Burning the trees has the same effect, because carbon dioxide is produced during combustion.

☑ **CHECK POINT** **Summarize Text** Describe the roles of producers and consumers in the oxygen cycle.

....

....

....

👆 **INTERACTIVITY**

Investigate and identify the cycles of matter.

Carbon dioxide (CO_2) in the air

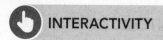
Nitrogen Cycle in Ecosystems

Like carbon, nitrogen is one of the necessary elements of life. Nitrogen is an important component for building proteins in animals and an essential nutrient for plants. In the nitrogen cycle, nitrogen moves from the air into the soil, into living things, and back into the air or soil. The air around you is about 78 percent nitrogen gas (N_2). However, most organisms cannot use nitrogen gas. Nitrogen gas is called "free" nitrogen because it is not combined with other kinds of atoms.

Nitrogen Fixation Most organisms can use nitrogen only after it has been "fixed," or combined with other elements to form nitrogen-containing compounds. Nitrogen fixation is the process of changing free nitrogen into a usable form of nitrogen, as shown in **Figure 5**. Certain bacteria perform most nitrogen fixation. These bacteria live in bumps called nodules on the roots of legume plants. Clover, beans, peas, alfalfa, peanuts, and trees such as mesquite and desert ironwood are all common legume plants. Nitrogen can also be "fixed" by lightning. About 10 percent of the nitrogen needed by plants is fixed by lightning.

Nitrogen Cycle

Figure 5 In the nitrogen cycle, free nitrogen from the air is fixed into compounds. Consumers can then use these nitrogen compounds to carry out their life processes.

CCC System Models
✏ Circle the steps where free nitrogen is changed to a form plants and animals can use.

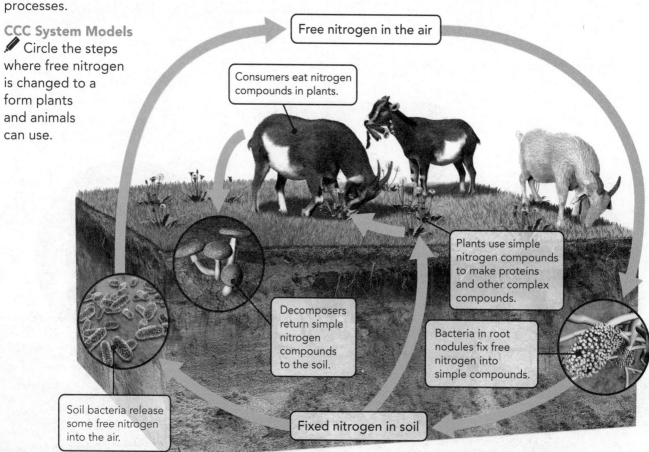

Free nitrogen in the air

Consumers eat nitrogen compounds in plants.

Plants use simple nitrogen compounds to make proteins and other complex compounds.

Decomposers return simple nitrogen compounds to the soil.

Bacteria in root nodules fix free nitrogen into simple compounds.

Soil bacteria release some free nitrogen into the air.

Fixed nitrogen in soil

Recycling Free Nitrogen Once nitrogen has been fixed, producers can use it to build proteins and other complex molecules. Nitrogen can cycle from the soil to producers and then to consumers many times. At some point, however, bacteria break down the nitrogen compounds into free nitrogen. The free nitrogen rises back into the air and the cycle begins again. This is also an example of the Law of Conservation of Mass. Throughout the cycling of nitrogen, the number of atoms remains constant. Nitrogen atoms may take the form of gas (free nitrogen) or they may take the form of nitrogen-containing compounds, but the atoms are never created or destroyed.

☑ CHECK POINT **Summarize Text** Why is nitrogen fixation necessary?

....

Math Toolbox

Dependent and Independent Variables

Soybean plants are legumes that host nitrogen-fixing bacteria in their root nodules. Researchers wanted to know whether the plants would produce more seeds if nitrogen-fixing bacteria called *Rhizobia* were added to the soil during planting. The graph below shows the results of the experiment.

1. **Analyze Relationships**
   ✏ Underline the independent variable and circle the dependent variable in the graph. Then explain their relationship.

   ....

   ....

2. **CCC Use Mathematics** Write an equation that represents the difference in seed yield between beans without treatment and beans with treatment.

   ....

   ....

   ....

   ....

   ....

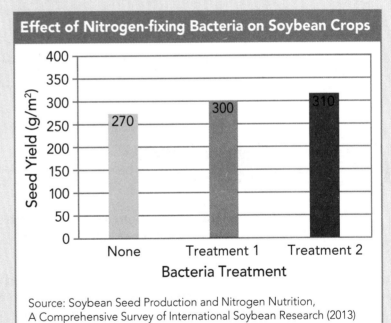

Effect of Nitrogen-fixing Bacteria on Soybean Crops

Source: Soybean Seed Production and Nitrogen Nutrition, A Comprehensive Survey of International Soybean Research (2013)

3. **SEP Interpret Data** Did the bacterial treatment have any effect? Use evidence from the graph and your equation to support your answer.

   ....

   ....

   ....

☑ LESSON 3 Check

MS-LS2-3, EP&CIIIa

1. **CCC Systems** What are the two roles of bacteria in the nitrogen cycle?

....

....

....

2. **SEP Construct Explanations** How does water get up to the atmosphere, and how does it get back down to Earth's surface?

....

....

....

....

3. **SEP Develop Models** ✏ Sketch and label a diagram showing how carbon cycles through an ecosystem.

4. **CCC Apply Concepts** How does the Law of Conservation of Mass apply to Earth's recycling of water, oxygen, carbon, and nitrogen. Give one example.

....

....

....

....

5. **CCC Energy and Matter** Compare the cycling of water and nutrients through an ecosystem to the cycling of blood in your cardiovascular system. What is the source of energy in each case?

....

....

....

....

....

....

....

....

....

Quest CHECK-IN

In this lesson, you explored the carbon, oxygen, and nitrogen cycles and learned about the roles that living things play in these cycles.

SEP Define Problems How are matter and energy cycled between plants and animals? How can you apply this information to help you determine what is happening to the pond?

....

....

....

....

INTERACTIVITY

Matter and Energy in a Pond

Go online to to investigate how matter and energy are cycled in a pond ecosystem.

MS-LS2-1, MS-LS2-3, EP&CIVb

An Appetite for Plastic?!

Organic materials, such as bone and leaves, get cycled through ecosystems by decomposers. Materials like rock and metal break down more slowly. Plastics, however, are manufactured products that cannot be broken down easily. Additionally, they are problematic for the environment. Scientists have been trying for decades to discover a way to degrade plastic. Now, it seems they may have found an answer inside the guts of two tiny larvae.

Wax worms live in beehives where they feed off beeswax. What is bad for bees, may be good for people who are looking for a way to deal with Earth's plastic problem. Scientists have found out that wax worms can digest plastic bags! How they do this isn't clear yet. It may be that bacteria living in the wax worm's gut allow it to break down the plastic. Another possibility is that the wax worm produces an enzyme, a substance that speeds up reactions in an organism's body, that helps it degrade the plastic.

Wax worms aren't the only ones getting attention for their eating habits! Mealworms are the larvae of a species of beetle. They are fed to pet reptiles, fish, and birds. Scientists have observed that mealworms can break down plastic foam, such as the kind used in coffee cups and packing materials.

Scientists are trying to figure out how these larvae are able to degrade plastic. It may be a long time before we figure out how to use that knowledge on a scale large enough to reduce global plastic pollution.

MY DISCOVERY

Use the Internet or other sources to investigate how wax worms and mealworms are able to break down different types of plastics. Create a presentation that includes a visual display that shows what type of plastic each larva can eat and how its body is able to break down plastic. Then, share your presentation with the class.

Mealworms are able to break down plastic foam.

A wax worm can munch its way through through a plastic shopping bag.

☑ TOPIC 2 Review and Assess

1 Living Things and the Environment

🔖 MS-LS2-1, EP&CIIb

1. Which statement describes a population?
   A. 85 great white sharks off Cape Cod
   B. thousands of dolphins and whales around Hawaii
   C. a mating pair of seagulls migrating to an island
   D. corals, sponges, algae, reef fish, lobsters, and giant clams

2. Which biotic factor might limit a population of mice?
   A. water for the mice to drink
   B. rainy weather that floods the mice's nests
   C. owls that prey on the mice
   D. rocks in which the mice can hide from predators

3. In terms of its effect on population, which factor is most similar to birth rate?
   A. immigration   **B.** density
   C. emigration   **D.** carrying capacity

4. CCC Apply Concepts Name two biotic and two abiotic factors you might find in a forest ecosystem.

....

....

....

5. SEP Construct Explanations Describe how the availability of water can limit the growth of a population that otherwise has unlimited resources.

....

....

....

....

....

2 Energy Flow in Ecosystems

🔖 MS-LS2-3, EP&CIIIa

6. Which term describes a straight series of connections among organisms that feed on each other?
   A. food web   **B.** ecosystem
   C. community   **D.** food chain

7. Mushrooms and bacteria are important
   A. predators.   **B.** decomposers.
   C. producers.   **D.** herbivores.

8. CCC System Models What does an energy pyramid show?

....

....

....

....

....

9. SEP Develop Models 🖊 Draw a food web to illustrate the relationships among grass, a grasshopper, a mouse, a rabbit, a coyote, and hawk. Use the following information:
   • grass is a producer
   • a grasshopper is a first-level consumer
   • a mouse and a rabbit are first- and second-level consumers
   • a coyote is a second- and third-level consumer
   • a hawk is a third-level consumer

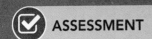
3 **Cycles of Matter**

 MS-LS2-3, EP&CIIIa

10. Distinguish Relationships What is different about how producers and consumers get energy?

....

....

....

....

....

....

11. Determine Similarities In terms of how they get energy, are decomposers more like producers or consumers? Explain.

....

....

....

....

12. SEP Consider Limitations In your opinion, is a food web or a food chain a more accurate representation of how energy and matter flow in an ecosystem? Explain.

....

....

....

....

....

....

....

13. What do consumers release as they break down food to obtain energy?
A. sugar
B. carbon dioxide and water
C. free nitrogen
D. oxygen

14. Rain, hail, and snow are all examples of
A. condensation.   B. evaporation.
C. erosion.   D. precipitation.

15. In one form of nitrogen fixation, the .... energy of .... splits nitrogen molecules into atoms.
A. chemical, water vapor
B. mechanical, consumers
C. electrical, lightning
D. released, bacteria

16. SEP Apply Scientific Reasoning Cite evidence to show that living systems follow the Laws of Conservation of Mass and Energy.

....

....

....

....

17. CCC Energy and Matter How is carbon cycled between organisms and the environment?

....

....

....

....

....

....

MS-LS2-3

Evidence-Based Assessment

A team of field biologists is studying energy roles and relationships among organisms in a tropical rainforest habitat in Southeast Asia. One of the biologists diagrams some of these relationships in a food web.

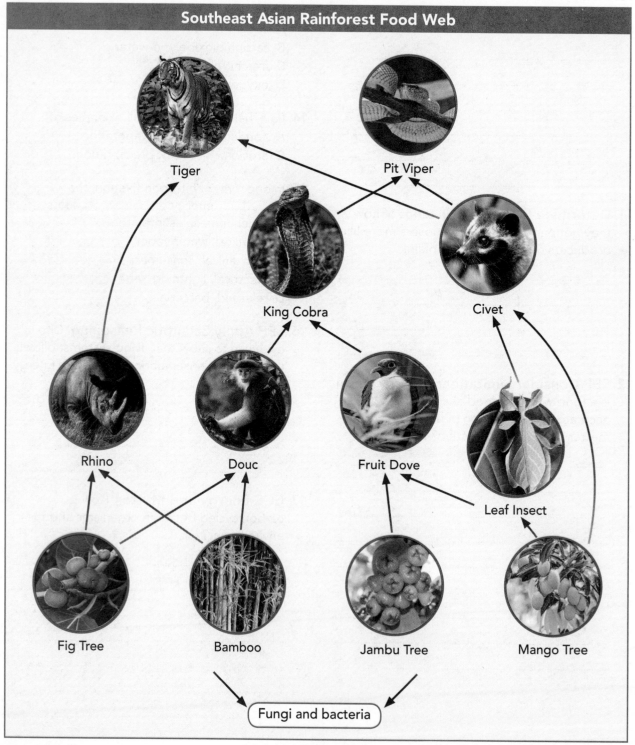

Southeast Asian Rainforest Food Web

Tiger

Pit Viper

King Cobra

Civet

Rhino

Douc

Fruit Dove

Leaf Insect

Fig Tree

Bamboo

Jambu Tree

Mango Tree

Fungi and bacteria

1. **SEP Use Models** Which organism from the food web is a producer?

A. bamboo   B. civet

C. douc   D. tiger

2. **CCC Energy and Matter** Why are there usually fewer organisms at the top level of a food web?

....

....

....

....

....

3. **CCC System Models** What is the role of decomposers in the cycling of matter between the living and nonliving parts of the Southeast Asian rainforest ecosystem? Select all that apply.

☐ Decomposers are producers.

☐ Decomposers break down matter from dead organisms.

☐ Decomposers only interact with living parts of the ecosystem.

☐ Decomposers return biotic matter to soil, water, and air.

4. **CCC Stability and Change** If the jambu tree were removed from the food web, how would it impact the Southeast Asian rainforest ecosystem? Order the events from 1 to 4, with 1 being the first event to take place after the removal of the jambu tree and 4 being the last.

.... The douc population would decrease.

.... The king cobra population would decrease.

.... The fruit dove population would decrease.

.... The pit viper population would decrease.

5. **SEP Construct Explanations** As matter is cycled and energy flows through this system, how are both conserved? Use details from the food web to support your response.

....

....

....

....

....

....

....

....

....

....

Quest FINDINGS

Complete the Quest!

Phenomenon Identify what you believe is the cause of the algal bloom at Pleasant Pond, and describe the impact it has had on the organisms in this ecosystem. Include a proposal about restoring the pond using evidence from your investigation.

CCC Cause and Effect What is the connection between the water in Pleasant Pond—an abiotic factor—and the biotic factors?

....

....

....

....

👆 **INTERACTIVITY**

Reflections on a Pond

Last Remains

How can you **confirm** an owl's role in a **food web**?

Background

Phenomenon Your neighborhood has a rodent problem! Squirrels and mice seem to be taking over. Some members of your neighborhood have suggested that introducing more barn owls into the neighborhood will bring the rodent population under control. But people want to be sure that barn owls do hunt and eat mice and squirrels before they go to the trouble of introducing these nocturnal birds to the area.

You will design and carry out an investigation by observing remains found in an owl pellet—undigested material an owl spits up. You will relate your findings to food webs and energy flow in the owl's ecosystem. Using the evidence you have collected, you will confirm whether or not the idea to introduce more barn owls into your area will help to bring the rodent population under control.

Materials

(per group)
- goggles, 2 pair
- gloves, 2 pair
- owl pellet, 1 per pair
- probes, 2
- tweezers, 1 pair
- hand lens
- paper towels
- bone identification charts

Safety

Be sure to follow all safety guidelines provided by your teacher. The Safety Appendix of your textbook provides more details about the safety icons.

Barn owl

House mouse

Gray squirrel

Design Your Investigation

1. Your investigation will involve observing an owl pellet, which is regurgitated or "spit up" remains of food. Owls generally eat their prey whole and then get rid of the parts of the organisms that they cannot digest, such as bones and fur.

HANDS-ON LAB

Demonstrate Go online for a downloadable worksheet of this lab.

2. Design a procedure for your investigation. Consider the following questions to help develop your plan:

   - How will you use the materials provided by your teacher?

   - What observations will you make?

   - How will you use the remains in the pellet to determine what the owl eats?

   - How can you use the bone identification charts to help you identify the remains of organisms?

3. Write the procedure for your investigation in the space provided.

4. Create a data table to record your observations. Include whether each organism you find inside the owl pellet is a herbivore, a carnivore, or an omnivore.

5. After receiving your teacher's approval for the procedure you developed, carry out your investigation.

Procedure

Data Table and Observations

Analyze and Interpret Data

1. **SEP Develop Models** Diagram the cycling of matter and energy in the barn owl's habitat. Begin by drawing a food chain. Then develop the food chain into a simple food web using additional organisms that you might find in the habitat. Include captions for your diagram that explain the cycling matter and flow of energy among the organisms.

2. **Claim** Do you think the introduction of more barn owls into your neighborhood will solve your mouse and squirrel problem? Use evidence from your investigation to support your response.

....

....

....

....

3. **Evidence** What information did you find out by observing the remains in the owl pellet?

....

....

....

....

4. **Reasoning** Owls hunt at night. Using your findings from the owl pellet, what conclusions can you draw about whether squirrels and mice are more active during the day or at night?

....

....

....

....

Populations, Communities, and Ecosystems

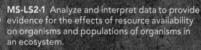
MS-LS2-1 Analyze and interpret data to provide evidence for the effects of resource availability on organisms and populations of organisms in an ecosystem.

MS-LS2-2 Construct an explanation that predicts patterns of interactions among organisms across multiple ecosystems.

MS-LS2-3 Develop a model to describe the cycling of matter and flow of energy among living and nonliving parts of an ecosystem.

MS-LS2-4 Construct an argument supported by empirical evidence that changes to physical or biological components of an ecosystem affect populations.

MS-LS2-5 Evaluate competing design solutions for maintaining biodiversity and ecosystem services.

MS-LS4-1 Analyze and interpret data for patterns in the fossil record that document

the existence, diversity, extinction, and change of life forms throughout the history of life on Earth under the assumption that natural laws operate today as in the past.

EP&CIc Students should be developing an understanding that the quality, quantity, and reliability of the goods and ecosystem services provided by natural systems are directly affected by the health of those systems.

EP&CIIb Students should be developing an understanding that methods used to extract, harvest, transport, and consume natural resources influence the geographic extent, composition, biological diversity, and viability of natural systems.

EP&CIIIa Students should be developing an understanding that natural systems proceed through cycles and processes that are required for their functioning.

EP&CIIIb Students should be developing an understanding that human practices depend upon and benefit from the cycles and processes that operate within natural systems.

EP&CIIIc Students should be developing an understanding that human practices can alter the cycles and processes that operate within natural systems.

EP&CIVc Students should be developing an understanding that the capacity of natural systems to adjust to human-caused alterations depends on the nature of the system as well as the scope, scale, and duration of the activity and the nature of its byproducts.

EP&CVa Students should be developing an understanding of the spectrum of what is considered in making decisions about resources and natural systems and how those factors influence decisions.

Why would these deer risk crossing a busy road?

GO ONLINE
to access your
digital course

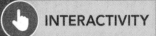 VIDEO

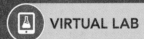 INTERACTIVITY

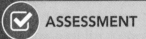 VIRTUAL LAB

 ASSESSMENT

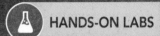 eTEXT

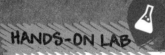 HANDS-ON LABS

HANDS-ON LAB

uConnect Explore how communities change in response to natural disasters.

The Essential Question

How do living and nonliving things affect one another?

SEP Construct Explanations Crossing a road can be dangerous business. What might the deer be trying to get to on the other side of the road that makes it worth the risk? List some living and nonliving resources that the road makes it difficult for the deer to get to.

....

....

....

....

Quest KICKOFF

Should an Animal Crossing Be Constructed in My Community?

STEM **Phenomenon** A company wants to build a new factory nearby, but wants the state to build a new highway to the location. The highway would allow employees and products to access the site. However, the highway would pass through an area with endangered species. Before the state decides, they contact a wildlife biologist to study the impact the highway would have on the local ecosystem. In this problem-based Quest activity, you will investigate how the construction of highways can affect organisms. By applying what you learn in each lesson, in a digital activity or hands-on lab, you will gather key Quest information and evidence. With the information, you will propose a solution in the Findings activity.

 **INTERACTIVITY**

To Cross or Not to Cross

MS-LS2-5, EP&CIIb, EP&CIIIa, EP&CIIIb, EP&CIIIc

NBC LEARN ▶ VIDEO

After watching the Quest kickoff video, where a wildlife biologist discusses animal crossings in Banff National Park, fill in the 3-2-1 activity.

3 organisms I think are at risk locally

....

....

....

2 ideas I have to help them

....

....

....

1 thing I learned from the wildlife biologist

....

....

....

Quest CHECK-IN

IN LESSON 1

How do animal crossings effect ecosystems? Analyze some effects then brainstorm ideas for your animal crossing and identify the criteria and constraints you need to consider.

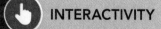 **INTERACTIVITY**

Research Animal Crossings

Quest CHECK-IN

IN LESSON 2

How does community stakeholder feedback impact your design ideas, criteria, and constraints? Evaluate your design.

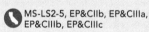 **INTERACTIVITY**

Community Opinions

Quest CHECK-IN

IN LESSON 3

STEM What are the criteria and constraints for the animal crossing? Evaluate competing design solutions.

 HANDS-ON LAB

Design and Model a Crossing

This crossing over the highway looks like it is part of the surrounding forest. It's a much safer route for the animals, and keeps the drivers who pass underneath safe as well.

IN LESSON 4

How could a highway affect local ecosystem services? Consider your animal crossing design and how it might also affect ecosystem services.

Quest FINDINGS

Complete the Quest!

Determine the best way to clearly present your claim with data and evidence, such as graphics or a multimedia presentation.

👆 **INTERACTIVITY**

Reflect on Your Animal Crossing

Guiding Questions

- How can resource availability affect interactions between organisms?
- How is population size affected by predation and symbiotic relationships?
- How are patterns of interactions between organisms similar in different ecosystems?

Connections

Literacy Determine Central Ideas

Math Construct Graphs

 MS-LS2-1 Analyze and interpret data to provide evidence for the effects of resource availability on organisms and populations of organisms in an ecosystem.

MS-LS2-2 Construct an explanation that predicts patterns of interactions among organisms across multiple ecosystems. (Also **EP&CIIb**)

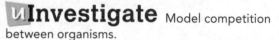

HANDS-ON LAB

uInvestigate Model competition between organisms.

Vocabulary

niche
competition
predation
symbiosis
commensalism
mutualism
parasitism

Academic Vocabulary

interactions
interdependent

Connect It !

✏ **Outline the organism hidden in the image. What adaptations do you notice?**

SEP Construct Explanations How do the animal's adaptations help it survive?

....

....

CCC Cause and Effect How does your body adapt to its environment?

....

....

....

....

Adaptations and Survival

Each organism in an ecosystem has special characteristics. These characteristics influence whether an individual can survive and reproduce in its environment. A characteristic that makes an individual better suited to a specific environment may eventually become common in that species through a process called natural selection.

In this process, individuals with characteristics that are well-suited to a particular environment tend to survive and produce more offspring. Offspring inheriting these characteristics also are more likely to survive to reproduce. Natural selection results in adaptations—the behaviors and physical characteristics that allow organisms to live successfully in their environments. As an example, a great white shark's body is white along its underside, but dark across the top. The shark blends with the surroundings in the water whether being looked at from below or above. **Figure 1** shows another example of how a species adapts to its environment.

Individuals with characteristics that do not help them survive in their environments are less likely to reproduce. Over time, these unhelpful characteristics may affect the survival of a species. If individuals in a species cannot adapt successfully to changes in their environment, the species can become extinct.

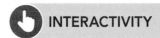

INTERACTIVITY

Identify competition in your daily life.

Student Discourse With a partner, discuss some ways that organisms in your local area have adapted to the environment. In your science notebook, describe characteristics that make the organism successful.

Adaptation and Survival

Figure 1 Different kinds of adaptations work together to aid in this Western screech owl's survival.

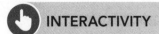

INTERACTIVITY

Model what competition looks like in nature.

Niche The organisms in any ecosystem have adaptations that help them fill specific roles or functions. The role of an organism in its habitat is called its niche. A **niche** includes how an organism obtains its food, the type of food the organism eats, and what other organisms eat it.

Remember that an organism's energy role in an ecosystem is determined by how it obtains food and how it interacts with other organisms. Adaptations by a species allow a population to live successfully on the available resources in its niche. Abiotic factors also influence a population's ability to survive in the niche it occupies. Lack of water or space, for example, may cause a population to decline and no longer fit well into that niche. Biotic factors, such as predators or a reduced food source, affect the populations in a niche and may change an organism's ability to survive.

A niche also includes when and how the organism reproduces and the physical conditions it requires to survive. Every organism has a variety of adaptations that suit it to specific living conditions and help it survive. Use **Figure 2** to describe characteristics of a giraffe's niche.

Niche Characteristics

Figure 2 This picture shows that organisms occupy many niches in an environment.

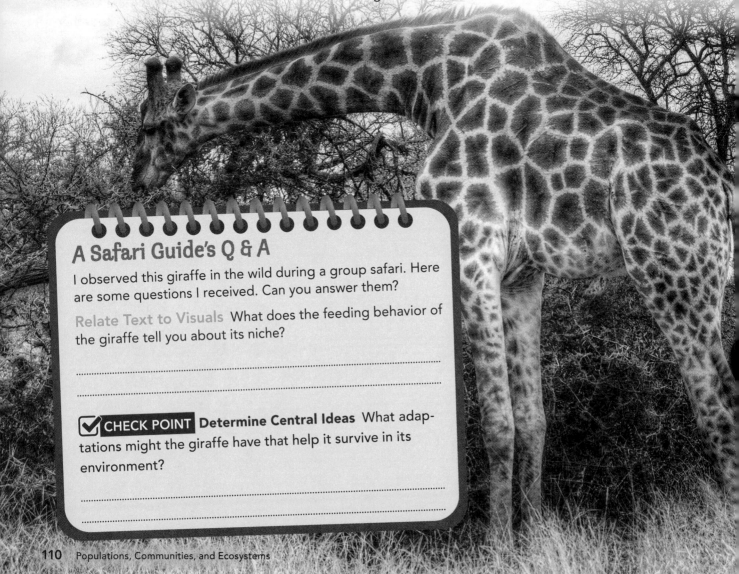

A Safari Guide's Q & A

I observed this giraffe in the wild during a group safari. Here are some questions I received. Can you answer them?

Relate Text to Visuals What does the feeding behavior of the giraffe tell you about its niche?

....

....

☑ CHECK POINT **Determine Central Ideas** What adaptations might the giraffe have that help it survive in its environment?

....

....

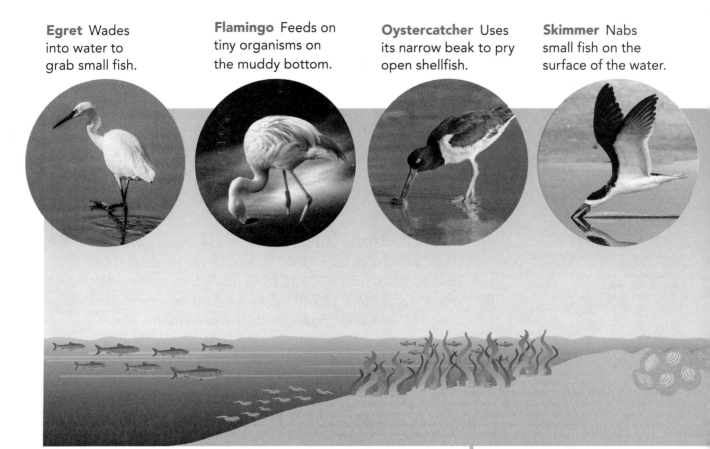

Egret Wades into water to grab small fish.

Flamingo Feeds on tiny organisms on the muddy bottom.

Oystercatcher Uses its narrow beak to pry open shellfish.

Skimmer Nabs small fish on the surface of the water.

Competition and Predation

In every type of ecosystem, a range of **interactions** takes place among organisms every day. Two major types of interactions among organisms are competition and predation.

Competition More than one species of organism can live in the same habitat and obtain the same food. For example, in a desert ecosystem, a flycatcher and an elf owl both live on the saguaro cactus and eat insects. However, these two species do not occupy exactly the same niche. The flycatcher is active during the day, while the owl is active mostly at night.

When two species share a niche, one of their populations might be affected. The reason for this is **competition**. The struggle between organisms to survive as they use the same limited resources is called competition. For example, different species of birds in a park compete for the same bugs and worms to eat. If one population of birds is more successful, it will increase while the other population decreases.

In any ecosystem, there are limited amounts of food, water, and shelter. Organisms that share the same habitat often have adaptations that enable them to reduce competition. Observe the shorebirds in **Figure 3** and discover how their niches vary in the shoreline habitat.

Shorebird Competition
Figure 3 🖉 Draw a line from each bird to the location where it feeds.

Academic Vocabulary
How have you heard the term *interactions* used in another subject and what does the word mean in that context?

....

....

....

....

....

Predation A tiger shark bursts through the water and grabs a sea snake swimming on the surface. An interaction in which one organism kills another for food or nutrients is called **predation**. In this interaction, one organism is the predator and the other is the prey. The tiger shark, for example, is the predator and the sea snake is the prey. Predator and prey interactions occur in all ecosystems. The species involved may be different, but the pattern of interaction is the same. Predation can reduce the number of organisms or eliminate populations.

Adaptations All species have ways of supporting their survival in their environment. Some predators have adaptations, such as sharp teeth and claws, well-developed senses, and the ability to run fast, which help them to catch and kill their prey **(Figure 4)**. Prey organisms may have protective coverings, warning coloration, or the ability to camouflage themselves to help them avoid being killed.

Model It

Predator and Prey Adaptations

Figure 4 In the Mojave Desert in California, the Mojave rattlesnake blends in with its surroundings so that it can ambush rodents it preys on. The snake's venom is considered to be the strongest rattlesnake venom in the world.

SEP Develop Models ✏ Consider a grassland ecosystem of tall, tan savanna grasses. Draw either a predator or a prey organism that might live there. Label the adaptations that will allow your organism to be successful.

Population Size Predation affects population size. Changes in population size occur when new members arrive or when members leave. Population size increases if more members enter than leave, and declines if more members leave than arrive. Too many predators in a area can decrease the prey population, leading to less food availability and possible predator population decline. In general, predator and prey populations rise and fall together in predictable patterns.

☑ CHECK POINT **Summarize Text** What effect do competition and predation have on population size?

....

....

Math Toolbox

Predator-Prey Interactions

Moose and Wolf
Populations on Isle Royale

On Isle Royale, an island in Lake Superior, the populations of wolves (the predator) and moose (the prey) rise and fall in cycles.

Year	Wolves	Moose
1985	22	976
1990	15	1,315
1995	16	2,117
2000	29	2,007
2005	30	540
2010	19	510
2015	2	1,300

1. **Construct Graphs** 🖊 Create a double line graph of the data above. Fill in the x-axis and both y-axes. Use a different color line for each animal and provide a key.

2. **Analyze and Interpret Data** Describe the relationship shown by your graph and suggest factors that impact it.

....

....

....

....

113

INTERACTIVITY

Classify symbiotic relationships.

VIDEO

Explore the three types of symbiotic relationships.

Academic Vocabulary

Break the adjective *interdependent* into two parts. Based on those word parts, what is an interdependent relationship among species?

....

....

....

....

....

Literacy Connection

Determine Central Ideas As you read, determine the central idea of the text. Note how this idea is developed through examples. Underline examples that you think most clearly explain the central idea.

Symbiotic Relationships

Symbiosis is a third type of interaction among organisms. **Symbiosis** (sim bee OH sis) is any relationship in which two species live closely together. There are three types of symbiotic relationships: commensalism, mutualism, and parasitism. Just like predation and competition, symbiotic interactions, occur in all ecosystems. All organisms share patterns of interactions with their environments, both living and nonliving. An organism cannot survive without relying on another for survival.

Mutualism In some interactions, two species may depend on one another. In California's chaparral ecosystem, Harvester ants build their mounds near Indian Rice Grass. The ants attack any organism that comes to eat the grass. The Harvester ants depend on the Indian Rice Grass to get food. The grass depends on the ants for protection. This relationship is an example of **mutualism** (MYOO choo uh liz um), which is a relationship in which both species benefit. Some mutually beneficial interactions can become so **interdependent** that each organism requires the other for survival.

Commensalism Birds build nests in trees to make a place to live. The tree is unharmed. This relationship is an example of **commensalism**. Commensalism (kuh MEN suh liz um) is a relationship in which one species benefits and the other species is neither helped nor harmed.

Commensalism is not very common in nature because two species are usually either helped or harmed a little by any interaction. Scientists may disagree on whether a particular relationship truly demonstrates commensalism.

Identifying examples of commensalism can be difficult. For example, sea otters wrap themselves in kelp in order to anchor themselves while they sleep. Because the kelp is not affected, this species interaction could be an example of commensalism. On the other hand, sea otters also eat sea urchins which eat kelp thus limiting their growth. Kelp forests with sea otters can grow as high as 250 feet, making it an example of mutualism. When kelp grows to its maximum height, it gets better access to sunlight, an important abiotic factor for their survival. **Figure 5** shows more examples of symbiotic relationships across multiple ecosystems.

Mutualism and Commensalism

Figure 5 Some relationships more clearly show benefits to one or both species than others.

1. **Synthesize Information** ✏ Read each image caption. Label each photo "M" for mutualism or "C" for commensalism in the circle provided.

2. **SEP Cite Evidence** ✏ Beneath each image, use evidence to justify how you classified the relationship.

Hummingbirds feed on nectar deep within a flower. While sipping, the flower's pollen rubs off on the hummingbird. The bird can carry it to another flower.

SEP Evidence

....

....

....

The banded mongoose feeds on ticks and other tiny animals that nestle in the warthog's fur and feed off of the warthog.

SEP Evidence

....

....

....

....

Barnacles feed by filtering tiny organisms from the water. They grow on objects below the surface, such as piers and rocks, and attach themselves to whales.

SEP Evidence

....

....

....

....

Remora attach themselves to the underside of a manta ray with a suction-cup-like structure. Mantas are messy eaters and remora feed on the food scraps.

SEP Evidence

....

....

....

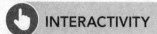
Parasitism If you've ever seen a dog continually scratching itself, then it may have fleas. This interaction is an example of **parasitism** (PAHR uh sit iz um). Parasitism is a relationship that involves one organism living with, on, or inside another organism and harming it.

The organism that benefits is called a parasite. The host is the organism that the parasite lives in or on. The parasite is generally smaller than its host. The fleas, for example, are parasites that harm the dog by biting it to feed on its blood for nourishment. Pets can suffer from severe health problems as a result of these bites. Study the examples of parasitism in **Figure 6**.

Parasitic Relationships

Figure 6 Unlike a predator, a parasite does not usually kill the organism it feeds on. If the host dies, the parasite could lose its source of food or shelter.

✓ CHECK POINT **Integrate with Visuals** 🖉 In each picture, label the host and the parasite shown.

SEP Construct Explanations How does parasitism differ from other symbiotic relationships?

....

....

....

....

....

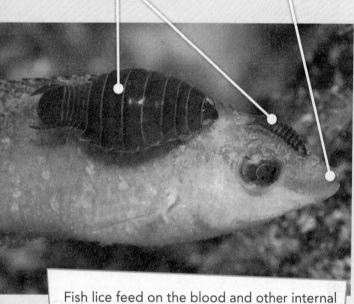

Fish lice feed on the blood and other internal fluids of the fish. Eventually the fish may quit eating and lose color from the stress caused by the lice.

A braconid wasp lays its eggs under the skin of the hornworm, a common pest in California gardens. As the larvae develop, they feed on the insides of the hornworm. Once fully developed, the larvae emerge and spin silk cocoons on the hornworm.

☑ LESSON 1 Check

MS-LS2-1, MS-LS2-2, EP&CIIb

1. Identify What are the five different types of interactions between organisms?

....

....

....

....

....

....

....

....

Use the graph you constructed on wolf and moose populations to help you answer Questions 2 and 3.

2. CCC Patterns What patterns do scientists observe between predator-prey relationships like the wolves and moose on Isle Royale?

....

....

....

....

....

3. SEP Interpret Data Use the data from your graph to provide evidence for the effects of resource availability on individuals and populations in an ecosystem.

....

....

....

....

4. SEP Construct Explanations Do the patterns of interactions between organisms, such as competition and predation, change when they occur in different ecosystems? Explain.

....

....

....

....

....

....

5. CCC Cause and Effect Predict the effects on a predator-prey relationship, such as the one between a frog and blue heron, in a wetland ecosystem in the midst of a drought.

....

....

....

Quest CHECK-IN

In this lesson, you learned how organisms in ecosystems interact with one another and how resource availability can affect these interactions. You also discovered that these interactions can influence population size.

CCC Analyze Systems Why is it important to maintain existing organism interactions and availability of resources when building a new highway?

....

....

....

👆 **INTERACTIVITY**

Research Animal Crossings

Go online to investigate the effects of highways and animals crossings.

Dynamic and Resilient Ecosystems

Guiding Questions

- How can changes to physical or biological components of an ecosystem affect organisms and populations?
- How do natural events impact the environment?
- How do human activities impact ecosystems?

Connection

Literacy Write Arguments

🕐 **MS-LS2-1** Analyze and interpret data to provide evidence for the effects of resource availability on organisms and populations of organisms in an ecosystem.

MS-LS2-2 Construct an explanation that predicts patterns of interactions among organisms across multiple ecosystems.

MS-LS2-4 Construct an argument supported by empirical evidence that changes to physical or biological components of an ecosystem affect populations.

(Also **EP&CIIb, EP&CIIIa, EP&CIIIb, EP&CIIIc**)

HANDS-ON LAB

u**Investigate** Identify examples of succession in a local ecosystem.

Vocabulary

succession
pioneer species

Academic Vocabulary

colonize
dominate

Connect It!

✏️ **Circle the living organisms in the photo. Think about why the number of living organisms is limited here.**

Predict How do you think this landscape will change in the future?

....

....

Succession

Ecosystems and their communities are dynamic in nature. They are always changing, because their characteristics can vary over time. Natural disasters, such as floods and tornadoes, can cause rapid change. Other changes occur over centuries or even longer. Humans can have a major impact on ecosystems as well. The series of predictable changes that occur in a community over time is called **succession**. **Figure 1** shows how organisms can establish habitats in even the harshest environments.

Primary Succession
Disruptions to the physical or biological components of an ecosystem can impact organism populations living there. For example, lava from a volcanic eruption is creating new land by the sea. When the lava cools and hardens, no organisms are present. Over time, living things will **colonize** these areas. Primary succession is the series of changes that occur in an area where no soil or organisms exist.

Pioneer Species
The first species to populate an area are called **pioneer species.** These species are usually mosses and lichens, carried to the area by wind or water. Lichens are fungi and algae growing in a symbiotic relationship. They give off acidic compounds that help dissolve rock into soil. As pioneer species die, their remains add nutrients to the thin soil and help build it up.

 **INTERACTIVITY**

Consider what happens when an ecosystem is disturbed.

Academic Vocabulary

Where else have you heard the term *colonize*, or the related term *colony*? Provide an example.

....

....

....

....

Succession

Figure 1 Harsh landscapes like this hardened lava flow transform over time as lichens and plants establish themselves.

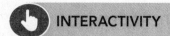

INTERACTIVITY

Investigate how ecosystems can change over time.

Ecosystem Disruption
Figure 2 In 2017, wildfires raged through California's drought-stricken regions.

Mature Communities Small changes in one part of a system can cause large changes in another part. For example, because lichens help to form a thin layer of soil, seed-producing plants can then establish themselves. Wind, water, and birds can bring seeds into the area. If the soil is adequate and there's enough rainfall, seedlings will emerge and may grow to adulthood. As the plants grow, they will shed leaves that will break down to make more soil. Plants also attract animals that will further enhance the soil by leaving waste and their own remains. Over time, the buildup of organic matter will improve the soil and allow for a more diverse community to establish itself in the area.

Succession demonstrates how all natural systems go through cycles and processes that are required for their functioning. While it can take centuries for a community to mature, once a community is established it can last for thousands of years or more if it is not disturbed or disrupted.

Secondary Succession Devastating fires, such as the one shown in **Figure 2**, can result from natural system processes or human activities. Regardless of their cause, fires lead to secondary succession. Secondary succession is the series of changes that occur in an area where the ecosystem has been disturbed, but where soil and organisms already exist. Natural disruptions that affect the physical and biological components of an ecosystem include fires, hurricanes, tsunamis, and tornadoes. Human activities may also disturb an ecosystem and cause secondary succession to occur.

Unlike primary succession (**Figure 3**), secondary succession occurs in a place where an ecosystem and community exist. Secondary succession usually occurs more rapidly than primary succession because soil is already present and seeds from some plants may remain in the soil. Over time, more and more organisms can live in the area and it starts to resemble places that were never disturbed in the first place.

Empirical evidence is what's based on experience or verified by observation. Scientists follow common rules for obtaining and evaluating empirical evidence. What we know about succession in natural ecosystems is based on both empirical evidence and on data that has been gathered and analyzed over years and even decades.

☑ **CHECK POINT** **Cite Textual Evidence** How is secondary succession different from primary succession?

....

....

....

Pioneers

Figure 3 The images show how pioneer species begin the process of succession, which changes an area over time.

Integrate Information 🖉 Draw pictures to represent the missing stages of primary succession.

1. **Claim** Identify a place in your community where succession might occur if people abandoned the area.

....

2. **Evidence** Describe what the location would look like years later after being abandoned.

....

....

....

3. **Reasoning** Explain how changes to the physical and biological components of the ecosystem would affect the populations that make up the community.

....

....

....

....

....

HANDS-ON LAB

Investigate Identify examples of succession in a local ecosystem.

INTERACTIVITY

Propose causes for a change in a population and predict future changes.

Academic Vocabulary

What does it mean when a sports team *dominates* its rival team?

....

....

....

Ecosystem Disruptions and Population Survival

Disruptions to any physical or biological component of an ecosystem can lead to shifts in all its populations. When changes occur suddenly or last for a long time, most populations in the ecosystem do not survive. However, some organisms do survive the changes. Organisms surviving a fast-changing ecosystem often have adaptations that help them thrive in the new conditions.

Georgia, South Carolina, and Florida have an ecosystem of the longleaf pine forest, as shown in **Figure 4.** Longleaf pine trees **dominate** this ecosystem. These trees grow in a pattern that permits sunlight to reach the forest floor. Longleaf pine seeds need a soil free from undergrowth and germinate quickly in the soil. Longleaf pines are dependent on regular forest fires from lightning strikes to burn away grasses and invasive hardwood trees such as oak to remain healthy and reproduce. Mature trees' bark and early growth are fire-resistant.

Longleaf pines support a healthy ecosystem. Red-cockaded woodpeckers depend on mature trees for nesting sites. If fires don't burn the undergrowth, predators can reach the nests. Swallowed-tailed kites build nests high in the trees. Bachmann's sparrows favor mature pine forests where underbrush has been removed by fires. These bird populations have been reduced due to logging of the longleaf pines and previous fire suppression practices, which opened space for invasive oaks.

Most organisms reappear at some point after the fire because of adaptations such as heat-resistant seeds that may sprout or underground roots that can grow. Young longleaf pines develop a long taproot that enables them to grow after a fire.

Changes to Populations
Figure 4 In the longleaf pine ecosystem, some organisms are adapted to survive fire and others are not.

CHECK POINT Determine Central Ideas How does a wildfire impact a population of oak trees?

....

....

CCC Cause and Effect How might a wildfire help the longleaf pine population survive a deadly fungal infection on the needles of seedlings?

....

....

The red-cockaded woodpecker flies away from the fire to safety.

As the thick, scaly bark burns, flakes fall off and take the heat with them.

A longleaf pine seedling is topped with a moist tuft of needles. As fire burns the needles, they produce steam that moves the heat away from the plant and extinguishes the fire. If the needles burn off entirely, the seedling can regrow from its root.

Fire burns the blades of bluestem grass, but its underground roots remain unharmed. After the fire, new shoots sprout from the roots.

The pine snake escapes fire by seeking shelter in a gopher burrow.

☑ LESSON 2 Check

MS-LS2-1, MS-LS2-2, MS-LS2-4, EP&CIIb, EP&CIIIa, EP&CIIIb, EP&CIIIc

1. SEP Construct Explanations What are pioneer species? How do they affect the variety of organisms in an ecosystem?

....

....

....

....

....

....

....

2. SEP Engage in Argument Support the argument that a forest fire impacts a population of birds that nest in the trees.

....

....

....

....

....

....

....

3. Connect to Environmental Principles and Concepts Explain how the physical and biological components of this ecosystem in Chico, California, are being disrupted.

....

....

....

....

....

....

Quest CHECK-IN

In this lesson you learned that changes to physical or biological components of an ecosystem can affect the populations of organisms that live there.

Apply Concepts How might mature communities of organisms be affected by the construction of a new highway? How does an animal crossing solve some of these problems?

....

....

....

....

....

☝ INTERACTIVITY

Community Opinions

Go online to learn about reactions to a proposed crossing from members of the community. Based on the feedback, consider the constraints the animal crossing should meet.

"A Bird came down the Walk"

Emily Dickinson

A Bird came down the Walk—
He did not know I saw—
He bit an Angle Worm in halves
And ate the fellow, raw.

And then, he drank a Dew
From a convenient Grass—
And then hopped sidewise to the Wall
To let a Beetle pass—

He glanced with rapid eyes
That hurried all abroad—
They looked like frightened Beads, I thought—
He stirred his Velvet Head.—

Like one in danger, Cautious,
I offered him a Crumb,
And he unrolled his feathers,
And rowed him softer home—

Than Oars divide the Ocean,
Too silver for a seam,
Or Butterflies, off Banks of Noon,
Leap, plashless as they swim.

CONNECT TO YOU

With a classmate, discuss what you think the poem is about. How is the speaker in the poem similar to a scientist?

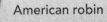

American robin

125

LESSON

(3) Biodiversity

GUIDING QUESTIONS

- What is the value of biodiversity?
- What factors affect biodiversity?
- How do human activities impact biodiversity?

Connections

Literacy Cite Textual Evidence

Math Use Ratio Reasoning

 MS-LS2-4 Construct an argument supported by empirical evidence that changes to physical or biological components of an ecosystem affect populations.

MS-LS2-5, Evaluate competing design solutions for maintaining biodiversity and ecosystem services.

MS-LS4-1 Analyze and interpret data for patterns in the fossil record that document the existence, diversity, extinction, and change of life forms throughout the history of life on Earth under the assumption that natural laws operate today as in the past. (Also **EP&CIc, EP&CIIb, EP&CIIIa, EP&CIIIb, EP&CIIIc, EP&CIVc, EP&CVa**)

HANDS-ON LAB

иInvestigate Explore the role of keystone species in maintaining biodiversity.

Vocabulary

biodiversity
keystone species
extinction
invasive species

Academic Vocabulary

value
economic

Connect It!

✏ **Circle the parts of the ecosystem shown here that you think are important to people.**

Identify Unknowns What do you think are two important ways that humans benefit from a healthy ecosystem? Explain.

....

....

The Value of Biodiversity

Earth is filled with many different ecosystems that provide habitats for each and every organism. Some organisms live in one ecosystem their entire lives. Other organisms are born in one ecosystem and migrate to another. Healthy ecosystems have biodiversity. The number and variety of different species in an area is **biodiversity**. Healthy ecosystems have biodiversity and also provide the opportunity for different species to interact. This is often essential for their survival, such as a predator finding prey.

Even small changes in an ecosystem's condition or available resources can produce larger changes that impact the entire ecosystem. Biodiversity increases as more resources are available. It decreases when fewer resources are available. When biodiversity changes, it impacts ecosystem processes. This impact may affect the health of an ecosystem.

Biodiversity also has both economic and ecological **value**. Healthy ecosystems, such as the one in **Figure 1**, provide resources and materials that we use. We consume food, fuel, medicines, and fibers from healthy ecosystems.

Healthy Ecosystems
Figure 1 Biodiversity determines the health of an ecosystem.

Economic Value Humans use ecosystems for our own profit. There is value in using ecosystems to fulfill our basic needs and wants. The products we take from ecosystems have **economic** value, such as providing a household income. People can profit from healthy ecosystems both directly or indirectly.

Resources that are consumed from an ecosystem provide a direct value. For example, the crops from the vineyard in **Figure 2** are direct value. The farmer used the land and grew the crops to make a profit on their sale. In addition to food, medicines and raw materials provide resources and income. Unfortunately, demand for resources can harm biodiversity and ecosystems. Humans can use too many resources at once. As a result, many ecosystems do not have time to recover and are damaged. This can hurt humans in the long run.

Some resources in an ecosystem are used, but not consumed. These indirect values also affect the economic value. Shade trees reduce utility bills and provide wind protection. Wetlands reduce soil erosion, control flooding, and reduce large temperature swings. Hiking, touring unique habitats, and recreational activities provide revenue. The key is using these ecosystem resources for profit without destroying them.

☑ CHECK POINT **Determine Central Ideas** What makes crops a direct value from an ecosystem?

....

....

Economic Loss

Figure 2 Disease and poor weather conditions can cause severe financial losses for farmers. This vineyard in Hopeland, California, flooded after historic rainstorms.

SEP Construct Explanations Would it be wise for a farmer to grow just one type of crop? Explain.

....

....

....

....

....

....

A Valuable Tree

Figure 3 Elephants eat the fruit of the balanite, or desert date, tree. The elephants then spread the seeds in their waste as they travel.

CCC Cause and Effect Consider the interdependence between the tree and the elephant. What would happen if one of the species were to decline in number?

....

....

HANDS-ON LAB

☑**Investigate** Explore the role of keystone species in maintaining biodiversity.

Ecological Value

All species function within an ecosystem. Each species performs a certain role. All species are connected and depend on each other for survival. A **keystone species** is a species that influences the survival of many other species in an ecosystem. One example of a keystone species is the African elephant.

African elephant herds appeared to be stripping vegetation from the ecosystem, thereby harming it. Some park officials wanted to control the elephant population by thinning the herds. Instead, they let the herds range freely. When the elephants uprooted trees, that made way for grasslands and smaller animals. Shrubs grew where the trees once stood and fed the animals unable to reach taller trees. Over time, the park ecosystem, **Figure 3**, returned to an ecological balance. Changes to physical and biological factors of an ecosystem, such as the number of elephants and trees, affect all of the populations within an ecosystem.

Biodiversity sustains ecosystems by protecting land and water resources, and aiding in nutrient cycling. Trees and vegetation hold soil in place to prevent erosion and landslides. Roots break up rocks to allow water to enter the soil. Animal waste sustains soil fertility. A diverse ecosystem is stable, productive, and can easily withstand environmental changes.

☑ CHECK POINT **Summarize Text** Why is the elephant considered a keystone species?

....

....

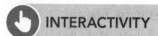

INTERACTIVITY

Explore the diversity of species that live in the Amazon.

Factors Affecting Biodiversity

There are numerous ecosystems on Earth. Biodiversity within these ecosystems varies from place to place. Various factors affect biodiversity, including niche diversity, genetic diversity, extinction, climate, and area.

Niche Diversity Every species in an ecosystem occupies a unique niche. The abiotic and biotic resources that a species needs to survive are provided by its niche. These resources include food, water, and habitat. The niches of different populations within an ecosystem interact with one another. Some species, like the panda in **Figure 4**, live in a narrow niche with only a few food sources. Species that have a narrow niche are more vulnerable to environmental changes. A niche can also be shared by two different species. When this happens, they compete for resources. If resources are low, one species may survive while the other must leave or die out. A healthy ecosystem reflects a balance among different populations and their unique niches.

A Narrow Niche

Figure 4 🖉 The panda's diet has no diversity. Its diet consists almost entirely of leaves, stems, and shoots from different bamboo species. Pandas can eat over 30 kg of bamboo a day. Circle the bamboo in the image.

CCC Analyze Systems What would happen to the panda population if there were a decrease in the amount of bamboo available? Explain.

....

....

....

....

....

....

Question It!

Endangered Species

Figure 5 Gray wolves are endangered. Scientists speculate that their near-extinction status could be due to low genetic diversity, loss of natural food resources, or loss of habitat.

SEP **Ask Questions** A group of scientists is visiting your school to discuss the importance of saving the gray wolf population. They need your help to design a solution to increase the number of gray wolves in California. However, you must first understand a little more about the endangered species. Each person is required to ask at least three questions of the experts. In the space below, write your questions. Consider constraints when developing your questions.

....

....

....

Genetic Diversity You may have heard the expression "gene pool." It is the number of genes available within a population. Genetic diversity, on the other hand, is the total number of inherited traits in the genetic makeup of an entire species. The greater its genetic diversity, the more likely it is that a species can adapt and survive. Species with low genetic diversity lack the ability to adapt to changing environmental conditions. The gray wolves you see in **Figure 5** could have low genetic diversity, which would contribute to their near-extinction status.

Species Extinction According to fossil evidence, about 99.9% of all species that have ever existed on Earth are now extinct. The disappearance of all members of a species from Earth is **extinction**. Species in danger of becoming extinct are endangered species. And species that could become endangered in the near future are threatened species. There are two ways in which species can become extinct. Background extinction occurs over a long period of time. It usually involves only one species. Environmental changes or the arrival of a competitor cause background extinctions. Mass extinction can kill many different species in a very short time. Mass extinctions are caused by rapid climate changes (such as from a meteoroid impact), continuous volcanic eruptions, or changes in the air or water.

☑ **CHECK POINT** **Summarize Text** Why are populations with low genetic diversity, like gray wolves, less likely to survive?

....

....

Other Factors The climate and size of an ecosystem also affect biodiversity. Scientists hypothesize that a consistent climate supports biodiversity. One of the most diverse places on Earth is the tropical rainforest. Temperatures do not fluctuate greatly and it receives a large amount of rainfall. Also, plants grow year-round, providing food for animals. An ecosystem's area, or the amount of space that an ecosystem covers, also determines its biodiversity. For example, more species are found in an ecosystem that covers 50 square kilometers, than in one that covers 10 square kilometers. An ecosystem with a larger area will generally have more biodiversity.

Math Toolbox

Room to Roam

A savanna is a grassland ecosystem with few trees. About 65 percent of Africa is covered by savannas. Lions roam where there are fewer than 25 people per square mile. As the human population in Africa increases, the amount of land where lions roam is decreasing. Use the chart and graphs to answer the questions.

1. Predict Describe how the green area of the pie chart would change to show the area where lions freely roam today.

....

2. Draw Conclusions How has the balance in the African lion population shifted over time? What caused this shift?

....
....
....

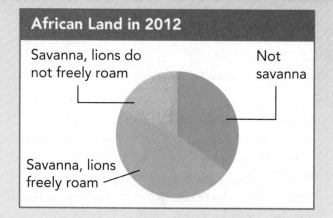

African Land in 2012

Savanna, lions do not freely roam

Not savanna

Savanna, lions freely roam

3. Use Ratio Reasoning Write a ratio comparing the lion population in 1950 to 2000. Explain the relationship between human population and the lion population.

....
....

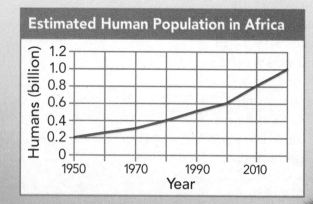

Estimated Human Population in Africa

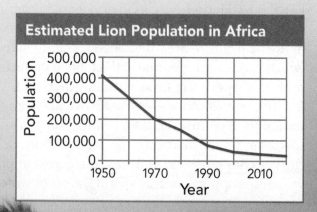

Estimated Lion Population in Africa

Human Impact

When an ecosystem is harmed in any way, its biodiversity is reduced. Human activities directly impact ecosystems and the organisms that live there. As you see in **Figure 6**, human activities can impact the environment.

Our Impact on Ecosystems

Figure 6 🖊 For each image, determine if the human activities are increasing or decreasing impacts on the environment. Place an "I" in the circle for an increased impact, and a "D" in the circle for a decreased impact. Then, in the space provided, provide evidence to support your determination.

Threats to Coral

Figure 7 ✎ These images show two different coral reef ecosystems. One image shows how an increase in water temperature can harm a coral reef through coral bleaching. When water gets too warm, coral can become stressed, causing the algae living in their tissue to leave. Because the coral relies on algae for food, it begins to starve. Circle the image that shows coral bleaching.

☑️ CHECK POINT
Determine Conclusions
What evidence is presented to show that a warming climate can impact biodiversity?

....

....

....

....

....

....

....

Damaging Biodiversity Human activities cause most of the harm to habitats and ecosystems. The result is a loss of biodiversity. For example, removing natural resources from an ecosystem can reduce its biodiversity.

Scientists agree that increased levels of carbon dioxide gas contribute to climate change. One way humans contribute to climate change is by the removal of resources from ecosystems. For example, people remove trees for farming, houses, and timber. The use of machinery to remove and process the trees increases the amount of carbon dioxide gas in our atmosphere. In addition, the deforested plants are not taking in carbon dioxide. Changes to the climate impact all of Earth's ecosystems. It is easy to observe changes in temperature on land, but ocean water temperature also changes. **Figure 7** shows how a changing climate threatens biodiversity.

Human activities can also introduce non-native species, called **invasive species**, into a habitat. Often, invasive species out-compete native species within an ecosystem. Humans also remove species when poachers illegally kill wildlife for clothing, medicine, or body parts such as horns for ivory.

Protecting Biodiversity We can all take action to protect wildlife on Earth. For example, **Figure 8** shows students collecting data for conservation projects. Captive breeding programs help endangered species reproduce and sustain diversity. States and countries can set aside land to safeguard natural habitats. Finally, international laws and treaties protect the environment and biodiversity.

Habitat Preservation The goal of habitat preservation is to maintain the natural state of an ecosystem. Sometimes, that requires restoring its biodiversity. National parks, marine fisheries, and wildlife refuges are areas that preserve habitats. These areas are wildlife sanctuaries. Laws prevent or severely restrict any removal of resources from wildlife sanctuaries.

INTERACTIVITY

Examine how humans can safeguard and preserve biodiversity.

Student Discourse With a partner, discuss what you value about being out in nature. Consider the number and variety of species you see there. What would happen if some of them disappeared?

Citizen Scientists

Figure 8 Scientists often seek help from people like you for preservation and conservation efforts. Citizens are trained to collect data on factors such as water quality, population numbers, and behavior of species. Scientists use the data to track populations and to monitor preservation efforts.

SEP Engage in Argument Do you think citizen volunteers should participate in citizen science projects? Explain.

....

....

....

....

Using Technology to Save a Species

Figure 9 ✏ Innovations in technology, such as cameras with artificial intelligence, let people learn about endangered marine species, like this vaquita. With that knowledge comes the desire to protect them.

Protecting Our Oceans

Figure 10 ✏ The Sea of Cortez is a protected marine ecosystem. It's also where the world's remaining one hundred vaquitas live in the wild today. Global support for protecting Earth's marine ecosystems is increasing. Circle two organisms that could be harmed without marine protection.

Global Cooperation

Habitat preservation is the most important way to protect the existing species on our planet. Two treaties are dedicated to preserving global biodiversity. The Convention on Biological Diversity focuses on conservation. The Convention on International Trade in Endangered Species of Wild Fauna and Flora ensures that the trade of plants and animals does not endanger them. These two treaties protect over 30,000 plant and animal species. We all benefit from global efforts that protect Earth's biodiversity. Protection and conservation ensure resources for future generations (**Figure 10**).

Technology and engineering play a key role in species conservation. Researchers at the University of California in San Diego have combined robotics and camera vision to track and study the rare and endangered vaquita (**Figure 9**), also known as the Gulf of California harbor porpoise.

✅ **CHECK POINT** **Determine Conclusions** Why is it important to protect marine ecosystems?

....

....

....

MS-LS2-4, MS-LS2-5, MS-LS4-1, EP&CIc, EP&CIIb, EP&CIIIa, EP&CIIIb, EP&CIIIc, EP&CIVc, EP&CVa

1. SEP Construct Explanations What is meant by the value of biodiversity?

....

....

....

....

2. Distinguish Relationships How is an ecosystem's biodiversity a measure of its health?

....

....

....

....

3. CCC Cause and Effect What consequences might occur if a particular species becomes extinct?

....

....

....

....

....

4. Apply Concepts When scientists analyze the rock record, they look for fossil evidence. How are scientists able to determine that the majority of all organisms are now extinct?

....

....

....

....

....

5. Connect to Environmental Principles and Concepts Support the argument that humans must take measures to protect biodiversity. Explain.

....

....

....

....

....

....

....

....

Quest CHECK-IN

In this lesson, you learned about the value of healthy ecosystems and the importance of biodiversity. You also learned about the factors affecting biodiversity.

Synthesize Information How can road construction affect the biodiversity of an ecosystem?

....

....

....

....

....

HANDS-ON LAB

Design and Model a Crossing

Go online for a downloadable worksheet of this lab. Build a model of your wildlife crossing. As a class, share your ideas. Evaluate how each model functions to protect biodiversity.

Ecosystem Services

Guiding Questions

- Why is it important to maintain healthy ecosystems?
- Which supporting services are necessary to all other ecosystem services?
- How does biodiversity impact ecosystem services?

Connections

Literacy Write Arguments

Math Graph Proportional Relationships

 MS-LS2-3 Develop a model to describe the cycling of matter and flow of energy among living and nonliving parts of an ecosystem.

MS-LS2-5 Evaluate competing design solutions for maintaining biodiversity and ecosystem services. (Also **EP&CIc, EP&CIIIa, EP&CIIIb, EP&CIIIc, EP&CIVc, EP&CVa**)

HANDS-ON LAB

ᴍInvestigate Model how wetlands help with water purification.

Vocabulary

ecosystem services
ecology
natural resource
conservation
sustainability
ecological restoration

Academic Vocabulary

regulation

Connect It!

✏️ **Circle three different organisms interacting with their environment.**

Distinguish Relationships Describe how each organism interacts with the environment. How would they be affected if the environment was disrupted?

....

....

....

....

Ecosystem Services

Ecosystems meet our needs by supplying us with water, fuel, and wellness. **Ecosystem services** are the benefits humans receive from ecosystems. They are often produced without help from humans, and they are free! Ecosystem services occur because systems in an ecosystem interact with one another. Plants interact with the air, sun, soil, water, and minerals. Animals interact with plants, other animals, the air, and water. Because services are exchanged when interactions occur, biodiversity is an important factor.

In an ecosystem, all organisms, including humans, interact with one another and benefit from those interactions. **Ecology** is the study of how organisms interact with their environment. Ecology helps us understand how services emerge from those interactions. For example, the bee in **Figure 1** is pollinating the flower, but it is also getting nectar from the flower. Both interactions can result in services that humans use. Further, their exchange is an example of cycling matter and energy within an ecosystem.

Humans rely on cycling of matter and energy that occurs in diverse ecosystems. Scientists have separated ecosystem services into four categories, based on how they benefit us. The categories are: cultural, provisional, regulatory, and supporting services. Identifying and protecting each service is vital for human life.

INTERACTIVITY

Explore the services provided by a healthy ecosystem.

Ecosystem Services

Figure 1 Organisms interact with and rely on one another. This bee pollinates the flower, which will turn into a strawberry. Consider some benefits you might get from this ecosystem. Some of these benefits might be obvious, while others may not be.

Cultural and Provisional Services

Figure 2 ✏ Cultural services make us feel well, while provisional services provide us with something to use. Circle any photo that shows a provisional service.

SEP Provide Evidence Which services, cultural or provisional, do humans pay the most money for? Explain.

....

....

....

....

....

....

Cultural Services Nature has a way of putting a smile on your face. When nature makes you happy, it is providing you with a cultural service. Cultural services include recreational services, such as paddling a canoe at a local lake or going on a hike, and educational services, such as exploring Earth's history in the rock layers. We use cultural services to rest and relax, or learn more about the world around us. We can even learn about history, such as the role of the Mississippi and Missouri Rivers in building our nation. **Figure 2** shows a few examples of the cultural services that give meaning to life and help our wellness.

Provisional Services *Provisional* means useful. Provisional services, also shown in **Figure 2**, are the products obtained from the natural resources in an ecosystem. Anything naturally occurring in the environment that humans use is a **natural resource**, such as drinking water, food, fuel, and raw materials. Filtered ground water and surface water are two sources we tap into for drinking water. Farming provides many of the meats, vegetables, and fruits we eat. Marine and freshwater ecosystems provide us with meat and vegetables. Fuel resources include oil, coal, and natural gas. Plants provide us with timber for buildings and plant-based medicines.

Restoring Water

The water flowing into New York Harbor is polluted due to waste and fertilizer runoff. Scientists have designed a solution that relies on natural filtration and purification. One oyster filters about 150 liters of water a day, while one mussel filters 65 liters a day.

1. **Write an Expression** Write a formula to show the amount of water filtered by 7 oysters in one day.

....

....

2. **Graph Proportional Relationships** Use your formula to calculate the amount of water 5, 10, 15, and 20 oysters can filter. Then, calculate the amount of water the same number of mussels can filter. Graph your data. Use a solid line to represent the oysters and a dashed line to represent the mussels.

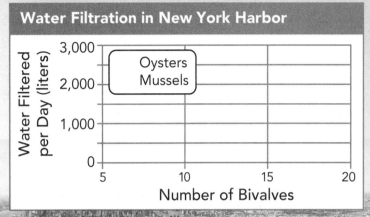

Water Filtration in New York Harbor

Oysters
Mussels

Water Filtered per Day (liters)

3,000

2,000

1,000

0

5   10   15   20

Number of Bivalves

Regulatory Services Benefits humans receive from natural processes are regulatory services. An ecosystem needs to function and operate properly to support life. Many of these processes, such as decomposition, go unseen. Regulatory services allow nature to resist or fix problems that may harm the ecosystem. These processes also protect humans from some of the same problems.

Plants and animals play a major role in the regulation of an ecosystem. Plants increase air quality by removing harmful chemicals and releasing useful chemicals. They regulate our climate by absorbing a greenhouse gas—carbon dioxide. The roots of plants prevent soil erosion. Bivalves, such as mussels and oysters, filter polluted and contaminated water. We have fruits to eat because animals pollinate flowers and help disperse seeds. Some animals naturally help with pest and disease control. This natural regulation of pests is biological control.

 VIRTUAL LAB

Test and evaluate competing solutions for preventing soil erosion to protect cropland.

☑ **CHECK POINT** **Cite Textual Evidence** How are regulatory services important for ecosystems?

....

....

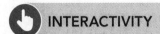

INTERACTIVITY

Explore the four key ecosystem services.

Interactions Between Cycles of an Ecosystem

Figure 3 ✏ Draw two arrows to show the flow of water in this ecosystem.

Explain Phenomena What would happen if any of these services were disrupted?

....

....

....

Supporting Services

The most important ecosystem services are the ones that support all the processes in nature. While supporting services do not directly impact humans, ecosystems would cease to function without them.

Supporting services cycle resources such as water, nutrients, gases, and soil throughout the ecosystem. In the water cycle, water evaporates, travels into the air and forms a part of a cloud, returns to Earth as precipitation, and the cycle continues. When an organism dies, it decomposes and forms nutrient-rich matter that becomes part of the soil. Plants take in the nutrients and store them in their cells. Atmospheric gases also cycle through ecosystems. During photosynthesis, plants take in carbon dioxide and release oxygen. Animals then take in oxygen and release carbon dioxide. Soil is also cycled. It is formed from weathered rock and organic matter. Rock sediment can reform into another rock with added heat and/or pressure. **Figure 3** shows how these different cycles interact with one another. The cycles ensure that matter and energy are endlessly transferred within a healthy ecosystem.

☑ **CHECK POINT** **Determine Central Ideas** Why are supporting services important to the ecosystem?

....

....

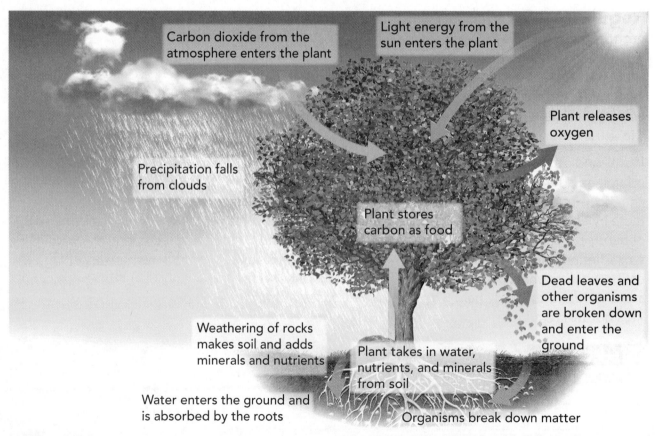

Carbon dioxide from the atmosphere enters the plant

Light energy from the sun enters the plant

Plant releases oxygen

Precipitation falls from clouds

Plant stores carbon as food

Dead leaves and other organisms are broken down and enter the ground

Weathering of rocks makes soil and adds minerals and nutrients

Plant takes in water, nutrients, and minerals from soil

Water enters the ground and is absorbed by the roots

Organisms break down matter

Figure 4 The survival of marine ecosystems, like this coral reef, is dependent on the diversity of organisms. Coral reefs provide every type of ecosystem service. But sometimes those services can be in conflict. People who snorkel and scuba dive can damage the corals. Boats can increase water pollution. People can also overfish the area.

Specify Design Constraints

Think about ways to preserve this ecosystem. What sort of management plan could maintain the ecosystem services a coral reef provides, while protecting it from the negative impact of human activities?

....

....

....

....

....

....

Factors Impacting Ecosystem Services

Earth needs diverse and healthy ecosystems. All organisms depend on their environment to get food, water, and shelter. Diverse ecosystems provide these basic needs for life.

Biodiversity Ecosystem production increases with biodiversity. When production increases, ecosystem services increase. Coral reefs, such as the one in **Figure 4**, cover less than one percent of the ocean. However, over 25 percent of the marine life lives among coral reefs. Each species plays a role within the ecosystem and they benefit from one another. Small fish eat algae, so the coral do not compete for resources with algae. Predators, such as sharks, keep the number of small fish from getting too large. Some fish eat parasites growing on other fish. Organisms like crabs feed on dead organisms.

As you can see, there are many more examples of biodiversity found at coral reefs. This biodiversity helps coral reefs survive changing conditions. However, coral reefs are increasingly threatened by our demand for their resources.

Avocado Farms

Figure 5 Avocado farmers in Mexico did not know that the roots of the native trees filter water. Avocado tree roots are not able to filter the ground water.

CCC Identify Patterns How has this impacted people who rely on naturally filtered drinking water?

....

....

....

....

Investigate Model how wetlands help with water purification.

Literacy Connection

Write Arguments Use the Internet to conduct research on the clearing of forests to create farmland. Research two opposing sides of the issue. Select one side of the issue to support. Cite specific claims and relevant evidence to explain why you chose that side.

Human Activities When humans alter or destroy habitats, the natural cycling of the ecosystem is disrupted. The severe impact of human activities is mostly due to our ignorance and greed. Removing species from ecosystems disrupts natural cycling, which decreases ecosystem services. However, many people are working to restore and protect the natural cycling of ecosystems.

Scientific knowledge might be able to describe the environmental consequences of our actions, but it does not determine or recommend the decisions that we take as a society. For example, we once thought that our oceans could handle anything we dumped in them, from sewage to nuclear waste. We also assumed that the ocean was an endless supply of goods. Now we know that by polluting our oceans, we have lost marine organisms. By overfishing the Atlantic cod, bluefin tuna, and Chilean sea bass, we have caused their populations to decline drastically.

Changing the ecosystem impacts humans because it reduces the ecosystem services we rely on. The development of cities and demand for food further harms ecosystems. When buildings replace wetlands and floodplains, flooding and loss of biodiversity often result. To grow crops, farmers strip the land of native plant species, decreasing biodiversity. In Mexico, this became a problem when avocado farmers cleared native oak and pine trees to grow avocado trees, as shown in **Figure 5**.

Conservation

Over the past 50 years, human activities have drastically changed Earth's ecosystems. Scientists and engineers are working to design solutions to help save Earth's ecosystems. One way is through **conservation**, or the practice of using less of a resource so that it can last longer. As concerned citizens, we can all participate in conservation to protect and restore Earth's ecosystems.

Protection Healthy ecosystems need protection from the loss of resources. **Sustainability** is the ability of an ecosystem to maintain biodiversity and production indefinitely. Designating protected areas and regulating the amount of resources humans can take from an ecosystem are two main efforts to promote sustainability. The **regulation** of protected areas can be difficult to enforce without monitors.

Restoration **Ecological restoration** is the practice of helping a degraded or destroyed ecosystem recover from damage. Some recovery efforts are easy, like planting native plants. Others are more difficult. For example, toxic chemical spills require bioremediation, a technique that uses microorganisms to breakdown pollutants. Restoring land to a more natural state, or land reclamation, also helps ecosystems (**Figure 6**).

☑ CHECK POINT **Determine Central Ideas** Why do scientists prefer to use bioremediation to clean up chemical spills?

....

....

👆 **INTERACTIVITY**

Investigate how biodiversity impacts ecosystem services.

Academic Vocabulary

Why is it important for the school to have regulations?

....

....

....

Design It!

Ecological Restoration

Figure 6 Restoring an ecosystem often takes several years and several regulations.

Design Your Solution Construction of a shopping mall has caused the deterioration of a wetland area. A study conducted showed that runoff from paved areas is disrupting the existing wetland. Create a plan to present to local officials outlining criteria for restoring the remaining wetland.

....

....

....

....

☑ LESSON 4 Check

MS-LS2-3, MS-LS2-5, EP&CIc, EP&CIIb, EP&CIIIa, EP&CIIIb, EP&CIIIc, EP&CIVc, EP&CVa

1. **Identify** What are the four categories of ecosystem services?

....

....

2. **SEP Provide Evidence** How do cultural services help humans?

....

....

3. **Distinguish Relationships** How are biodiversity and the cycling of matter related to maintaining ecosystem services?

....

....

....

....

4. **SEP Design Solutions** What are several ways that you could conserve water?

....

....

....

....

....

5. **Explain Phenomena** What are supporting services and why are they important to cultural, provisional, and regulatory services?

....

....

....

....

....

....

....

6. **Evaluate Proportion** Using your data from the math toolbox, which bivalve is more efficient at filtering water? Provide support.

....

....

....

....

7. **SEP Construct Explanations** What are some other organisms, aside from bivalves, that could be used to purify water? Explain the benefits of using this organism.

....

....

....

....

....

8. **Connect to Environmental Principles and Concepts** A giant factory farm uses large open lagoons to treat waste from the buildings where hogs are housed. The problem is that the lagoons smell awful and during rainstorms they are at risk of spilling into surrounding river systems. Design a solution that resolves the smell and water contamination risk, and allows the farm to continue to raise hogs.

....

....

....

....

....

....

....

....

....

....

MS-LS2-4, MS-LS2-5, ETS1-1, EP&CIc, EP&CIVc, EP&CVa

FROM BULLDOZERS
To Biomes

▶ **VIDEO**

Explore different types of ecosystem services.

Do you know how to transform an old clay pit into lush biomes? You engineer it! The Eden Project in Cornwall, England shows us how.

➤ **The Challenge:** To renew and transform land after humans have damaged it.

Phenomenon A clay pit in Cornwall had been mined for over a hundred years to make fine china and was shutting down. Mining provides access to resources, but can damage ecosystems by removing vegetation and topsoil. Mining can threaten biodiversity by destroying or fragmenting habitats, and increasing erosion and pollution.

Eden Project planners chose the clay pit to build a giant greenhouse to showcase biodiversity and the relationship between plants, people and resources.

The greenhouse represents two biomes: the rain forest biome and the Mediterranean biome. These biomes contain over a million plants and more than 5,000 different species. By comparison, in the California Floristic Province, a Mediterranean-type climate, there are over 2,000 different native plant species. Visitors can learn how plants are adapted to different climates, how plants play a role in their daily lives, and how to use resources sustainably.

The top photo shows the clay pit that was transformed into the biome structures and lush vegetation of the Eden Project below.

DESIGN CHALLENGE

Can you build a model of a biome structure? Go to the Engineering Design Notebook to find out!

You have limited materials to work with: 30 toothpicks and 15 balls of clay

☑TOPIC 3 Review and Assess

1 Interactions in Ecosystems

🕐 MS-LS2-1, MS-LS2-2, EP&CIIb

1. To reduce competition, the role of an organism in its habitat is called its
   A. adaption.   B. host.
   C. niche.   D. parasite.

2. In which type of interaction do both species benefit?
   A. predation   B. mutualism
   C. commensalism   D. parasitism

3. Four different mammals all live among oak and maple trees in a forest. They don't seem to compete for the same foods or nesting places. Which is a likely explanation for this lack of competition?
   A. The four species occupy different niches.
   B. Their small size is a limiting factor that reduces competition among them.
   C. There is no shortage of food.
   D. There is no shortage of space.

4. **CCC Cause and Effect** Why is it in the best interest of a parasite not to kill its host? Explain.

   ....

   ....

   ....

5. **SEP Construct Explanations** Describe what a predatory relationship would look like in a forest ecosystem and a wetland ecosystem. Identify any similarities and differences.

   ....

   ....

   ....

   ....

   ....

   ....

2 Dynamic and Resilient Ecosystems

🕐 MS-LS2-1, MS-LS2-2, MS-LS2-4, EP&CIIb, EP&CIIIa, EP&CIIIb, EP&CIIIc

6. The series of predictable changes that occur in a community over time is called
   A. natural selection.   B. ecology.
   C. commensalism.   D. succession.

7. A disruption to an established ecosystem can lead to
   A. new organisms being prevented from moving into the area.
   B. changes in the populations of the community.
   C. more resources for all the organisms that make up the community.
   D. hurricanes or volcanic eruptions.

8. A former farmland that is now home to shrubs and small trees is undergoing
   A. pioneer succession.
   B. primary succession.
   C. secondary succession.
   D. adaptive succession.

9. After a long time, a mature community is established in an ecosystem. This community will not change unless a component of the ecosystem is ....

10. **Apply Scientific Reasoning** When a disrupted part of a wetland ecosystem is left alone so that nature can help restore it to what it once was, what are people counting on occurring? Explain.

    ....

    ....

    ....

    ....

    ....

    ....

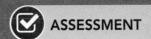
3 Biodiversity

MS-LS2-4, MS-LS2-5, MS-LS4-1, EP&CIc, EP&CIIIa, EP&CIIIb, EP&CIIIc, EP&CIVc, EP&CVa

11. A(n) .... is a species that influences the survival of many other species in an ecosystem.

12. A(n) .... is a non-native species that is introduced into an ecosystem and severely disrupts it by competing with native species.

13. CCC Cause and Effect Why are species with low genetic diversity at more risk of becoming extinct than species with high genetic diversity?

....

....

....

....

....

....

....

14. Apply Concepts Describe an example in which humans overuse an ecosystem's resources for their economic value.

....

....

....

....

....

....

....

....

4 Ecosystem Services

MS-LS2-3, MS-LS2-5, EP&CIc, EP&CIIIa, EP&CIIIb, EP&CIIIc, EP&CIVc, EP&CVa

15. Going for a hike in a forest where you can breathe fresh air, observe wildlife, and relax is an example of a .... service that an ecosystem can provide.

16. The water cycle, photosynthesis, nutrient cycling, and soil formation are examples of
A. cultural services.
B. provisioning services.
C. regulating services.
D. supporting services.

17. Analyze Properties What are some examples of provisioning services humans get from plants?

....

....

....

18. Synthesize Information Describe an example of when land reclamation may be needed on a beach.

....

....

....

....

....

....

19. Explain Phenomena How can bioremediation play a role in cleaning up an oil spill?

....

....

....

....

MS-LS2-1, MS-LS2-4, MS-LS4-1, EP&CIIb, EP&CIIIc

Evidence-Based Assessment

Like organisms in an ecosystem, the microscopic organisms, or microbiota, living in the human mouth are affected by environmental conditions. One way the human oral environment can change is by a changing diet.

Scientists use fossil evidence to compare the oral microbiota of our ancestors with people living today. Their goal is to gain a better understanding of how the human diet has changed over time. First, they studied the diversity of oral microbiota species. They found that two cavity-causing bacteria appeared more often through time (*S. mutans* and *P. gingivalis*). Then they studied the frequency, or rate, of the two cavity-causing bacteria.

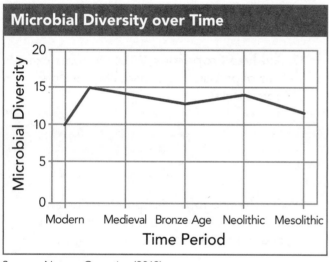

Source: Nature Genetics (2013)

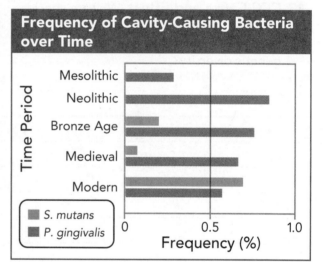

Source: Nature Genetics (2013)

The scientists also considered the changes in human diet and culture that have taken place since ancient times.

- During the Mesolithic period (7,550–5,450 BP), humans were hunter-gatherers.

- During the Neolithic period (7,400–4,000 BP), humans developed farming and adopted a carbohydrate-rich diet.

- During the Bronze Age (4,200–3,000 BP), humans manufactured bronze tools, but did not change their diet.

- During the Medieval period (1,100–400 BP), human diet was based on agricultural products.

- In modern times, human diet shifts to mass-produced, high processed food filled with flour, salt, and sugar.

1. **SEP Analyze Data** According to the study, in which period were mouth microbiota the least diverse?
   A. Mesolithic period
   B. Neolithic period
   C. Bronze Age
   D. Medieval era
   E. Modern times

2. **CCC Identify Patterns** Complete the sentences to show how the frequency of each cavity-causing bacteria changed over time.

   (P. gingivalis / S. mutans) was found in every sample, but was present in a (lower / higher) percentage in the oldest sample.

   (P. gingivalis / S. mutans) appeared during the Bronze Age and is still present in a much (smaller / larger) percentage.

3. **Explain Phenomena** According to the information presented in the graphs and text, what is the relationship between diet and the diversity of oral microbiota populations throughout time? Cite evidence from the graph and text.

   ....
   ....
   ....
   ....
   ....
   ....
   ....
   ....
   ....

4. **SEP Communicate Information** Based on the data and information presented, how did the availability of resources cause changes in the population size of cavity-causing bacteria? Explain.

   ....
   ....
   ....
   ....
   ....
   ....
   ....
   ....
   ....
   ....
   ....

Quest FINDINGS

Complete the Quest!

Phenomenon Determine the best way to clearly present your claim with data and evidence, such as graphics or a multimedia presentation.

CCC Cause and Effect If new homes or businesses are constructed when new highways are built, how would an animal crossing affect the changes to the physical and biological components of the ecosystem?

....
....
....
....

🖑 **INTERACTIVITY**

Reflect on Your Animal Crossing

MS-LS2-1, MS-LS2-2, MS-LS2-3, MS-LS2-4,
EP&CIIB, EP&CIIIa, EP&CIIIb, EP&CIIIc

Changes in an Ecosystem

How can you use a **model** to determine the effects of a **forest fire** on a **rabbit population?**

Background

Phenomenon Forest fires have a bad reputation! Many of these fires damage or destroy habitats and impact the populations of organisms that live there. But forest fires can also play an important role in maintaining the overall health of ecosystems. In this lab, you will develop and use a model to investigate how a forest fire might affect a population of rabbits 50 years after the fire.

Materials

(per group)

- tree-shadow circles handout
- scissors
- transparent tape

Young
Longleaf Pine

Tree Shadow As
Seen From Above

Mature
Longleaf Pine

Tree Shadow As
Seen From Above

Safety

Be sure to follow all safety guidelines provided by your teacher. The Safety Appendix of your textbook provides more details about the safety icons.

Oak Tree

Tree Shadow As
Seen From Above

Procedure

1. Predict what will happen to the rabbit population 50 years after the fire. Will the population be smaller, the same size, or larger? Record your prediction.

2. The graph paper represents the forest floor where each square is equal to 10 square meters (m^2). Calculate the total area of the forest floor. Create a data table in the space provided and enter this area in the table.

3. ✂ Cut out the tree shadow circles from the tree-shadow circles handout. Design a longleaf pine forest by arranging the mature pine and oak tree shadow circles on the forest floor. (Do not use the young pine tree shadows yet.) Tape the mature pine tree shadows in place, but not the oak tree shadows.

4. Determine the area of forest floor in sunlight. Add this data to your table.

5. Using a similar method, determine the square meters of shadow. Calculate the percentage of forest floor in shadow and in sunlight. Add this data to your table.

6. Suppose a lightning strike ignites a forest fire. Here's what would happen to some of the populations in the forest:

   - **Oak trees** are not adapted to survive fire so they burn and are destroyed; new trees will grow only if seeds are carried into the forest after the fire

   - **Longleaf pine trees** survive and continue to grow; seeds are released from pine cones and can germinate

   - **Bluestem grasses** are burned, but roots survive

7. Fast forward 50 years. The oak trees did not survive the forest fire, but the longleaf pines did. Use the young pine tree shadows to model the areas where young pine trees have likely grown. Repeat Steps 4 & 5 to gather evidence from your model about what the forest looks like 50 years after the fire.

HANDS-ON LAB

ᵘ**Demonstrate** Go online for a downloadable worksheet of this lab.

Prediction

....

....

....

....

....

....

Observations

....

....

....

....

....

....

....

Data Table

Analyze and Interpret Data

1. **Explain** What resources are the trees and grass competing for?

....

....

....

2. **SEP Analyze Data** Was your prediction correct? How did resource availability 50 years after the fire impact the rabbit population? (Hint: The rabbits are herbivores that primarily feed on grasses.)

....

....

....

....

....

3. **SEP Cite Evidence** Use the data you have collected as evidence to support the claim you made in Question 2.

....

....

....

....

....

4. **SEP Engage in Argument** Longleaf pine forests are important habitats, home to several endangered species. Oak trees are invasive (non-native) species in longleaf pine forests. When there are too many oak trees, they block the sunlight that pine trees need. Construct an argument that it is sometimes necessary to set forest fires in these habitats in order to preserve these endangered species.

....

....

....

....

....

....

....

MS-LS2-1, EP&CIIa, EP&CIIb, EP&CIIc, EP&CIVa, EP&CIVc

THE CASE OF THE DISAPPEARING

Cerulean Warbler

The cerulean warbler is a small, migratory songbird named for its blue color. Cerulean warblers breed in eastern North America during the spring and summer. The warblers spend the winter months in the Andes Mountains of Colombia, Venezuela, Ecuador, and Peru in northern part of South America.

The population of cerulean warblers is decreasing very quickly. No other population of songbirds is decreasing more rapidly in eastern North America. Populations of warblers have been declining at a rate of about 3 percent a year. This means that there are 3 percent fewer warblers from one year to the next. Habitat loss, especially in the region where the birds spend the winter, is thought to be the main reason. Look at the Cerulean Warbler Range Map.

Cerulean Warbler Range Map

EQUATOR

KEY

- Breeding range (April–Spetember)
- Wintering range (October–March)
- Migration route

Habitat Loss in the Wintering Range

By 2025, there will be 100 million more people in South America than there were in 2002. As human population size increases, the demands on the land and local habitats also increase. Forests are cleared and habitats for native plants and animals are lost to make room for planting crops and for raising cattle. These crops and cattle are needed to feed the increased population of people in the area.

Cerulean warblers inhabit the dense, evergreen forests that grow at middle elevations in the Andes Mountains. Their preferred habitat is tall, mature trees where they can feed on insects.

However, this habitat is also the preferred area to grow shade-coffee crops. The tall trees provide shade for the shorter coffee plants. Shade-coffee takes longer to grow and produces less coffee than sun-grown coffee crops. Forested areas are often cleared to make room for sun-grown coffee and other more profitable crops needing direct sunlight. This reduces the size of the warbler's habitat. As shown in the graph, the rate of clearing has decreased in recent years because the forests that are left are on steep slopes. These steep slopes and high elevations are not suitable for farming. Look at the bar graph below.

Use the graph to answer the following questions.

1. CCC Patterns Describe any patterns you see in the graph.

2. Predict What do you think the data will look like for each country in the future? Why?

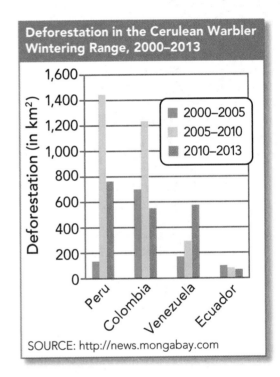

Deforestation in the Cerulean Warbler Wintering Range, 2000–2013

SOURCE: http://news.mongabay.com

3. SEP Construct Explanations Explain how you think changing levels of deforestation in the wintering range affects the cerulean warbler population.

4. SEP Design Solutions What are some strategies that you think can be used in northern South America to stabilize and protect the warbler populations?

MS-LS2-2, MS-LS2-4, EP&CIIa, EP&CIIb, EP&CIIc, EP&CIVc, EP&CVa

The Dependable Elephant

The African elephant is the largest land mammal on Earth. It can grow to weigh more than 4,500 kilograms (10,000 pounds) and spend most of its days eating. This huge creature often lives in herds of 12 to 15 individuals that are led by a dominant female. An African elephant gives birth every 3 to 4 years, producing one calf after a two-year pregnancy. A calf can weigh about 110 kilograms (250 pounds) at birth.

Elephants serve an ecological role as big as their size. As a keystone species, they directly impact the structure, composition, and biodiversity of their ecosystem—where the vast grassy plains of the African savannas and woodlands meet. Elephants affect the variety and amount of trees that make up a forest. By pulling down trees and tearing up thorny bushes, they create grassland habitats for other species. Elephant dung enriches the soil with nutrients and carries the seeds of many plant species. In fact, some of the seeds need to pass through the elephant's digestive system to germinate! Other seeds are removed from the dung and eaten by other animals. Scientists estimate that at least one-third of Africa's woodlands depend on elephants for their survival in one way or another.

African elephants once numbered in the millions, but the numbers have been dropping. This dramatic decline is a result of poaching. Hunters kill the elephants for their ivory tusks. The valuable ivory is sold or used to make decorative items.

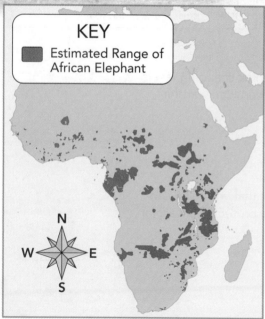

KEY

Estimated Range of African Elephant

N
W E
S

Saving the Elephants

Various elephant conservation groups suggest that there are scattered pockets of African elephants throughout the southern portions of the continent. While there are efforts being made to protect the elephants, there are just too few people and too much land to cover to be very effective.

The graph to the right shows the estimated African elephant population from 1995 through 2014. Use the graph to answer the questions.

1. **CCC Patterns** Describe any patterns you see in the graph.

   ....

   ....

   ....

   ....

2. **Predict** Do you think the trend shown in the graph will continue? Explain.

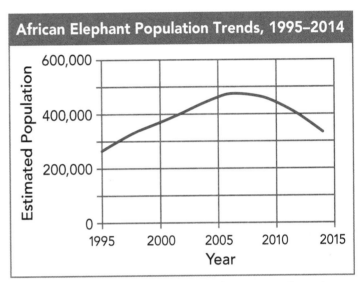

Source: Chase MJ, et. al. (2016) Continent-wide survey reveals massive decline in African savannah elephants. *PeerJ* 4:e2354

   ....

   ....

   ....

3. **CCC Stability and Change** Based on the data, how might the rest of the elephant's ecosystem be affected long term?

   ....

   ....

   ....

   ....

4. **SEP Construct Explanations** What are some ways elephants could be protected in order to preserve the biodiversity of an ecosystem?

   ....

   ....

   ....

   ....

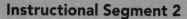
MS-LS1-1, MS-LS1-2, MS-LS1-3,
MS-LS1-8, EP&CIIa, EP&CIIc,
EP&CIIIa, EP&CIIIb, EP&CIIIc, EP&CIVb

Guiding Questions

- How do the parts of a cell sustain life?
- How do cells work together to make a complex organism?
- How do environmental conditions affect the proper functioning of the human body?

Topics

Before the Topics
Identify the Problem

California Wildfires

Phenomenon Wildfires are common in California from April to October. The California Department of Forestry and Fire Prevention (Cal Fire) responds to an average of 5,600 wild land fires each year. But the fires that struck in the fall of 2017 were the worst ever seen in the state.

What are the natural and human causes of these fires, how do wildfires affect living things, and what can people do to reduce their impact?

This firefighter works to put out a fire along Highway 29 near Calistoga. This fire was just one of the hundreds of fires that burned in the fall of 2017.

Fuel for Fires

Organisms need food for their cells to use as fuel for proper functioning. Similarly, fires must have fuel to burn. The fuel for wildfires is usually plant material. Manufactured materials such as cars and plastics also provide fuel for wildfires.

In California, the winter of 2016–2017 was unusually wet. That moisture allowed plants to grow very rapidly. Very hot weather in 2017, especially in the northern part of the state, caused many plants to lose water and die. Dried plants make excellent fuel for fires. This pattern of a wet winter followed by a hot, dry summer is dangerous. It only takes a spark from an electrical line or an unattended campfire to start a wildfire. Based on the conditions, forecasters predicted that 2017 would be a bad year for wildfires in California.

Winds Fan the Flames

Each autumn, recurring wind patterns blow through different parts of California at 56 to 64 km/h (35 to 40 mi/h). The Santa Ana winds generally affect southern California, while the Diablo winds affect north-central California.

In 2017, those winds reached 110 km/h (70 mi/h). High winds blew down power lines and whipped small wildfires into raging infernos, or large fires that are out of control, around the state. The winds carried burning embers to new areas with fresh fuel. The Santa Rosa fire, for example, traveled as fast as 80 km/h (50 mi/h) at times. Cal Fire workers had their hands full getting people out of danger. It took days before they could start to bring the fires under control.

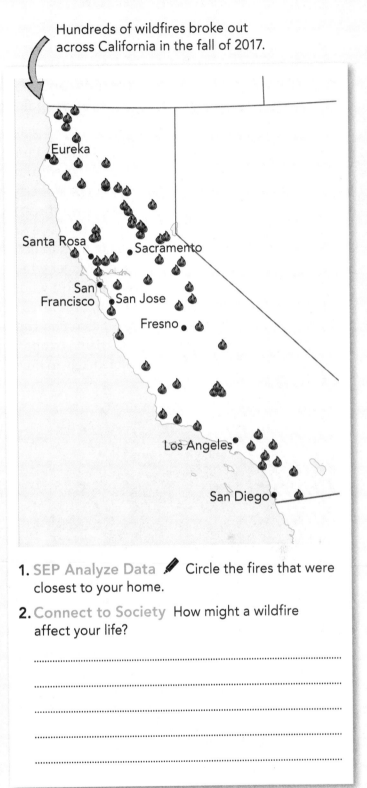

Hundreds of wildfires broke out across California in the fall of 2017.

1. **SEP Analyze Data** Circle the fires that were closest to your home.

2. **Connect to Society** How might a wildfire affect your life?

....

....

....

....

....

Making Wildfires Worse

Cycles of wildfires existed in California since long before the first humans arrived in the area. Prior to humans, lightning usually started wildfires. Over time, new plants sprang up from the ashes and renewed the landscape. Then, the same area might burn again in another 30–50 years.

Human actions disrupt the natural cycle in several ways. First, humans build homes and businesses, such as vineyards, in shrub areas that are at high risk for fire. Then, people try to protect property from damage by preventing the natural cycle of wildfires. As a result, more dead vegetation builds up, providing more fuel for future fires. In addition, global warming due to human activities has caused record high temperatures and stronger winds. Both factors increase the risk of wildfires. Finally, most wildfires are now the result of human activity. Arson, campfires, and downed electrical lines are some of the most common causes. The combination of more fuel, high winds, and rising temperatures means that wildfires are now much more likely to burn out of control.

Because these homes in southern California are built on top of shrub land, they are in greater danger from wildfires.

CCC Cause and Effect What could be done to help protect these homes from a wildfire? Explain.

....

....

....

....

Wildfires and Public Health

The number of people harmed by wildfires is much greater than the deaths reported on the news. The greatest health risk from wildfires is air pollution that comes from smoke, ash, and soot. Inhaling these substances causes respiratory issues.

Wildfire smoke contains gases produced by burning matter and tiny particles floating in the air. The gases can be toxic to cells and body systems. Burning plastic releases carbon monoxide into the air. When inhaled, it enters the blood and limits the amount of oxygen delivered to cells. Tiny particles, referred to as particulate matter (PM), make people cough and can burn the eyes and nose. PM can paralyze and damage the cilia of lungs cells, preventing cilia from clearing airways. Healthy people can recover quickly from breathing in smoke. People with lung or heart conditions take longer to recover.

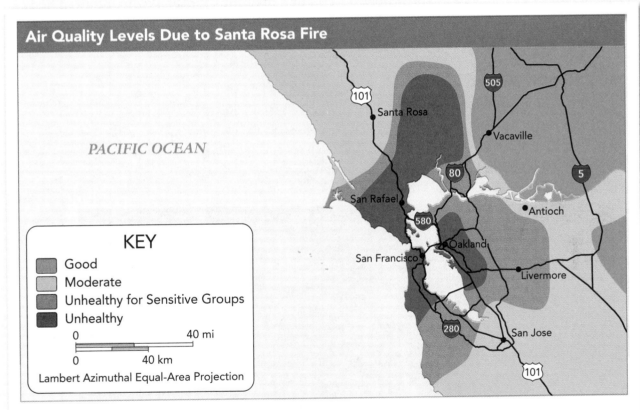

Air Quality Levels Due to Santa Rosa Fire

KEY
- Good
- Moderate
- Unhealthy for Sensitive Groups
- Unhealthy

0   40 mi
0   40 km
Lambert Azimuthal Equal-Area Projection

1. SEP Interpret Data According to the map, which cities had unhealthy air quality during the Santa Rosa fire?

....

2. CCC Energy and Matter One of the biggest wildfires burned near Santa Rosa. Why do you think the air quality east of Santa Rosa is worse than the air quality around Santa Rosa?

....

....

163

Fire's Impact on Ecosystems

Ecosystems in California are well adapted to wildfires. Animals such as deer and bats move out of the way of danger. Snakes and gophers burrow underground and wait for the fires to pass. After a fire, many plants grow back from their roots or new plants grow from seeds. Rain washes away ash. Animals move back when there is enough food for them to eat again. While individual animals and plants die in fires, the ecosystem recovers within a few years or decades.

As you read the two topics in this segment, think about how each one relates to the different causes of wildfires and the effects of these fires on living things. Consider these questions: How do wildfires impact habitats and the organisms that live there? How are organisms affected at the cellular level by the fires? What effects do the fires have on humans and the proper functioning of organs that make up different body systems?

Mt. Diablo State Park near Berkeley, California, is using a high-tech approach to study the recovery of an ecosystem after a wildfire. In September 2013, the Morgan fire burned about 3,200 acres of the park. The park now asks visitors to take photos from specific locations to provide crowdsourced data about the ecosystem's recovery.

A bulldozer attempts to create a fire break on the Morgan fire on Mt. Diablo.

After the Topics
Conduct an Investigation

Evidence **Now that you have completed the two topics in this segment, do the following tasks.**

Promote Collaborative Conversations ✏ With a partner, discuss what you have learned in this segment. Consider the causes and effects of the devastating 2017 wildfires. Fill in the first concept map to explore how wildfires affect living things, cell systems, and body systems. Then, fill in the second map to explore how each natural system contributed to the 2017 wildfires.

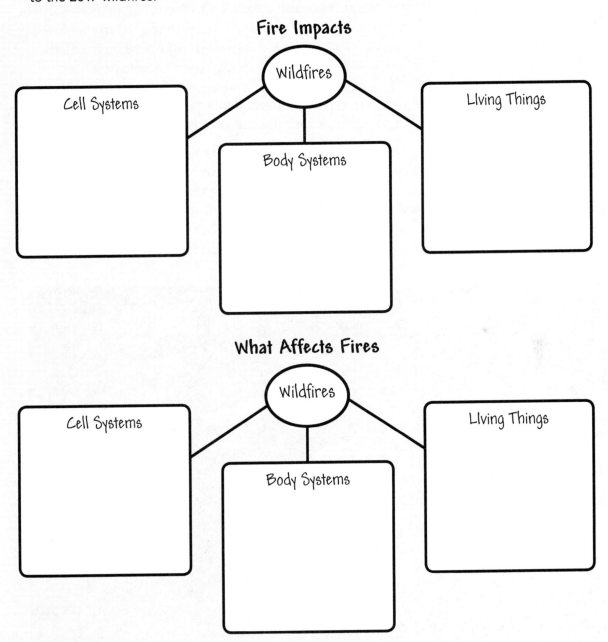

Fire Impacts

Wildfires

Cell Systems

Body Systems

Living Things

What Affects Fires

Wildfires

Cell Systems

Body Systems

Living Things

Reducing the Impacts of Wildfires

Case Study In less than a week, it is estimated that the wildfires in the fall of 2017 released over 10,000 tons of PM into the atmosphere. This amount is close to the amount of PM release from cars in California every year. As the wildfires continued through the end of 2017, air quality declined.

As a class, make a list of the sources of PM from the 2017 wildfires. Add to your list the sources of toxic gases. Next, work with a partner or in a small group. Each pair or group should choose one item from the list and research the harmful health impact on humans and a solution to the problem. For example, if you choose "plastic burned," then research what is emitted when plastics burn, how it impacts humans when inhaled, and how to decrease the impact. Based on your research, recommend one action that might reduce the harmful health impact. You may want to read news articles about the wildfire pollutants or look for information from experts.

The majority of the homes in this development provided fuel for the fire. As the homes burned to the ground, they released particles and toxic gases into the air.

Present your recommended action to the class. Include an explanation of the cost of this action. How would you convince Californians to follow your suggestion? After all groups have completed their presentations, hold a class discussion about the ideas that were presented. Decide which actions are most likely to reduce the harmful health effects from wildfires in the future.

Santa Rosa, California

Communicate a Solution

Based on your research and class discussion, answer the following questions.

1. **SEP Use Models** How can developing and using models of living systems such as cell systems and body systems help you make recommendations for reducing the health effects from wildfires?

....

....

....

....

2. **Connect to Society** What did you find to be the most effective actions Californians could take to reduce harmful health effects from future wildfires?

....

....

....

....

....

3. **CCC Cause and Effect** Identify some possible reasons why your recommendation or suggested actions were not put into place in the state before 2017.

....

....

....

....

4. **SEP Communicate Information** ✎ What steps would be needed to put your recommendation or plan into action? Sketch or outline the process in the space provided.

The Cell System

HANDS-ON LAB

uConnect Explore how an object's appearance changes when different tools are used.

MS-LS1-1 Conduct an investigation to provide evidence that living things are made of cells; either one cell or many different numbers and types of cells.

MS-LS1-2 Develop and use a model to describe the function of a cell as a whole and ways parts of cells contribute to the function.

MS-LS1-3 Use argument supported by evidence for how the body is a system of interacting subsystems composed of groups of cells.

MS-LS1-6 Construct a scientific explanation based on evidence for the role of photosynthesis in the cycling of matter and flow of energy into and out of organisms.

MS-LS1-7 Develop a model to describe how food is rearranged through chemical reactions forming new molecules that support growth and/or release energy as this matter moves through an organism.

EP&CIIIa Students should be developing an understanding that natural systems proceed through cycles and processes that are required for their functioning

EP&CIIIb Students should be developing an understanding that human practices depend upon and benefit from the cycles and processes that operate within natural systems

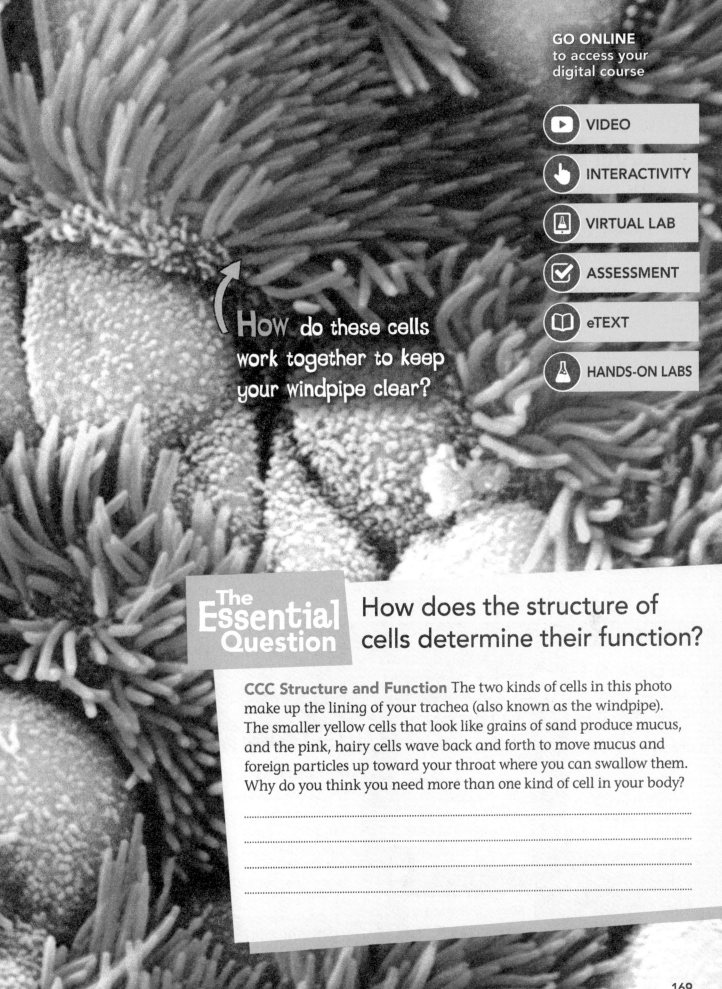

GO ONLINE
to access your
digital course

▶ VIDEO

👆 INTERACTIVITY

🧪 VIRTUAL LAB

☑ ASSESSMENT

📖 eTEXT

⚗ HANDS-ON LABS

How do these cells work together to keep your windpipe clear?

The Essential Question

How does the structure of cells determine their function?

CCC Structure and Function The two kinds of cells in this photo make up the lining of your trachea (also known as the windpipe). The smaller yellow cells that look like grains of sand produce mucus, and the pink, hairy cells wave back and forth to move mucus and foreign particles up toward your throat where you can swallow them. Why do you think you need more than one kind of cell in your body?

....

....

....

....

169

Quest KICKOFF

How can you design a model exhibit for a science museum?

Phenomenon Cells are often called "the building blocks of life." But that makes us think of wooden or plastic blocks that simply sit next to each other or stack neatly. In fact, cells have moving parts. And they interact with each other. To help people understand impossible-to-see processes such as these, museum staff—both scientists and engineers—try to engage and educate visitors with easy-to-see and hands-on models. In this problem-based Quest activity, you will plan and design a science exhibit on cells. By applying what you learn in each lesson, digital activity, and hands-on lab, you will gather information that will assist you in creating your exhibit. Then, in the Findings activity, you assemble, organize, and present your exhibit.

 INTERACTIVITY

Cells on Display

MS-LS1-1 Conduct an investigation to provide evidence that living things are made of cells; either one cell or many different numbers and types of cells.

MS-LS1-2 Develop and use a model to describe the function of a cell as a whole and ways parts of cells contribute to the function.

MS-LS1-3 Use argument supported by evidence for how the body is a system of interacting subsystems composed of groups of cells.

NBC LEARN ▶ VIDEO

After watching the Quest Kickoff video on how museum models are planned and built, think about the qualities of a good science museum display. Record your thoughts in the graphic organizer.

Qualities of a Science Museum Display	
Good Qualities	**Bad Qualities**

IN LESSON 1
What will your exhibit teach the public about cell theory? Consider the challenges of explaining and modeling things that are hard to observe.

Quest CHECK-IN

IN LESSON 2
What do cells look like? How can you represent different cell parts? Design and build a model cell.

 HANDS-ON LAB

Make a Cell Model

Quest CHECK-IN

IN LESSON 3
What cell parts are involved in cellular transport? Create an animation that shows how materials enter and leave the cell.

INTERACTIVITY

Put Your Cells in Motion

IN LESSON 4
Why is cell division important? Think about how to incorporate information about cell division into your exhibit.

The Body Fantastic exhibit at the Odyssium, a science museum in Edmonton, Alberta, Canada.

Quest CHECK-INS

IN LESSON 6

What factors affect cellular respiration? Research a disease and its impact on cell function. Consider how cell function affect the body at the atomic level.

HANDS-ON LAB

Accounting for Atoms

INTERACTIVITY

The Importance of Cells

Quest FINDINGS

Complete the Quest!

Determine the best way to present your museum exhibit. Then share your exhibit with museum guests. Evaluate and compare the different exhibits.

INTERACTIVITY

Reflect on Your Museum Exhibit

IN LESSON 5

What is necessary for photosynthesis to take place? Explore the components necessary for photosynthesis.

1 Structure and Function of Cells

Guiding Questions

- What evidence is there that cells make up all living things?
- How do cells determine the structure of living things?

Connections

Literacy Determine Central Ideas

Math Represent Quantitative Relationships

 MS-LS1-1 Conduct an investigation to provide evidence that living things are made of cells; either one cell or many different numbers and types of cells.

MS-LS1-2 Develop and use a model to describe the function of a cell as a whole and ways parts of cells contribute to the function.

HANDS-ON LAB

иInvestigate Observe objects using a microscope.

Vocabulary

cell
microscope
cell theory

Academic Vocabulary

distinguish

Connect It!

✎ **Circle the different structures you observe in the photograph.**

CCC Cause and Effect With microscopes, we can see the cells inside us and around us. What reactions do you think people had when they first learned that they were surrounded by tiny living organisms?

....

....

....

Cells

What do a whale, a rose, bacteria, a ladybug, and you have in common? You are all living things, or organisms. All are made of **cells**, the basic unit of structure and function in living things. Cells form the parts of an organism and carry out its functions. The smallest organisms, such as the bacteria in **Figure 1,** are made of one cell, while the largest organisms may have trillions of cells.

Cell Structure The structure of an object refers to what it is made of and how its parts are put together. For example, the structure of a car depends on how materials such as plastic, metal, and rubber are arranged. The structure of a living thing is determined by the amazing variety of ways its cells are put together.

Cell Function A single cell has the same needs as an entire organism. For a cell to stay alive, it must perform biological functions. Those functions include obtaining energy, bringing in nutrients and water, and getting rid of wastes. Most organisms have bodies with many different cells that work together to help the organism to stay alive, grow, and reproduce. For example, blood cells in your circulatory system carry oxygen around your body. This blood provides you with fresh oxygen and removes the waste product carbon dioxide. Cells in your heart pump blood to every part of you. Your body's cells work together to keep you alive.

✓ **CHECK POINT** **Determine Central Ideas** How is a single cell similar to a gray wolf?

....

....

....

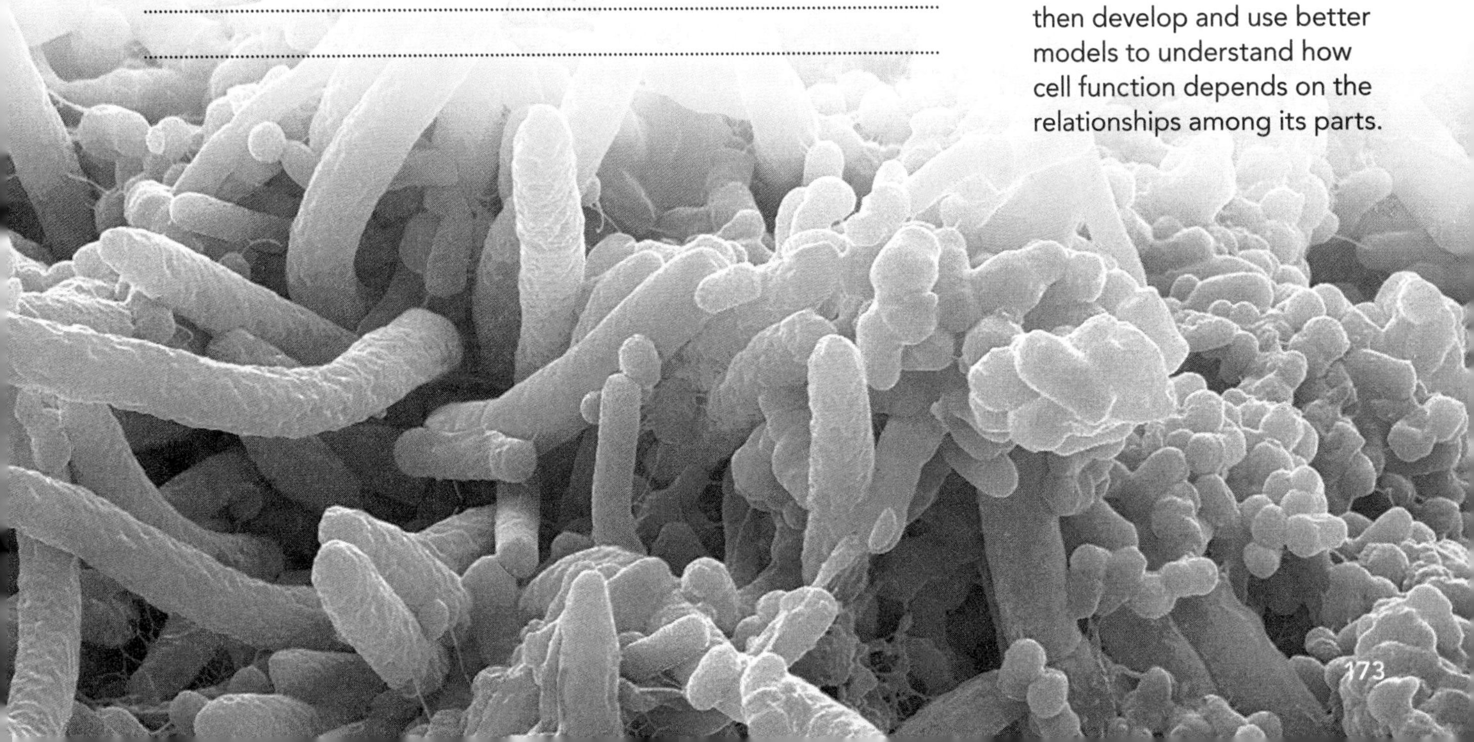

INTERACTIVITY

Explore the function of different cell types in unicellular and multicellular organisms.

Studying Cell Function
Figure 1 If you were to take a swab from someone's tongue, you might see this under this microscope. Microscope visualizations such as these help scientists study complex cell structures. Scientists can then develop and use better models to understand how cell function depends on the relationships among its parts.

VIDEO

Learn more about the scientists who helped to develop the cell theory.

Cell Theory

It wasn't until the 1600s that scientists realized living organisms are made of cells. The invention of the **microscope**, an instrument that makes small objects look larger, made this discovery possible. The technology of the microscope led to new knowledge of how life is organized. As this technology improved over time, scientists were able to gather new information about cells and how they function. Scientists put all these discoveries together to develop a theory about cells.

Observing Cells In the mid-1600s, English scientist Robert Hooke built his own microscopes to learn about nature. He made drawings of what he saw when he looked at the bark of cork oak trees (**Figure 2**). Hooke thought that the empty spaces he observed in the tree bark looked like tiny rooms, so he named them "cells." Tree bark, however, contains only dead cells.

Early Cell Observations

Figure 2 🖊 Hooke drew what he saw through his microscope in great detail. Draw a circle around one of Hooke's "cells."

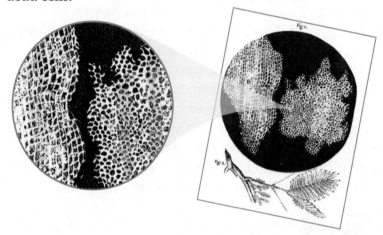

In 1674, Dutch businessman Anton van Leeuwenhoek (LAY von hook) was the first person to observe living cells through a microscope. He saw many tiny organisms swimming and hopping around in a drop of pond water. He named them "animalcules," or little animals.

By 1838, Matthias Schleiden, a scientist working with plants, noticed that all plants are made of cells. A year later, Theodor Schwann came to the conclusion that animals are made of animal cells. The timeline in **Figure 3** shows how the improvement of the microscope furthered the study of cells.

Before Schleiden and Schwann's suggestion that organisms are made up of cells, not much was known about the structure of organisms. These two scientists are credited with the development of the cell theory. Each scientist proposed a hypothesis (plural: hypotheses), a possible answer to a scientific question. Their hypotheses, supported through the observations and experiments of other scientists, led to a theory about cells and all living things.

Literacy Connection

Determine Central Ideas How did early modern scientists learn about cells without performing experiments?

....

....

....

....

....

Microscopes & Cell Theory

Anton van Leeuwenhoek observes living microorganisms under the microscope.

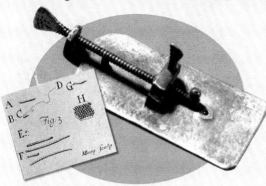

1650

Robert Hooke studies bark and fossils with microscopes and coins the term "cells".

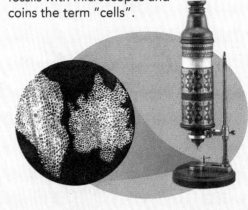

1663

1674

1675

1825

Matthias Schleiden concludes that all plants are made of cells.

1838

1839

Theodor Schwann reaches the conclusion that all animals are made of cells.

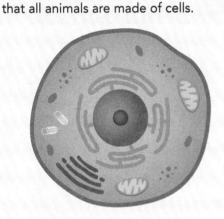

1850

1855

Rudolf Virchow proposes that cells are only made from other cells.

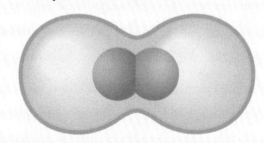

Scientists developed several types of electron microscopes that are 5,000 times more powerful than light microscopes.

1875

1925

1930s

Magnifying the Power of Discovery

Figure 3 This timeline shows how technology and science advance together.

Infer Why didn't Robert Hooke recognize that cells are alive?

....

....

....

1950

Giant Cells

Figure 4 Bubble algae, or sea pearls, look like rubber balls. The bubble shown in this life-sized photo is a single cell! Some scientists consider eggs to be single cells as well. An ostrich egg is 15 cm long and a human egg is about the size of the period at the end of this sentence.

HANDS-ON LAB

Investigate Observe objects using a microscope.

Principles of Cell Theory One of the most important ideas in biology, **cell theory** is a widely accepted explanation of the relationship between cells and living things. According to this theory:

- All living things are made of cells.
- Cells are the basic units of structure and function in living things.
- All new cells are produced from existing cells.

Even though living things differ greatly from one another, they are all made of one or more cells. Cells are the basic unit of life. Most cells are tiny. But some, like those shown in **Figure 4**, can be surprisingly large. The cell theory holds true for all living things, no matter how big or how small they are. Organisms can be made of one cell or of many cells. We can study how one-celled organisms remove wastes to sustain life. Then we can use this information to understand how multi-celled organisms carry out the same task. And, because all new cells are produced from existing cells, scientists can study cells to learn about growth and reproduction.

✓ **CHECK POINT** **Cite Textual Evidence** According to cell theory, how are bubble algae, or sea pearls, made?

....

....

Microscopes The cell theory could not have been developed without microscopes. The microscopes we use today have the same function as those used 200 years ago—to view tiny specimens. These specimens are now known as "microscopic." The advanced technology in the modern microscope, however, provides far greater detail and much clearer visualization. Light microscopes focus light through lenses to produce a magnified image. Electron microscopes are more complex. To create an image, electron microscopes use beams of electrons that scan the surface of the specimen. Look at the two different images of the same cells in **Figure 5**. Both types of microscopes do the same job in different ways, and both rely on two important properties—magnification and resolution.

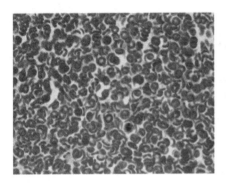 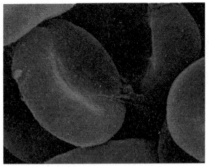

Different Views

Figure 5 Red blood cells look very different when viewed using a light microscope (left) and an electron microscope (right).

Apply Concepts How could scientists today use current technologies to further support the cell theory?

....

....

....

....

....

....

....

Plan It !

Plastic or Wood?

Two students in a science classroom are debating about whether the tables are made of wood or plastic. As the teacher passes by, she suggests, "Use cell theory to find the truth!"

SEP Plan an Investigation Propose a scientific investigation to determine whether the tables are wooden or plastic. Include your hypothesis, what steps the students should take, and any materials they might need to carry out the procedure.

....

....

....

....

....

....

....

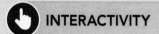
INTERACTIVITY

Explore how to use a microscope to observe specimens under different magnifications.

Magnification

The compound light microscope you see in **Figure 6** magnifies an image using two lenses at once. One lens is fixed in the eyepiece. A second lens, called the objective, is located on the revolving nosepiece. A compound microscope usually has more than one objective lens. Each objective lens has a different magnifying power. By turning the nosepiece, you select the lens with the magnifying power you need. A glass rectangle called a slide holds a thin sample to be viewed. A light shines up and passes through the slide and the sample. The light then passes through the lens in the nosepiece and the eyepiece lens. Each lens magnifies the sample. Finally, the light reaches your eye and you get to see the sample in detail!

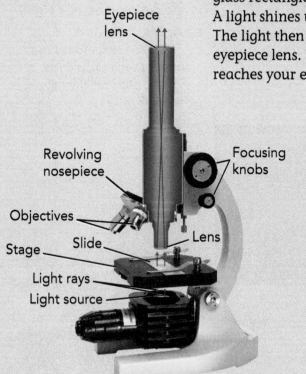

Eyepiece lens

Revolving nosepiece

Focusing knobs

Objectives

Stage — Slide

Lens

Light rays

Light source

Compound Light Microscope

Figure 6 This microscope has a 10× lens in the eyepiece. The revolving nosepiece holds three different objective lenses: 4×, 10×, and 40×.

CCC Scale, Proportion, and Quantity
Which magnification would you select to look at a penny? Which would you select to look at a sample of pond water?

Academic Vocabulary
The verb *distinguish* has more than one meaning: "to manage to recognize something you can barely see" or "to point out a difference." What distinguishes technology from science?

Resolution

A microscope image is useful when it helps you to see the details of an object clearly. The higher the resolution of an image, the better you can **distinguish** two separate structures that are close together, for example. Better resolution shows more details. In general, for light microscopes, resolution improves as magnification increases. Electron microscopes provide images with great resolution and high magnification. As you can see in **Figure 7**, greater resolution and higher magnification makes it relatively easy to study tiny objects.

✓ CHECK POINT **Summarize Text** How does the resolution of a microscope help you to observe different structures of the cell?

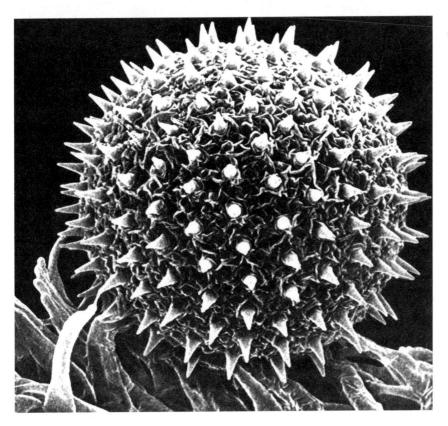

INTERACTIVITY

Investigate a sample to determine if it is living.

Extreme Close-Up

Figure 7 These plant pollen grains are magnified thousands of times.

SEP Make Observations Look closely at the image. Describe some of the details you can distinguish at this very high resolution.

....

....

....

....

Math Toolbox

Getting the Right Magnification

The total magnification of the image from a microscope equals the magnifications of the two lenses multiplied together. If the objective lens magnifies the object 10 times, and the eyepiece lens also magnifies the object 10 times, the total magnification of the microscope is 10 x 10, or 100 times (expressed as "100×"). The image you see will be 100 times larger than the actual sample.

1. SEP Use Mathematics Calculate the total magnification of a microscope with eyepiece lens 10× and objective lens 4×.

....

2. CCC Evaluate Scale If you use that microscope to view a human hair that is 0.1 mm across, how large will the hair appear in the image?

....

3. Represent Quantitative Relationships ✎ Your lab partner examined some items under the compound microscope at 40x and began entering her data in this table. Based on the equations in questions 1 and 2, fill in the missing data.

Item	Actual size	Size at 40x
A	0.3 mm	
B		4.8 mm
C		2 mm

☑ LESSON 1 Check

MS-LS1-1, MS-LS1-2

1. Identify What are three functions of all cells?

2. Describe What are the three key points of cell theory?

3. CCC Apply Concepts Scientists discover new kinds of life in the deep ocean every year. What does the cell theory tell them must be true about every new organism?

4. SEP Construct Explanations Use evidence to explain how advancements in technology influenced cell theory.

5. CCC Relate Structure and Function Compare and contrast the structure and function of a unicellular organism to that of a multicellular organism.

6. SEP Use Models In the first circle, draw a small, simple picture of something that is big enough to see without magnification. In the second circle, draw it again under 5x magnification. If it is too big to fit in the circle, draw only the part of the object that fits inside.

7. SEP Apply Scientific Reasoning Hooke and Van Leeuwenhoek made their discoveries around the same time. More than 150 years later, Schleiden, Schwann, and Virchow all made breakthroughs within a few years of each other. What are some possible reasons for the sudden development of the cell theory after such a long break?

180 The Cell System

Viewing cells through a
"Thermal Lens"

Cells have complex functions. Researchers have been trying to figure out how to target cells as a way to deliver drugs and medicines. The mid-infrared photothermal microscope is a new technology that lets scientists peer directly into living cells.

Until now, research into how cells use chemicals has been limited. Infrared imaging techniques could only use samples of dried tissue. Because the water in live cells kept the infrared signals from passing all the way through, scientists could not get detailed images. But engineering advances have led to a new imaging technology that works by shining a laser onto the surface of the tissue. This creates a phenomenon called a "thermal lens" effect, much like a mirage seen over a hot road. The result is a detailed three-dimensional image of the cell.

The photothermal microscope will be essential for discovering different ways cancer treatment drugs reach and affect cancer cells. And scientists can learn more about the chemistry of living systems and find better ways to treat many diseases.

This T-cell attacks cancer cells.

Biomedical engineers are constantly developing new technologies that help save lives. The mid-infrared photothermal microscope lets researchers see how various drug treatments affect cancer cells (left).

MY DISCOVERY

Investigate other conditions and diseases that could be better understood or treated using the new photothermal microscope.

2 Cell Structures

Guiding Questions

- What are some special structures within a cell?
- How do the different parts of a cell help it function?
- How are animal cells different from plant cells?

Connection

Literacy Integrate with Visuals

 MS-LS1-2 Develop and use a model to describe the function of a cell as a whole and ways parts of cells contribute to the function.

MS-LS1-3 Use argument supported by evidence for how the body is a system of interacting subsystems composed of groups of cells.

HANDS-ON LAB

ɴInvestigate Observe objects using a microscope.

Vocabulary

organelle
cell wall
cell membrane
cytoplasm
nucleus
mitochondria
chloroplast
vacuole

Academic Vocabulary

structure
function

Connect It !

✏ **Circle three different structures inside this plant cell.**

Describe This plant cell has been sliced in half and you are looking into one of the halves. How would you describe the structure of the cell?

....

....

....

....

Parts of a Cell

Humans, mushrooms, and plants are all made of many parts. If you've ever taken apart a flower, a leaf, or a nut, you've seen that it also contains smaller parts. You could keep dividing the plant up into parts until you got all the way down to the individual cells. As you learned in your study of the cell theory, cells are the smallest functional units of living organisms. But within each cell there are working structures that help the cell function like an entire organism. Each **organelle** is a tiny cell structure that carries out a specific function within the cell. You can see that the cell in **Figure 1** may have many of the same organelles, but different organelles have a different **structure**. This is because each of the different organelles has a different **function**. Also, some organelles are found only in plant cells, some only in animal cells, and some are found in both plant and animal cells. Bacteria are unicellular organisms that do not contain as many different types of cell parts as plant or animals cells. Together, all the parts of a cell keep the cell contributing to the function of whole organism.

Academic Vocabulary

Have you heard the terms *structure* and *function* used before? Using what you already know, identify two structures in your classroom and state their function.

....

....

....

Working as a Team

Figure 1 Many structures, or organelles, in this plant cell work together to help the cell survive. The cells, in turn, work together to help the plant survive and grow.

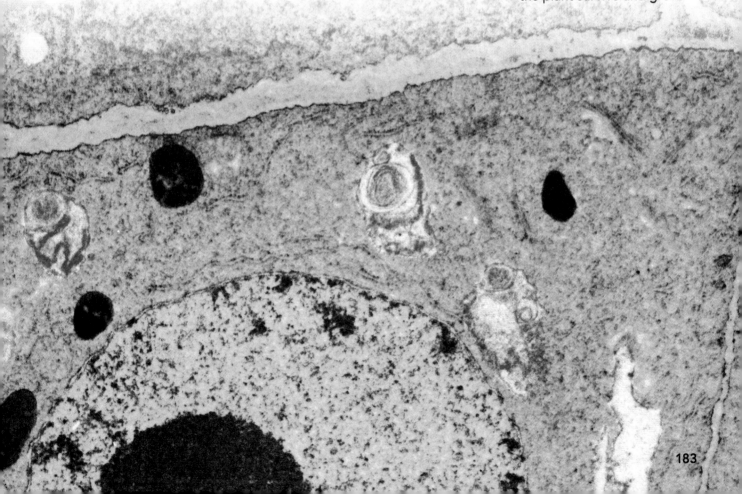

Plant and Animal Cell Differences

Figure 2 These illustrations show typical structures found in plant and animal cells. The functions of some organelles are also included.

1. **SEP Develop Models** ✎ Fill in the functions of the cell wall and the cell membrane in the boxes provided.

2. **Identify** ✎ Draw a circle around the structure *inside* the plant cell that is not inside the animal cell.

3. **Use an Analogy** How would you describe the shape of the plant cell compared to the shape of the animal cell?

....

....

....

....

....

....

....

....

....

....

Plant Cell

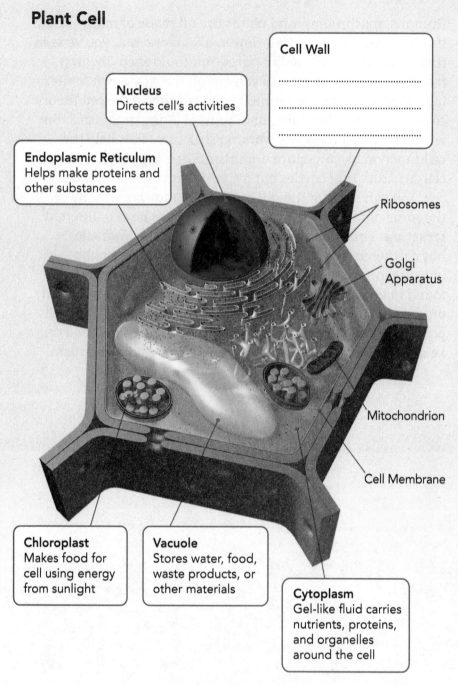

Cell Wall

....

....

....

Nucleus
Directs cell's activities

Endoplasmic Reticulum
Helps make proteins and other substances

Ribosomes

Golgi Apparatus

Mitochondrion

Cell Membrane

Chloroplast
Makes food for cell using energy from sunlight

Vacuole
Stores water, food, waste products, or other materials

Cytoplasm
Gel-like fluid carries nutrients, proteins, and organelles around the cell

Cell Wall The rigid supporting layer that surrounds the cells of plants and some other organisms is the **cell wall**. While plants, protists, fungi, and some bacteria have cell walls, the cells of animals do not have cell walls. One function of the cell wall is to help protect and support the cell. The cell walls of plant cells are made mostly of a strong material called cellulose. The cell walls of fungi are made of chitin, the same material that forms the hard, outer skeleton of insects. Observe in **Figure 2** that there are small holes, or pores, in the plant cell wall. Pores allow materials such as water and oxygen to pass through the cell wall.

Animal Cell

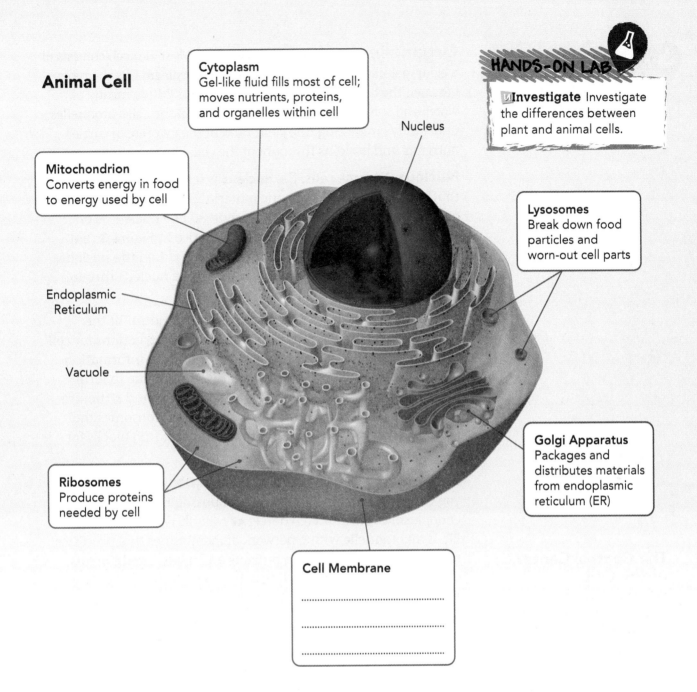

Cytoplasm
Gel-like fluid fills most of cell; moves nutrients, proteins, and organelles within cell

Nucleus

HANDS-ON LAB

☐ **Investigate** Investigate the differences between plant and animal cells.

Mitochondrion
Converts energy in food to energy used by cell

Lysosomes
Break down food particles and worn-out cell parts

Endoplasmic Reticulum

Vacuole

Golgi Apparatus
Packages and distributes materials from endoplasmic reticulum (ER)

Ribosomes
Produce proteins needed by cell

Cell Membrane

....

....

....

Cell Membrane The **cell membrane** is a thin, flexible barrier that surrounds a cell and controls which substances pass into and out of a cell. All cells have a cell membrane. In plant cells, the cell membrane is a fluid-like layer between the cell and the cell wall. As you can see in **Figure 2**, animal cells do not have a cell wall, so the cell membrane is the outermost layer. For all cells without a cell wall, the cell membrane forms the border between the cell and its environment. Think about how a dust mask allows you to breathe, but keeps harmful particles outside your body. One of the functions of the cell membrane is similar to that of a dust mask—it prevents harmful materials from entering the cell. Everything a cell needs, such as food particles, water, and oxygen, enters through the cell membrane. Waste products leave the same way.

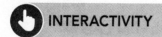

INTERACTIVITY

Explore the different functions of organelles.

Organelles in the Cytoplasm

Most of a cell consists of a clear, gel-like fluid called cytoplasm. **Cytoplasm** fills the region between the cell membrane and the nucleus. Made mostly of water and some salt, the cytoplasm holds all the cell's organelles. Constantly circulating, the clear fluid of the cytoplasm carries nutrients and proteins throughout the cell.

Nucleus In some cells, the **nucleus** is a large oval organelle that contains the cell's genetic material in the form of DNA and controls many of the cell's activities. The nucleus is one of the largest of the cell's organelles. Notice in **Figure 3** that the nucleus is surrounded by a membrane called the nuclear envelope. Materials pass into and out of the nucleus through pores in the nuclear envelope.

Thin strands of genetic material called chromatin fill the nucleus. This genetic material contains the instructions for cell function. For example, chromatin helps to store information that will later make sure leaf cells grow and divide to form more leaf cells. Also in the nucleus is a dark, round structure called the nucleolus. The nucleolus produces ribosomes that produce proteins. Proteins are important building blocks for many parts of the body.

Endoplasmic Reticulum and Ribosomes In **Figure 3**, you can see a structure like a maze of passageways. The endoplasmic reticulum (en doh PLAZ mik rih TIK yuh lum), or ER, is an organelle with a network of membranes that processes many substances, including proteins and lipids. Lipids, or fats, are an important part of cell structure. They also store energy. Ribosomes dot some parts of the ER, while other ribosomes float in the cytoplasm. The ER and its attached ribosomes make proteins for use in the cell.

The Control Center of the Cell

Figure 3 The nucleus acts as the control center of the cell. Folds of the endoplasmic reticulum (ER) surround the nucleus.

1. Identify 🖊 On the electron microscopy photo, label the nucleus, nuclear envelope, and ER.

2. Apply Concepts Why is the nucleus called the cell's "control center"?

....

....

....

....

....

....

....

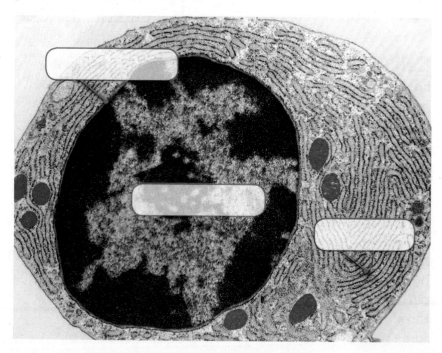

Golgi Apparatus As proteins leave the ER, they move to the Golgi apparatus, a structure that looks like flattened sacs and tubes. Considered the cell's warehouse, the Golgi apparatus receives proteins and other newly formed materials from the ER, packages them, and distributes them to other parts of the cell or to the outside of the cell.

Mitochondria Floating in the cytoplasm are rod-shaped structures. Look again at **Figure 2**. **Mitochondria** (myt oh KAHN dree uh; singular: mitochondrion) convert energy stored in food to energy the cell can use to live and function. They are the "powerhouses" of the cell.

Chloroplasts The **chloroplast** is an organelle in the cells of plants and some other organisms that captures energy from sunlight and changes it to an energy form that cells can use in making food. The function of the chloroplast is to make food, in the form of sugar, for the cell. Cells on the leaves of plants typically contain many green chloroplasts. Animal cells do not have chloroplasts because animals eat food instead of making their own food from sunlight.

☑ CHECK POINT **Determine Conclusions** Suppose there is a drought and a plant cannot get enough water. What happens to the cytoplasm and the organelles in the plant cells?

....

....

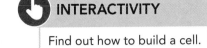
INTERACTIVITY

Find out how to build a cell.

📓 **Student Discourse** In a small group, brainstorm real-world models for a mitochondrion and a chloroplast. Consider their functions and how these parts of the cell help keep the whole cell alive. What structures do you know in everyday life that function like them? Record your ideas in your science notebook.

Model It !

The Substance of Life
Earth is often called the water planet because water covers 75 percent of its surface. Cytoplasm, a gel-like fluid, is about 80 percent water. Cytoplasm has three important functions: it gives the cell form, it houses the other organelles in the cell, and it stores chemicals that the cell needs.

SEP Develop Models What could you use to model cytoplasm? What would you use to represent each organelle? List the items you would use.

....

....

....

....

Organelles Up Close

Figure 4 Advanced microscopes capable of very high magnification allow scientists to see organelles in very fine detail. The actual images are not colored. All of these images have been colorized to help you see details.

1. **Claim** 🖊 For each organelle, fill in the small circle with A if it is found only in animal cells, P if it is found only in plant cells, or B if it is found in both kinds of cells.

2. **Evidence** Fill in the blank under each image with the name of the organelle. Make changes to your claim as needed.

3. **Reasoning** Explain how your evidence supports your claim.

....

....

....

....

....

....

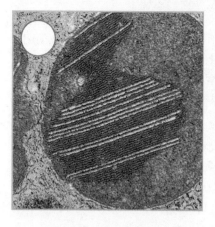

....

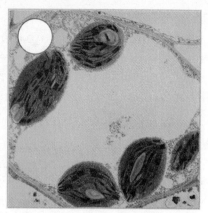

....

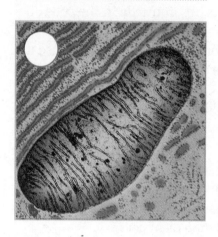

....

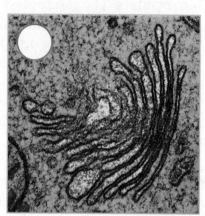

....

▶ **VIDEO**

Take a tour of the major structures of a cell.

Lysosomes You can think of lysosomes as a cell's recycling centers. Refer to the animal cell in **Figure 2**. Notice the small, round organelles? These are called lysosomes (LY suh sohmz). Lysosomes contain substances that break down large food particles into smaller ones. Lysosomes also break down old cell parts and release the materials so they can be used again.

Vacuoles Plant cells often have one or more large, water-filled sacs floating in the cytoplasm along with the other organelles shown in **Figure 4**. In some animals cells these sacs are much smaller. This structure is a **vacuole** (VAK yoo ohl), a sac-like organelle that stores water, food, or other materials needed by the cell. In addition, vacuoles store waste products until the wastes are removed. In some plants, vacuoles also perform the function of digestion that lysosomes perform in animal cells.

☑ **CHECK POINT** **Integrate with Visuals** Use **Figure 2** to describe the main differences between lysosomes and vacuoles.

....

....

....

Cells Working Together

A unicellular organism must perform every function for the survival, growth, and reproduction of the organism. A bacterium is one example of a unicellular organism that performs all the functions that sustain life. When the only cell that makes up the bacterium dies, the organism dies. In a multicellular organism, there are many different types of cells with different functions. Whether a cell is an entire organism or one of billions, all its parts contribute to its function.

Specialized Cells Multicellular organisms are more complex than unicellular organisms. Because they are more complex, they are composed of different types of cells that perform different functions. One type of cell does one kind of job, while other types of cells do other jobs. For example, red blood cells are specialized to deliver oxygen to cells throughout your body. However, they would not travel through your body without the specialized cells of the heart, which send them to other cells needing oxygen. Just as specialized cells differ in function, they also differ in structure. **Figure 5** shows specialized cells from plants and animals. Each type of cell has a distinct shape. For example, a nerve cell has thin, thread-like extensions that reach toward other cells. These structures help nerve cells transmit information from one part of your body to another. The nerve cell's shape would not help a red blood cell fulfill its function.

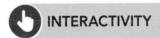

INTERACTIVITY

Investigate the functions of different specialized cells.

Literacy Connection

Integrate with Visuals Which image in **Figure 5** shows you evidence that the cells are relaying information to each other? What does it remind you of?

....

....

....

....

Functions of Specialized Cells

1. Animal cells that bend and squeeze easily through narrow spaces	**2.** Animal cells that relay information to other cells	**3.** Plant root cells that absorb water and minerals from the soil	**4.** Plant cells that make food

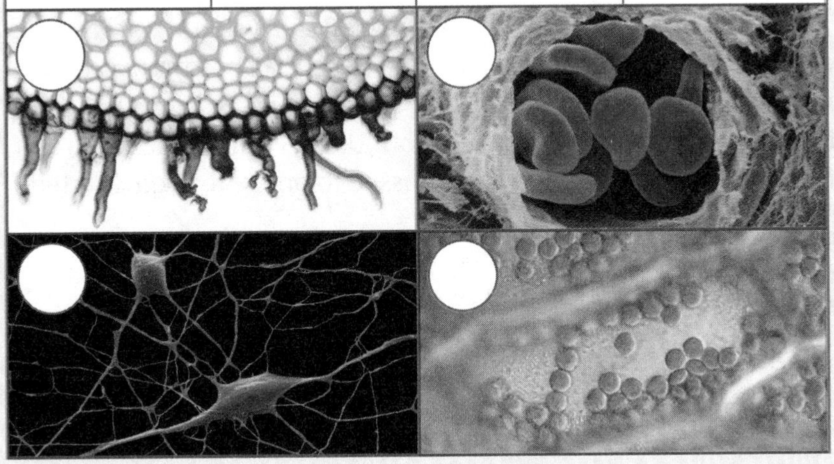

The Right Cell for the Job

Figure 5 Different cells carry out different functions.

1. **Draw Conclusions** 🖊 Match each function to a cell. Write the number of the function in the corresponding image.

2. **SEP Consider Limitations** Recall the animal cell in **Figure 2**. Why is that model not a true representation of different types of animal cells?

....

....

....

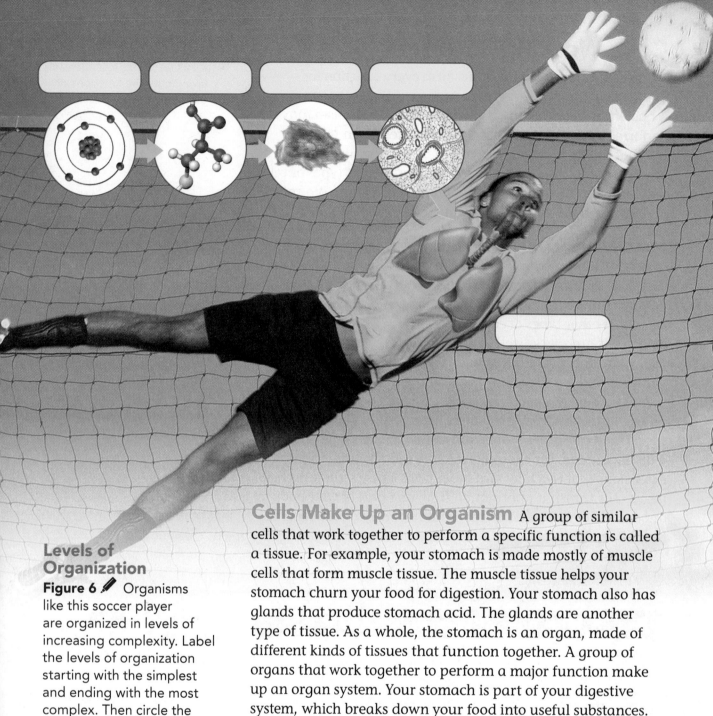

Levels of Organization

Figure 6 ✏ Organisms like this soccer player are organized in levels of increasing complexity. Label the levels of organization starting with the simplest and ending with the most complex. Then circle the organ system.

📓 **Reflect** Consider a time when you worked on a team. In your science notebook, describe how members of your team had special skills that helped you all work together as a group to overcome a challenge.

Cells Make Up an Organism A group of similar cells that work together to perform a specific function is called a tissue. For example, your stomach is made mostly of muscle cells that form muscle tissue. The muscle tissue helps your stomach churn your food for digestion. Your stomach also has glands that produce stomach acid. The glands are another type of tissue. As a whole, the stomach is an organ, made of different kinds of tissues that function together. A group of organs that work together to perform a major function make up an organ system. Your stomach is part of your digestive system, which breaks down your food into useful substances. The body is a system made up of many subsystems, such as the digestive system, and all are made of cells. These subsystems interact to run the whole body system. **Figure 6** shows how the body, a multicellular organism, builds up complex structures from atom to molecule to cell to tissue to organ to organ system.

✅ **CHECK POINT** **Determine Central Ideas** Could a single part of a multicellular organism survive on its own? Explain.

....

....

....

✅ LESSON 2 Check

🕐 MS-LS1-2, MS-LS1-3

1. Interpret Photos What is the yellow structure, and what role does it play in a cell?

....

....

....

2. SEP Explain Phenomena Why do cells have so many different organelles and structures?

....

....

....

....

3. SEP Determine Differences What are the main differences between cell walls and cell membranes?

....

....

....

....

....

4. CCC Structure and Function What are three differences between plant cells and animal cells?

....

....

....

....

5. SEP Construct Explanations Are there more tissues or more organs in your body? Explain your reasoning.

....

....

....

Quest CHECK-IN

In this lesson, you learned about the different structures of plant and animal cells and how they function.

SEP Develop Models How can a model help visitors to the exhibit better understand cell structures and their functions?

....

....

....

....

....

HANDS-ON LAB

Make a Cell Model

Go online for a downloadable worksheet of this lab. Design and build a model of a plant cell.

3 Obtaining and Removing Materials

Guiding Question

- What is the primary role of the cell membrane in cell function?

Connections

Literacy Integrate with Visuals

Math Analyze Proportional Relationships

 MS-LS1-2 Develop and use a model to describe the function of a cell as a whole and ways parts of cells contribute to the function.

HANDS-ON LAB

и**Investigate** Model the way that water moves into and out of a cell.

Vocabulary

selectively
    permeable
diffusion
osmosis
endocytosis
exocytosis

Academic Vocabulary

maintain

Connect It !

✏️ **Circle the area on the photo where you think the skunk spray odor will be strongest.**

Hypothesize How do you think it's possible for you to detect skunk spray from inside your house or from inside a moving car?

....

....

....

Moving Materials Into and Out of Cells

INTERACTIVITY

Discuss how objects move in and out of an area.

One afternoon, you are out walking near your home. You spy something moving around on the ground. Look at **Figure 1**. Is it a black and white cat? As you move closer to get a better look, the animal fluffs up and raises its tail. It's a skunk! You hurriedly turn around and go in the other direction. You know that if you get sprayed by a skunk, people will be able to smell the stink from far away. Odor molecules will travel through the air to be inhaled by everyone around you.

Cells rely on the movement of surrounding gases, liquids, and particles to supply them with nutrients and materials. In order to live and function, cells must let certain materials enter and leave. Oxygen and water and particles of food must be able to move into a cell, while waste materials must move out. The same mechanism that lets materials in and out of a cell also lets those skunk spray molecules—the chemical makeup of odor— seep into the specialized cells in your nose that perceive smell.

Stinky Defense

Figure 1 Striped skunks are found throughout most of California. If one finds you, you'll remember it for a long time! The long-lasting smell travels through the air by diffusion. Diffusion also carries useful molecules to the cells of every living organism.

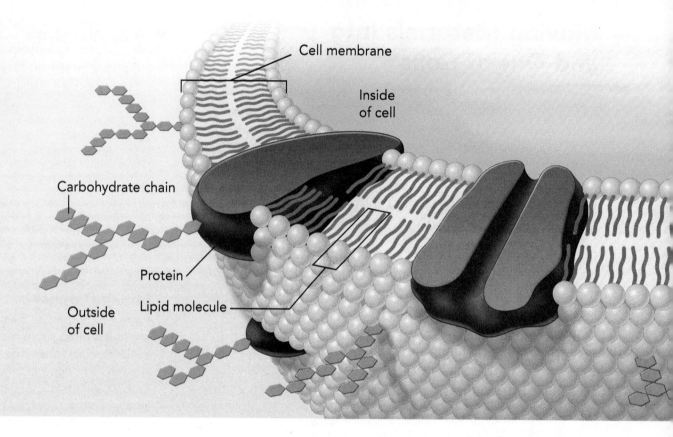

Cell membrane

Inside of cell

Carbohydrate chain

Protein

Lipid molecule

Outside of cell

A Selective Barrier

Figure 2 Carbohydrates, proteins, and lipids are important molecules that make up the structure of the cell membrane. They help move materials into and out of the cell through the cell membrane.

SEP Use Models In what way is the cell membrane like a security guard?

....

....

....

....

....

....

Function of the Cell Membrane
Every cell is surrounded by a cell membrane that lets substances in and out. This movement allows the cell to maintain homeostasis (a stable internal environment) and get all the chemicals needed to support life. The cell membrane is not rigid, but flexible. In **Figure 2**, you can see that different types of molecules play important roles in helping materials move across the cell membrane.

A permeable membrane allows liquids and gases to pass through it. Some materials move freely across the cell membrane. Others move less freely or not at all. The cell membrane is **selectively permeable**, which means some substances can cross the membrane, while others cannot. Substances that move into and out of a cell do so by means of one of two processes: passive transport or active transport.

Passive Transport
Moving materials across the cell membrane sometimes requires no energy. At other times, the cell has to use its own energy. Consider this analogy: If you pour a bucket of water down a slide, the water flows down easily with no effort on your part. Your role is passive. Now, suppose you have to push that same water back up the slide. You would have to use your own energy to move the water. The movement of dissolved materials across a cell membrane without using the cell's energy is called passive transport.

Diffusion Molecules are always moving. As they move, they bump into one another. Crowded, or concentrated, molecules collide more often. Collisions cause molecules to push away from one another. Over time, as molecules continue colliding and moving apart, they spread evenly throughout the space and become less concentrated. **Diffusion** (dih FYOO zhun) is the process by which molecules move from an area of higher concentration to an area of lower concentration. Consider a cell in the lining of your lungs. The cell is in contact with the air that you breathe. The air outside the cell has a higher concentration of oxygen. What happens? Oxygen moves easily into the cell. The diffusion of oxygen into the cell does not require the cell to use any of its energy. Diffusion is a form of passive transport. **Figure 3** shows how insects use spiracles instead of lungs to diffuse oxygen into their cells.

☑ CHECK POINT **Write Informative Texts** Why is it important for a cell membrane to be selectively permeable?

....

....

....

....

....

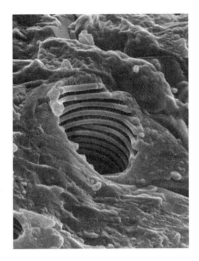

No Lungs Necessary
Figure 3 Spiracles are holes in the exoskeleton, or outer shell, of insects that allow oxygen to enter and diffuse into the cells of the insect. Spiracles connect to air passages that lead into all parts of the insect.

CCC Relate Function and Structure ✏ Circle the area where air can enter the insect's body.

Math Toolbox

Giant Ancient Insect

The largest insects ever discovered were giant dragonflies that lived 300 million years ago. These dragonflies had a wingspan of 67 cm! Today the largest dragonfly has a wingspan of about 20 cm. The giant dragonflies existed at a time when the oxygen level in the atmosphere was about 35 percent, compared to 21 percent today. Use this information to answer the following questions.

1. Analyze Proportional Relationships Express the size of the giant dragonfly as a percentage of the size of the modern dragonfly. Show your work.

....

2. CCC Infer Structure from Function Refer to the spiracle in **Figure 3**. What do you think the relationship is between the spiracles, insect size, and air oxygen levels?

....

....

Model It !

Raisins No More

Figure 4 In the U.S., most raisins grow in California—as grapes! Raisins are grapes with most of the water removed. The cells of raisins are dead. If you soak raisins in water, the cells will take up water by the process of diffusion.

SEP Develop Models ✏ Use the grape cell shown below as a reference. In the empty circles, first draw a raisin cell and then draw what the cell looks like after soaking the raisin in water overnight.

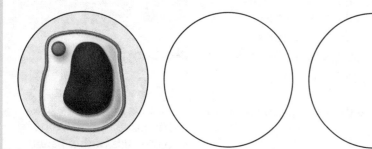

Literacy Connection

Integrate with Visuals ✏
The Great Salt Lake in Utah is so salty that large clumps of salt crystallize out of the water. Imagine yourself soaking in the lake. Draw a diagram below to show the flow of water by osmosis between the lake water and the cells of your body.

Osmosis Like oxygen, water passes easily into and out of a cell across the cell membrane. **Osmosis** is the diffusion of water molecules across a selectively permeable membrane. Many cellular processes depend on osmosis to bring them the water they need to function. Without enough water, most cells will die. Because it requires no energy from the cell, osmosis is a form of passive transport.

Osmosis can have important effects on cells and entire organisms. The soaked raisins in **Figure 4** are lighter in color and appear plumper due to a flow of water into their cells. Under certain conditions, osmosis can cause water to move out of the cells more quickly than it moves in. When that happens, the cytoplasm shrinks and the cell membrane pulls away from the cell wall. If conditions do not change, the cells can die.

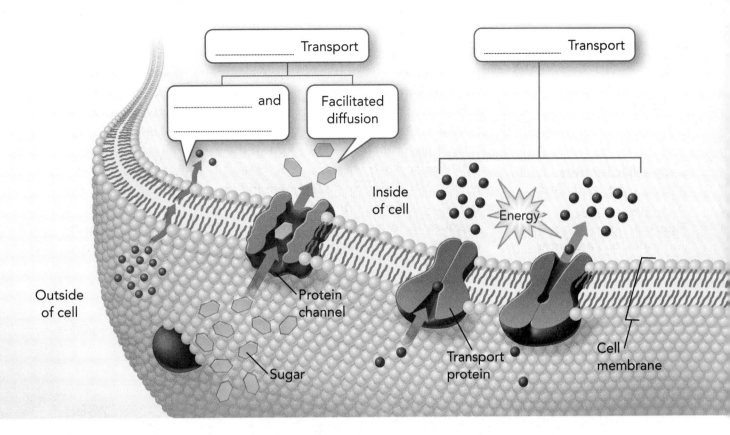

Transport

_____ and | Facilitated diffusion

Transport

Outside of cell

Inside of cell

Energy

Protein channel

Sugar

Transport protein

Cell membrane

Facilitated Diffusion Oxygen, carbon dioxide, and water freely diffuse across the cell membrane. Some molecules, such as sugar, cannot easily cross the cell membrane. In a process called facilitated diffusion, proteins in the cell membrane form channels through which the sugars can pass. The word *facilitate* means "to make easier." As shown in **Figure 5**, these proteins provide a pathway for the sugars to diffuse. The proteins function much the way downspouts guide water that flows from the roof of a house to the ground. Facilitated diffusion uses no cell energy and is a form of passive transport.

Active Transport During diffusion, molecules move randomly in all directions. A few molecules move by chance from areas of low concentration to areas of high concentration, but most molecules move toward areas of lower concentration. In many cases, cells need the concentration of a molecule inside the cell to be higher than the concentration outside the cell. In order to **maintain** this difference in the concentration of molecules, cells use active transport. Cells supply the energy to do this work—just as you would supply the energy to pedal your bike uphill. Active transport is the movement of materials across a cell membrane using cellular energy. As in facilitated diffusion, proteins within the cell membrane play a key role in active transport. Using the cell's energy, transport proteins "pick up" specific molecules passing by the cell and carry them across the membrane. Calcium, potassium, and sodium are some substances that are carried into and out of cells by active transport.

Crossing the Cell Membrane
Figure 5 Molecules move into and out of a cell by means of passive or active transport.

Interpret Diagrams 🖍
Complete the labels. Fill in the missing words.

Academic Vocabulary
To *maintain* means to keep in an existing state. When have you had to maintain something?

....

....

....

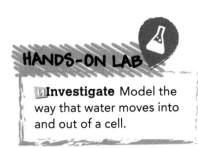

HANDS-ON LAB

Investigate Model the way that water moves into and out of a cell.

197

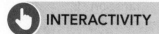

INTERACTIVITY

Investigate diffusion through a cell.

Large Molecules Move Into and Out of Cells

Figure 6 Both endocytosis and exocytosis are forms of active transport. These processes require energy from the cell.

CCC Structure and Function Fill in the blanks by labeling each process shown below.

Moving Large Particles

Some materials, such as food particles, are too large to cross the cell membrane. In a process called **endocytosis** (en doh sigh TOH sis), the cell membrane takes particles into the cell by changing shape and engulfing the particles. Once the food particle is engulfed, the cell membrane fuses, pinching off a vacuole within the cell. The reverse process, called **exocytosis** (ek soh sigh TOH sis), allows large particles to leave a cell. This process is shown in **Figure 6**. During exocytosis, the vacuole surrounding the food particles fuses with the cell membrane, forcing the contents out of the cell. Both endocytosis and exocytosis are forms of active transport that require energy from the cell.

☑ **CHECK POINT** **Draw Conclusions** Why don't cells use endocytosis to transport all substances across the cell membrane?

....

....

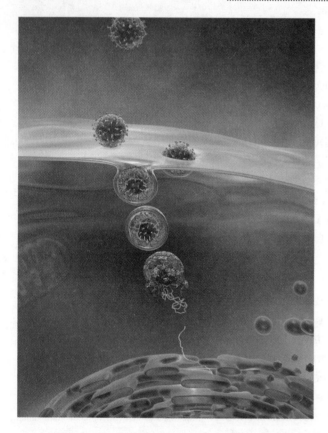

Large Molecules Entering the Cell
Large food particles are close to the cell. In order to bring food into the cell, the membrane wraps itself around a particle and draws it into the cytoplasm.

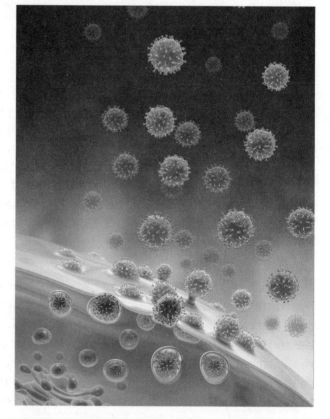

Large Molecules Leaving the Cell
Vacuoles carrying large particles of waste move toward the cell membrane. The vacuoles fuse with the membrane in order to push the waste particles out of the cell.

....

MS-LS1-2

1. SEP Explain Phenomena Why do cells need to maintain homeostasis?

....

....

....

2. SEP Determine Differences How is facilitated diffusion different from diffusion?

....

....

....

....

....

3. SEP Construct Explanations What would happen to a cell placed in extremely salty water?

....

....

....

....

....

4. Compare and Contrast ✏ Fill in the Venn diagram below with the following terms: exocytosis, diffusion, endocytosis, osmosis

Into Cell   Out of Cell

5. SEP Apply Scientific Reasoning How could disease-causing bacteria get inside a cell without damaging the cell membrane?

....

....

....

....

....

Quest CHECK-IN

In this lesson, you learned about the cell membrane and how cells take in the substances they need in order to function. You also learned how cells remove waste products through cellular processes.

CCC Relate Structure and Function Consider which structures of the cell membrane function to help materials move into and out of the cell. How can you best model this information in your animation?

....

....

....

INTERACTIVITY

Put Your Cells in Motion

Go online to plan an animation that shows the ways materials enter and leave the cell. Then create your animation for the exhibit.

4 Cell Division

Guiding Questions

- What are the four functions of cell division?
- Which structures in a cell help it to reproduce?

Connections

Literacy Summarize Text

Math Analyze Quantitative Relationships

 MS-LS1-2 Develop and use a model to describe the function of a cell as a whole and ways parts of cells contribute to the function.

HANDS-ON LAB

ɥInvestigate Model how a cell divides.

Vocabulary

cell cycle
interphase
replication
mitosis
cytokinesis

Academic Vocabulary

sequence

Connect It!

🖊 **Using the x-ray image as a guide, place a circle on the biker to show where the broken bone is.**

SEP Construct Explanations Where will the bike rider's body get new cells to repair the broken bones?

....

....

The Functions of Cell Division

The bike rider in **Figure 1** really took a tumble! Thankfully, he was wearing a helmet and only suffered a broken arm and a scraped elbow. His body will immediately begin to repair the bones, muscles, and skin. Where will his body get so many new cells to repair the damage? Recall that cells can only be produced by other cells. The new cells will come from older cells that divide in two, over and over again, until there are enough healthy cells to restore full function. Similarly, cell division can replace aging cells and those that die from disease.

Cell division also allows an organism to grow larger. A tiny fertilized egg cell splits into two, two into four, and so on, until a single cell becomes a multicellular organism. Another function of cell division is reproduction. Many single-celled organisms, such as yeasts, reproduce simply through cell division. Other organisms reproduce when cell division leads to the growth of new structures. For example, a strawberry plant can grow new stems and roots. These structures then break away from the parent plant and become a separate plant. Most organisms reproduce when specialized cells from two different parents combine, forming a new cell. This cell then undergoes many divisions and grows into a new organism.

CHECK POINT **Determine Central Ideas** What are four functions of cell division?

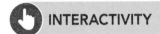**INTERACTIVITY**

Reflect on where you think cell division is occurring in your body.

Reflect Think of a time when you injured yourself. In your Science Notebook, describe the appearance and feeling of the injury when it first happened and then how the injured area changed as your body healed.

Cell Division to the Rescue

Figure 1 As soon as you break a bone, your body sets to work repairing it. Many new cells are produced to clean up the mess and produce new tissues.

Phases of the Cell Cycle

Figure 2 The series of diagrams represents an entire cell cycle.

Interpret Diagrams What happens to the cell's genetic information during the cell cycle?

....

....

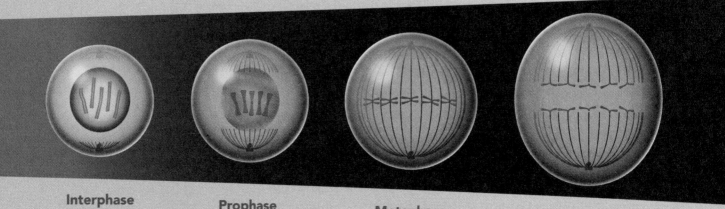

Interphase

Prophase (Mitosis)

Metaphase (Mitosis)

Anaphase (Mitosis)

HANDS-ON LAB

☑**Investigate** Model how a cell divides.

Academic Vocabulary

Cell division follows a careful sequence of events. Describe the sequence of events on one of your typical school days.

....

....

....

....

....

The Cell Cycle

Most of the time, cells carry out their regular functions, but everything changes when a cell gets the signal to divide. At that point, the cell must accomplish several tasks to be ready for the big division into two "daughter cells." **Figure 2** summarizes those tasks.

First, the cell must grow in size and double its contents. This phase is called interphase. Next, the cell must divide up its contents so that the two daughter cells will have roughly equal contents. This second phase is called mitosis, and it has several stages.

Finally, the cell's cytoplasm physically divides in two in a phase called cytokinesis. The regular **sequence** of events in which the cell grows, prepares for division, and divides to form two daughter cells is known as the **cell cycle**. After the division is complete, each of the daughter cells begins the cycle again.

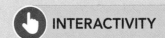

INTERACTIVITY

Explore the cell cycle and learn why living things go through the cell cycle.

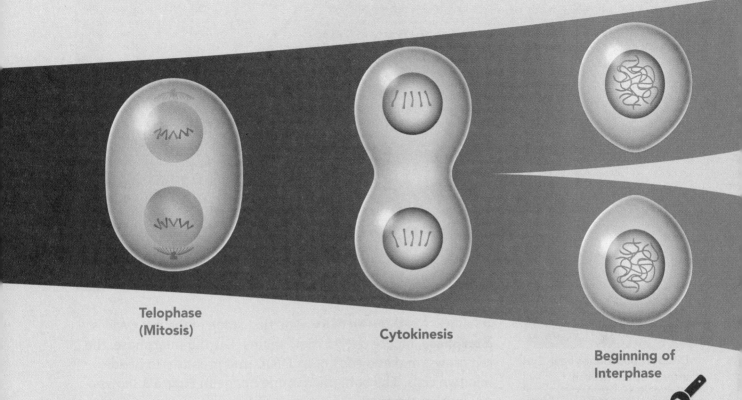

Telophase (Mitosis)

Cytokinesis

Beginning of Interphase

Math Toolbox

Dividing Cells

Every cell division produces two daughter cells. You can see in the diagram that after one division, the single cell has become two cells.

🖊 Fill in the last two squares to show the results from two more cell divisions.

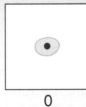

0 Divisions

1 Division

2 Divisions

3 Divisions

1. **Analyze Quantitative Relationships** How does the number of cells increase with each new division of the cells?

....

2. **SEP Use Mathematics** How many cells would there be after five divisions?

....

3. **Hypothesize** Do you think all human cells divide at the same rate throughout life? Explain your reasoning.

....

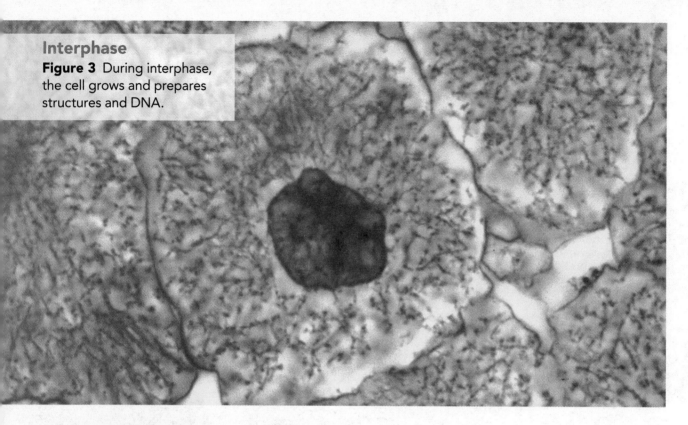

Interphase
Figure 3 During interphase, the cell grows and prepares structures and DNA.

INTERACTIVITY

Discover how bones heal after they are broken.

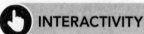

VIDEO

Find out more about how cell division allows living things to grow.

Stage 1: Interphase The first stage of the cell cycle is **interphase**, before cell division begins. During interphase, the cell grows, makes a copy of its DNA, and prepares to divide into two cells. The light microscope image in **Figure 3** shows a cell in interphase.

Growing Early in interphase, a cell grows to its full size and produces the organelles that both daughter cells will need. For example, plant cells make more chloroplasts. All cells make more ribosomes and mitochondria. Cells also make more enzymes, substances that speed up chemical reactions in living things.

Replication Recall that chromatin in the nucleus holds all the genetic information that a cell needs to carry out its functions. That information is in a complex chemical substance called DNA (deoxyribonucleic acid). In a process called **replication**, the cell makes a copy of the DNA in its nucleus before cell division. DNA replication results in the formation of threadlike structures called chromosomes. Each chromosome inside the nucleus of the cell contains two identical sets of DNA, called chromatids.

Preparing for Division Once the DNA has replicated, preparation for cell division begins. The cell produces structures that will help it to divide into two new cells. In animal cells, but not plant cells, a pair of centrioles is duplicated. The centrioles help later with dividing the DNA between the daughter cells. At the end of interphase, the cell is ready to divide.

Stage 2: Mitosis Once interphase ends, the second stage of the cell cycle begins. During **mitosis** (my TOH sis), the cell's nucleus divides into two new nuclei and one set of DNA is distributed into each daughter cell. Scientists divide mitosis into four parts, or phases: prophase, metaphase, anaphase, and telophase.

During prophase, DNA condenses into separate chromosomes. Recall that during replication, chromosomes formed. The two chromatids that make up the chromosome are exact copies of identical DNA. The nuclear membrane that surrounds the DNA begins to break apart. In metaphase, the chromosomes line up along the center of the cell. The chromatids that will go to each daughter cell are lined up on that side of the cell. Next, in anaphase, fibers connected to the centrioles pull the chromatids apart into each side of the cell. The final phase of mitosis is telophase. During telophase, the chromatids are pulled to opposite ends of the cell. The nuclear membrane reforms around the DNA to create two new nuclei. Each nucleus contains a complete, identical copy of DNA. Test your knowledge of the phases of mitosis in **Figure 4**.

☑ CHECK POINT **Summarize Text** What are the three things that a cell has to complete in order to be ready for cell division?

....

....

Literacy Connection

Summarize Text As you read, underline each phase of mitosis. Write a short description of each phase of mitosis.

....

....

....

....

....

....

....

....

....

....

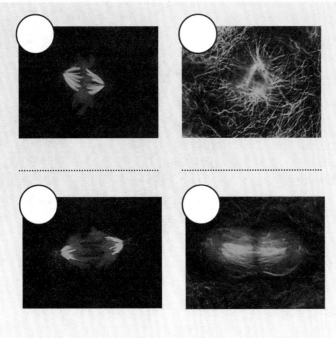

Scrambled Mitosis

Figure 4 These dividing cells have been marked with a dye that glows under fluorescent light. The dye makes it easy to see the DNA, stained blue, and fibers, stained green. The pictures are in the wrong order.

Identify 🖊 Label each phase of mitosis in the space provided. Then, write the numbers 1 to 4 in the circles to show the correct order of the phases in mitosis.

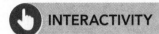

INTERACTIVITY

Apply the cell cycle to animal cells and plant cells.

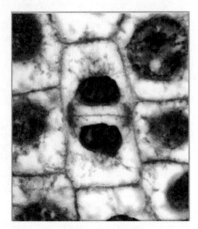

Plant Cytokinesis

Figure 5 One of these plant cells is dividing.

Identify ✎ Find the cell that is dividing. Place an *X* on each daughter cell and trace the cell plate.

Stage 3: Cytokinesis

The final stage of the cell cycle is called **cytokinesis** (sy toh kih NEE sis). This stage completes the process of cell division. During cytokinesis, the cell's cytoplasm divides, distributing the organelles into each of the two new daughter cells. Cytokinesis usually starts at about the same time as telophase. When cytokinesis is complete, each daughter cell has the same number of chromosomes as the parent cell. Next, each cell enters interphase and the cell cycle begins again.

Cytokinesis in Animal Cells During cytokinesis in animal cells, the cell membrane squeezes together around the middle of the cell. The cytoplasm pinches into two cells. Each daughter cell gets about half of the organelles of the parent cell.

Cytokinesis in Plant Cells Cytokinesis is somewhat different in plant cells. A plant cell's rigid cell wall cannot squeeze together in the same way that a cell membrane can. Instead, a structure called a cell plate forms across the middle of the cell, as shown in **Figure 5**. The cell plate begins to form new cell membranes between the two daughter cells. New cell walls then form around the cell membranes.

☑ CHECK POINT **Determine Conclusions** What would happen if cytokinesis did not occur?

....

....

Question It !

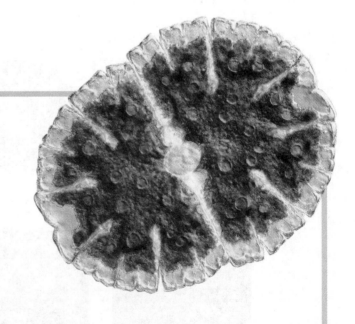

A Two-Celled Organism?

Two students examining a sample of lake water find an unusual-looking organism.

SEP Ask Questions What kinds of questions would you have if you saw the organism shown here? List three questions and two resources you could use to help you to answer them.

....

....

....

....

☑LESSON 4 Check

1. **Explain** Why is it important for the cells in your body to go through the cell cycle?

....

....

....

....

2. **SEP Construct Explanations** How does a plant cell accomplish cytokinesis?

....

....

....

....

....

....

3. **Apply Concepts** When you look at cells under a microscope, how can you recognize cells that are dividing?

....

....

....

....

4. **SEP Explain Phenomena** Why does the cell need to replicate its DNA during interphase?

....

....

....

....

5. **Draw Conclusions** If a single-celled organism is unable to undergo cell division, what will happen to that organism?

....

....

....

6. **SEP Make Observations** What is happening during this part of the cell cycle?

....

....

....

7. **CCC Predict** What would happen to a cell that didn't replicate its DNA before cell division?

....

....

....

8. **SEP Develop Models** 🖊 What happens during cytokinesis? Use the space below to sketch and label a diagram of an animal cell undergoing cytokinesis.

5 Photosynthesis

Guiding Questions

- How do plants and other organisms use photosynthesis to make food?
- What are the roles of light, carbon dioxide, water, and chlorophyll in photosynthesis?
- What role does photosynthesis play in cycling materials and energy through ecosystems?

Connections

Literacy Summarize Text

Math Represent Relationships

🧭 **MS-LS1-6** Construct a scientific explanation based on evidence for the role of photosynthesis in the cycling of matter and flow of energy into and out of organisms.

MS-LS1-7 Develop a model to describe how food is rearranged through chemical reactions forming new molecules that support growth and/or release energy as this matter moves through an organism.

HANDS-ON LAB

🔬**Investigate** Explore why one stage of photosynthesis can take place in the dark.

Vocabulary

photosynthesis
autotroph
heterotroph
chlorophyll

Academic Vocabulary

equation

Connect It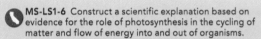

🖊️**In the boxes, write the direct source of energy for each organism.**

SEP Evaluate Evidence Which of the organisms shown does not eat another organism for food?

....

Apply Scientific Reasoning What do you think would happen to each species if the water became too cloudy for sunlight to penetrate?

....

....

....

....

Living Things and Energy

Off the Pacific coast, from Alaska to California, sea urchins graze on kelp beds under water. A sea otter begins the hunt for lunch as they always have and hopefully always will. The otter will take urchins off kelp to eat them at the surface.

Both the sea urchins and the otter in **Figure 1** use the food they eat to obtain energy. Every living thing needs energy. All the cells in every organism need energy to carry out their functions, such as making proteins and transporting substances into and out of the cell. Energy used by living things comes from their environment, similar to the raw materials cells use to function. Meat from the sea urchin provides the otter's cells with energy, while kelp provides energy for the cells of the sea urchin. Where does the energy in the kelp come from? Plants, algae, phytoplankton (floating algae), and some microorganisms including bacteria, obtain their energy differently. These organisms use the energy from sunlight to make their own food.

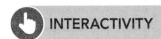
INTERACTIVITY

Identify what items are considered food.

Energy for Life

Figure 1 All living things—such as California sea otters, sea urchins, and kelp—need energy to survive.

CCC Cause and Effect What would likely happen to the kelp if the otters died off?

....

....

....

....

....

kelp

sea urchins

otter

Summarize Text In your own words, summarize the main idea of the passage on this page.

....

....

....

....

....

....

....

....

Energy From the Sun Cells capture energy in sunlight and use it to make food in a process called **photosynthesis.** The term *photosynthesis* comes from the Greek words *photos*, which means "light," and *syntithenai*, which means "putting together." Plants and other photosynthetic organisms link molecules together into useful forms using photosynthesis.

Nearly all living things obtain energy directly or indirectly from the sun's energy. This energy is captured from the sunlight during photosynthesis. In **Figure 2,** the leaf obtains energy directly from sunlight because plants use sunlight to make their own food during photosynthesis. When you eat an apple, you get energy from the sun that has been stored in the apple. You get the sun's energy indirectly from the energy that the apple tree gained through photosynthesis.

An Energy Chain

Figure 2 The energy of sunlight passes from one organism to another.

Explain Phenomena ✏ Draw arrows showing the flow of energy from the sun.

Making and Obtaining Food Plants make their own food through the process of photosynthesis. **Autotrophs**, or producers, are able to create their own food in the form of glucose, an energy-giving sugar. Plants and algae, as well as some bacteria, are autotrophs. An organism that cannot make its own food, such as the sea urchin or otter, is a consumer, or a **heterotroph.** Many heterotrophs, like the fox in **Figure 3**, obtain food by eating other organisms. Some heterotrophs, such as fungi, absorb their food from other organisms.

☑ **CHECK POINT** **Summarize Text** What is the difference between heterotrophs and autotrophs?

....

....

....

▤ **Reflect** How is sunlight important to plant growth? In your science notebook, list some questions you have about the effects of sunlight on growing plants.

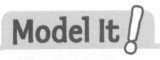
Model It !

Trace Energy to the Source
Figure 3 A California gray fox captures and eats prey like rabbits and hares that depend on plants for food.

SEP Develop Models 🖉 Draw a diagram that tracks how the sun's energy gets to the fox. In your diagram, label each organism as a heterotroph or an autotroph.

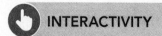

INTERACTIVITY

Describe the cycling of matter and energy that occurs during photosynthesis.

HANDS-ON LAB

Investigate Explore why one stage of photosynthesis can take place in the dark.

Student Discourse

After reading about Stage 1 of photosynthesis and completing Figure 4, form a small group with classmates. Write down two questions about Stage 1. Then each group member should offer a question for the group to discuss.

Photosynthesis

Photosynthesis is a chemical reaction in plants that uses light energy to convert certain types of matter into another they can use as food. It takes place mostly in chloroplasts, as shown in **Figure 4.** When plants use the sun's energy to convert carbon dioxide from the atmosphere and water into sugar, oxygen is produced. Because photosynthesis is a chemical reaction, several different factors affect the rate of chemical change. The availability of sunlight, water, and carbon dioxide are all factors required for photosynthesis.

Stage 1: Trapping the Sun's Energy

Chloroplasts, the green organelles in plant cells, use chlorophyll to absorb sunlight during the first stage of photosynthesis. The green color comes from pigments, which are colored chemical compounds that absorb light. The green photosynthetic pigment found in the chloroplasts of plants, algae, and some bacteria is **chlorophyll**.

Picture solar cells in a solar-powered calculator. Chlorophyll functions in a similar way. Chlorophyll captures light energy that the chloroplast uses to create oxygen gas and sugar (**Figure 4**).

During Stage 1, sunlight splits water molecules in the chloroplasts into hydrogen and oxygen. The hydrogen combines with other atoms during Stage 2 and the oxygen is released into the environment as a waste product. A product is the substance formed after a reaction takes place. Some oxygen gas exits a leaf through openings on the leaf's underside. Almost all the oxygen in Earth's atmosphere is produced by living things through the process of photosynthesis.

Photosynthesis: Stages 1 and 2

Figure 4 Photosynthesis takes place in the chloroplasts. Specialized structures in each chloroplast contain chlorophyll.

Translate Information ✐
Add labels to the arrows in the diagram to indicate whether water, carbon dioxide, sugar, or oxygen is entering or leaving.

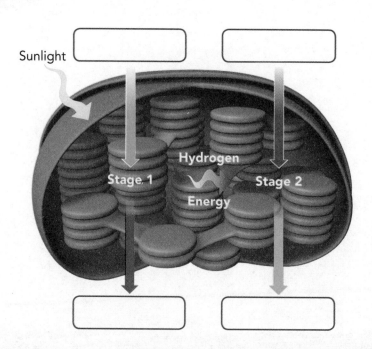

Stage 2: Making Food

In Stage 2 of photosynthesis, cells produce sugar. Sugars are carbon-based organic molecules that are useful for storing chemical energy or for building larger molecules. Glucose, which has the chemical formula $C_6H_{12}O_6$, is one of the most important sugars produced in photosynthesis. The energy stored in the chemical bonds of glucose allows cells to carry out vital functions.

The production of glucose is shown in **Figure 5.** Hydrogen (H) that came from splitting water molecules in Stage 1 is one reactant, the substance undergoing a change during a reaction. The other reactant is carbon dioxide (CO_2) from the air. Carbon dioxide enters the plant through the small openings on the underside of each leaf and moves into the chloroplasts. Powered by the energy captured in Stage 1, hydrogen and carbon dioxide undergo a series of reactions to produce glucose.

☑ **CHECK POINT** **Integrate with Visuals**
🖊 On the picture, write R in the circles for the three raw materials, or reactants, of photosynthesis, and P in the circles of the two products.

Light energy

Oxygen

Carbon dioxide

Glucose

The Big Picture of Photosynthesis
Figure 5 This view of photosynthesis is from outside the plant. Plant cells also break down glucose to release the energy they need to grow and reproduce.

Water

213

INTERACTIVITY

Determine what factors influence photosynthesis in modern and ancient plants.

Expressing Photosynthesis

The events of photosynthesis that lead to the production of glucose can be expressed as the following chemical **equation**:

$$\text{light energy} + 6\,CO_2 \text{ carbon dioxide} + 6\,H_2O \text{ water} \longrightarrow C_6H_{12}O_6 \text{ glucose} + 6\,O_2 \text{ oxygen}$$

Academic Vocabulary

How is a chemical equation similar to a mathematical equation, and how do they model a natural phenomenon?

....

....

....

....

....

....

....

....

Notice that six molecules of carbon dioxide and six molecules of water are in the equation to the left of the arrow. These compounds are raw materials, or reactants. One molecule of glucose and six molecules of oxygen are on the right side of the arrow. These compounds are products. An arrow, which means "yields," points from the reactants to the products. Energy is not a reactant, but it is written on the left side of the equation to show that it is used in the reaction. There are the same number of atoms of each element on both sides of the equation—no matter is gained or lost.

Plant cells use some glucose produced in photosynthesis for food. The cells break down sugar molecules in a process called cellular respiration. The energy released from glucose can be used to carry out a plant's functions (**Figure 6**), such as growth. Other glucose molecules are stored for later use. When you eat food from plant roots, such as potatoes or carrots, you are eating the plant's stored energy.

☑ CHECK POINT **Determine Central Ideas** What happens to glucose and oxygen that is produced by plants during photosynthesis?

....

....

....

Photosynthesis Is the Key

Figure 6 Green plants use the sugars produced in photosynthesis in many ways.

Interpret Diagrams ✎ Label the leaves, roots, and seeds in the diagram. Then fill in the boxes with some of the ways plants use the products of photosynthesis.

Importance of Plant Cells

Plant cells were the first cells to be seen with a microscope. Because plant cell walls are like rigid boxes, plant cells do not burst when placed in an aquatic environment. The ability to store water is one reason that marshes are so important (**Figure 7**). During storms with heavy rainfall, such as hurricanes, marsh plants soak up water. For this reason, marshland is considered a natural flood control.

Plants and algae that live in water absorb about one sixth of all the sun's energy that falls on Earth. Ocean plants play an essential role in recycling oxygen. In fact, 85 percent of the oxygen in Earth's atmosphere comes from ocean plants. They perform photosynthesis much like land plants. They collect the sun's energy and take in carbon dioxide. They always have water. They use these reactants to produce food (energy) for themselves and to release oxygen into the water for use by other organisms.

Marsh Plants

Figure 7 The marsh in the Vic Fazio Yolo Wildlife Area is managed to help protect Sacramento, California, from flooding. It also provides prime habitat to nearly 200 species of birds and other wetland wildlife.

SEP Construct Explanations How do marshes control flooding?

....

....

Math Toolbox

All in the Balance

The photosynthesis equation states that 6 CO_2 and 6 H_2O molecules combine to form 1 $C_6H_{12}O_6$ molecule and 6 O_2 molecules. For every 6 carbon dioxide molecules, the reaction produces 1 glucose molecule.

1. **Represent Relationships** Write an equation using two variables to model how many glucose molecules are produced by 6 CO_2 molecules. Use x for the number of glucose molecules and y for the number of CO_2 molecules.

....

2. **SEP Use Mathematics** ✏ Calculate how many glucose molecules are produced by 6, 12, 18, and 24 CO_2 molecules. Plot these points on the graph. What is the relationship between the two variables?

....

....

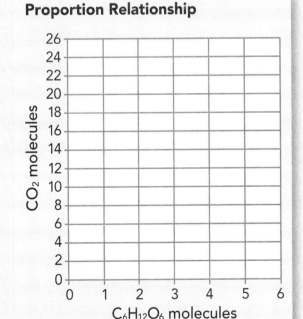

Proportion Relationship

Graph: y-axis labeled "CO_2 molecules" with values 0, 2, 4, 6, 8, 10, 12, 14, 16, 18, 20, 22, 24, 26; x-axis labeled "$C_6H_{12}O_6$ molecules" with values 0, 1, 2, 3, 4, 5, 6.

☑ LESSON 5 Check

MS-LS1-6, MS-LS1-7

1. **CCC Analyze Systems** Where does a plant get the energy necessary to drive the chemical reaction in photosynthesis?

....

2. **SEP Cite Evidence** How do you know an organism is a heterotroph? Name three heterotrophs.

....

....

....

....

....

3. **Identify** What are the raw materials, or reactants, for Stage 2 of photosynthesis, and where do these materials come from?

....

....

....

4. **SEP Construct Explanations** How does chlorophyll help the functioning of chloroplasts?

....

....

....

....

5. **CCC Cause and Effect** What are the roles of light, carbon dioxide, and water molecules in the production of food and oxygen in photosynthesis?

....

....

....

....

....

....

6. **SEP Develop Models** Draw the same plant on a sunny day and a cloudy day. In your model, show on which day it would likely produce less oxygen. In your labels, show which part of the chemical reaction of photosynthesis would be affected. (Smaller versions of **Figure 5** might be good starting points.)

Engineering Artificial
PHOTOSYNTHESIS

VIDEO

Examine how the different parts of an artificial leaf work.

How do you make photosynthesis more efficient? You engineer it!

The Challenge: To create a more efficient form of photosynthesis.

Phenomenon Photosynthesis is an important process for all life on Earth. However, it isn't very efficient. Only 1 percent of the sunlight that hits a leaf is used during the process of photosynthesis.

Scientists at the Joint Center for Artificial Photosynthesis (JCAP) in California hope to engineer ways of improving that efficiency. Founded in 2010 by the U.S. Department of Energy, the center has one main goal: to find a way to produce fossil fuel alternatives using just sunlight, water, and carbon dioxide. The center is led by a team of scientists and researchers at the California Institute of Technology in partnership with the Lawrence Berkeley National Laboratory. JCAP's facilities have state-of-the-art tools and technologies at its disposal for scientists to conduct investigations and experiments of just about any kind as they relate to photosynthesis.

In his 2011 State of the Union address to Congress, President Obama singled out the work of JCAP researchers: "We're issuing a challenge. We're telling America's scientists and engineers that if they assemble teams of the best minds in their fields, and focus on the hardest problems in clean energy, we'll fund the Apollo projects of our time. At the California Institute of Technology, they're developing a way to turn sunlight and water into fuel for our cars."

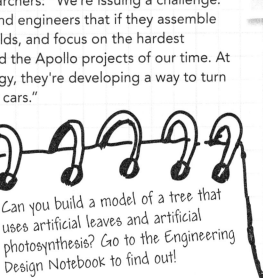

JCAP scientists are developing solar fuel generators (shown here) that mimic the process of photosynthesis with greater efficiency.

DESIGN CHALLENGE

Can you build a model of a tree that uses artificial leaves and artificial photosynthesis? Go to the Engineering Design Notebook to find out!

LESSON 6 Cellular Respiration

Guiding Questions

- How does cellular respiration break down food to produce energy and carbon dioxide?
- How can cells release energy without using oxygen?
- How are matter and energy conserved during cellular respiration?

Connections

Literacy Translate Information

Math Analyze Quantitative Relationships

 MS-LS1-6 Construct a scientific explanation based on evidence for the role of photosynthesis in the cycling of matter and flow of energy into and out of organisms.

MS-LS1-7 Develop a model to describe how food is rearranged through chemical reactions forming new molecules that support growth and/or release energy as this matter moves through an organism.

HANDS-ON LAB

ᵘInvestigate Examine a product of cellular respiration.

Vocabulary

cellular respiration
fermentation

Academic Vocabulary

produce
source

Connect It!

✏ **Draw arrows on Figure 1 to show the flow of energy from the food into the bikers, and then out into the environment as heat and motion.**

Construct a Graph ✏ Sketch on the graph to show how the bikers' energy level may change over time as they start biking, stop for a snack, start biking again, and finish their ride.

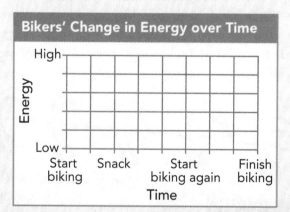

Bikers' Change in Energy over Time

Energy (High / Low) vs. Time (Start biking, Snack, Start biking again, Finish biking)

Energy and Cellular Respiration

You and your friend have been biking all morning. The steepest part of the road is ahead. You'll need a lot of energy to get to the top! The food shown in **Figure 1** will provide some of that energy.

Plants and animals break down food into small, usable molecules, such as glucose. Energy stored in these molecules is released so the cell can carry out functions. **Cellular respiration** is the process in which oxygen and glucose undergo a complex series of chemical reactions inside cells, releasing energy. All living things need energy. Therefore, all living things carry out cellular respiration.

Using Energy A hot water heater stores hot water. To wash your hands, you turn on the faucet and draw out the needed hot water. Your body stores and uses energy in a similar way. When you eat, you add to your body's energy account by storing glucose, fat, and other substances. When cells need energy, they "draw it out" by breaking down the energy-rich compounds through cellular respiration.

Respiration People often use the word *respiration* when they mean *breathing*, the physical movement of air in and out of your lungs. In the study of the life sciences, however, respiration and breathing are not interchangeable. Breathing brings oxygen into your lungs. Cells use oxygen in cellular respiration. Exhaling removes the waste products of that process from your body.

HANDS-ON LAB

Investigate how yeast carry out cellular respiration.

Reflect "Respiration" can also refer to breathing. Is some sort of "breathing" required for cellular respiration to occur? Do plants "breathe"?

Food for Energy
Figure 1 Biking takes a lot of energy! Your body uses cellular respiration to get energy from the food you eat, such as trail mix.

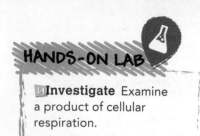

Cellular Respiration Process

Like photosynthesis, cellular respiration is a two-stage process. **Figure 2** shows both stages of cellular respiration. Stage 1 occurs in the cell's cytoplasm, where glucose is broken down into smaller molecules. Oxygen is not involved in this stage, and only a small amount of energy is released. Stage 2 occurs in a mitochondrion and uses oxygen. The smaller molecules produced in Stage 1 are broken down even more. Stage 2 releases a great deal of energy that the cell can use for all its activities.

Academic Vocabulary

How can the terms *produce* and *source* be used to describe a nation's economy?

....

....

....

....

Cellular Respiration Equation

The raw materials for cellular respiration are glucose and oxygen. Heterotrophs get glucose from consuming food. Autotrophs carry out photosynthesis to **produce** their own glucose. Air is the **source** of oxygen. The products of cellular respiration are carbon dioxide and water. Although respiration occurs in a series of complex steps, the overall process can be summarized in the equation:

$$C_6H_{12}O_6 + 6\,O_2 \longrightarrow 6\,CO_2 + 6\,H_2O + energy$$

glucose + oxygen → carbon dioxide + water + energy

Releasing Energy

Figure 2 Cellular respiration takes place in two stages.

Integrate Information ✏
Fill in the missing terms in the spaces provided.

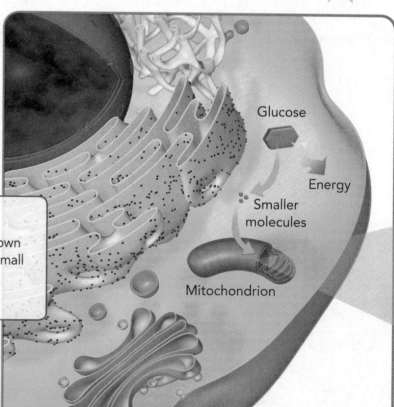

Glucose

Energy

Smaller molecules

Mitochondrion

Stage 1 In the cytoplasm,

.... is broken down into smaller molecules, releasing a small

amount of ....

Role of Mitochondria It may be a small organelle, but the mitochondrion (plural, mitochondria) is well known as the cell's powerhouse. The function of the mitochondrion is to create large amounts of energy. In **Figure 2**, notice how the mitochondrion is structured. The folds inside the organelle create more surface area. Chemical reactions occur on these folds. Because of this increased surface area, many more chemical reactions can occur. In turn, more energy is created. Cells that need a great deal of energy may have thousands of mitochondria. If a cell needs more energy to survive, it can create more mitochondria.

Not all organisms use glucose and oxygen to carry out cellular respiration. Some organisms rely on a type of cellular respiration that uses fructose instead of glucose to create energy. For this chemical reaction, they do not need oxygen to break down the fructose.

☑ **CHECK POINT** **Determine Conclusions** Think about the job of the mitochondria. Which cells in your body would you expect to have the most mitochondria? Explain your reasoning.

....

....

INTERACTIVITY

Explore what happens when the body breaks down glucose.

Literacy Connection

Translate Information 🖊
In **Figure 2**, circle the folds in the mitochondrion that increase the organelle's surface area.

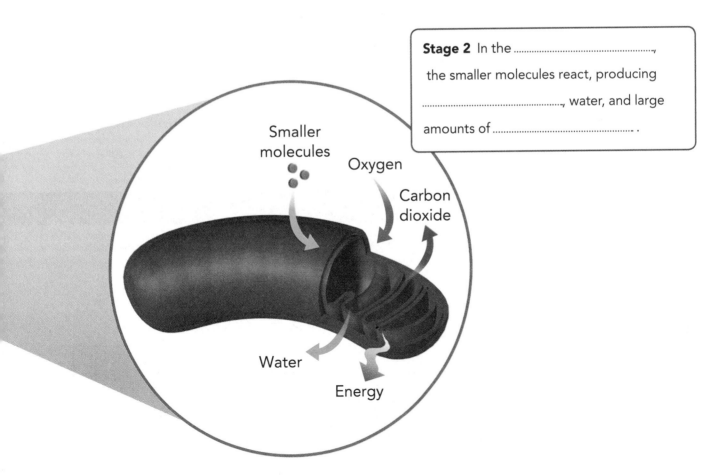

Smaller molecules

Oxygen

Carbon dioxide

Water

Energy

Stage 2 In the ....,
the smaller molecules react, producing
...................................., water, and large
amounts of ....

Comparing Two Energy Processes

If you think the equation for cellular respiration is the opposite of the one for photosynthesis, you're right! Photosynthesis and cellular respiration can be thought of as opposite processes. The two processes form a cycle, keeping the levels of oxygen and carbon dioxide molecules relatively stable in Earth's atmosphere. As shown in **Figure 3**, living things cycle both gases repeatedly. The energy released through cellular respiration is used or lost as heat. Matter and energy is neither created or destroyed in this cycle.

Related Processes

Figure 3 Carbon dioxide and oxygen cycle through cellular respiration and photosynthesis.

CCC Relate Structure and Function ✎ Label the diagram to complete each of the processes.

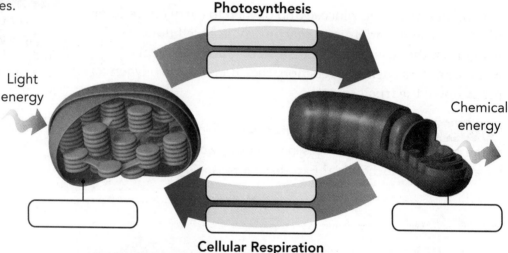

Photosynthesis

Light energy

Chemical energy

Cellular Respiration

✓ CHECK POINT **Translate Information** Look at **Figure 3.** How are photosynthesis and cellular respiration opposite chemical reactions?

....

....

Math Toolbox

Conservation of Matter in the Balance

In a chemical reaction, matter is neither created nor destroyed. For this reason, every chemical equation is balanced. You will find the same number of each kind of atom on both sides of the equation for cellular respiration.

Analyze Quantitative Relationships ✎ Do the math to prove that the equation for cellular respiration is balanced for oxygen and carbon. Review the equation for cellular respiration below and complete the table.

$$C_6H_{12}O_6 + 6\,O_2 \longrightarrow 6\,CO_2 + 6\,H_2O$$

	Atoms on left side	Atoms on right side	Balanced? Yes or No
Oxygen (O)			
Carbon (C)			

Fermentation

Yeast, bacteria, and your own muscle cells can release energy from food without oxygen. The release of energy from food without using oxygen is called **fermentation**. Fermentation is very useful in environments with limited oxygen, such as in the intestines. However, fermentation releases much less energy than cellular respiration with oxygen.

Alcoholic Fermentation When you eat a slice of bread, you are eating a product of fermentation. Alcoholic fermentation takes place in live yeast cells—unicellular fungi—and in other single-celled organisms. This type of fermentation produces alcohol, carbon dioxide, and a small amount of energy. Bakers use these products of fermentation. Carbon dioxide creates gas pockets in bread dough. This causes the dough to rise.

Lactic Acid Fermentation Have you ever run as fast and hard as you could, like the sprinter in **Figure 4**? Although you started to breathe faster, your muscle cells used up oxygen faster than it could be replaced. Without enough oxygen, fermentation takes place. Your body supplies energy to your muscle cells by breaking down glucose without using oxygen. A compound called lactic acid is a product of fermentation in muscles. One popular misconception is that lactic acid "builds up in the muscles" and causes "muscle burn" as well as any lingering soreness. However, lactic acid actually fuels your muscles and goes away shortly after the workout. During exercise and intense physical activity, your body needs ATP—a substance the cells use as an energy source to meet high demands for energy. When the cells use ATP, it produces a proton. As protons pile up, the immediate area becomes acidic. The nerves near the muscles sense this acidity as muscle burn. But that sensation has nothing to do with lactic acid.

☑ CHECK POINT **Determine Central Ideas** How does fermentation that causes dough to rise differ from fermentation in muscles?

....

....

Running Out of Oxygen

Figure 4 Your breathing and blood circulation can supply enough oxygen for cellular respiration when you exercise gently. During a sprint, your cells run low on oxygen and switch to lactic acid fermentation for energy.

Interpret Diagrams ✎ For each activity, label the source of energy for the muscle cells. Is it oxygen or lactic acid?

standing

jogging

sprinting

223

Respiration and Fermentation in Bacteria

Figure 5 There are bacteria adapted to eat almost anything and live anywhere. Bacteria use every available process for getting energy from food.

These bacteria live in oxygen-free environments. In fact, oxygen would poison some of them! These bacteria are sometimes used to produce bread and pickled vegetables.

....

....

....

1. Synthesize Information
🖊 Read each image caption. In the circles provided, label each photo "LAF" for lactic acid fermentation, "AF" for alcoholic fermentation, or "CR" for cellular respiration.

2. Construct Arguments
Under each description, use evidence to justify how you classified the process.

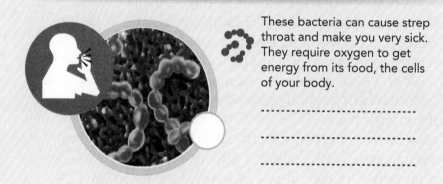

Yogurt is made from milk sugar by bacteria. The lactic acid produced in this reaction gives yogurt its sharp taste.

....

....

....

These bacteria can cause strep throat and make you very sick. They require oxygen to get energy from its food, the cells of your body.

....

....

....

Plan It!

Long-Distance Space Travel

Many scientists and engineers are working toward the goal of sending astronauts to Mars. The trip is estimated to take about 9 months each way. It is very expensive to take enough oxygen to last the whole trip. The astronauts also need enough food, and there has to be a way to get rid of excess carbon dioxide created by their cellular respiration.

Implement a Solution Present a plan for the astronauts. Explain how growing food during space flight will help regulate carbon dioxide and oxygen levels. List the supplies the astronauts would need.

....

....

....

....

MS-LS1-6, MS-LS1-7

1. **Identify** Where does cellular respiration take place in the cell?

....

....

2. **SEP Develop Models** ✏ In the space below, sketch and label a diagram showing the relationship between photosynthesis and cellular respiration.

3. **SEP Engage in Argument** Do plants and animals both use cellular respiration? Explain.

....

....

....

4. **Apply Concepts** How do heterotrophs get energy? Explain.

....

....

....

....

5. **CCC Energy and Matter** A classmate states that both energy and matter can be created during photosynthesis and cellular respiration. Use the chemical equations for the processes to respond to your classmate.

....

....

....

....

....

Quest CHECK-INS

In this lesson, you learned about the process of cellular respiration, in which the cells of an organism rearrange food molecules such as sugars and oxygen to produce energy, carbon dioxide, and water through chemical reactions. You also learned how cellular respiration works with photosynthesis to cycle matter and energy.

Analyze Systems Why is cellular respiration necessary for the functioning of a healthy cell? Why is it necessary for the health of other organisms?

....

....

....

....

HANDS-ON LAB

Accounting for Atoms

👆 **INTERACTIVITY**

The Importance of Cells

Go online to explore the importance of cell structure and healthy cell function.

Do the hands-on lab to investigate how matter is conserved in the processes of photosynthesis and cellular respiration.

☑ TOPIC 4 Review and Assess

1 Structure and Function of Cells

🕐 MS-LS1-1, MS-LS1-2

1. Which of the following is *not* stated in the cell theory?
   A. Cells are the basic unit of structure and function in all living things.
   B. Animal cells are generally more complex than plant cells.
   C. All living things are composed of cells.
   D. All cells are produced from other cells.

2. Reproduction is a function of both

.... and organisms.

3. Apply Concepts How did technology impact the development of the cell theory?

....

....

....

....

2 Cell Structures

🕐 MS-LS1-2, MS-LS1-3

4. Which of these structures is considered the "control center" of the cell?
   A. vacuole   B. endoplasmic reticulum
   C. nucleus   D. mitochondrion

5. The outermost layer in a plant cell is the

.... The outermost layer in

an animal cell is the ....

6. SEP Construct Explanations Plant cells have a cell wall and cell membranes, but animal cells have only cell membranes. How does this difference benefit plants?

....

....

....

3 Obtaining and Removing Materials

🕐 MS-LS1-2

7. A cell can bring in a large particle of food using the process of
   A. endocytosis.
   B. facilitated diffusion.
   C. osmosis.
   D. exocytosis.

8. Osmosis is the diffusion of ....

9. CCC Relate Structure and Function What are the benefits of a selectively permeable cell membrane?

....

....

....

....

4 Cell Division

🕐 MS-LS1-2

10. What happens when a cell reproduces?
   A. Two similar daughter cells are created.
   B. One mother cell and one daughter cell are created.
   C. One mother and two similar daughter cells are created.
   D. One father and one mother cell are created.

11. SEP Construct Explanations What is the purpose of cell division?

....

....

12. Apply Concepts At what point during the cell division process does one cell become two?

....

....

....

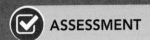
5 Photosynthesis

MS-LS1-6, MS-LS1-7

13. What provides the energy for the photosynthesis process?
A. glucose   B. sunlight
C. carbon dioxide   D. oxygen

14. Which organism is NOT a heterotroph?
A. rabbit   B. yeast
C. tomato plant   D. fungus

15. .... is a chemical that captures energy for photosynthesis.
A. glucose   B. lactic acid
C. carbon dioxide   D. chlorophyll

16. Describe What are two ways that plants use the carbohydrates produced in photosynthesis?

....

....

17. CCC Energy and Matter What is the relationship between the raw materials and the products in photosynthesis?

....

....

....

....

18. CCC Cause and Effect The concentration of carbon dioxide in the atmosphere has been gradually increasing for many years. How might this increase affect photosynthesis?

....

....

....

....

....

6 Cellular Respiration

MS-LS1-6, MS-LS1-7

19. The second stage of cellular respiration takes place in the
A. mitochondria.   B. root nodules.
C. chloroplast.   D. atmosphere.

20. .... and .... can be considered opposite processes.
A. fermentation, cellular respiration
B. photosynthesis, nitrogen fixation
C. evaporation, fermentation
D. photosynthesis, cellular respiration

21. SEP Use Models Why do you think plants hold on to a small amount of the oxygen produced during photosynthesis for use during cellular respiration?

$$\underset{\text{glucose}}{C_6H_{12}O_6} + \underset{\text{oxygen}}{6\,O_2} \longrightarrow \underset{\text{carbon dioxide}}{6\,CO_2} + \underset{\text{water}}{6\,H_2O} + \text{energy}$$

....

....

....

22. CCC Energy and Matter How do the raw materials of photosynthesis compare to the products of cellular respiration?

....

....

....

....

....

....

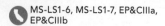 MS-LS1-6, MS-LS1-7, EP&CIIIa, EP&CIIIb

Evidence-Based Assessment

In late 2013, California was in the midst of a severe drought. Farms, ranches, and vineyards were suffering. Agriculture is an important part of the state's economy and it was suffering. In January 2014, the governor issued an official State of Emergency, with the goal of easing the impact of the drought on citizens, crops, and the environment. It stated that:

> State agencies, led by the Department of Water Resources, will execute a statewide water conservation campaign to make all Californians aware of the drought and encourage personal actions to reduce water usage. This campaign will coordinate with local water agencies, [and] . . . call on Californians to reduce their water usage by 20 percent.

Fortunately, the drought ended in late 2016. Governor Brown lifted the State of Emergency in April 2017. Estimating annual runoff helps to analyze the moisture level of an area to determine a drought. *Annual runoff* is water that is released by the land, or "runs off," in one year. Runoff is mostly precipitation that remains after water has evaporated, been used by plants, and seeped into soil. Runoff will make its way to bodies of water.

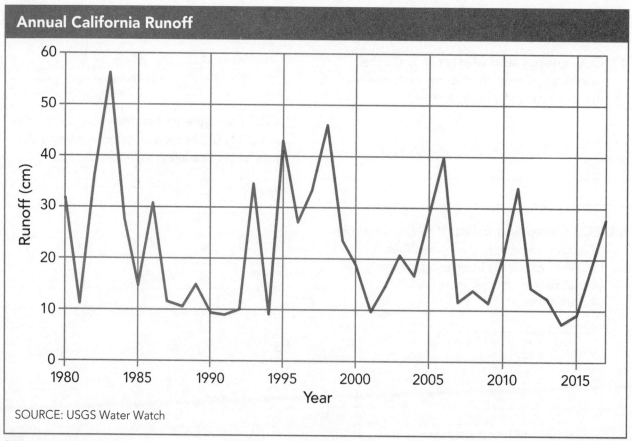

Annual California Runoff

SOURCE: USGS Water Watch

Use the graph to answer the questions.

1. **SEP Analyze Data** What do the data indicate about California's climate?
   A. It is steadily becoming wetter.
   B. It is steadily becoming drier.
   C. It has wetter and drier cycles.
   D. It does not change.

2. **SEP Evaluate Evidence** Where does the water a land plant uses for photosynthesis come from? Why would that water be scarce during a drought? Select the answers to make the statement true.

   The water comes from ....
   A. evaporation   B. condensation
   C. precipitation

   During a drought, soil is ....
   A. wetter   B. drier

   due to ....
   A. excess rain or snow
   B. little rain or snow
   C. less water vapor in the air

3. **CCC Energy and Matter** If a plant is considered drought-resistant, does it require more water or less water to perform photosynthesis? Explain.

   ....
   ....
   ....

4. **SEP Engage in Argument** Low-lying areas like river valleys can dry out in droughts but may also flood in unusually rainy periods. Suppose you were a valley tomato farmer in California. Based on your knowledge of photosynthesis and the data, would you buy seeds that were regular, drought-resistant, flood-resistant, or some combination? Explain.

   ....
   ....
   ....
   ....
   ....
   ....

5. **Connect to Environmental Principles and Concepts** The processes of photosynthesis and cellular respiration are continually cycling matter: carbon dioxide, water, and oxygen. How can a drought affect both processes in that cycle? Select all that apply.
   ☐ Less available water means photosynthesis slows down.
   ☐ Less oxygen is produced, so more cellular respiration can occur.
   ☐ Less oxygen is produced and cellular respiration slows down.
   ☐ More cellular respiration occurs, producing more carbon dioxide.
   ☐ Less carbon dioxide in the atmosphere can slow photosynthesis in plants.
   ☐ Plants have more carbon dioxide and photosynthesis occurs at a faster rate.

Quest FINDINGS

Complete the Quest!

Phenomenon Take the time to evaluate your exhibit and add finishing touches.

Optimize Performance Consider how you want to present your information. What sorts of changes could you make to your exhibit so that it is accessible to people with all sorts of information processing styles?

....
....
....
....
....

👆 **INTERACTIVITY**

Reflect on Your Museum Exhibit

MS-LS1-1, MS-ETS1-1, MS-ETS1-2, MS-ETS1-3, MS-ETS1-4

Design and Build a Microscope

Can you **design** and build your own **microscope** to **examine** small objects?

Materials

(per group)

- book
- 2 hand lenses; one low-power and one high-power
- metric ruler
- cardboard tubes
- tape
- scissors
- rubber bands
- other common materials for building your microscope

Safety

Be sure to follow all safety guidelines provided by your teacher. The Safety Appendix of your textbook provides more details about the safety icons.

Background

Phenomenon Have you ever used a magnifying glass to read the date on a small coin more easily? What do you think would happen if you used a second magnifying glass to look through the first magnifying glass?

That's the basic idea behind a compound microscope—using one lens to look through a second lens to get a better view of small objects. This view often gives scientists the ability to understand how the structure of an organism helps with its function. In this activity, you will design and build your own microscope to examine small objects.

Herald Moth The wings on this Herald moth allow it to fly. Viewing the moth's wings up close could explain how the wing's structure enables the moth to fly.

Procedure

Part 1: Define the Problem

☐ 1. **Student Discourse** Work with a partner to discuss and explore how lenses can be used to magnify objects. Using only your eyes, examine words in a book. Then use the high-power lens to examine the same words. Draw your observations in the space provided.

☐ 2. Hold the high-power lens 5 to 6 cm above the words in the book. Keep the high-power lens about the same height above the words. Hold the low-power lens above the high power lens.

☐ 3. Move the high-power lens up and down until the image is in focus and upside down. Once the image is in focus, experiment with raising and lowering both lenses. Your goal is to produce the highest magnification while keeping the image in clear focus.

☐ 4. Measure and record the distance between the book and the high-power lens, and between the two lenses. Draw your observations through both lenses together.

Part 2: Design a Solution

☐ 5. Using this information, design your own compound microscope. Think of creative ways to use the available materials. Your microscope should meet all the criteria shown.

☐ 6. Sketch your design. Obtain your teacher's approval for your design. Then construct your microscope.

Part 3: Test and Evaluate Your Solution

☐ 7. Test your microscope by examining printed words or a printed photograph. Then, examine other objects such as a leaf or onion skin. Record your observations. Did your microscope meet the criteria listed in Step 5?

☐ 8. Examine microscopes made by other students. Based on your tests and your examination of other microscopes, identify ways you could improve your microscope.

HANDS-ON LAB

▣**Demonstrate** Go online for a downloadable worksheet of this lab.

Your microscope should:

- contain one low-power lens and one high-power lens
- allow the distance between the two lenses to be easily adjusted
- focus to produce a clear, enlarged, and upside-down image of the object

Part 1: Research and Investigate

Sketch what you observed:

eyes only   high-powered lens   both lenses

Measurements:

....

....

Part 2: Design and Build

Sketch of proposed microscope design:

Part 3: Evaluate and Redesign

Observations: Ideas to improve microscope:

....

....

....

....

....

....

Analyze and Interpret Data

1. **SEP Evaluate Your Solution** When you used two lenses, how did moving the top lens up and down affect the image? What was the effect of moving the bottom lens up and down?

....

....

....

2. **CCC Cause and Effect** Compare the images you observed using one lens with the image from two lenses. What do you think accounts for these differences?

....

....

....

3. **SEP Cite Evidence** How do you think that the compound microscope contributed to the development of the cell theory? Use evidence from your investigation to support the claim.

....

....

....

4. **SEP Use Models** How did modeling a microscope with the two lenses in Part 1 help you determine the design and function of your microscope? What types of limitations did you encounter as you designed and built your prototype?

....

....

....

....

5. **SEP Engage in Argument** Imagine you are living in the year 1675. Write a letter to a scientific magazine that will convince scientists to use your new microscope rather than the single-lens variety used by Van Leeuwenhoek. Support your points with evidence from your investigation.

....

....

....

....

MS-LS1-3 Use argument supported by evidence for how the body is a system of interacting subsystems composed of groups of cells.

MS-LS1-8 Gather and synthesize information that sensory receptors respond to stimuli by sending messages to the brain for immediate behavior or storage as memories.

EP&Clc Students should be developing an understanding that the quality, quantity, and reliability of the goods and ecosystem services provided by natural systems are directly affected by the health of those systems.

HANDS-ON LAB

uConnect Use a model to explore how the human body is organized.

How does this person maintain his balance on the slackline?

GO ONLINE to access your digital course

▶ VIDEO

👆 INTERACTIVITY

🧪 VIRTUAL LAB

☑ ASSESSMENT

📖 eTEXT

🧪 HANDS-ON LABS

The Essential Question

How do systems interact in the human body?

CCC Systems and System Models Walking on a slackline requires good balance and coordination. What different actions are taking place in the the body of the person on the slackline?

....

....

....

....

....

235

Quest KICKOFF

How do your body systems interact when you train for your favorite sport?

 NBC LEARN ▶ VIDEO

Phenomenon Nutritionists and physical trainers study human body systems and how they interact to help athletes maintain peak performance. In this Quest activity, you will develop a training plan for an athlete. In digital activities and labs, you will investigate how body systems interact to supply energy, manage materials, and control processes in order to develop a well-rounded plan. By applying what you have learned, you will produce a training and nutrition presentation for the athlete.

After watching the video, which explores a typical day in the life of a teen athlete, think about the requirements of playing a physically demanding sport. List the following in order of importance, with the first being the most important: strength, endurance, flexibility.

1 ....

2 ....

3 ....

 👆 **INTERACTIVITY**

🕐 MS-LS1-3, MS-LS1-8

Peak Performance Plan

IN LESSON 1

What are the functions of body systems? Think about the body systems that are most important to the athlete's performance.

Quest CHECK-IN

IN LESSON 2

What skills, movements, and processes are involved in the athlete playing the sport? Identify the system interactions that are required by the sport.

 👆 **INTERACTIVITY**

Training Systems

Quest CHECK-IN

IN LESSON 3

What are the athlete's nutritional needs? Design a nutrition plan for your athlete that maximizes his or her performance.

 👆 **INTERACTIVITY**

Training Table

A training program designed for this athlete prepared his body to accomplish his personal goal of running through a desert.

Quest CHECK-IN

IN LESSON 4

What effect does the body's demand for more energy have on the circulatory and respiratory systems? Determine how different activities affect heart and respiration rates.

HANDS-ON LAB

Heart Beat, Health Beat

Quest CHECK-IN

IN LESSON 5

What is muscle memory? Consider how training the nervous system can improve the athlete's performance.

INTERACTIVITY

Why Practice Makes Perfect

Quest FINDINGS

Complete the Quest!

Organize your findings about system interactions and nutrition to develop a presentation for your athlete.

INTERACTIVITY

Reflect on Peak Performance Plan

1 Body Organization

Guiding Questions

- How do groups of cells form interacting subsystems in the body?
- How do the structures of specialized organs relate to their functions in the body?

Connections

Literacy Support Author's Claim

Math Identify Equivalent Expressions

 MS-LS1-3 Use argument supported by evidence for how the body is a system of interacting subsystems composed of groups of cells.

HANDS-ON LAB

Investigate Consider how the structures of cells and tissues relate to their functions in the body.

Vocabulary

tissue
organ
organ system

Academic Vocabulary

organized

Connect It!

✏ **Circle an instrument panel that the co-pilot might control. The co-pilot sits on the right side.**

Use an Analogy If an airplane has parts that function like a person's parts, then what part of the body does the pilot represent? Explain your reasoning.

....

....

....

Organization of the Body

Driving a car safely requires constant attention, even in the best road conditions. Controlling an airplane is even more demanding. For a plane to fly safely to its destination, all of its systems must be in good working order. The plane's steering system, brake system, lights, tires, and jet engines are all vital to a safe flight. The pilot and the co-pilot must be skilled at operating the instrument panels shown in **Figure 1**. They have to be able to steer the plane safely through all sorts of conditions. At times, they must fly the plane while relying on the instruments and screens in the cockpit, because they cannot see where the plane is headed.

Like an airplane, your body is a large system **organized** into subsystems that work together. For example, when you walk up the stairs or ride a bike, your nervous, skeletal, and muscular systems are subsystems working together to move your body. Each subsystem in your body system is made up of groups of cells. Cells form the basic units of every living thing. Just as an airplane is a large system that cannot function properly without subsystems, such as its landing gear or electrical system, the same is true for your body: You need each of your subsystems to work together so that you can survive and grow.

☑ **CHECK POINT** **Support Author's Claim** How is the human body similar to an airplane?

....

....

HANDS-ON LAB

Examine the levels of organization in a multicellular organism.

Academic Vocabulary

What steps do you take to get organized for an upcoming project?

....

....

....

....

All Systems Go

Figure 1 All systems in an airplane, including the pilot and co-pilot, must function properly in order to operate the plane.

Levels of Organization

The smooth functioning of your body depends on its organization. Recall that the levels of organization in the human body are cells, tissues, organs, and organ systems. All tissues are made up of cells. Organs are made of different kinds of tissues. And organ systems are made from organs that work together to perform bodily functions.

Cells and Tissues You are alive because specialized cells are performing their functions throughout your body. When similar cells that perform the same function are grouped together they form a **tissue.** Muscle tissue, for example, contracts, or shortens, to make parts of your body move. Nerve tissue carries electrical signals from the brain all over the body and back again. Connective tissue, such as bone and fat, provides support for your body and attaches all of its parts together. Skin, the largest organ in the human body, has epithelial (ep uh THEE lee ul) tissue that protects your insides from damage. Epithelial tissue covers the inner and outer surfaces of your body.

Math Toolbox

Counting Cells in the Body

Scientists and mathematicians have wondered about the number of cells in the human body for centuries. Estimates of the number of cells have ranged from 100 billion to 1 quadrillion, or a 1 followed by 15 zeros! It's easier to write one quadrillion using exponents: 1×10^{15} where the exponent 15 is the number of zeros.

A team of European scientists recently completed a new estimate of the human cells in an average person. Their estimate is about 37 trillion cells per person.

Name	Number	Written with Power of Ten Exponent
million	1,000,000	1×10^{6}
billion	1,000,000,000	1×10^{9}
trillion	1,000,000,000,000	1×10^{12}
quadrillion	1,000,000,000,000,000	1×10^{15}

1. **Identify Equivalent Expressions** How do you write 37 trillion as a number and using the power of ten exponent?

....

2. **SEP Reason Quantitatively** How does the new European estimate compare to the smallest and largest estimates of other research groups?

....

....

Organs and Systems Your kidneys, heart, brain, and skin are all organs. An **organ** is a body structure composed of different kinds of tissues that work together. Each organ has a specific function in the body. Because its structure is more complex, the job of an organ is usually more complex than that of a tissue. For example, kidneys remove waste from your blood and form urine. Each kidney contains muscle, connective, and epithelial tissues. In addition, nervous tissue connects to the kidney and helps to control its function. Look at **Figure 2** to see where the different kinds of tissue are found in the kidney. Each tissue contributes in a different way to the kidney's job of filtering blood.

Every organ is part of an **organ system**, which is a group of organs that work together, performing major functions. For example, your kidneys are part of your excretory system. The excretory system also includes the skin, lungs, and liver. The body is a system of several interacting subsystems, such as organ systems.

HANDS-ON LAB

Investigate Consider how the structures of cells and tissues relate to their functions in the body.

Many Tissues Make an Organ

Figure 2 Kidneys filter blood to remove waste and excess water.

SEP Explain Phenomena What might happen to a kidney if the muscle tissue does not function properly?

....

....

....

....

Epithelial tissue in the renal cortex gives the kidney structure and protects the nephrons that filter the blood.

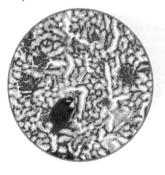

Renal capsules of connective and fat tissue protect the kidney and maintain its shape.

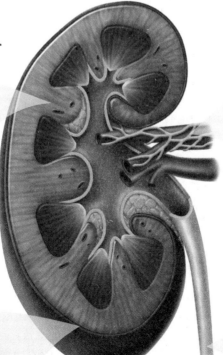

Nerve cells help the kidney pump and filter blood.

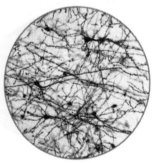

Muscle cells in the ureter drain urine to the bladder.

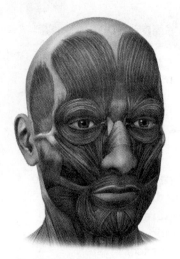

Make a Face

Figure 3 A multitude of facial muscles allows for a variety of expressions.

Interpret Diagrams
Draw an X on the muscles involved in blinking your eyes.

 VIDEO

Find out how your body is like an orchestra.

Human Organ Systems

Eleven major organ subsystems keep the human body system running smoothly. All of the organ subsystems work together.

Control Systems To function properly, each part of your body must be able to communicate with other parts of your body. Your body communicates using the nervous system, which is made up of the brain, spinal cord, and nerves. The nervous system sends information through nerve cells to control your actions.

Many body functions are controlled through the endocrine system, a collection of glands that produces important chemicals. The chemicals in turn affect your energy level, body temperature, digestion, and even your moods!

Structural Systems Three organ systems work to shape, move, and protect your body. The skeletal system includes your bones and connective tissues. The main functions of the skeletal system support your body, protect your organs, make blood cells, and store minerals. Connective tissues cushion the bones and attach bones to muscles.

The muscular system includes 650 muscles that control your movements, help you to stand up straight, and allow you to breathe. The muscles that control your face are shown in **Figure 3**. The muscular system also keeps your blood and your food moving through your body.

The integumentary system protects your body from outside damage. Skin, hair, and nails are all parts of the integumentary system. Oil and sweat glands under the skin help to keep your skin waterproof and your temperature comfortable. Your skin is attached to muscles, which are anchored to bones by connective tissue. Together, these three systems provide your shape and allow you to move your body in many ways.

Oxygen and Transport Systems The respiratory system brings in oxygen and moves out carbon dioxide by way of the lungs. As you breathe in fresh air, oxygen diffuses into the red blood cells. When you breathe out, carbon dioxide diffuses back into the air.

The circulatory system carries oxygen-rich blood to all the parts of your body. Your heart pumps the blood through your blood vessels. Blood cells pass oxygen to your cells and pick up carbon dioxide. Your veins then bring the blood back to your heart and lungs. The circulatory system also transports nutrients, wastes, endocrine chemicals, and disease-fighting cells all over your body through your bloodstream.

Food and Waste Processing Systems Food you put into your mouth begins a journey through your digestive system. Your esophagus squeezes the food down into the stomach, where the food is crushed and broken down by acids. Next, the food travels into the intestines. Useful substances pass through the intestinal walls into the blood. The liver and pancreas produce substances that help to break down food. So do trillions of bacteria that live in your intestines. Some parts of the food cannot be digested. Those parts pass out of your body as waste. You can think of the digestive system as a long tube that runs through your body. Some food parts pass through the tube and back out into the world without ever entering other tissues of your body.

The excretory system gets rid of waste products and toxic substances in your body. Kidneys produce urine, sweat glands in your skin make sweat, and lungs release wastes from the body into the air. Meanwhile, the liver breaks down toxic chemicals into substances that the kidneys can pull out of your blood.

☑ **CHECK POINT** **Determine Conclusions** What would happen if your organ systems stopped functioning properly?

....

....

Literacy Connection

Support Author's Claim
Is it true that the human body can make its own chemicals? Cite evidence from the text.

....

....

....

....

Model It!

What? No Bones?
Figure 4 Most of the known animals on Earth are invertebrates. These organisms lack the backbone found in humans, birds, reptiles, and other vertebrates.

SEP Develop Models ✐ Choose a kind of invertebrate— snail, insect, worm, octopus, water bear (shown here), and spider are just a few. Consider how an animal maintains its structure with no bones. Then sketch a diagram to explain how your animal moves with no bones connected to its muscles.

Organ Systems in the Human Body

Figure 5 The structures of different body systems all work together to allow you to grow, obtain energy, move, stay healthy, and reproduce.

CCC Analyze Systems ✏ Use the key on the right to label each body system. There may be more than one function for each system.

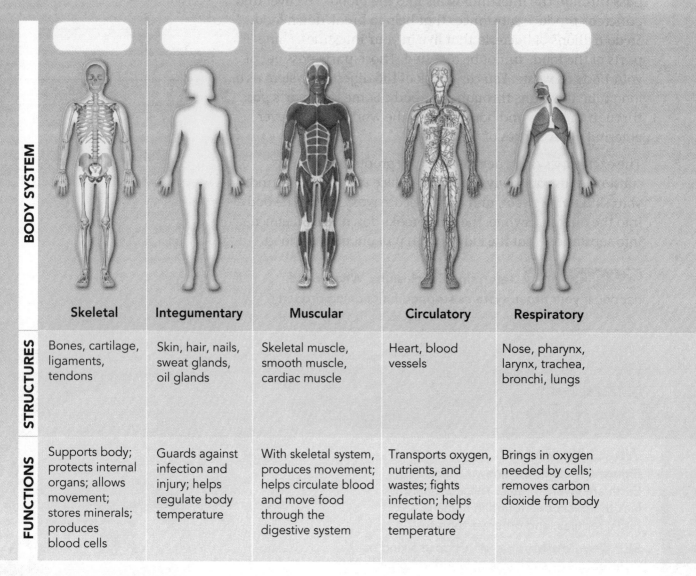

BODY SYSTEM	Skeletal	Integumentary	Muscular	Circulatory	Respiratory
STRUCTURES	Bones, cartilage, ligaments, tendons	Skin, hair, nails, sweat glands, oil glands	Skeletal muscle, smooth muscle, cardiac muscle	Heart, blood vessels	Nose, pharynx, larynx, trachea, bronchi, lungs
FUNCTIONS	Supports body; protects internal organs; allows movement; stores minerals; produces blood cells	Guards against infection and injury; helps regulate body temperature	With skeletal system, produces movement; helps circulate blood and move food through the digestive system	Transports oxygen, nutrients, and wastes; fights infection; helps regulate body temperature	Brings in oxygen needed by cells; removes carbon dioxide from body

 **INTERACTIVITY**

Explore the structures and functions of different body systems.

Defense System The immune system is your defense system against infections. Lymph nodes and lymph vessels trap bacteria and viruses. "Swollen glands" are lymph nodes that have grown larger to fight off an infection. White blood cells produced inside your bones also attack and destroy bacteria and other causes of disease. As shown in **Figure 5** above, many different organs work together to help to fight off invading disease organisms.

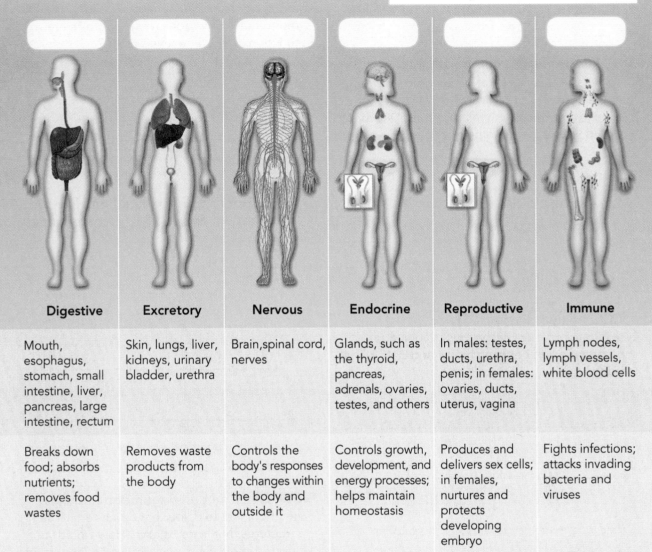

Digestive	Excretory	Nervous	Endocrine	Reproductive	Immune
Mouth, esophagus, stomach, small intestine, liver, pancreas, large intestine, rectum	Skin, lungs, liver, kidneys, urinary bladder, urethra	Brain, spinal cord, nerves	Glands, such as the thyroid, pancreas, adrenals, ovaries, testes, and others	In males: testes, ducts, urethra, penis; in females: ovaries, ducts, uterus, vagina	Lymph nodes, lymph vessels, white blood cells
Breaks down food; absorbs nutrients; removes food wastes	Removes waste products from the body	Controls the body's responses to changes within the body and outside it	Controls growth, development, and energy processes; helps maintain homeostasis	Produces and delivers sex cells; in females, nurtures and protects developing embryo	Fights infections; attacks invading bacteria and viruses

Reproductive System The reproductive system is responsible for producing sperm and eggs and (in females) for nurturing the fetus until birth. Male reproductive organs include the testes (also known as testicles) and the penis. Female reproductive organs include the ovaries, uterus, and vagina. A cell can reproduce itself to make a new cell, but it takes a whole organ system to make a new human.

 INTERACTIVITY

Explain how the human body is organized and how different body systems work together.

✓ CHECK POINT **Cite Textual Evidence** Identify an example of how the human body's multiple subsystems interact to perform a specific function.

....

....

☑ LESSON 1 Check

1. **CCC Patterns** What are the levels of organization in the human body from the least to the most complex?

....

2. **SEP Distinguish Relationships** If you are relating the levels of organization of the human body to the levels of organization of a city, what would you relate cells to? What would you relate the other levels to?

....

....

....

....

3. **CCC Analyze Systems** Explain how the respiratory system exchanges oxygen and carbon dioxide between the air and cells in the body?

....

....

....

....

....

4. **Apply Concepts** How could you tell if your immune system were not functioning well?

....

....

5. **SEP Construct Explanations** If the brain is the control center of the body, why does it have nerves connected to your organs?

....

....

....

6. **CCC Relate Structure and Function** The thin layer of epithelial tissue in the small intestines works somewhat like a cell membrane. How does its structure relate to its function in the digestive system?

....

....

....

....

....

7. **SEP Support Your Explanation** How does learning about organs help us understand how organ systems work?

....

....

....

....

....

....

....

8. **SEP Construct an Argument** A younger neighbor just told you that organs are large structures that keep us alive. How would you support their claim, and explain the importance of cells in keeping us alive?

....

....

....

....

....

....

MS-LS1-3

Artificial SKiN

This artificial skin (genetically modified to "glow" green) is able to function just like real skin. It can grow hair and is able to sweat.

INTERACTIVITY

Identify criteria, constraints, and materials that need to be considered when building an artificial limb.

How do you help people who suffer due to severely damaged skin? You engineer new skin for them! Bioengineers may have solved a big problem.

The Challenge: To grow artificial skin that functions like the real thing.

Phenomenon Until recently, patients who lost skin because of burns and injuries had to donate skin from other parts of their bodies. But using their own skin was risky. Artificial skin, with no hair follicles or sweat glands, could not help maintain homeostasis, the process that keeps internal conditions in the body stable. New developments in cell research and bioengineering may have overcome this obstacle.

To make improved artificial skin, bioengineer Takashi Tsuji and his team took cells from the mouths of mice. After treating the cells with chemicals, they were able to form clumps of cell types that you would find in a new embryo. When they placed these cells into other mice, the cells gradually changed into specialized tissue. When transplanted into the skin tissue of other mice, the tissues developed normally, with hair follicles and oil glands. The tissue also made connections with the surrounding nerve and muscle tissue, allowing the different body systems to interact normally. Someday, fully functional engineered skin "donations" may be saving lives all over the world.

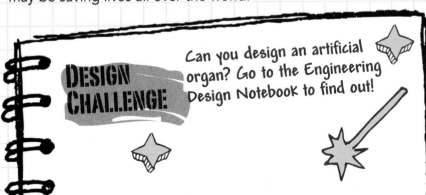

DESIGN CHALLENGE

Can you design an artificial organ? Go to the Engineering Design Notebook to find out!

Guiding Questions

- How do organ systems interact to carry out all the necessary functions for an organism's growth and survival?
- How do organ systems interact to maintain homeostasis?

Connection

Literacy Cite Textual Evidence

 MS-LS1-3 Use argument supported by evidence for how the body is a system of interacting subsystems composed of groups of cells.

HANDS-ON LAB

ⁿInvestigate Identify the body systems used to perform specific actions.

Vocabulary

stimulus
response
gland
hormone
stress

Academic Vocabulary

interactions
stable

Connect It!

In the space provided on the image, list the body systems that you think are involved in skateboarding.

CCC Predict   If one of these body systems were to stop interacting with the other systems, would this activity still be possible? Explain.

....

....

....

Systems Working Together

All the systems in the human body work together to perform all the necessary functions for life. Cells need oxygen provided by the respiratory system and carried by the circulatory system. Organs carry out commands from the nervous system. And every part of the body changes its activities based on signals from the endocrine system.

Movement How is the skateboarder in **Figure 1** able to do what she does? **Interactions** between the skeletal, muscular, and nervous systems make it possible. Skeletal muscles are attached to the bones of the skeleton and provide the force that moves bones. Muscles contract and relax. When a muscle contracts, it shortens and pulls on the bones to which it is attached.

Try standing on one leg and bending the other leg at the knee. Hold that position. You can feel that you are using the muscles at the back of your thigh. Your nervous system controls when and how your muscles act on your bones.

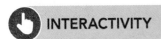
INTERACTIVITY

Explore how joints function in the human body.

Academic Vocabulary

What kinds of interactions are there between people in your neighborhood?

....

....

....

....

Poetry in Motion
Figure 1 This skater in Venice, California, is accomplishing impressive feats because his body's systems are working together properly.

Literacy Connection

Cite Textual Evidence
The central idea of this text is that the body is organized into systems that interact with each other. As you read, underline evidence that organ systems interact with each other.

Controlling Body Functions
The nervous system has two ways of controlling body functions: electrical signals from nerves and chemical signals from the endocrine system. Both methods help you to respond to your environment.

Transporting Materials
All cells need oxygen and nutrients, and they need to get rid of carbon dioxide and other wastes. But most cells are locked into position with no way to move in search of food. So how can they stay alive? The answer is that blood vessels from the circulatory system carry nutrients to and waste from the cells in the body. Blood vessels divide into smaller and smaller branches until the tiniest, called capillaries, are only as wide as one blood cell. Capillaries, visible in **Figure 2**, pass near every cell in the body.

Blood picks up oxygen from the lungs and food molecules from the intestines and delivers them to needy cells. At the same time, blood collects carbon dioxide and waste from the cells. The carbon dioxide is returned to the lungs to be released into the air. Waste products are filtered from the blood by the kidneys in the excretory system and passed out of the body in urine.

☑ CHECK POINT **Determine Meaning** Why do the capillaries have to be so small?

....

....

Special Delivery
Figure 2 Blood cells, like those shown in the inset, travel through a network of blood vessels to transport materials to and from every part of the body.

CCC Predict How do you think a blocked blood vessel would affect an organism?

....

....

....

....

....

....

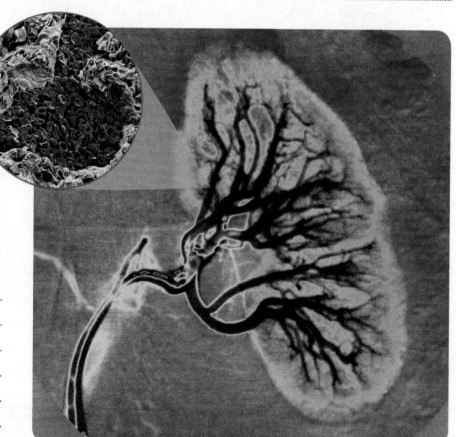

Stimulus and Response Your eyes, ears, skin, nose, and taste buds all send information about your environment to your nervous system. Your senses let you react to loud noises, hot objects, and the odor of your favorite food. Any change or signal in the environment that can make an organism react in some way is called a **stimulus** (plural: stimuli). A **response** is an action or change in behavior that occurs as a result of a stimulus. Responses are directed by your nervous system but often involve other body systems as well. Your muscular and skeletal systems help you reach for food, and your digestive system releases saliva before the food even reaches your mouth. **Figure 3** shows an example of stimulus and response used in an American Sign Language expression.

INTERACTIVITY

Investigate how different body systems work together.

Plan It!

Reaction Time

The time that passes between a stimulus and a response is the reaction time. A short reaction time could save you from a fall or a burn, and it might help you beat video games.

SEP Plan Your Investigation Plan an investigation to measure reaction times under different conditions. Choose two or three factors that you suspect may influence reaction time, such as time of day, type of stimulus, environmental conditions, or state of mental alertness. How could you display your results?

....

....

....

....

....

....

....

....

....

....

....

....

....

....

Don't Burn Your Mouth

Figure 3 The American Sign Language expression for *hot* shows a reaction to hot food.

SEP Communicate Use the terms *stimulus* and *response* to explain what the sign is expressing.

....

....

....

....

HANDS-ON LAB

☑ **Investigate** Identify the body systems used to perform specific actions.

Hormonal Control The endocrine system uses chemical signals instead of nerves to control body functions. The endocrine system is made up of many **glands**, organs that produce and release chemicals either through tiny tubes called ducts or directly into the bloodstream. For example, when something startles you, your adrenal glands send signals that prepare you to fight or run away. Your heart pumps faster, your lungs let in more air, and your ability to feel pain decreases. The pupils of your eyes even grow larger and allow in more light. You are ready for action.

The chemical produced by an endocrine gland is called a **hormone**. Hormones are carried through your body by the circulatory system. These chemicals affect many body processes. One hormone interacts with the excretory system and the circulatory system to control the amount of water in the bloodstream. Another hormone interacts with the digestive system and the circulatory system to control the amount of sugar in the bloodstream. Hormones also affect the reproductive systems of both males and females. **Figure 4** shows some of the effects of hormones on boys during puberty.

☑ CHECK POINT **Cite Textual Evidence** What text on this page supports the idea that the endocrine system functions differently from the nervous system?

....

....

....

Hormones and Puberty

Figure 4 Hormones can have dramatic and long-lasting effects.

SEP Make Observations Identify some of the changes you see between the before-puberty and after-puberty pictures.

....

....

....

Interacting Organ Subsystems

Figure 5 This swimmer's body systems work together as she pushes herself to excel.

CCC Systems   Read the descriptions of functions happening in the swimmer's body. Then identify the subsystems involved.

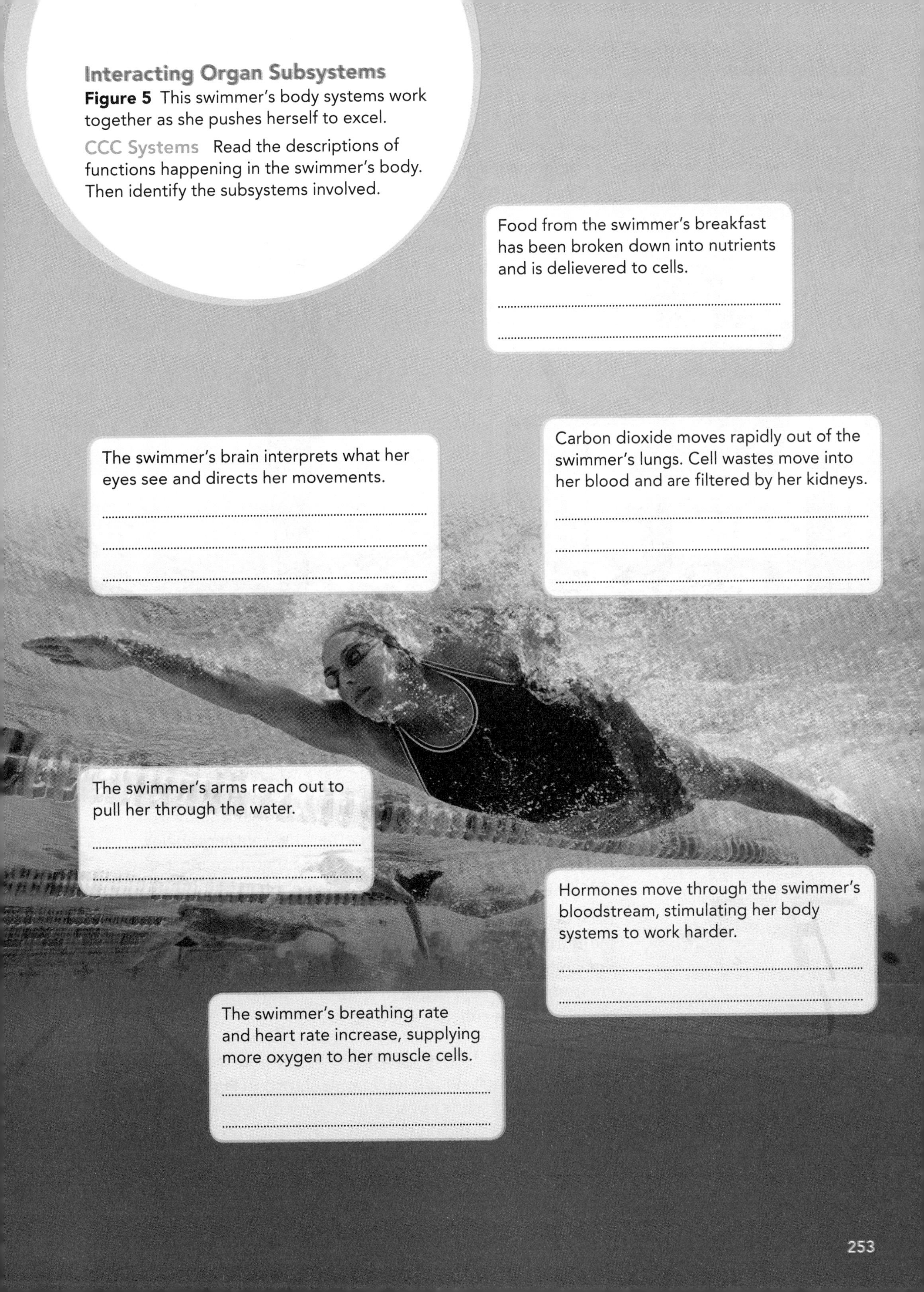

Food from the swimmer's breakfast has been broken down into nutrients and is delievered to cells.

....

....

The swimmer's brain interprets what her eyes see and directs her movements.

....

....

....

Carbon dioxide moves rapidly out of the swimmer's lungs. Cell wastes move into her blood and are filtered by her kidneys.

....

....

....

The swimmer's arms reach out to pull her through the water.

....

....

Hormones move through the swimmer's bloodstream, stimulating her body systems to work harder.

....

....

The swimmer's breathing rate and heart rate increase, supplying more oxygen to her muscle cells.

....

....

Cooling Down

Figure 6 The woman in the first image is using several different ways to warm up.

CCC Apply Concepts Identify some ways the woman in the second drawing might cool her body and maintain a constant body temperature.

....

....

....

Academic Vocabulary

Stable is a common word to describe something that hasn't changed much and isn't expected to change much in the future. Make a list of some things you have heard described as stable.

....

....

....

....

 VIDEO

Find out how a house's heating system is like your body.

Homeostasis

What happens when you go outside in the cold? Does your body temperature fall to meet the outside temperature? It does not, and that's a very good thing! Your body only functions well around 37°C. It is vitally important for your body to maintain that temperature. Whether the weather is below freezing or roasting hot, your body's temperature must stay **stable** and remain close to 37°C to function well.

Each organism requires specific conditions to function. Maintaining those conditions is necessary for life to continue. Remember that the condition in which an organism's internal environment is kept stable in spite of changes in the outside environment is called homeostasis.

Regulating Temperature When your body temperature starts to fall too low, as shown in **Figure 6**, your nervous system sends out signals to your other systems to take action to warm you up. Your skin, which is part of the integumentary system, develops goosebumps. Your muscles cause you to shiver. You tend to move your large muscles to generate heat. All of these actions help to raise your temperature back to normal.

Keeping Balance Structures in your inner ear sense the position of your head. They send this information to your brain, which interprets the signals. If your brain senses that you are losing your balance, then it sends messages to your muscles to move in ways that help you stay steady. **Figure 7** shows the cycle of how your body keeps its balance.

Meeting Energy Needs When the cells in your body need more energy, hormones from the endocrine system signal the nervous system to make you feel hungry. After you eat, other hormones signal your brain to make you feel full.

Maintaining Water Balance All the chemical reactions that keep you alive take place within the watery environment of your cells. If your body needs more water, then your nervous system causes you to feel thirsty. Your senses, muscles, and skeleton take you to a source of water. After you have had enough water, your nervous system causes your thirst to end. Soon after, the water passes through your digestive system to your circulatory system and from there into your cells. Water balance is restored!

INTERACTIVITY

Explain how body systems interact to maintain homeostasis.

Maintaining Homeostasis

Figure 7 Interactions among your ears, brain, and muscular system make up the balance cycle.

Sequence ✏ Fill in the missing steps to create a diagram of the thirst cycle.

☑ **CHECK POINT**

Translate Information What role does the nervous system play in maintaining homeostasis? Explain.

....

....

....

....

....

....

....

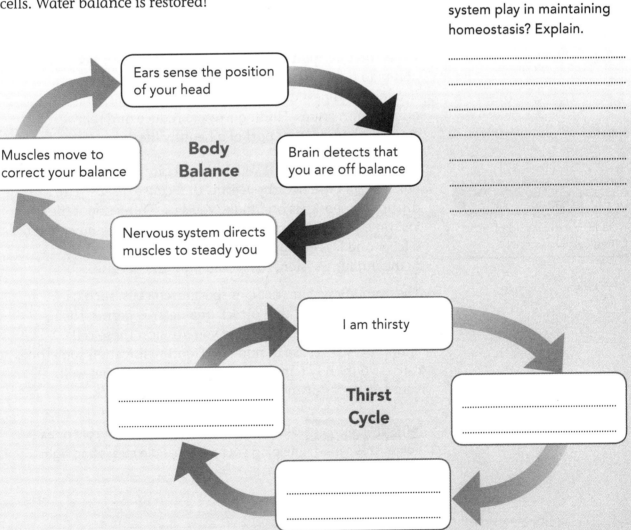

255

Defense Against Disease

Figure 8 The green cell is an immune cell. It engulfs the orange and blue bacteria cells, and destroys them.

CCC Analyze Systems How do you think the immune system is affected by stress?

....

....

....

....

....

....

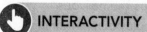

INTERACTIVITY

Analyze symptoms to see what body systems are affected by an illness.

VIDEO

Go inside the world of a medical illustrator.

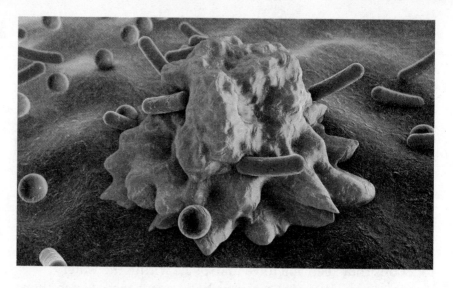

Managing Stress In general, **stress** is the reaction of a person's body to potentially threatening, challenging, or disturbing events. Each person experiences stress differently. One person may enjoy taking on the challenge of a math test, while someone else might freeze with fear.

Some stress is unavoidable. If stress is over quickly, then the body returns to its normal, healthy condition. However, too much stress for too long a time can be unhealthy. Ongoing stress can disrupt homeostasis and weaken your body's ability to fight disease. Stress also can cause depression, headaches, digestion problems, heart problems, and other health issues. Finding ways to reduce and relieve stress is an important part of a healthy lifestyle.

Fighting Disease When your body systems are in balance, you are healthy. Germs that cause disease can disrupt homeostasis and make you sick. Think about the last time you had a cold or strep throat. You may have had a fever and less energy. Your body was devoting resources to the immune system so it could fight the disease.

The immune system includes specialized cells, such as the one in **Figure 8**, that attack and destroy germs, such as viruses and bacteria. When you are sick, these cells temporarily increase in number. Fighting infection sometimes causes your body temperature to go up. As you get well, your fever goes away and your energy comes back.

☑ **CHECK POINT** **Determine Central Ideas** What role does homeostasis play in helping your body handle stress and fight disease?

....

....

....

MS-LS1-3

1. Define What is a hormone?

....

....

2. CCC Analyze Systems What are four conditions in the body related to maintaining homeostasis?

....

....

3. Compare and Contrast How are chemical signals and electrical signals alike? How are they different?

....

....

....

....

4. CCC Cause and Effect Explain how getting sick can affect the body's ability to maintain homeostasis.

....

....

....

....

5. SEP Communicate Pick one material that is moved within the body by the organ systems. Describe which systems are involved and how they work together.

....

....

....

....

....

....

6. SEP Construct Explanations How does the circulatory system interact with other body systems to maintain homeostasis?

....

....

....

....

....

....

7. SEP Develop Models 🖊 Start with the sentence "I feel hungry." In the space below, draw a cycle diagram to show how your body would respond to this situation.

Quest CHECK-IN

In this lesson, you learned about how body systems interact with one another to carry out functions necessary for growth and survival. You also explored how body systems interact to maintain homeostasis.

CCC Systems Why is it important to understand how different body systems interact when developing a training plan?

....

....

....

INTERACTIVITY

Training Systems

Go online to identify body systems with their functions and use that information to begin a training plan.

3 Supplying Energy

Guiding Questions

- What are the important nutrients your body needs to carry out its processes?
- How does food become the materials your body can use?
- How do your body's systems process the food you eat?

Connections

Literacy Write Arguments

Math Analyze Proportional Relationships

MS-LS1-3 Use argument supported by evidence for how the body is a system of interacting subsystems composed of groups of cells. (Also EP&Clc)

HANDS-ON LAB

иInvestigate Discover how Calories in different foods are measured.

Vocabulary

digestion
nutrients
carbohydrates
peristalsis
saliva
enzyme

Academic Vocabulary

absorption
elimination

Connect It

✏ **Circle the food choice the runner should make to get the most energy for the race.**

SEP Make Observations Consider your daily activities. Which require the most energy? What would happen if you did not eat enough food?

....

....

Make Generalizations Why are your food choices important?

....

....

....

Food and Energy

What have you done so far today? You woke up, got dressed, ate breakfast, and came to school. Later today, you may have karate, dance, or basketball. You may be running in a race like the people in **Figure 1**. All of these activities require energy. In fact, your cells require energy for all the processes that go on inside your body, including breathing, thinking, and growing.

Living things get energy from food. Plants make their own food. Animals and decomposers get their food by eating other organisms and breaking it down into its component parts. **Digestion** is the process by which your body breaks down food into small nutrient molecules.

Nutrients are the substances in food that provide the raw materials the body's cells need to carry out all their essential processes. Some nutrients are broken down and used for energy. Other nutrients are used to repair damaged cells or to help you grow. Your body needs nutrients to perform every function. Therefore, you constantly need nutrients from food to keep up with the body's demand.

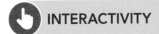

INTERACTIVITY

Learn how our bodies get energized.

Literacy Connection

Write Arguments A classmate claims that an apple and cupcake, both about the same size, give you the same amount of energy. Do you agree or disagree with this statement? Explain.

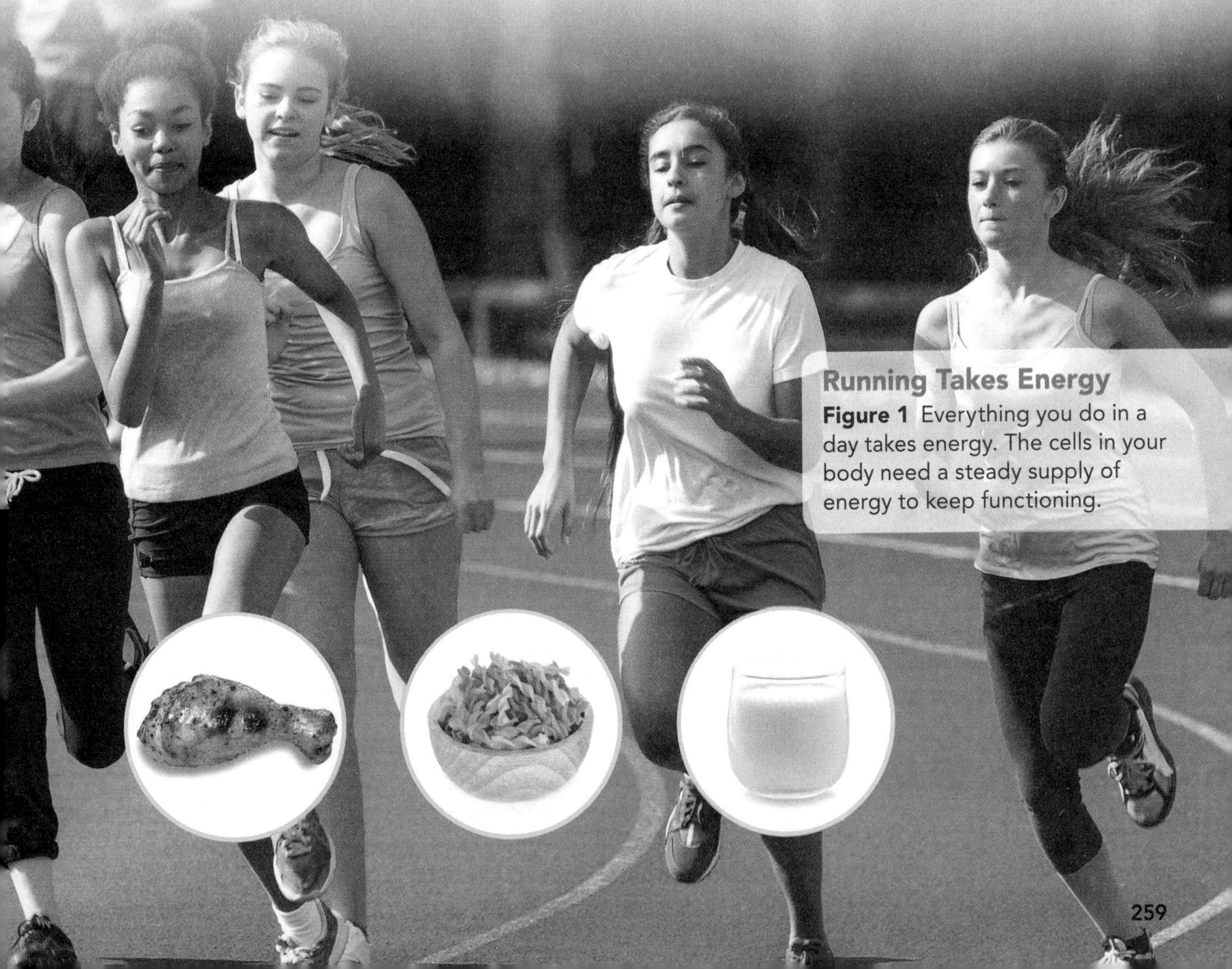

Running Takes Energy

Figure 1 Everything you do in a day takes energy. The cells in your body need a steady supply of energy to keep functioning.

How Sweet It Is

Figure 2 Our bodies can digest simple carbohydrates very quickly so they can give a quick burst of energy.

SEP Defend Your Claim ✏️
Circle a simple carbohydrate that you think makes a healthy snack. Then, explain why you think that's a better choice than some others.

....
....
....
....
....
....
....

Academic Vocabulary

The base word of *absorption* is *absorb*. What else can absorb materials? How does this help you understand the term *absorption*?

....
....
....
....
....

HANDS-ON LAB

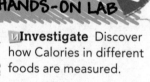

🔬**Investigate** Discover how Calories in different foods are measured.

Main Nutrients The purpose of digestion is the **absorption** of six important nutrients you get from food: carbohydrates, proteins, fats, vitamins, minerals, and water.

Carbohydrates An energy-rich organic compound, such as sugar or a starch, that is made of the elements carbon, hydrogen, and oxygen, is called a **carbohydrate**. They can be quickly broken down and the body can use the energy released in this process. This energy is measured in Calories. High Calorie foods can give you more energy than low Calorie foods.

A carbohydrate can be simple or complex, depending on the size of its molecules. Simple carbohydrates, such as the ones shown in **Figure 2**, are smaller molecules and taste sweet. Complex carbohydrates, such as fiber, are larger molecules. Whole grains, such as brown rice, are considered healthy sources of complex carbohydrates. They are high in fiber and nutrients.

Proteins Your body needs protein for growth and body repair. Proteins are made of smaller components called amino acids. Beans, beef, chicken, eggs, fish, and nuts are all protein sources.

Fats While carbohydrates provide quick energy, fats provide a concentrated energy source and the body also uses fats for long-term energy storage. There are two main types—saturated fat and unsaturated fat. Saturated fats usually come from animal products, such as lard. They are solid at room temperature. People should limit saturated fat intake because they are linked to heart disease and other illnesses. Unsaturated fats usually come from plant products and are oils, such as olive oil. They are liquid at room temperature.

Vitamins Vitamins are nutrients that help your body with chemical reactions. They do not provide any energy or building materials, but without them, you would not be able to function. Your body can make small amounts of some vitamins, such as vitamins D and K, but most come from your diet. Vitamins can be fat-soluble or water-soluble. Fat-soluble vitamins, such as A and K, are stored in the fatty tissues of the body and released when needed. Water-soluble vitamins, such as vitamin C, dissolve in water and are not stored in large amounts by the body. Citrus fruits, such as oranges, are high in vitamin C.

Minerals Minerals are nutrients that are not made by the body, but are needed to carry out chemical processes. Calcium for bones and iron for blood are two examples of minerals that are taken in through the diet. Calcium is common in dairy products, such as milk and cheese. Iron is found in meat and leafy green vegetables, such as spinach.

Water Of the six nutrients you need, water is the most important. While the human body can go a few weeks without eating food, it can only survive a few days without water. Survival time without water hinges on both environmental conditions and level of activity. For example, someone hiking in the desert under a blazing sun needs more water than someone in cooler conditions. You get water from much of the food you eat, but you still need to drink water every day.

INTERACTIVITY

Discover how food is broken down into bits and pieces in the digestive system.

Reflect Consider the different types of food you eat every day. Are they all equally nutritious?

CHECK POINT **Cite Textual Evidence** Underline some recommended sources of the main nutrients your body needs.

Question It

California's State Organic Program (SOP) ensures that California families can get healthy produce from farms that meet strict organic standards. The California Organic Food and Farming Act of 2017 requires farmers who want to sell products labeled organic to register with the California Department of Food and Agriculture.

1. **Conduct Research** Go to HYPERLINK "https://www.cdfa. ca.gov/" and search for "organic program fact sheet."

2. **SEP Obtain Information** According to the fact sheet, how many states have their own organic program? What percentage of organic food sold in the US comes from California?

....

3. **SEP Ask Questions** What would you like to know about California's SOP and its regulations?

....

....

The Digestive Process

Digestion can be classified into two main types—mechanical and chemical. Mechanical digestion involves the physical breakdown and movement of food. Chemical digestion, as the name suggests, involves the chemical breakdown of food.

Mechanical Digestion The mouth and stomach are the main places where mechanical digestion happens. The movement of the food through the esophagus and the intestines is also part of mechanical digestion. Waves of smooth muscle contractions that move food through the esophagus toward the stomach are called **peristalsis**.

Math Toolbox

Monitoring Sodium Intake

Sodium is a mineral that our bodies need to function. It helps our muscular and nervous systems work and it helps us stay hydrated. In certain people, too much salt may lead to high blood pressure, which puts them at risk for heart disease, stroke, and other illnesses.

1. **Analyze Proportional Relationships** According to the nutrition facts for these potato chips, a serving has 170 mg of sodium, or 7% of the daily recommended value for an average adult. Based on this information, how many milligrams of sodium should an average adult consume in a day? Show your work.

   ....

2. **SEP Calculate** How many servings of potato chips would it take for you reach the maximum amount of sodium you should consume in a day? Show your work.

   ....

   ....

3. **SEP Apply Mathematical Concepts** The American Heart Association recommends that adults consume no more than 1500 mg of sodium a day for optimal heart health. How would this change the percentage of the daily recommended \value? How many servings of chips would it take to reach this adjusted maximum daily value?

   ....

   ....

   ....

Nutrition Facts
Serving Size 1 oz (28g/About 15 chips)

Amount Per Serving

Calories 160	Calories from Fat 90

	% Daily Value*
Total Fat 10g	**16%**
Saturated Fat 1.5g	**8%**
Trans Fat 0g	
Cholesterol 0mg	**0%**
Sodium 170mg	**7%**
Potassium 350mg	**10%**
Total Carbohydrate 15g	**5%**
Dietary Fiber 1g	**5%**
Sugars less than 1g	
Protein 2g	

Vitamin A 0%	•	Vitamin C 10%
Calcium 0%	•	Iron 2%
Vitamin E 6%	•	Thiamin 4%
Niacin 6%	•	Vitamin B$_6$ 10%

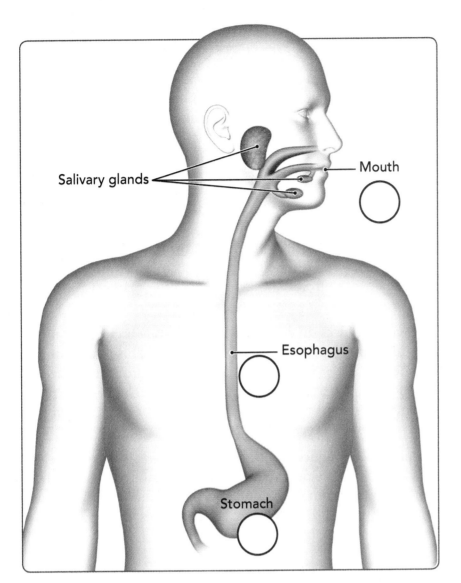

Salivary glands

Mouth

Esophagus

Stomach

Upper Digestive System

Figure 3 The upper digestive system includes the mouth, esophagus, and the stomach.

SEP Synthesize Information

🖊 For each part of the digestive system, write M if mechanical digestion takes place and write C if chemical digestion occurs.

Chemical Digestion

As shown in **Figure 3**, chemical digestion begins in the mouth. Fluid called **saliva** is released from glands in the mouth and plays an important role in both mechanical and chemical digestion. Your saliva contains chemicals. Some of these chemicals are called enzymes. **Enzymes** are proteins that speed up chemical reactions in the body. Enzymes cause the food to break down faster. Chemical digestion starts in the mouth, which is shown in **Figure 3**, with an enzyme found in saliva. This acts specifically on the carbohydrate starch. Saliva also moistens the food so it can be easily swallowed. Chemical digestion continues in the stomach, where other enzymes and hydrochloric acid further break down food. The partially-digested material then passes into the small intestine, where most chemical digestion takes place.

✅ CHECK POINT **Determine Central Ideas** What role do enzymes play on the process of digestion? Explain.

....

....

The Lower Digestive System

By the time food leaves the stomach, it has been broken into very small parts and some of the nutrients have been released. Most of the carbohydrates and proteins have been digested, but fats still remain as large molecules.

The Small Intestine, Liver, and Pancreas

The majority of chemical digestion and nutrient absorption into the blood takes place in the small intestine. Other organs, including the liver and pancreas, shown in **Figure 5**, secrete enzymes into the small intestine to aid with the breakdown of fats and any remaining proteins and carbohydrates. These organs play other roles in the body, but their primary role is to help with the digestion process.

The liver produces an enzyme called bile. Bile breaks down fat into small fat droplets in the small intestine. This allows fat to be digested. Bile is stored in another small organ called the gall bladder. When needed, the gall bladder releases bile into the small intestine. The liver is also responsible for filtering blood and storing certain vitamins.

The pancreas produces an enzyme called trypsin, which breaks down proteins. The pancreas also makes insulin, a chemical involved in a system that monitors blood sugar levels. When a person has Type 1 diabetes, the pancreas does not produce as much insulin as it should.

Got Greens?

Figure 4 Fiber is an important part of a healthy diet. Vegetables are an excellent source of fiber. Because the human body cannot break down fiber, it passes through the digestive system virtually unchanged.

CCC Apply Concepts Why is it important to get plenty of fiber in your diet?

....

....

....

Lower Digestive System

Figure 5 Most chemical digestion takes place in the small intestine.

Interpret Diagrams Why does the gall bladder need to be close to the liver?

....

....

....

....

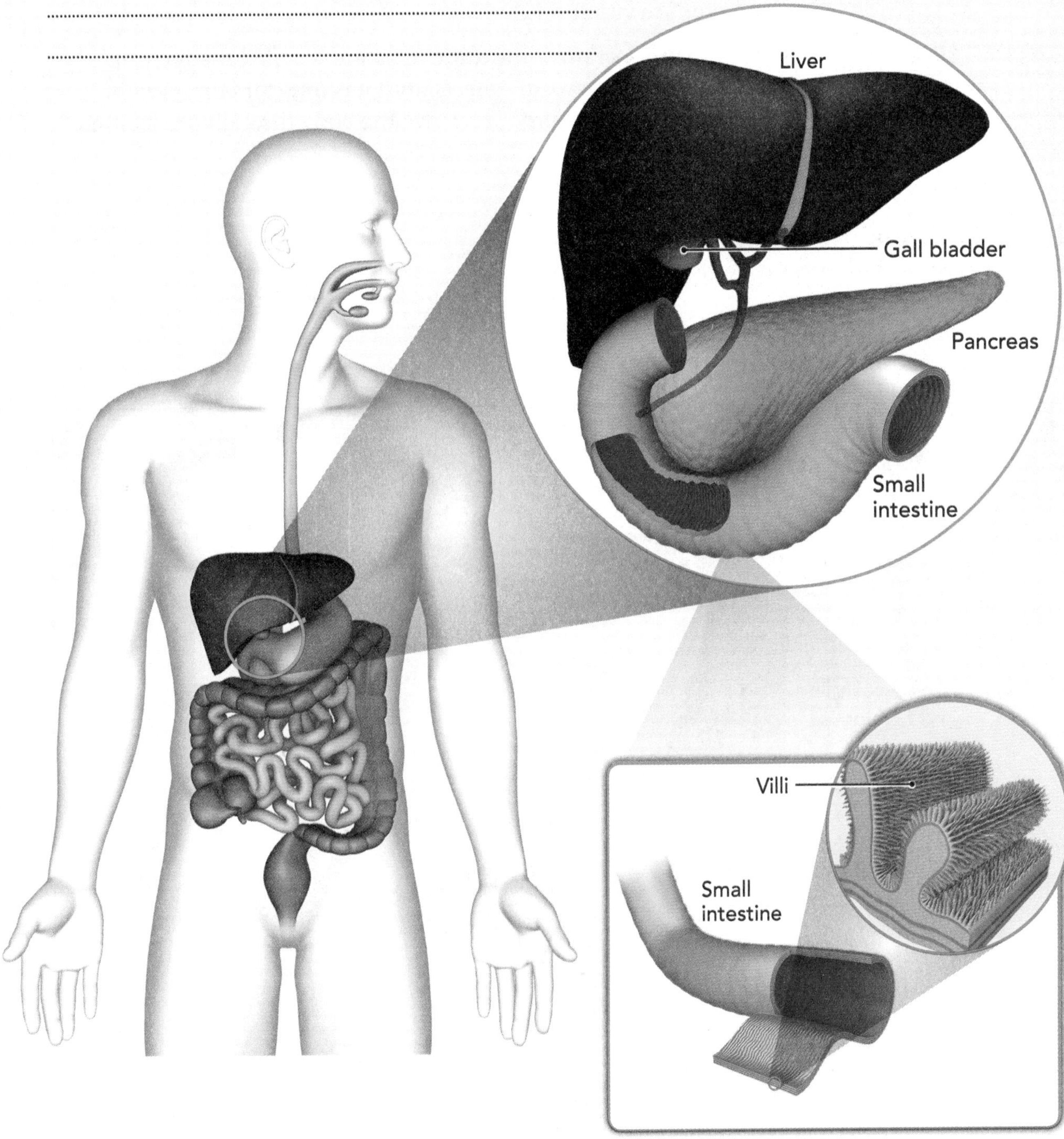

The Large Intestine

As shown in **Figure 6**, the last stage of digestion occurs in the large intestine. The large intestine is actually shorter than the small intestine—1.5 m versus 6–8 m. It is in the large intestine that water from food is reabsorbed and waste products are compacted and prepared for **elimination** from the body. There are many bacteria present in the large intestine. Fortunately, most of them are not dangerous. In fact, many of them are useful. Some of the bacteria produce vitamin K.

The last section of the large intestine is called the rectum. This is where waste collects until it is time for elimination. The solid waste products leave the body through an opening called the anus.

Academic Vocabulary

Use *elimination* in a sentence that uses a context other than digestion.

....

....

....

....

Large Intestine

Figure 6 The large intestine is the last section of the digestive system.

SEP Use Models ✏ Draw a line that shows the pathway waste takes through the large intestine.

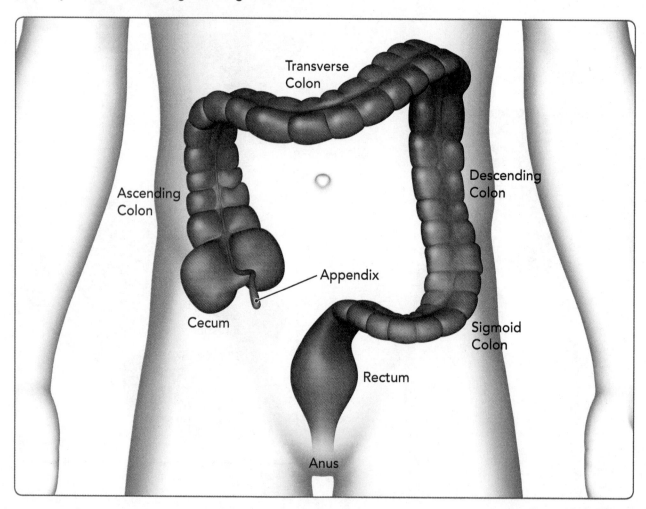

Transverse Colon

Descending Colon

Ascending Colon

Appendix

Cecum

Sigmoid Colon

Rectum

Anus

Human Digestive System

Figure 7 Like all body systems, the digestive system relies on many organs working together.

CCC Analyze Systems ✏ Circle the names of the organs that provide chemicals for your body to perform chemical digestion. Then, place the pathway of food through the body in sequential order from 1 through 6.

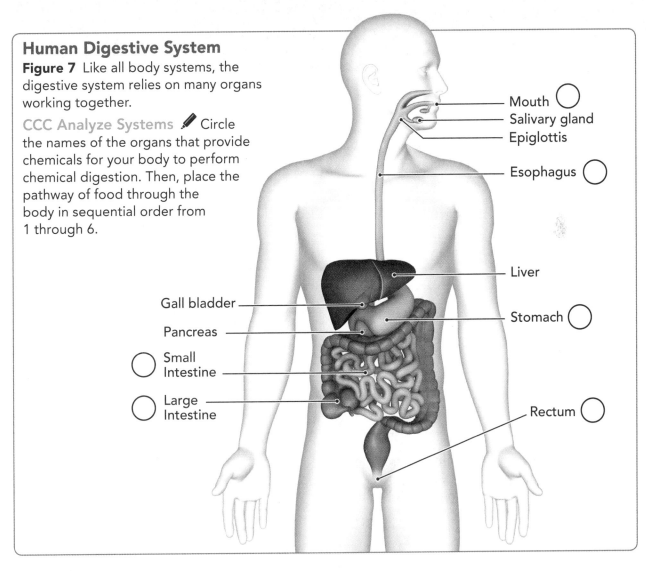

- Mouth ○
- Salivary gland
- Epiglottis
- Esophagus ○
- Liver
- Gall bladder
- Stomach ○
- Pancreas
- ○ Small Intestine
- ○ Large Intestine
- Rectum ○

The Digestive System as a Whole

You have read about the functions of the different organs that make up the digestive system, which are shown in **Figure 7**. It is important to realize that the digestive system is related to many other systems in the human body. For example, after nutrients are absorbed in the small intestine, they are transported around the body in the blood. The pumping of the heart and the rest of the circulatory system make sure all of your cells get the nutrients they need.

INTERACTIVITY

Find out what a day in the life of a cell is like.

☑ CHECK POINT **Write Arguments** Your sister claims that the digestive system works by itself to give your body energy. She states that small branches from the stomach get food to the body cells. Use evidence to support or refute her statement.

....

....

....

....

....

🕐 MS-LS1-3

1. CCC Analyze Systems Suppose your immune system needed help killing a bacterial infection. You took a prescribed antibiotic that killed off all the bacteria in your body. How would this affect your digestive system?

....
....
....
....

2. SEP Cite Evidence How can food labels help determine the amount of nutrients in a food?

....
....
....

3. SEP Construct an Argument By analyzing the nutrients in a food, how would you persuade a classmate that the food is healthy or not? Support your claim.

....
....
....
....
....

4. SEP Distinguish Relationships How does the release of energy and nutrients from digestion help the rest of the body's systems?

....
....
....
....
....

5. Compare and Contrast Both the liver and the pancreas are responsible for producing enzymes that aid in digestion. What other functions do each perform for the body system as a whole?

....
....
....
....
....
....

Quest CHECK-IN

In this lesson, you learned about nutrients that help maintain a healthy body. You also learned about the digestive system and how it supports other body systems.

SEP Evaluate Reasoning Consider how your dietary needs might differ from someone else's and how you might need to modify your diet based on a day's activities. Why is it important to eat a variety of different foods?

....
....
....

👆 **INTERACTIVITY**

Training Table

Go online to investigate the ideal nutrients for different athletes.

MS-LS1-3

Nutritionist

You Can't Order
OUT IN SPACE

Nutritionists and dieticians promote healthy eating habits and develop nutrition plans tailored to an individual's dietary or medical needs. But what if your client is an astronaut?

Space is a microgravity environment, which means astronauts experience near-weightlessness. While floating around seems like fun, it has serious consequences for the human body. Microgravity affects muscle mass, bone density, and cardiovascular health. It also impacts how the body digests food and processes essential vitamins and minerals.

At NASA, nutritionists work with food scientists to develop meals that counteract the harmful effects of living in space. Nutrients such as iron are added to meals to help deal with bone and muscle loss. The challenge for the nutritionists is creating meals that can be prepared and consumed in microgravity!

 VIDEO

Find out how a nutritionist helps people make healthy diet choices.

MY CAREER

Type "nutritionist" or "dietician" into an online search engine to learn more about these careers.

Space food is often packaged in individual meal pouches, similar to the chicken the astronaut is eating.

Chicken

269

Managing Materials

Guiding Questions

- How are materials transported in the body?
- How does the respiratory system interact with other systems to exchange gases?
- How does the excretory system interact with other systems to remove wastes from the body?

Connections

Literacy Draw Evidence

Math Represent Quantitative Relationships

 MS-LS1-3 Use argument supported by evidence for how the body is a system of interacting subsystems composed of groups of cells.

HANDS-ON LAB

ʉInvestigate Find out how your body's systems work together.

Vocabulary

circulatory system
artery
capillary
vein
lymph
bronchi
alveoli
excretion
nephron

Academic Vocabulary

contract

Connect It!

✎ **Draw an arrow to show in which direction the ants are carrying the food.**

Form an Opinion How do you think actions in the human body might be like the system the ants use to transport food?

....

....

....

....

The Circulatory System

Ants, such as the ones in **Figure 1**, are known for cooperating to transport food to their colonies. Your body has a similar system that transports nutrients and other life-sustaining resources. It is called the **circulatory system**, and it includes the cardiovascular system and the lymphatic system. In addition to bringing nutrients and oxygen to the cells, the circulatory system also removes waste products and helps to fight off diseases and infections.

The main structure of the circulatory system is the heart. This fist-sized organ has the never-ending job of pumping blood around the body. The heart is a muscle that **contracts** and relaxes constantly in order to do its job. Your heart beats around 100,000 times every day. Blood moves from the heart to the lungs and then back to the heart again before it is transported out to the body. Blood moving through the vessels allows for the exchange of gases and brings nutrients to all the cells. For this reason, blood is often called the "river of life."

HANDS-ON LAB

Explore the connection between your heart and breathing.

Academic Vocabulary

What are some other words you can think of that are synonyms for *contracts*?

....

....

Transporting Materials
Figure 1. Just as the circulatory system moves materials in your body, these ants transport food to their colony

INTERACTIVITY

Explore the highways and byways that make up the body's circulatory system.

Reflect Trace the journey of a molecule of oxygen from the time it enters your body until it reaches a muscle in your fingertip. Describe each step of the process.

The Cardiovascular System

The part of the circulatory system that pumps blood throughout the body is the cardiovascular system. In this system, the heart pumps blood through the body using the various blood vessels. Start on the right side of **Figure 2**.

Blood travels from the lungs to the left atrium down to the left ventricle. It then takes nutrients and oxygen to the cells of the body, where it picks up waste products, such as carbon dioxide. The blood returns through the right atrium. It goes down to the right ventricle, and out to the lungs where gas is exchanged. Then, the process starts all over again.

This continuous process of pumping blood is a double loop system, as shown in **Figure 3**. In loop one, the blood travels from the heart to the lungs and then back to the heart. In loop two, the oxygenated blood moves from the heart out to the body and deoxygenated blood is returned to the heart.

Special cells called red blood cells play a key role in transporting oxygen throughout the body. They take up oxygen in the lungs and deliver it to cells throughout the body. Red blood cells also absorb carbon dioxide in the body and transport it to the lungs, where it is released from the body.

Structure of the Heart

Figure 2 The human heart has four main chambers. Each upper chamber is called an atrium and each lower chamber is called a ventricle. The right ventricle has a special collection of cells called the pacemaker that keeps the heart beating in a regular rhythm. Label the four chambers of the heart.

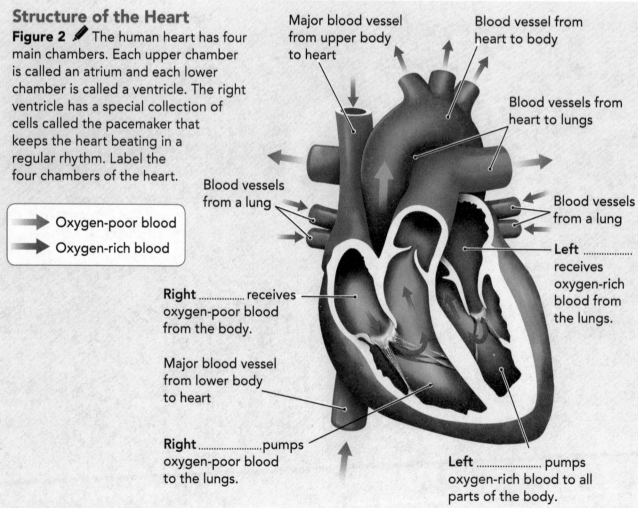

Oxygen-poor blood

Oxygen-rich blood

Major blood vessel from upper body to heart

Blood vessel from heart to body

Blood vessels from heart to lungs

Blood vessels from a lung

Blood vessels from a lung

Left .... receives oxygen-rich blood from the lungs.

Right .... receives oxygen-poor blood from the body.

Major blood vessel from lower body to heart

Right .... pumps oxygen-poor blood to the lungs.

Left .... pumps oxygen-rich blood to all parts of the body.

Double Loop System

Figure 3 ✏ Blood flows from the right atrium to the right ventricle and then to the lungs through a special artery called the pulmonary artery. Here it gets oxygenated and then is pumped back to the heart by way of the pulmonary vein. Draw arrows to show the direction of the blood flow.

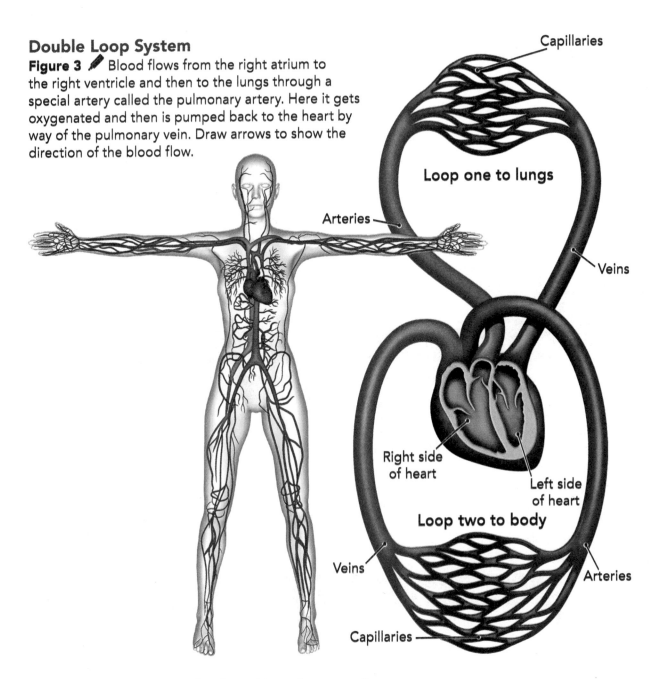

Capillaries

Loop one to lungs

Arteries

Veins

Right side of heart

Left side of heart

Loop two to body

Veins

Arteries

Capillaries

Transport Through the Circulatory System

You know that the main function of the circulatory system is to move materials, such as nutrients and oxygen, to all of the cells of the body. A series of vessels makes this process possible.

Blood Vessels Your heart is connected to the rest of your body through a system of vessels, which are illustrated in **Figure 3**. Not all vessels in the body are the same. Different vessels have different structures and functions. An **artery** carries blood away from the heart. It is a thick-walled and muscular vessel. On the other hand, a **vein** carries blood back to the heart. It has thinner walls than arteries. A **capillary** is a tiny vessel where substances are exchanged between the blood and body cells. Capillaries can be thought of as connecting arteries and veins.

CHECK POINT

Summarize Text What are the three main types of blood vessels and what are their jobs?

....

....

....

....

....

Diffusion Oxygen and other materials move through capillary walls by diffusion. In diffusion, materials move from an area of high concentration to one of lower concentration. For example, blood contains more glucose than cells do. As a result, glucose diffuses from the blood into body cells

Blood Pressure The force with which ventricles of the heart contract is what creates blood pressure. This pumping action is what you feel when you are aware of your heartbeat or pulse. The pumping action of the ventricles is strong enough to push blood throughout your body. Without blood pressure, blood would not be able to reach all parts of your body.

Math Toolbox

Exercise and Blood Flow Rate

Your heart pumps more blood through your body when you exercise. The rate of blood flow, however, does not increase in all parts of your body. The table shows how the rate of blood flow changes for different parts of the body during intense exercise.

Represent Quantitative Relationships

✏️ Draw a bar graph to represent the data in the table. Show the difference between the blood flow rate while the body is resting and exercising intensely.

Body Part	Blood Flow Rate, cm^3/min	
	Resting	Intense Exercise
Brain	750	750
Heart Muscle	250	750
Kidneys	1,100	600
Skeletal Muscle	1,200	12,500
Skin	500	1,800

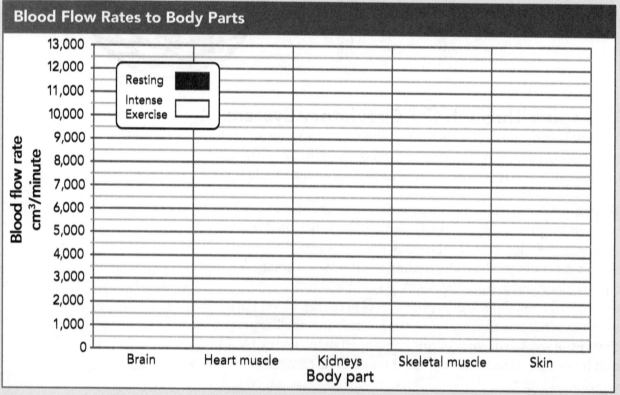

Blood Flow Rates to Body Parts

The Lymphatic System

Figure 4 🖊 The lymphatic system is part of the circulatory system. Its main function is to transport components of blood back into the circulatory system. On the diagram, label the lymph nodes and the lymph vessels.

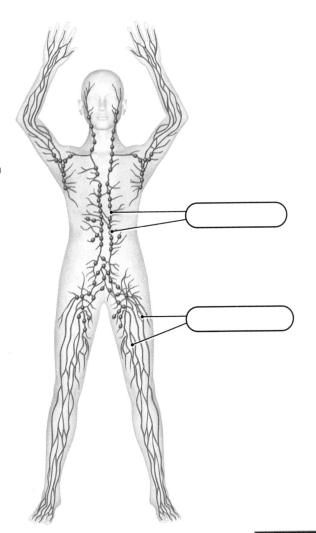

The Lymphatic System

In addition to red blood cells, blood also contains white blood cells, platelets, and plasma. White blood cells fight off diseases. Platelets help clot wounds. Plasma is the liquid part of the blood. As these components of blood move through the cardiovascular system, the fluid moves into the surrounding tissues. From here it needs to move back into the bloodstream. This job is done by the other component of the circulatory system—the lymphatic system. As shown in **Figure 4**, the lymphatic system is a network of vessels that returns fluid to the bloodstream.

Once the fluid is inside the lymphatic system, it is called **lymph** and consists of water, white blood cells, and dissolved materials such as glucose. Lymph flows through vessels called lymph vessels. The vessels connect to small knobs of tissue called lymph nodes, which filter lymph, trapping bacteria and other disease-causing microorganisms in the fluid.

☑️ CHECK POINT **Determine Central Ideas** The lymphatic system helps to remove bacteria and other microorganisms from the body. Why would this be important for you?

....

....

Literacy Connection

Draw Evidence Summarize the evidence on this page that supports the statement that the systems of the body work together to keep the body healthy.

....

....

....

....

....

....

....

....

....

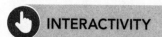

INTERACTIVITY

Investigate how the circulatory and respiratory systems respond to changes in the environment.

Respiratory System

Take a deep breath in. Now let it out. You have just used your respiratory system, shown along with the circulatory and digestive systems in **Figure 5**. It is the job of the respiratory system to bring air containing oxygen into your body and remove carbon dioxide and water from your body. The lungs are the main organs of the system. Other structures include the nose, which moistens the air you breathe, the trachea (windpipe), the **bronchi** (the two passages that direct air into to the lungs), and the **alveoli** (tiny thin-walled sacs of lung tissue where gases can move between air and blood).

The terms *respiration* and *breathing* are often used interchangeably. However, while they are related, they are different processes. *Respiration* refers to cellular respiration, the process cells use to break down glucose in order to produce energy. Cellular respiration requires oxygen and produces carbon dioxide as a waste product. Breathing is the exchange of gases between the inside and outside of the body. The gases exchanged are oxygen and carbon dioxide. Cellular respiration could not occur without breathing.

Systems Work Together

Figure 5 ✏ Cellular respiration and breathing both require body systems working together. Circle the body system responsible for the exchange of gases. Complete the labels.

Form an Opinion How do you think having a strong respiratory system helps the circulatory system?

....

....

....

....

....

....

....

....

....

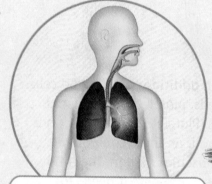

.... **system**
This system moves................,
which contains ....,
into the body.

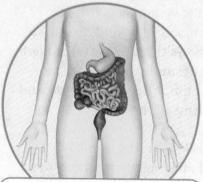

.... **system**
This system provides glucose used in ....

.... **system**
The blood picks up....................
and .... and delivers them to body cells.

Breathing and Gas Exchange

Figure 6 🖊 Complete the diagram labels on the right. In each diagram below, draw an arrow below the diaphragm to show the direction the lungs and diaphragm move when we breathe.

Apply Concepts Pneumonia is an infection people can get in their lungs. It causes the alveoli in your lungs to fill with fluid. How do you think this disease affects breathing?

....

....

....

....

Capillary

.... moving
.... alveolus
into ....

....
moving.................the
alveolus from blood

alveolus

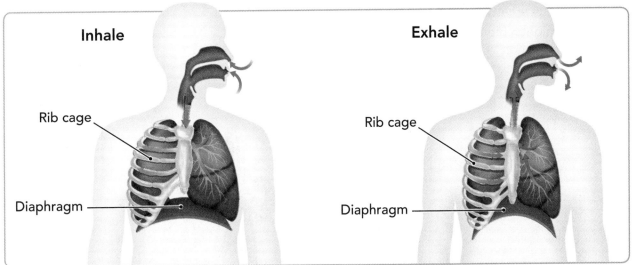

Inhale

Rib cage

Diaphragm

Exhale

Rib cage

Diaphragm

The Breathing Process

When you inhale, your rib muscles and diaphragm contract as shown in **Figure 6**. The chest moves upward and outward as it expands. The air pressure within the lungs lowers, so air moves in. When you exhale, the opposite happens. The muscles relax and the chest lowers. The pressure within the lungs is increased, so air is forced out.

Process of Gas Exchange

Gases move between the alveoli and the blood. After air enters the alveoli, oxygen passes through the capillary walls into the blood. At the same time, carbon dioxide and water pass from the blood into the alveoli. This continual exchange maintains the correct concentrations of gases within the blood.

✓ CHECK POINT **Draw Evidence** How is the respiratory system interconnected with other systems of the body?

....

....

....

INTERACTIVITY

Investigate how human body systems work together to maintain homeostasis during long-term physical activity.

Excretory System

The process of removing wastes is called **excretion**. The excretory system, which is illustrated in **Figure 7**, removes waste chemicals from the body. The main organs of this system are the kidneys, urinary bladder, urethra, lungs, skin, and liver. All of these organs work together to rid the body of waste. As your cells perform their various functions, they produce waste products. These include carbon dioxide, excess water, and other materials. These wastes need to be removed from the body in order to maintain homeostasis.

Excretion and the Kidneys

Figure 7 🖊 The kidneys are two of the main organs of the excretory system. Label the kidneys and the urinary bladder.

Infer How might a blockage in the ureter impact the excretion of wastes from the body?

....

....

....

....

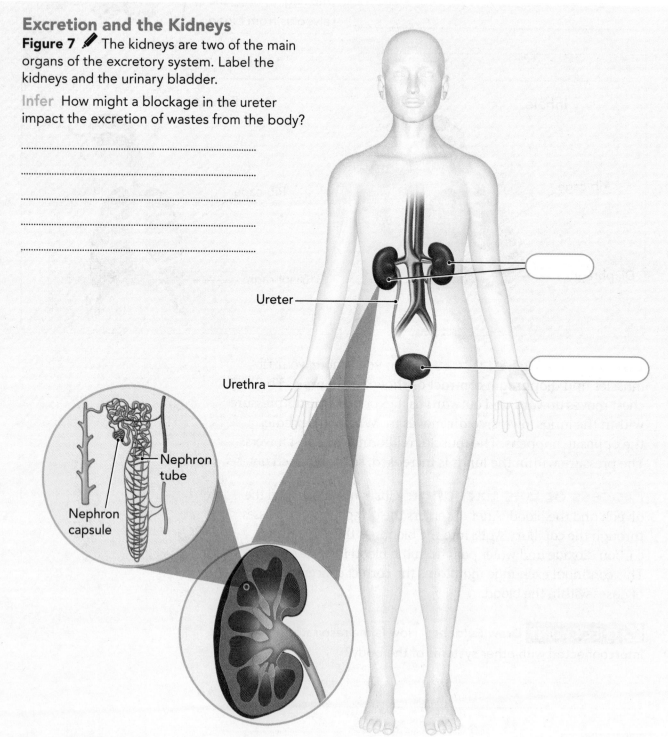

Kidneys The kidneys are two bean-shaped organs that filter blood and regulate the amount of water in the body. The kidneys remove water and urea, a chemical produced from the breakdown of proteins. While the lungs remove some water, most water is excreted from the body in the form of urine, which includes water and urea. Liquid waste collects in the urinary bladder and is expelled through the urethra.

Each kidney is composed of millions of tiny tubes called nephrons. A **nephron** is a small filtering structure in the kidneys that removes wastes from blood and produces urine. This filtration process happens in two stages. First, the nephrons filter both the wastes and the needed materials from the blood. Next, the needed materials are returned to the blood and wastes are excreted.

Like all organs, kidneys can be damaged or diseased. Causes of kidney disease include birth defects, uncontrolled diabetes, or high blood pressure. Humans have two kidneys, and a healthy donor can live comfortably with one. But you do need one healthy kidney. For those reasons, kidneys are the most often transplanted organ in the U.S. More than 17,000 kidneys were transplanted in a recent year, but that left more than 80,000 people waiting for kidney transplants.

HANDS-ON LAB

Investigate Find out how your body's systems work together.

California Centers
Figure 8 California is home to several internationally known organ donation and transplant centers. They include the Stanford Kidney and Pancreas Transplant Building, the UC Davis Transplant Center, and the California Pacific Medical Center in San Francisco.

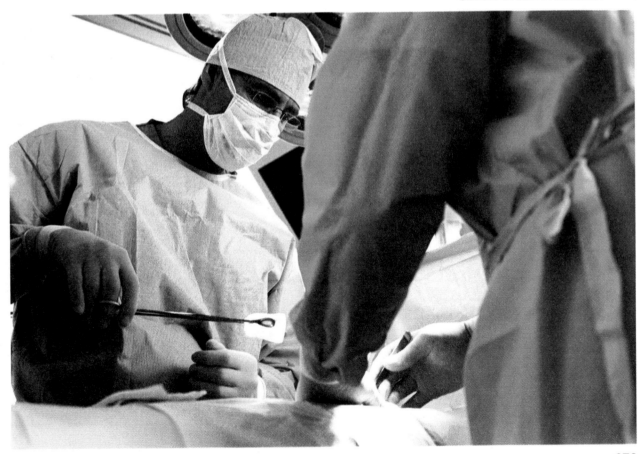

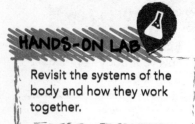
The Lungs, Skin, and Liver

The respiratory system, digestive system, and integumentary system work with the excretory system to remove wastes from the body. When you exhale, you are not only removing carbon dioxide from the body, but some water as well. Your integumentary system, which includes your skin (**Figure 9**), also removes waste. Sweat glands in your skin release water from your cells to help cool your body. Sweat also contains a small amount of urea. The liver produces urea from proteins and other wastes, including pieces of old red blood cells. Removing waste products from the body helps maintain homeostasis. However, if a disease or some blockage prevents these products from being removed, the body's internal environment can become toxic.

✅ **CHECK POINT** **Read and Comprehend** What are three ways your body excretes waste?

....

....

....

....

....

....

Skin and Excretion

Figure 9 🖊 As your body temperature rises, your sweat glands release water to help cool you off. Sweat is a form of excretion. Circle where a bead of sweat would form on the surface of the skin.

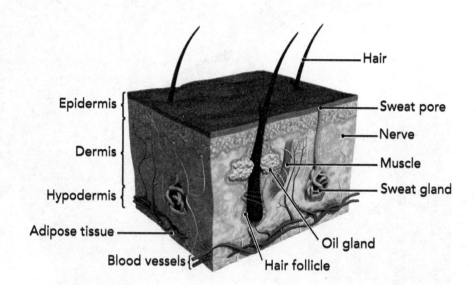

Epidermis

Dermis

Hypodermis

Adipose tissue

Blood vessels

Hair

Sweat pore

Nerve

Muscle

Sweat gland

Oil gland

Hair follicle

☑ LESSON 4 Check

MS-LS1-3

1. **Identify** What are the major organs of the circulatory system?

....
....
....
....
....

2. **SEP Use Mathematics** Using the Math Toolbox table, complete the equation below to calculate how much more blood flows per minute to the skeletal muscles during intense exercise than during rest.

exercising = ... cm³/minute

resting = 1,200 cm³/minute

1,200

3. **SEP Cite Evidence** How do the circulatory and respiratory systems work together to transport gases to all parts of the body?

....
....
....
....
....
....
....
....
....

4. **CCC Analyze Systems** How does the excretory system remove wastes from the blood of the circulatory system?

....
....
....
....

Quest CHECK-IN

In this lesson, you learned about the structures and functions of the circulatory, respiratory, and excretory systems. You also learned how these systems work together to manage materials that go into and out of your body.

CCC Analyze Systems Consider how your body systems interact when you train for your favorite sport. How does physical exertion impact your heart, lungs, and kidneys?

....
....
....
....
....

HANDS-ON LAB

Heart Beat, Health Beat

Go online and download the lab to explore how physical activity affects heart and perspiration rates.

Controlling Processes

Guiding Questions

- Which systems control processes in the human body?
- How does the body sense and respond to stimuli in the environment?
- How do the cells that make up the nervous system respond to stimuli?

Connection

Literacy Integrate with Visuals

 MS-LS1-8 Gather and synthesize information that sensory receptors respond to stimuli by sending messages to the brain for immediate behavior or storage as memories.

HANDS-ON LAB

Investigate Explore the different parts of the nervous system.

Vocabulary

neuron
synapse
brain
spinal cord
gland
negative
  feedback
reflex

Academic Vocabulary

impulse

Connect It !

✏ **Circle the stimulus in the image that may cause the diver to respond.**

SEP Construct Explanations What senses is the diver using to receive information about this encounter? Explain.

....

....

CCC Cause and Effect Why would the diver know to respond to the stimulus? Explain.

....

....

....

Nervous System

The Internet allows us to communicate quickly with friends near and far. The nervous system is your body's communication network. Your nervous system receives information about what is happening both inside and outside your body. Then it directs how your body responds to this information. For example, in **Figure 1**, the diver's nervous system responds to the information it receives about the sharks. Your nervous system also helps maintain homeostasis, which keeps your internal environment stable. Your nervous system consists of your brain, spinal cord, and nerves.

Like any system, the human nervous system is made up of organs and tissues. A cell that carries information through the nervous system is called a nerve cell, or **neuron**. The structure of a neuron helps it function. Neurons are made up of dendrites and axons. A dendrite is the branched structure that picks up information. The axon receives information from the dendrite and sends it away from the cell.

The nervous system is divided into two systems: the central nervous system (CNS) and the peripheral nervous system (PNS). The brain and spinal cord make up the CNS. The job of the CNS is to control most of the functions of the body and mind. The PNS is a network of nerves that branches out from the CNS and connects to the rest of the body.

HANDS-ON LAB

Test how your knee responds to an external stimulus.

Reflect In your notebook, describe three instances in which your body seems to react to something in the environment, without any thought or conscious decision on your part.

Reacting to the Environment

Figure 1 The diver's encounter with sharks provides stimuli that will result in both immediate reactions and lasting memories.

Student Discourse

Choose a partner and brainstorm the meanings of the terms electromagnetic, mechanical, and chemical. Then for each, come up with a type of stimulus, and a type of sensory receptor in your body that stimulus might affect. (For example, sunlight is an electromagnetic stimulus that affects your eyes.)

Academic Vocabulary

Many people say, "that was an impulse purchase." Use your understanding of the word *impulse* to explain the context in which the author is using the term in the paragraph.

....

....

....

Neurons

The nervous system is made up of three kinds of neurons. A sensory neuron in a sensory receptor (such as an eye) picks up an electromagnetic, mechanical, or chemical stimulus from inside or outside the body. It then converts the stimulus into a message. An interneuron carries this message from one neuron to another. A motor neuron sends the message to a muscle or gland, which reacts.

Nerve Impulses

The function of a neuron is to transmit information. When the dendrite receives information, the neuron sends the information along the cell through the long axon. The message carried by the neuron is called a nerve impulse. The axon transmits the **impulse** to nearby cells.

Synapse

As shown in **Figure 2**, the junction where one neuron can transfer an impulse to another neuron is called a **synapse**. At the axon tips, electrical signals change to chemical signals. This allows the signal to bridge the gap and continue to the next neuron. The impulse is converted to an electrical signal again, and travels through the neuron to another neighboring one.

☑ CHECK POINT **Interpret Visuals** Identify the path that the nerve impulse will take, starting and ending with the dendrite.

....

....

Signal and Synapse

Figure 2 ✏ Synapses are gaps between neurons where the impulse changes from electrical to chemical and back again. Draw an arrow on the diagram to indicate the direction the nerve impulse is traveling.

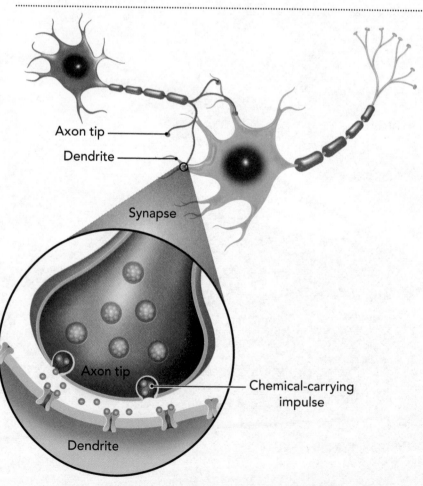

Axon tip

Dendrite

Synapse

Axon tip

Chemical-carrying impulse

Dendrite

Parts of the Nervous System

Figure 3 The brain sits atop the human nervous system, with bundled neurons branching out from the spinal cord.

CCC Cause and Effect What could happen if the brain stem were damaged?

....

....

....

....

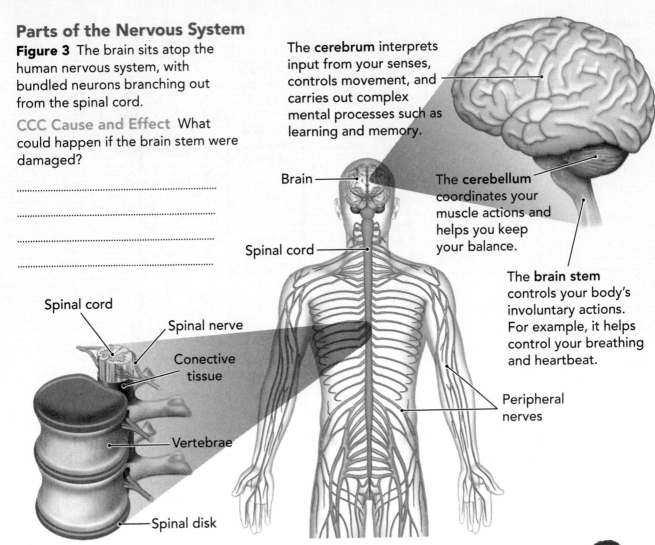

The **cerebrum** interprets input from your senses, controls movement, and carries out complex mental processes such as learning and memory.

Brain

The **cerebellum** coordinates your muscle actions and helps you keep your balance.

Spinal cord

The **brain stem** controls your body's involuntary actions. For example, it helps control your breathing and heartbeat.

Peripheral nerves

Spinal cord

Spinal nerve

Conective tissue

Vertebrae

Spinal disk

Central Nervous System The central nervous system, which is shown in **Figure 3**, controls the functions of the body. The **brain** is the part of the CNS that is located in the skull and controls most functions of the body. The **spinal cord** is a thick column of nervous tissue that links the brain to most of the nerves that branch out through the body. Most stimuli travel through the spinal cord to the brain. The brain then directs a response, usually back out through the spinal cord.

The Brain The human brain has about 100 billion neurons, all of which are interneurons. These interneurons handle thousands of messages each day. The brain is covered by layers of connective tissue and fluid that help protect the brain from injury. The brain itself has three main components. These control voluntary and involuntary actions such as heart rate, memory, and muscular coordination.

The Spinal Cord The vertebral column that you can feel with your fingers down the length of your neck and back contains the spinal cord. Like the brain, layers of connective tissue surround the spinal cord, along with a layer of fluid.

HANDS-ON LAB

Investigate Explore the different parts of the nervous system.

Nerve Pairs

Figure 4 Each nerve pair is connected to specific parts of the body.

SEP Obtain Information Referring back to Figure 3, which parts of the body do you think the thoracic nerve pairs communicate with?

....

....

....

....

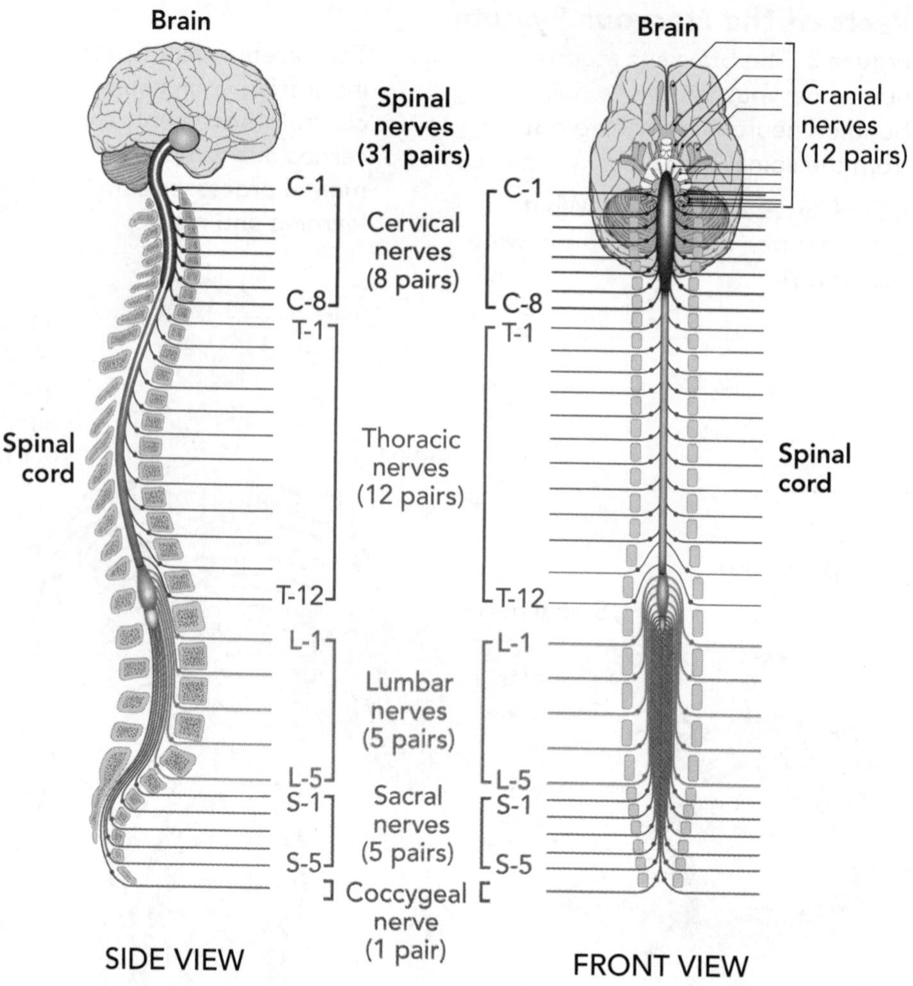

Brain

Spinal nerves (31 pairs)

Spinal cord

C-1

Cervical nerves (8 pairs)

C-8
T-1

Thoracic nerves (12 pairs)

T-12
L-1

Lumbar nerves (5 pairs)

L-5
S-1

Sacral nerves (5 pairs)

S-5

] **Coccygeal nerve (1 pair)** [

SIDE VIEW

Brain

Cranial nerves (12 pairs)

C-1

C-8
T-1

Spinal cord

T-12
L-1

L-5
S-1

S-5

FRONT VIEW

Autonomic Response

Figure 5 🖉 One of these pupils is responding to darkness, while the other is responding to light. Circle the eye that is responding bright light.

Contraction of round muscles of the iris constricts pupil.

Contraction of radial muscles of the iris dilates pupil.

Peripheral Nervous System
The network of nerves that connects the central nervous system to the rest of the body is called the peripheral nervous system. It has 43 pairs of nerves, as shown in **Figure 4**, and controls both involuntary and voluntary actions. Twelve pairs of nerves begin in the brain and branch out to parts of the head, while the other pairs begin in the spinal cord and branch out through the torso from the spine. In each nerve pair, one nerve goes to the left side of the body and the other goes to the right. Each spinal nerve has axons of sensory and motor neurons. Sensory neurons bring impulses to the central nervous system. Motor neurons carry impulses from the central nervous system out to the body.

Somatic and Autonomic Systems
The peripheral nervous system has two groups of nerves. The somatic nervous system controls voluntary actions, like typing a text message or throwing a ball. The autonomic nervous system controls involuntary actions, such as digestion or pupil dilation (**Figure 5**).

Reflexes The involuntary reaction of jumping when you hear a loud noise is called a **reflex**. It is an automatic response that occurs without conscious control. While skeletal muscles are largely within your conscious control through the somatic nervous system, some skeletal muscle contractions occur without the brain's involvement.

Pain is one type of stimulus that can trigger what is known as a reflex arc. Sensory neurons detect a pain stimulus, such as sticking your finger on a sharp object (**Figure 6**), and send impulses to the spinal cord. Interneurons in the spinal cord carry the impulses directly to motor neurons in the arm and hand. These motor neurons trigger muscle contractions in the hand to bring the fingertip away from the painful stimulus. At the same time, pain impulses travel to the brain, where they can be interpreted and stored as memories. This is how we learn to not press our fingertips against things like cactus spines and fishhooks.

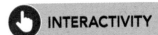

INTERACTIVITY

Find out how the human brain stacks up against a computer.

✅ CHECK POINT **Sequence** What is the sequence of neurons involved in a reflex arc?

Model It

Learning from Experience

Figure 6 The hooks on this fishing lure would cause pain if you accidentally snagged them on your fingertip.

SEP Develop Models ✏ In the space, draw a diagram of a brain, spine, arm, and hand. Use arrows and labels to model a reflex arc showing how a person would react to getting snagged by a hook. Also show how pain impulses would reach the brain and result in a memory of the experience.

Gigantism

Figure 7 If a person ends up with too much or too little growth hormone, his or her height will be affected.

SEP Identify Unknowns What do you think are some possible health problems of someone with gigantism? Explain.

....

....

....

....

Endocrine System

The human body has two systems that maintain homeostasis: the nervous system and the endocrine system. The nervous system maintains homeostasis by sending nerve impulses throughout the body. The endocrine system regulates the body by releasing chemicals called hormones, such as those that regulate height (**Figure 7**). The endocrine system is made up of different glands. A **gland** is an organ that produces and releases chemicals through ducts or into the bloodstream. The hormones of the endocrine system and the glands that regulate them are shown in **Figure 8**.

Regulators One of the links between the nervous system and the endocrine system is the hypothalamus. This gland is located deep inside the brain, just above the spinal cord. Its function is to send out nerve and chemical signals. Its nerve signals control sleep, hunger, and other basic body processes. It produces hormones—chemicals signals that regulate other glands and organs of the endocrine system.

Below the hypothalamus is the pituitary gland. This pea-sized gland receives signals from the hypothalamus and releases hormones. Some of these hormones are signals to other endocrine glands. Others, such as growth hormone, go to work directly on different body tissues.

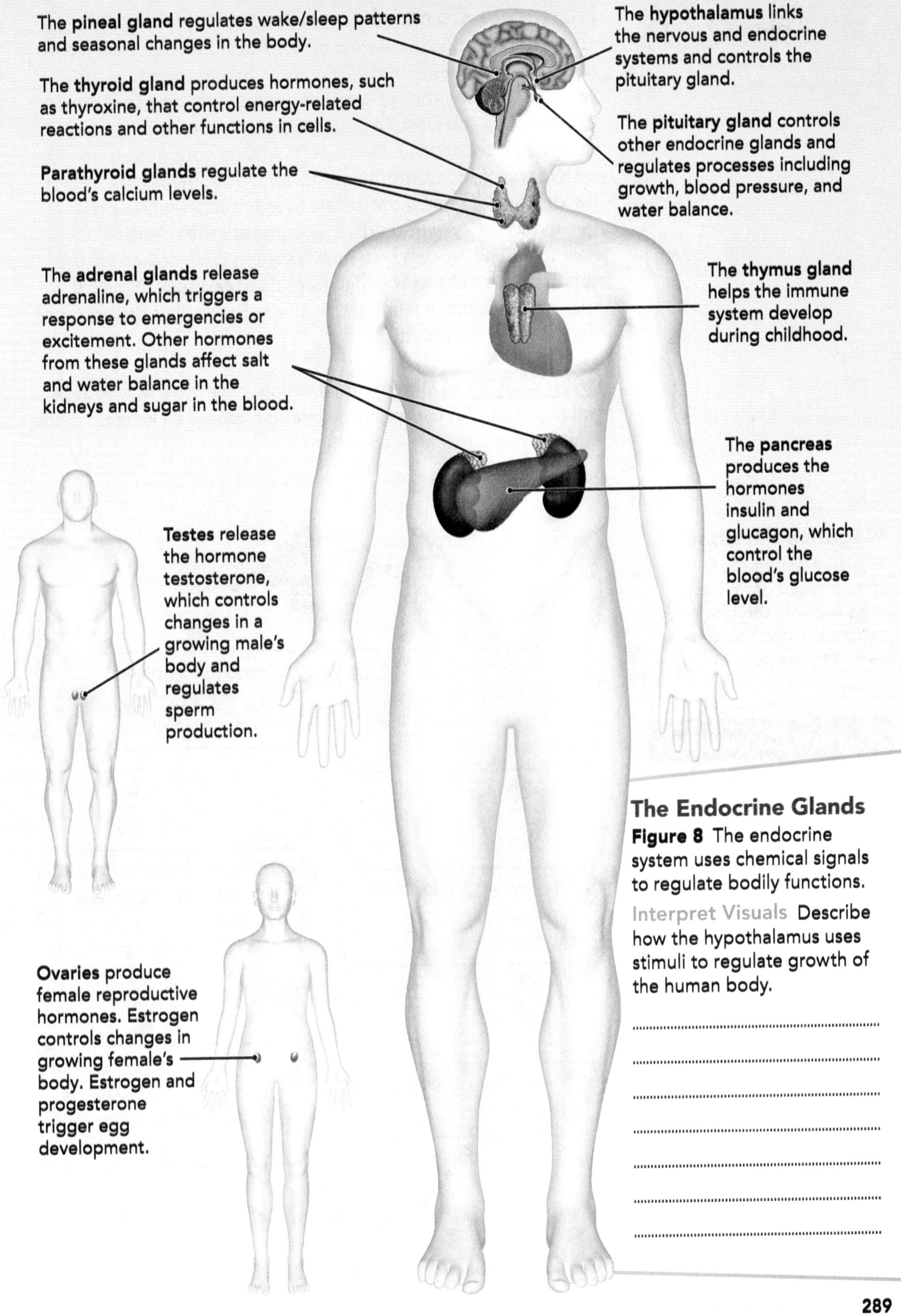

The **pineal gland** regulates wake/sleep patterns and seasonal changes in the body.

The **thyroid gland** produces hormones, such as thyroxine, that control energy-related reactions and other functions in cells.

Parathyroid glands regulate the blood's calcium levels.

The **adrenal glands** release adrenaline, which triggers a response to emergencies or excitement. Other hormones from these glands affect salt and water balance in the kidneys and sugar in the blood.

Testes release the hormone testosterone, which controls changes in a growing male's body and regulates sperm production.

Ovaries produce female reproductive hormones. Estrogen controls changes in growing female's body. Estrogen and progesterone trigger egg development.

The **hypothalamus** links the nervous and endocrine systems and controls the pituitary gland.

The **pituitary gland** controls other endocrine glands and regulates processes including growth, blood pressure, and water balance.

The **thymus gland** helps the immune system develop during childhood.

The **pancreas** produces the hormones insulin and glucagon, which control the blood's glucose level.

The Endocrine Glands

Figure 8 The endocrine system uses chemical signals to regulate bodily functions.

Interpret Visuals Describe how the hypothalamus uses stimuli to regulate growth of the human body.

....

....

....

....

....

....

....

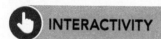

INTERACTIVITY

Test your reflexes.

Hormone Control Suppose you open the refrigerator and grab the milk. While you pour yourself a glass, you leave the door open. Because this increases the temperature inside your refrigerator, the compressor will turn on and cool the interior after you close the door. Once it is cool enough, the compressor turns off. Like the refrigerator, your endocrine system works to maintain equilibrium, or homeostasis. When the amount of a hormone in the blood reaches a certain level, the endocrine system sends signals to stop the release of that hormone. The process by which a system is turned off by the condition it produces is called **negative feedback**. **Figure 9** shows how negative feedback regulates the level of the hormone thyroxine in the blood.

✓ CHECK POINT **Determine Meaning** What type of feedback would you call it if the resulting condition caused an increase in the effect that produces the condition?

Negative Feedback
Figure 9 When the level of a released hormone is high enough, the feedback causes the body to stop releasing the hormone.

Literacy Connection

Integrate with Visuals
✐ Underline the names of endocrine glands in the diagram, and circle the caption that describes when negative feedback is provided.

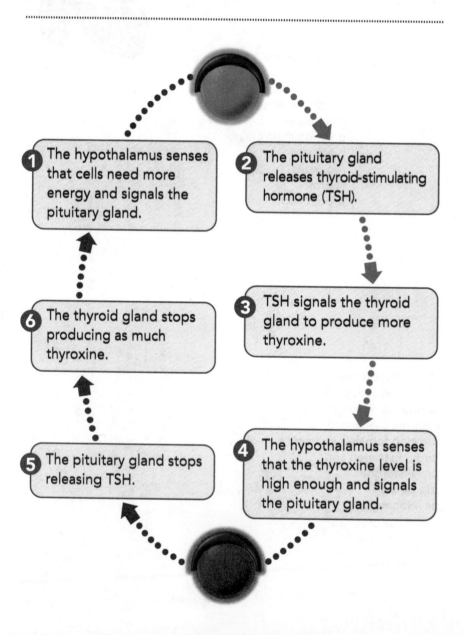

1 The hypothalamus senses that cells need more energy and signals the pituitary gland.

2 The pituitary gland releases thyroid-stimulating hormone (TSH).

3 TSH signals the thyroid gland to produce more thyroxine.

4 The hypothalamus senses that the thyroxine level is high enough and signals the pituitary gland.

5 The pituitary gland stops releasing TSH.

6 The thyroid gland stops producing as much thyroxine.

☑LESSON 5 Check

1. **Identify** What is the name for the division of the nervous system that handles involuntary actions and processes of the body?

....

2. **CCC Analyze Systems** What are the two main physical components of the central nervous system?

....

3. **CCC Cause and Effect** Describe the two signals and pathways that are activated when you touch something and experience pain.

....
....
....
....
....
....
....
....
....

4. **SEP Obtain Information** Describe the role chemical signals play in both the nervous system and the endocrine system.

....
....
....
....
....
....

5. **SEP Synthesize Information** Why would it be advantageous to have two separate pathways to react to and learn from (memories of) pain?

....
....
....
....
....
....
....
....

Quest CHECK-IN

In this lesson, you learned how the nervous system and endocrine system regulate the body and respond to stimuli from the environment.

SEP Communicate The brain is able to learn and make memories. How does this ability, along with motor neuron coordination, help you to improve physical performance?

....
....
....
....

☝ INTERACTIVITY

Why Practice Makes Perfect

Go online to explore how athletes develop muscle memory.

1 Body Organization

MS-LS1-3

1. Because its structure is more complex,
   A. a tissue can have a more complex function than an organ.
   B. a cell can have a more complex function than a tissue.
   C. an organ can have a more complex function than a tissue.
   D. a cell can have a more complex function than an organ.

2. **CCC Patterns** What is the relationship among organs, cells, and tissues?

....

....

....

....

2 Systems Interacting

MS-LS1-3

3. The main purpose of homeostasis is to
   A. fight disease-causing organisms.
   B. keep internal conditions stable.
   C. produce offspring.
   D. replicate DNA.

4. **SEP Explain Phenomena** Suppose you sit in the same position so long that your leg starts to hurt. How do the body's different parts interact to stop the pain?

....

....

....

....

....

....

3 Supplying Energy

MS-LS1-3

5. The liver helps the circulatory system by
   A. filtering blood of harmful substances.
   B. helping blood vessels to absorb nutrients.
   C. storing bile that is released into the bloodstream.
   D. releasing chemicals that begin to break down food in the mouth.

6. .... in the stomach are responsible for the mechanical digestion that takes place there.

7. **SEP Develop Models** Draw a flow chart to show how the digestive, circulatory, and excretory systems work together to process food and supply nutrients to the body.

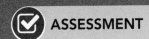
4 Managing Materials

MS-LS1-3

8. Which of the following organs function as both a respiratory organ and an excretory organ?
  A. liver   **B.** skin
  C. kidneys   **D.** lungs

9. Organs such as the kidneys, lungs, skin, and liver work together to
  A. remove carbon dioxide.
  B. eliminate excess water.
  C. help maintain homeostasis.
  D. filter out urea.

10. One role of rib bones in the .... system is to protect the heart from physical injury.

11. CCC Relate Structure and Function How does the structure of the alveoli in the lungs help with their function in the respiratory system?

....

....

....

....

....

12. SEP Construct Explanations Explain how the respiratory and circulatory systems work together to manage materials in the body.

....

....

....

....

....

....

....

5 Controlling Processes

MS-LS1-8

13. The spinal cord is a thick column of
  A. blood vessels that helps to support and hold up the body.
  B. bony discs that protects nervous tissue.
  C. muscle tissue that connects nerve cells in the brain with nerve cells in the body.
  D. nervous tissue that connects the brain to the body's nerves.

14. The .... system releases hormones that .... processes in the body.

15. CCC Analyze Systems How does the nervous system regulate basic body processes?

....

....

....

....

....

....

16. SEP Apply Scientific Reasoning Suppose you're riding a bike to a friend's house. On the way, you see a pothole in the street. Explain how your brain functions to protect you from injury both at that moment as well as in the future.

....

....

....

....

....

....

....

293

MS-LS1-3, MS-LS1-8

Evidence-Based Assessment

Crigler-Najjar syndrome is a rare inherited disorder with about 100 confirmed cases worldwide. Children born with the syndrome do not produce a certain liver enzyme. As a result, a toxic substance builds up in the body, which causes damage to other body systems.

The diagram below details some of the major effects of this disorder.

2 As the bilirubin level increases, it enters the bloodstream and builds up in the eyes and skin. This causes them to become yellow, a condition known as jaundice.

3 Eventually, bilirubin builds up in the brain and nervous tissue and causes neurological damage.

1 After about 115 days in the bloodstream, red blood cells are broken down in the liver. This produces a toxic substance called bilirubin. Without the enzyme, the liver cannot convert the bilirubin into a form that can be safely removed from the body.

4 Children with acute cases can also suffer from difficulty in coordination, muscle weakness, and muscle spasms.

1. **CCC Cause and Effect** Which body systems are directly affected by the syndrome? Select all that apply.
   - ☐ circulatory system
   - ☐ nervous system
   - ☐ skeletal system
   - ☐ respiratory system
   - ☐ muscular system

2. **SEP Develop Models** Order the events from first (1) to last (4).
   - .... Various systems in the body are damaged.
   - .... Child inherits Crigler-Najjar syndrome.
   - .... Bilirubin builds up and becomes toxic.
   - .... Liver cells cannot produce an enzyme.

3. **SEP Construct Explanations** How are cells and tissue in the liver affected by Crigler-Najjar syndrome?

   ....
   ....
   ....
   ....
   ....
   ....
   ....
   ....

4. **CCC Analyze Systems** How does Crigler-Najjar syndrome affect the circulatory system?

   ....
   ....
   ....
   ....
   ....
   ....
   ....

5. **SEP Engage in Argument** How does Crigler-Najjar syndrome demonstrate that the body is a system that depends on interacting subsystems in order to function properly?

   ....
   ....
   ....
   ....
   ....
   ....
   ....
   ....

Quest FINDINGS

Complete the Quest!

Phenomenon Organize your data and determine the best way to present your training and nutrition plan.

CCC Cause and Effect Why is it important to consider how one body system impacts other body systems when designing a successful training plan?

....
....
....
....
....

👆 **INTERACTIVITY**

Reflect on Peak Performance Plan

MS-LS1-3, MS-LS1-8

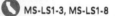

Reaction Research

How can you **design** and **conduct** an **investigation** about reaction times?

Background

Phenomenon You've been hired by a video game company to do some research and gather data on reaction times. Reaction time refers to the amount of time it takes for a person to recognize a stimulus and then direct the body to respond with an action. The developers are working on a new rhythm game in which the player presses buttons on the controller in time with visuals and music. They want to know how quickly a player might react to different stimuli, such as a shape changing color on the screen, a musical beat, or a vibration or rumble in the controller.

You will design and conduct an investigation to explore how different factors affect reaction times. Then you will analyze the data you have collected and draw some conclusions to share with the game developers.

Materials

(per group)
- meter stick (with centimeters marked)
- calculator

Safety

Be sure to follow all safety guidelines provided by your teacher. The Safety Appendix of your textbook provides more details about the safety icons.

Design Your Investigation

1. You and your partner can test reaction times with the meter stick. The subject sits at a table with a hand extended beyond the edge of the table as shown. The researcher holds up the meter stick so that the 0 lines up with the top of the subject's hand. The meter stick is dropped and the subject grabs it as quickly as possible. Measure the distance the meter stick falls by recording the centimeter mark closest to the top of the subject's hand.

2. You can use an equation to calculate how long it takes an object to fall based on how far an object falls. In the following equation, t is time, d is distance, and a is acceleration. To calculate the reaction time, use a calculator to solve the equation. (Note: A falling object accelerates due to gravity at a rate of 980 cm/s².)

$$t = \sqrt{(2d/a)}$$

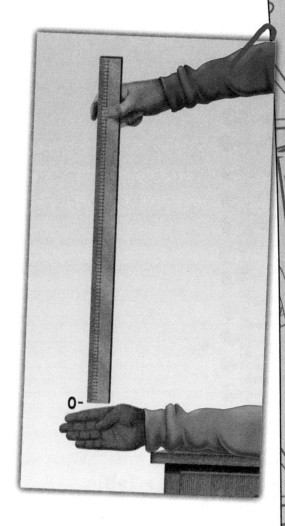

3. Based on the data that the developers want, identify the three types of stimuli that you will test in your investigation.

   - ....
   - ....
   - ....

4. Develop a procedure for your investigation based on the three stimuli you identified.
   Write your procedure in the space provided.
   As you plan your investigation, consider these questions.

   - How will you use the meter stick to determine reaction times?
   - What tests will you perform to collect data about reaction times for each type of stimulus?
   - How many trials of each test will you perform?
   - What data will you record?

5. After getting your teacher's approval, carry out the investigation. Make a table in the space provided to record your data.

Procedure

....

....

....

....

....

....

....

....

....

....

....

....

Data Table

Analyze and Interpret Data

1. **SEP Reason Quantitatively** Show the equations you used to calculate average reaction times to the visual, auditory, and tactile stimuli.

....

....

....

....

2. **SEP Defend Your Claim** Based on the trends or patterns you notice in the data, what claims can you make about reaction times to different stimuli? Explain.

....

....

....

....

3. **SEP Evaluate Evidence** Choose one stimulus that you tested in the investigation. Identify the body systems that are involved in responding to that stimulus. Then, draw a flow chart to diagram the process and explain how the systems interact.

....

4. **SEP Apply Scientific Reasoning** What conclusions would you share with the game developers? Which types of cues in the game would likely increase the chances of a player doing better? Explain.

....

....

....

....

....

MS-LS1-3

AGENTS OF
Infection

Your immune system is constantly working to fight off infections. Most of the time, the lymph nodes, lymph vessels, and white blood cells that are part of your immune system are able to attack invading viruses and bacteria to fight off infection. But some agents of infection are harder to conquer than others...

There are thousands of living and nonliving things that cause infections. The living ones include bacteria, fungi, worms, and single-celled organisms called protists. A bacterium is responsible for strep throat. Ringworm is caused by a fungus. Dysentery can result from a bacterial infection as well as amoebas. The good news about being infected with one of these organisms is that, for the most part, the infections they cause can be cured with medical treatment. There are also a number of ways that you can protect yourself from infections. For example, you can reduce your chances of getting or spreading an infection by washing your hands and by avoiding touching your face if your hands are not clean.

Nonliving viruses also cause infections. Viruses can cause diseases such as HIV, the common cold, and chicken pox. Only a few medications can treat them. A virus is hard to treat because it uses living cells to make copies of itself. These cells are damaged or destroyed when the new virus particles are released. The virus particles then infect other cells. Depending on the type of infection, people may get better over time. Sometimes a viral infection is so severe that symptoms never go away and conditions worsen.

You may have heard of the Zika virus or the flesh-eating bacterium *Vibrio vulnificus*. Each of these causes serious symptoms in people, often requiring hospitalization. Read about some of these infections in the table.

Medical professionals and patients need to take safety precautions, such as hand washing, to prevent the spread of infection.

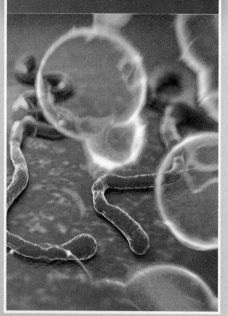

This bacterium is responsible for causing strep throat.

Infectious Agent	Type of Organism	Cause/Transmission	Symptoms	Treatment
Zika	Virus	Mosquito bites or transmission from infected person	Fever, rash, joint pain	There is no specific medicine or vaccine for Zika virus.
Brain-eating *Naegleria fowleri*	Amoeba	Infection occurs most often from diving, water skiing, or other water sports when water is forced into the nose.	Headache, fever, stiff neck, loss of appetite, seizures, coma	A number of drugs kill *N. fowleri* amoebas in the test tube. But even when treated with these drugs, very few patients survive.
Flesh-eating *Vibrio vulnificus*	Bacterium	It releases a toxin that causes the immune system to release white blood cells that destroy the individual's flesh.	Sweats, fever, and chills with red, swollen, blister-like patches on the body	Either the affected tissue has to be amputated, or antibiotics have to be administered.

Use the text and the table to answer the following questions.

1. CCC Structure and Function How are viruses different from other infectious agents, such as bacteria and fungi?

2. SEP Construct Arguments Do you think science and medicine will ever be able to discover a cure for Zika? Explain.

3. CCC Cause and Effect What are some steps you can take to protect yourself against an infectious disease?

MS-LS1-4, MS-LS1-5, MS-LS3-1, MS-LS3-2, MS-LS4-4, MS-LS4-5, MS-ETS1-1, EP&CIIc, EP&CIVb

Guiding Questions

- How do cells know what to do and how to accomplish it?
- Why do children look like their parents?
- What causes differences between individuals?

Topics

6 Reproduction and Growth

7 Genes and Heredity

Before the Topic
Identify the Problem

When Salmon Don't Run

Phenomenon Chinook salmon and steelhead trout once flourished in California. For several millennia, these native fish species lived in rivers that were very different from the ones that flow through California today. Human activities have altered fish habitats, and low genetic diversity is to blame for their decline in number. Climate change, for instance, has affected the health of many river ecosystems.

Some native trout and salmon populations are on the decline in California.

Every year, salmon from the ocean travel up river to their birthplace to spawn, or lay eggs, in freshwater. This yearly mass movement of fish up river is called a run.

Many game fishers practice catch-and-release with steelhead trout to help increase their probability of surviving and reproducing.

Changing Conditions and Permanent Change

California is home to a great diversity of salmon and trout species. To support the diversity of species and increase their chance of survival, fish need a place to spawn. The snow melt that runs off mountain ranges like the Sierra Nevadas provides fresh cold water for rivers and streams needed for spawning. But those conditions are changing, and many of California's fish are affected. Dams, which humans construct to control the flow of water, destroyed their habitat. Dams stop the run and isolate fish from one another downstream as water disappears. This isolation decreases genetic diversity. They also could not compete with the non-native fish that were introduced into the river system.

Due to climate change, river water is getting warmer. For some native fish species, low genetic diversity makes this change intolerable. They do not inherit traits that favor a change in temperature. Look at the table to see how warmer temperatures are impacting both native and non-native fish species.

The common carp is a non-native species. It now outnumbers native California species, such as the steelhead trout and salmon.

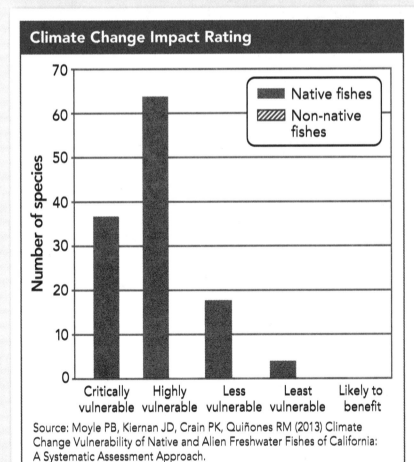

Source: Moyle PB, Kiernan JD, Crain PK, Quiñones RM (2013) Climate Change Vulnerability of Native and Alien Freshwater Fishes of California: A Systematic Assessment Approach.

If a species is vulnerable, that means hotter temperatures can harm it.

1. **SEP Use Mathematics** ✏ About 8 non-native species are highly vulnerable to climate change, 14 are less vulnerable, 16 are least vulnerable, and 6 are likely to benefit. Use the data to complete the histogram.

2. **SEP Interpret Data** How does the data for native fishes compare to the data for non-native fishes?

....

....

....

....

....

Changing Landscapes and Habitat Loss

Human activities, including burning fossil fuels and others that have contributed to global warming, have seriously impacted rivers and harmed many native fish species. When people divert water for farm use, they change the natural course of that water and isolate the fish. When people build dams, they change habitats both up and downstream. When gravel is mined out of riverbeds, humans are removing safe areas for fish to lay their eggs.

Six thousand miles of rivers and creeks flowing through California's Central Valley once provided safe fish habitats. Every spring, 600,000 Chinook salmon could run upstream to the place they were born. There, they would start the cycle of life all over again. But that changed when humans started building dams. By 1997, the number of Chinook salmon dropped below 6,000. Today, the spring-run Chinook salmon inhabit less than 300 river miles, mostly in the Sacramento River. And there are no more spring-run Chinook in the San Joaquin River. Look at the map to see the historic range of spring-run Chinook salmon.

In the Central Valley, the spring run for Chinook salmon takes place in the Antelope, Beegum, Butte, Deer, and Mill Creeks. These five creeks feed the Sacramento River.

SEP Analyze Data

Highlight the creeks on the map and then draw a circle around them.

Historic Run of Central Valley Chinook Salmon

One River, Many Habitats

Salmon and steelhead trout are anadromous (UH-nad-ru-mus) fish. Because of their genetic make-up, they spend most of their lives in salty ocean water but reproduce in fresh water. Rivers offer safe places for each phase of life. Young salmon eat insects. Streams flowing through areas with overhanging tree branches and grasses provide plenty of food. River beds with old logs and branches offer shelter. When Chinook move back to the ocean, they stop at marshes. These natural borders between freshwater and salt water give their bodies a chance to get used to being in salt water.

The Sacramento and San Joaquin rivers share a delta. The estuary, or area of water where a river meets the ocean, provides places where young fish can develop.

Salmon River in western Siskiyou County, California

Salmon and steelhead both need specific and various sizes of gravels to lay their eggs.

A New Lease on Life

In this segment you will learn about the reproduction and growth of plants and animals. You will investigate how animal behaviors increase their chances of reproducing. You will learn about how traits are inherited. You will also learn about the importance of genetic diversity and how differences can help, hurt, or not affect a population. You will also explore different genetic technologies. Scientists and wildlife managers study reproduction and inheritance so they can figure out the best ways to save a species.

Humans can help salmon, trout, and other native freshwater fish survive the impacts of global warming. People can also help undo some of the harm they have already caused. Many environmental groups specialize in fish conservation. Some rescue fish stranded in streams when water is running too low. Others work to restore native habitats. Some groups are advocates. For example, during the drought in 2014, the Hoopa Valley Tribe in northwestern California urged the federal government to release water from the Trinity River dam in Weatherville. They took action to protect the fish downstream.

These Department of Fish and Game workers are in the process of relocating trout from Caples Lake near Kirkwood, California.

SEP Construct Explanations What impact does relocating fish species have on the population Explain.

....

....

After the Topic
Conduct an Investigation

Evidence **Now that you have completed the two topics in this segment, do the following tasks.**

Make Generalizations The Sacramento River is the longest in California. It draws from many watersheds. The first map shows current habitat for spring-run Chinook salmon. Outside this zone, river water conditions cannot support healthy populations or the rivers are not accessible by the fish. The second map shows the locations of dams across the state.

There are more than 1,400 dams across the state.

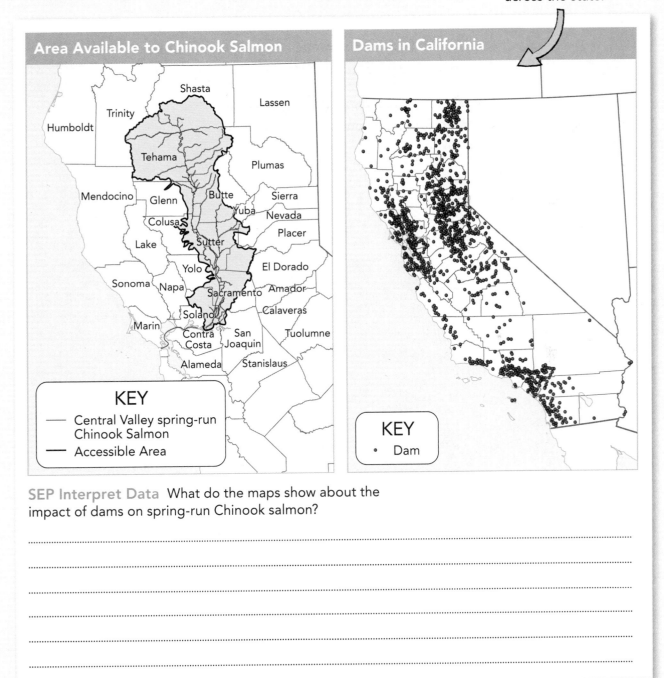

Area Available to Chinook Salmon

KEY
— Central Valley spring-run Chinook Salmon
— Accessible Area

Dams in California

KEY
• Dam

SEP Interpret Data What do the maps show about the impact of dams on spring-run Chinook salmon?

....

....

....

....

....

....

Design a Solution

Team up with a small group of classmates. Together, list the issues facing native fish species in California today. Talk about the factors that affect their growth and reproduction. Which factors have the greatest impact on the health of the species? Are the factors environmental, genetic, or a combination of both?

Make a plan to help an endangered native California fish species.

1. Go to this website to see a list of fish species in California: http://calfish.ucdavis.edu/species/

2. Find a native species.

3. Click on the name of the fish to read about its life history.

SEP Develop Models 🖊 In the space provided, sketch and describe your plan. Then, explain how your solution will help the fish population to survive.

Based on your analysis of the data and your research, answer the following questions.

1. **SEP Communicate Information** Which fish species did you choose? Briefly describe any inherited traits of fish, their habitat, and any behaviors that help them to reproduce.

....
....
....
....
....

2. **CCC Cause and Effect** How might climate change and low genetic diversity impact your fish species?

....
....
....
....
....

3. **SEP Engage in Argument** During long droughts, fresh water is very precious. Farmers need the water for their crops. People need fresh drinking water. Do you think it's important to provide water to fish during droughts by releasing dam water? Explain.

....
....
....
....

4. **SEP Design a Solution** Some of the ways that human use natural resources have long-term consequences. Consider some of the reasons humans build dams. One is to generate electricity. Another is to provide fresh drinking water. Some people suggest removing dams to help restore ecosystems. What could people do instead to get the fresh water they need in a way that limits these consequences?

....
....

Reproduction and Growth

Can desert animals
be affected by
drought?

MS-LS1-4 Use argument based on empirical evidence and scientific reasoning to support an explanation for how characteristic animal behaviors and specialized plant structures affect the probability of successful reproduction of animals and plants respectively.

MS-LS1-5 Construct a scientific explanation based on evidence for how environmental and genetic factors influence the growth of organisms.

MS-LS3-2 Develop and use a model to describe why asexual reproduction results in offspring with identical genetic information and sexual reproduction results in offspring with genetic variation.

EP&CIIc Students should be developing an understanding that the expansion and operation of human communities influences the geographic extent, composition, biological diversity, and viability of natural systems.

EP&CIVb Students should be developing an understanding that the byproducts of human activity are not readily prevented from entering natural systems and may be beneficial, neutral, or detrimental in their effect.

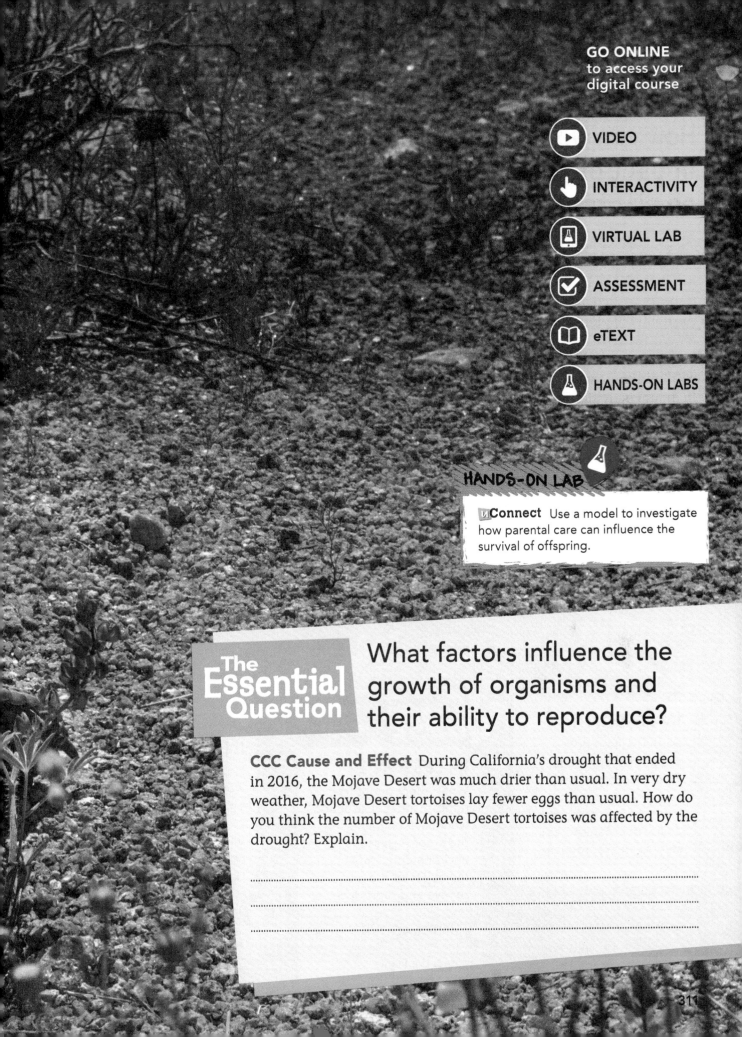

GO ONLINE
to access your
digital course

▶ VIDEO

👆 INTERACTIVITY

🧪 VIRTUAL LAB

☑ ASSESSMENT

📖 eTEXT

🧪 HANDS-ON LABS

HANDS-ON LAB

uConnect Use a model to investigate how parental care can influence the survival of offspring.

The Essential Question

What factors influence the growth of organisms and their ability to reproduce?

CCC Cause and Effect During California's drought that ended in 2016, the Mojave Desert was much drier than usual. In very dry weather, Mojave Desert tortoises lay fewer eggs than usual. How do you think the number of Mojave Desert tortoises was affected by the drought? Explain.

....

....

....

Quest KICKOFF

How can we reduce the impact of construction on plants and animals?

 STEM **Phenomenon** Environmental scientists study habitats and the organisms that live there. They investigate how the availability of resources—such as water, food, and space—affects the ability of plants and animals to survive and reproduce. In this Quest activity, you will consider how to build a basketball court on school grounds, with minimal impact on local plants and animals. In digital activities, you will explore the factors that affect plant and animal growth and reproduction. By applying what you have learned, you will develop a construction proposal for the basketball court.

MS-LS1-5, EP&CIIc

 INTERACTIVITY

Construction Without Destruction

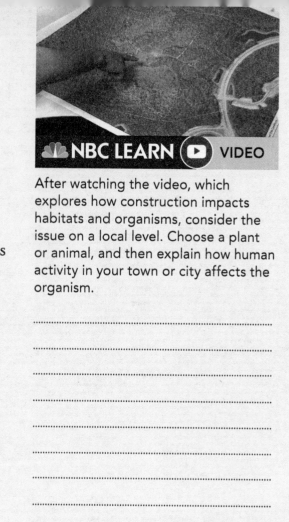

NBC LEARN ▶ **VIDEO**

After watching the video, which explores how construction impacts habitats and organisms, consider the issue on a local level. Choose a plant or animal, and then explain how human activity in your town or city affects the organism.

....
....
....
....
....
....
....
....
....

IN LESSON 1

How do different organisms reproduce? Think about how the court's impact on the habitat might affect the ability of organisms to survive and reproduce there.

Quest CHECK-IN

IN LESSON 2

What effect might tree removal and construction work have on plants in the area? Assess the environmental impact on the ability of the plants to survive and reproduce.

 INTERACTIVITY

Protect the Plants

Quest CHECK-IN

IN LESSON 3

How does construction work impact animals? Think about how construction noise might interfere with the ability of an organism to reproduce successfully.

 INTERACTIVITY

The Mating Game

Before construction begins for a facility, such as a basketball court, professionals complete a construction proposal. It often outlines how organisms may be impacted once the construction is complete.

Quest CHECK-IN

IN LESSON 4

STEM How can the impact of the court's location and construction be minimized? Develop a plan that ensures the successful survival and reproduction of plants and animals.

👆 INTERACTIVITY

Make Your Construction Case

Quest FINDINGS

Complete the Quest!

Present your construction plan using the information and data that you have collected as evidence to support your recommendations.

👆 INTERACTIVITY

Reflect on Your Basketball Court Plans

Patterns of Reproduction

Guiding Questions

- How do organisms reproduce and transfer genes to their offspring?
- How do offspring produced by asexual reproduction and sexual reproduction compare?
- Why do different offspring of the same parent usually look different?

Connections

Literacy Cite Textual Evidence

Math Summarize Distributions

 MS-LS3-2 Develop and use a model to describe why asexual reproduction results in offspring with identical genetic information and sexual reproduction results in offspring with genetic variation.

HANDS-ON LAB

µInvestigate Explore traits in an imaginary organism.

Vocabulary

asexual
 reproduction
sexual
 reproduction
fertilization
trait
gene
inheritance
allele

Academic Vocabulary

dominant

Connect It!

✏️ **The pictures show offspring with their mothers. Circle the offspring you think might look like the father.**

SEP Construct Explanations Summarize what you already know about how the three kinds of animals in the picture produce offspring.

....

....

....

....

....

Asexual and Sexual Reproduction

Living things reproduce. Giraffes make more giraffes, hermit crabs make more hermit crabs, and bald eagles make more bald eagles. Some animals produce offspring that look exactly like the parent. Others, such as humans and the animals in **Figure 1,** produce offspring that look different from the parents.

Animals use one of two main methods—asexual or sexual reproduction—to produce offspring. Reproduction guarantees that a species' genes are passed on to the next generation.

Asexual Reproduction
A reproductive process that involves only one parent and produces offspring that are genetically identical to the parent is called **asexual reproduction**. It is the simplest form of reproduction. Animals such as sponges, corals, and certain jellyfish reproduce asexually.

One form of asexual reproduction is fragmentation. During fragmentation, a new organism forms from a piece of the original. For example, in some sea star species, a whole new sea star can develop from a single arm (**Figure 2**). Another method of asexual reproduction is called budding. In this process, a new animal grows out from the parent until it fully matures and breaks off. Sponges and some sea anemones reproduce in this way.

INTERACTIVITY

Consider the traits that make you unique.

Reflect What do you think is the benefit of reproducing asexually? In your science notebook, explain how asexual reproduction could give some animals an advantage.

Reproduction Results in Offspring
Figure 1 All living things have the ability to reproduce.

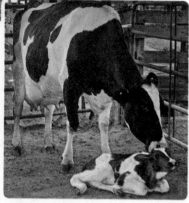

Sexual Reproduction

Consider the variety of trees, birds, fish, and plants in the world around you. Clearly, many life forms are unique. When organisms reproduce sexually, their offspring display a variety of traits. Even members of the same family are not exact copies of each other. Sexual reproduction is responsible for the variety of life you see.

In **sexual reproduction**, two parents combine their genetic material to produce a new organism that differs from both parents. Sexual reproduction involves an egg cell and a sperm cell joining to form a new cell in a process called **fertilization**. Sperm cells are from the father and contribute the father's half of the chromosomes. Egg cells are from the mother and contribute the mother's half of the chromosomes. When fertilization occurs, a full set of chromosomes is present in the new cell.

Because offspring receive roughly half their genetic information from each parent, they receive a combination of specific characteristics. A specific characteristic that an organism can pass to its offspring through its genes is called a **trait**. A **gene** is a sequence of DNA that determines a trait and is passed from parent to offspring. As a result, offspring may look very similar to their parents, or they may look very different, like the California dairy cows in **Figure 2**. These differences are known as variations, and they are what make you different from your siblings. Individual variations depend on which genes were passed on from each parent.

Sexual vs. Asexual Reproduction

Figure 2 (top) A new sea star is developing from its parent's arm. (bottom) A California dairy calf and her mother.

1. **Claim** 🖉 Circle the image of sexually reproducing organisms.

2. **Evidence** What evidence did you use to support your claim?

....

....

3. **Reasoning** Explain how your evidence supports your claim.

....

....

....

....

....

....

Model It

SEP Develop Models 🖉 Suppose two neighborhood dogs produce offspring. Draw a picture of the mother and the father. Draw one offspring that might result from the parents. Label the traits the father passed on to the offspring and the traits the mother passed on to the offspring.

Comparing Types of Reproduction Both methods of reproduction have advantages and disadvantages. Organisms that reproduce asexually do not have to find a mate. They can also produce many offspring fairly quickly. The downside is that all of the offspring have exactly the same genetic makeup as the parent. This can be a problem if the environment changes. If one individual organism is unable to survive the change, then chances are the rest of the identical offspring will not be able to survive it either.

Organisms that reproduce sexually pass on chromosomes with genetic variation. This variation may increase the chances their offspring could survive a changing environment. It is possible that they received a gene from a parent that would help them adapt to the changing environment. One potential downside of sexual reproduction is that the organism needs to find a mate. This can sometimes be a problem for animals, such as polar bears, that live in remote areas.

VIDEO

Compare asexual reproduction and sexual reproduction.

✔ CHECK POINT **Cite Textual Evidence** What are some advantages of organisms reproducing sexually?

....

....

....

Math Toolbox

Sexual Reproduction

Gestation is the time period between fertilization and birth. The data in the table are based on recorded observations from hundreds of pregnant individuals in each species.

Animal	Gestation Range (days)	Median Gestation Time (days)	Bottom Quartile Median (days)	Top Quartile Median (days)
Hamster	16–23	20	17	22
Red Fox	49–55	52	50	53
Gerbil	22–26	24	23	25
Leopard	91–95	93	92	94

1. **Distinguish Relationships** What is the relationship between the size of the animal and how long it takes for its offspring to develop?

....

....

2. **Summarize Distributions** ✏ Choose two species from the table and construct a box plot for each one.

Figure 3 Fur color, like human hair color, depends on which genes are inherited from the parents.

▶ **VIDEO**

Explore the relationship between inheritance and alleles.

Inherited Traits

When sperm and egg cells come together, genetic information from the mother and father mix. **Inheritance** is the process by which an offspring receives genes from its parents. Genes are located on chromosomes and describe the factors that control a trait. Each trait is described by a pair of genes, with one gene from the mother and one from the father. Sometimes the pair of genes are the same. At other times, there are two different genes in the pair.

For example, imagine a mouse with white fur and a mouse with brown fur have offspring. The genes for fur color from each parent are different. As shown in **Figure 3,** some of the offspring produced may be brown, some may be white, and others may be combinations of more than one color. Each offspring's fur color depends on how its inherited genes combine.

An **allele** is a different form of the same gene. One allele is received from each parent, and the combination of alleles determines which traits the offspring will have. In the simplest case, alleles are either dominant or recessive. If an offspring inherits a **dominant** allele from either parent, that trait will always show up in the offspring. But, if the offspring inherits recessive alleles from each parent, a recessive trait will show. This relationship allows parents with two dominant alleles to pass on recessive alleles to their offspring. For example, two brown-eyed people may have a blue-eyed child. However, most genetic traits do not follow these simple patterns of dominant and recessive inheritance.

Academic Vocabulary

Describe a situation in which you have been dominant.

....

....

....

....

....

....

Incomplete Dominance Sometimes intermediate forms of a dominant trait appear. This means that mixing of colors or sizes occurs. Incomplete dominance may occur when a dominant allele and recessive allele are inherited. The offspring will have a mixture of these two alleles. For example, in some species of sheep, gray fleece results from a dominant white-fleece allele and a recessive black allele. Incomplete dominance also occurs in petal color in some species of plants. **Figure 4** shows how petal color can result in the blending of two colors.

Incomplete Dominance
Figure 4 ✏️ Circle the flowers that demonstrate incomplete dominance in petal color.

Codominance Unlike incomplete dominance, which shows blending of traits, codominance results in both alleles being expressed at the same time. In cattle, horses, and dogs, there is a color pattern called roan. This color pattern appears when a dominant white-hair allele and a dominant solid-color allele is inherited. The offspring has hairs of each color intermixed, giving the solid-color a more muted or mottled look.

Model It ✏️

Integrate Information ✏️ Draw the parents of this flower in the box. Assume that the flower's color is determined by codominance.

		Father's blood type				Child's blood type must be
		A	B	AB	O	
Mother's blood type	A	A or O	A, B, AB, or O	A, B, or AB	A or O	
	B	A, B, AB, or O	B or O	A, B, or AB	B or O	
	AB	A, B, or AB	A, B, or AB	A, B, or AB	A or B	
	O	A or O	B or O	A or B	O	

Human Blood Types

Figure 5 Human blood type is on a gene with multiple alleles two of which are codominant.

Integrate Information What are the alleles for human blood type?

....

Multiple Alleles

Every offspring inherits one allele from each parent for a total of two alleles. However, sometimes one trait has more than two alleles. For example, there are three alleles for blood type—A, B, and O. The A and B blood types are codominant and O is recessive. As you see in **Figure 5**, you receive two of the multiple alleles from each parent, but each possible combination of alleles results in one of four different blood types. Multiple alleles are not found only in blood types. **Figure 6** shows how fur color in some rabbits is the result of multiple alleles.

Multiple Alleles

Figure 6 These rabbits all came from the same litter.

SEP Cite Evidence What evidence from the picture demonstrates that the fur color of these rabbits results from multiple alleles?

....

....

....

....

Polygenic Inheritance

Some traits are controlled by more than one gene. In polygenetic inheritance, these different genes are expressed together to produce the trait. Human height is an example of this. If the mother is 5 feet 2 inches tall and the father is 6 feet tall, then you might think that all of the offspring would be 5 feet 7 inches. However, there can be a large variation among the heights of the children. This fact is due to multiple genes working together to produce the trait.

✓ CHECK POINT **Determine Central Ideas** How do alleles influence inherited traits? Explain with an example of incomplete dominance.

....

....

....

Genes and the Environment

What kinds of things have you learned in your life? Maybe you know how to paint. Maybe you can ride a unicycle. Or maybe you know how to solve very complicated math problems. Whatever your abilities, they are acquired traits that are the result of learned behaviors.

Acquired Traits The traits you inherited can be affected by your experience. For example, humans are born with teeth, vocal cords, and tongues—all of which enable us to speak. The language you learn to use depends on your environment. You were not born speaking a particular language, but you were born with the capacity to learn languages, whether a spoken language or sign language. The ability for language is an inherited trait. The language or languages you use, however, are acquired traits.

The combination of inherited traits and acquired traits helps many organisms to survive in their environment. The fox squirrel in **Figure 7** has inherited traits from its parents that help it survive in its environment. The squirrel also acquired traits that help it survive, by learning behaviors from its parents and by interacting with its environment.

INTERACTIVITY

Find out how we learn about genes and traits from studying twins.

HANDS-ON LAB

Investigate Explore traits in an imaginary organism.

Acquired Traits

Figure 7 This fox squirrel, common in the Los Angeles area in California, has traits that were inherited as well as traits that were acquired through learning.

1. **Relate Text to Visuals** List two inherited traits and two acquired traits of the fox squirrel.

....
....
....
....

2. **Synthesize Information** How does the fox squirrel use its traits to survive?

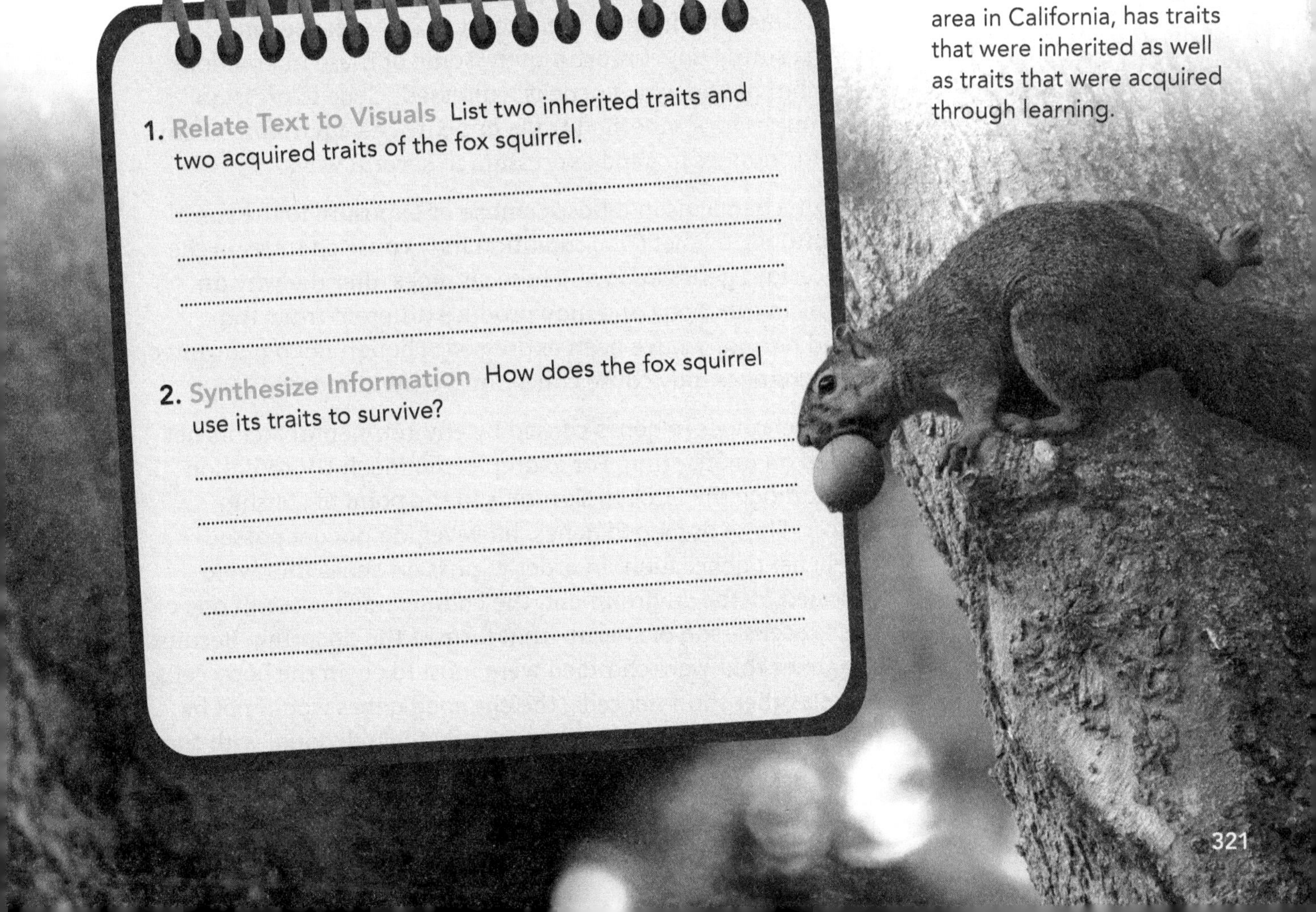

....
....
....
....
....

Environmental Interactions

Figure 8 Protection from the sun when you are outside all day is important.

Implement a Solution List three acquired behaviors that people have learned to protect themselves from ultraviolet light.

....

....

....

....

....

Environmental Factors Organisms interact with their environment on a regular basis. **Figure 8** shows some of the ways you interact with your environment. You may spend time with friends, breathe fresh air, exercise, and enjoy a sunny day. Unfortunately, some of these interactions may change the way a gene is expressed. Gene expression determines how inherited traits appear. The environment can lead to changes in gene expression in several ways.

Certain chemicals in tobacco smoke or exposure to the sun's harmful ultraviolet (UV) radiation may cause changes in the way certain genes behave. These changes alter the way an organism functions and may produce different traits than would normally have been expressed. Though not a guarantee, these changes may cause cancer and other diseases.

Not all changes in genes caused by environmental factors get passed on to offspring. For example, too much UV radiation can damage the DNA in skin cells to the point of causing cancer. These damaged genes, however, do not get passed to the next generation. In order to pass on genes that were changed by the environment, the change must occur in one of the sex cells—egg or sperm—that formed the offspring. Because the genes that were changed were most likely in the body cells, or cells other than sex cells, the changed genes would not be passed on to you, and would affect only the individual with the changed genes.

☑LESSON 1 Check

MS-LS3-2

1. **Distinguish Relationships** What does inheritance mean in terms of reproduction?

....

....

....

2. **Explain Phenomena** What happens if an offspring inherits a dominant allele from one of its parents?

....

....

....

3. **SEP Construct Explanations** What is a possible benefit to an organism expressing codominant or incomplete dominant traits?

....

....

....

....

....

....

4. **CCC Patterns** A species of butterfly has alleles for wing color that are either blue or orange. But, when a blue butterfly and an orange butterfly mated, the wings of the offspring were blue and orange. Explain the type of dominance through which wing color was expressed.

....

....

....

....

5. **SEP Evaluate Evidence** Human hair color is a trait with very broad variation. Which pattern of inheritance could account for human hair color? Explain your answer.

....

....

....

....

6. **SEP Use Models** ✏ In the space below, draw a Venn diagram comparing and contrasting asexual reproduction and sexual reproduction.

LESSON
2
Plant Structures for Reproduction

Guiding Questions

- How do plants reproduce?
- How do seeds become new plants?
- Which specialized plant structures affect the probability of successful reproduction?

Connection

Literacy Cite Textual Evidence

 MS-LS1-4 Use argument based on empirical evidence and scientific reasoning to support an explanation for how characteristic animal behaviors and specialized plant structures affect the probability of successful reproduction of animals and plants respectively.

HANDS-ON LAB

иInvestigate Demonstrate how flower structures relate to successful reproduction.

Vocabulary

zygote
pollination
cones
ovule
fruit
germination

Academic Vocabulary

disperse

Connect It

✎ **Circle the fruits shown here.**

SEP Construct Explanations Where in the fruit are seeds found and what do seeds do?

....

....

Plant Reproduction

Have you ever run from a bee buzzing around a garden? Have you taken the time to appreciate the pleasant scent and beautiful colors of a rose? Have you challenged a friend to see who could spit a watermelon seed the farthest? If you have done any of these things, you are already familiar with some of the methods plants use to reproduce.

When a seed, like ones from the fruits and vegetables in **Figure 1**, is planted in healthy soil and gets plenty of water and sunlight, it can grow into an adult plant. But this is just one part in the process of how plants reproduce. A lot must first happen in a plant's life before it can produce a seed that can grow into a plant. Surprisingly to some, plants are like animals in that reproduction requires a sperm cell fertilizing an egg cell for a new organism to begin.

Plants have evolved specialized structures over time that increase the probability of successful reproduction. Different types of plants have different structures and methods that help them reproduce. But the result is the same: producing new generations of plants.

INTERACTIVITY

Explore the relationship between seeds and the food we eat.

Find the Fruit

Figure 1 Fruits may not look alike, but they function much the same. They carry seeds with partially developed plants.

Plant Life Cycles

Figure 2 ✏ Complete the diagrams. Identify the sporophyte and gametophyte stage in each diagram.

The Life Cycle of a Moss Plant

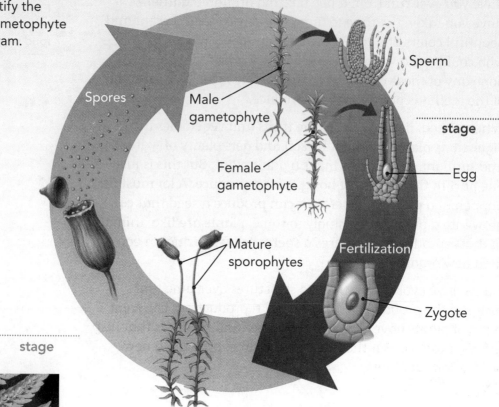

Spores

Male gametophyte

Female gametophyte

Mature sporophytes

Sperm

stage

Egg

Fertilization

Zygote

.... stage

Spore Production

Figure 3 Fern sporophytes are the recognizable parts of the plant.

SEP Use Models What is the result of the sporophyte stage?

....

....

....

....

....

Plant Life Cycles

Plants have complex life cycles that include two different stages: the sporophyte (SPOH ruh fyt) and gametophyte (guh MEE tuh fyt) stages. During the sporophyte stage, a plant produces the spores that will eventually develop into gametophytes. During the gametophyte stage, male and female gametophytes produce sex cells that will eventually be involved in the process of fertilization, which occurs when a sperm cell unites with an egg cell to produce a new organism.

Nonvascular and Seedless Vascular Plants

Mosses and other nonvascular plants produce sporophytes that resemble small trees or flowers. The sporophytes release spores that grow into male and female gametophytes. These gametophytes produce the sperm and egg cells that are needed for a **zygote**, or fertilized egg, to form and develop into a new sporophyte as is shown in **Figure 2**.

The life stages of seedless vascular plants, such as ferns, are similar to nonvascular plants in some ways. Sporophytes produce spores that develop into gametophytes. But fern gametophytes have both male and female structures that produce sex cells. When a sperm cell fertilizes an egg cell, a new sporophyte begins to develop.

The Life Cycle of an Angiosperm

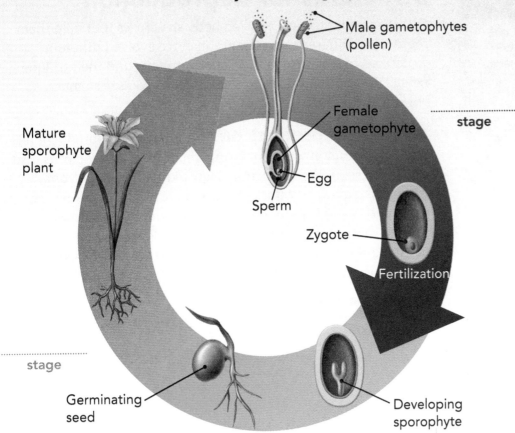

Male gametophytes (pollen)

Female gametophyte

stage

Egg

Sperm

Zygote

Fertilization

Mature sporophyte plant

stage

Germinating seed

Developing sporophyte

Other Vascular Plants The two other types of vascular plants are gymnosperms and angiosperms. Unlike both ferns and mosses, gymnosperm and angiosperm gametophytes actually develop inside structures within a larger sporophyte. In gymnosperms, they develop inside cones, and in an angiosperm like the one shown in **Figure 2**, they develop inside flowers.

The male gametophyte in these types of plants is called pollen. Pollen contains cells that will mature into sperm cells. For reproduction to occur, pollen must travel to the female gametophyte so it can fertilize egg cells. This process of transferring pollen from male reproductive structures to female reproductive structures in plants is called **pollination**. Pollination must occur in these plants before fertilization can occur.

☑ CHECK POINT **Determine Central Ideas** How do the sporophyte stage and gametophyte stage make a cycle?

....

....

....

....

Structures for Reproduction

Over time, plants have evolved body structures that help them reproduce. Different types of plants have evolved different structures in response to their environments and their unique needs. Reproduction is one of the reasons you see so much variety in the different plant types.

Asexual Reproduction Though sexual reproduction is the most common way that plants reproduce, many plants also undergo asexual reproduction. New plants can grow from the roots, leaves, or stems of a parent plant. If conditions are favorable, a single plant can quickly spread by producing many exact copies of itself. As shown in **Figure 4**, scientists can use a plant's ability to reproduce asexually in order to grow plants with favorable characteristics.

☑CHECK POINT **Summarize Text** What is the benefit of asexual reproduction?

....

....

Apple Tree Grafting

Figure 4 Grafting is one way that humans can control the traits of plants. Part of a plant's stem is cut and then attached to another plant. These apple trees in a California orchard have been grafted to ensure that desired traits from the original plant are maintained while new desired traits from the grafted plant grow on the new stem.

Apply Concepts Is grafting a form of sexual or asexual reproduction?

....

Male and Female Cones

Figure 5 Male cones, such as the ones to the right, hold pollen. Female cones, such as the two shown below, open when the weather is warm and dry. They close when conditions are cold and wet.

Apply Scientific Reasoning How do you think the cone's ability to open and close helps with reproduction?

....

....

....

....

....

Gymnosperms Trees such as pines, redwoods, firs, cedars, and hemlocks are all classified as gymnosperms. Many gymnosperms have needle-like leaves and deep roots. However, all have cones and unprotected seeds. These two characteristics set them apart from other vascular plants.

The structures in **Figure 5** are **cones** , which are the reproductive structures of gymnosperms. Male cones hold pollen, whereas the female cone has an **ovule**, the structure holding the egg. The female cone also makes a sticky substance on the outside of the cone, needed for pollination. Pollen from the male cone is light enough to be carried by the wind. When the wind blows, pollen may land on the sticky female cone. When this happens, the egg may become fertilized. The ovule seals off and the zygote develops into a plant embryo in the seed. Seeds can remain in the female cone for a few years, until they mature.

The seeds of gymnosperms are "naked," meaning they are unprotected. Once the female cone matures, the scales open, exposing the seeds. As wind blows, the exposed seeds are blown out of the cone and spread by the wind.

Literacy Connection

Cite Textual Evidence
Which detail in the text helped you understand what gymnosperms are?

....

....

....

....

....

....

....

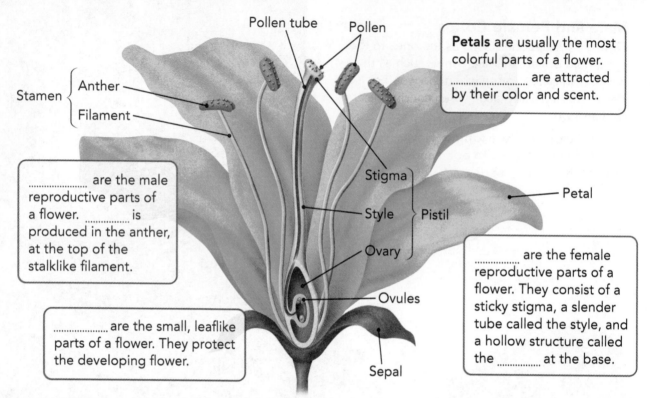

Pollen tube   Pollen

Petals are usually the most colorful parts of a flower. .... are attracted by their color and scent.

Stamen { Anther
        { Filament

.... are the male reproductive parts of a flower. .... is produced in the anther, at the top of the stalklike filament.

Stigma

Style } Pistil

Ovary

Petal

.... are the female reproductive parts of a flower. They consist of a sticky stigma, a slender tube called the style, and a hollow structure called the .... at the base.

.... are the small, leaflike parts of a flower. They protect the developing flower.

Ovules

Sepal

Flower Parts and Their Jobs

Figure 6 🖊 Flowers contain the reproductive structures of angiosperms. Complete the diagram by filling in the missing words.

CCC Relate Structure and Function How are a flower's petals important to reproduction?

....

....

....

....

....

....

HANDS-ON LAB

🔬**Investigate**
Demonstrate how flower structures relate to successful reproduction.

Angiosperms

All angiosperms share two important characteristics. They all produce flowers and fruits that contain seeds. The angiosperm life cycle begins when pollen forms in the flower's anthers. These structures are found at the end of the stamens, which are the male reproductive structure. The female reproductive structure is the pistil and has three parts: the stigma, style, and ovary. When pollen falls on the stigma, pollination may occur, which can lead to fertilization.

Some angiosperms are pollinated by the wind, but most rely on animals called pollinators, such as bees and hummingbirds. When an organism enters a flower to obtain food, it becomes coated with pollen. Some of the pollen can drop onto the flower's stigma as the animal leaves. The pollen can also be brushed onto the stigma of the next flower the animal visits. If the pollen falls on the stigma of a similar plant, fertilization can occur. A sperm cell joins with an egg cell inside an ovule within the ovary at the base of the flower. The zygote then begins to develop into the seed's embryo. Other parts of the ovule develop into the rest of the seed.

Additional structures help a flowering plant to reproduce successfully. Colorful, often pleasantly-scented petals surround the plant's reproductive organs and attract pollinators. Green sepals protect the growing flower. The flower is what develops into the **fruit**—the ripened ovary and other structures of an angiosperm enclosing one or more seeds.

Seed Dispersal Fruits are the means by which angiosperm seeds are **dispersed**. Often the scent and color of fruit attracts animals to the plant. Animals eat the fruit and then the seeds in it pass through the animal's digestive system. As the animal moves around, seeds are deposited in different areas in the animal's dung, or droppings. The droppings have an added benefit of providing nutrients and moisture for the seed.

In other cases, seeds disperse by falling into water or being carried by the wind. Seeds with barbs attach to fur or clothing and are carried away. Others are ejected by the seed pods and scattered in different directions. Seeds dispersed far from the parent plant have a better chance of surviving. Distance keeps the new plant from competing with the parent plant for light, water, and nutrients. When a seed lands in a spot with suitable conditions, germination may occur. **Germination** occurs when the embryo sprouts out of the seed.

☑ CHECK POINT **Cite Textual Evidence** How do the examples of seed dispersal given in the text help you understand the role of seed dispersal in plant reproduction?

....

....

....

Academic Vocabulary
Use *dispersed* in another sentence that uses a context other than seeds and plants.

....

....

....

....

 INTERACTIVITY

Explore the relationship between plants and pollinators.

Model It

Flower to Fruit

The male and female flower parts enable reproduction to take place. They contain structures to form the egg and sperm that will join to create the zygote.

SEP **Develop Models** ✏ Draw a sequence of pictures to show the steps that must take place for a flowering plant to reproduce and form a new seedling.

☑ LESSON 2 Check

MS-LS1-4

1. Communicate What is a fruit?

....

....

....

2. Draw Conclusions How are flowers with brightly-colored petals and attractive scents helpful to plants?

....

....

....

....

....

3. Determine Differences How does seed dispersal in angiosperms differ from seed dispersal in gymnosperms?

....

....

....

....

....

....

4. SEP Construct Explanations In what ways are sexual and asexual reproduction in plants similar, and in what ways do they differ?

....

....

....

....

....

....

....

5. SEP Engage in Argument A classmate tells you he read on the Internet that plants need flowers to produce seeds. Respond using evidence from this text.

....

....

....

....

....

....

Quest CHECK-IN

In this lesson, you learned about plant structures that help them reproduce successfully.

SEP Design Solutions How might knowing about the ways the local plants reproduce help in the planning and design of the basketball court?

....

....

....

....

....

INTERACTIVITY

Protect the Plants

Go online to assess the impact of the construction project on plants.

MS-LS1-4

GARDENING in Space

▶ VIDEO

Learn more about growing plants in space.

Do you know how to grow plants in space? You engineer it! NASA engineers and astronauts show us how.

The Challenge: To grow plants on long space flights.

Phenomenon Future space-flight missions will take months, years, and eventually multiple lifetimes, to reach their distant destinations. These missions will rely on growing plants in space as a source of food for astronauts, a method for recycling carbon dioxide into breathable oxygen, and potentially as part of the process that recycles, filters, and purifies water.

Plant structures and their functions are adapted to life on Earth. Leaves grow toward sunlight and roots grow down, due to gravity. In space, with no sunlight and very little gravity, plants do not grow easily. Because water floats away without gravity, watering plants in space is also tricky. Astronauts grow some plants directly in water. Other plants grow in a spongy clay-like material that allows water to reach all the roots.

NASA engineers have designed plant growth chambers used on the International Space Station (ISS) to investigate the effects of space on plant growth. The systems use LED lights and have multiple sensors to track data on temperature, moisture, and oxygen levels.

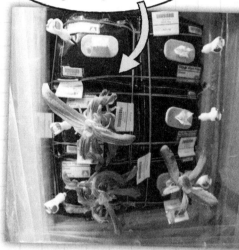

This is not a picture taken from above. These plants are growing sideways!

The Veggie System was installed in 2014. It allows the astronauts to grow their own food aboard the ISS.

 **DESIGN CHALLENGE** Can you design and build a model of a lunar growth chamber for plants? Go to the Engineering Design Notebook to find out!

LESSON 3 Animal Behaviors for Reproduction

Guiding Questions

- What causes animals to behave in certain ways?
- What are some different ways in which animals reproduce?
- How can the behavior of animals increase their chances of reproducing?

Connections

Literacy Summarize Text

Math Draw Comparative Inferences

 MS-LS1-4 Use argument based on empirical evidence and scientific reasoning to support an explanation for how characteristic animal behaviors and specialized plant structures affect the probability of successful reproduction of animals and plants respectively.

HANDS-ON LAB

иInvestigate Explore how salmon migrate from the ocean back to their home river.

Vocabulary

behavior
instinct
pheromone
mating system
migration

Academic Vocabulary

typically

Connect It!

✎ Circle a vulnerable member of this wood duck family.

SEP Construct Explanations Why do you think the ducks travel this way?

....

....

Animal Behavior

Have you ever noticed how busy animals are? Most are constantly looking for food or trying to avoid other animals that think of them as food. Many also spend a lot of time looking for mates and caring for their young. All of these actions are examples of an animal's behavior. The way an organism reacts to changes in its internal conditions or external environment is **behavior**. Like body structures, the behaviors of animals are adaptations that have evolved over long periods of time.

Some behaviors are learned while others are known without being taught. An **instinct** is a response to a stimulus that is inborn and that an animal performs correctly the first time. For example, when sea turtles hatch from their eggs, they know by instinct to travel to the ocean. Other behaviors are learned. Learning is the process that leads to changes in behavior based on practice or experience.

The goal of most animal behaviors is to help them survive or reproduce (**Figure 1**). When an animal looks for food or hides from a predator, it is doing something that helps it stay alive. When animals search for mates and build nests for their young, they are behaving in ways that help them reproduce.

HANDS-ON LAB

Consider how animals can communicate without words.

Wood Duck Behavior
Figure 1 These wood ducklings on Lindo Lake in Lakeside, California, stay close to their mother for protection.

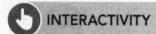 **INTERACTIVITY**

Find out more about animal behavior.

Mating Behaviors When animals mate, a male animal fertilizes a female animal's egg cells with his sperm cells. The fertilized egg will eventually develop into a new organism. This process is an important part of ensuring the continued survival of the species. Scientists believe that the drive to reproduce evolved in animals over time as a way to ensure the success of their species and their own individual genes.

The behavior patterns related to how animals mate are called **mating systems**, and they vary from species to species. Some species of animals are monogamous. That means that they only mate with one other organism for a period of time, which can range from just a season or to their entire lives. In other animal species, such as baboons, a male has multiple female mates at one time. There are other species in which females have multiple male mates. Honeybees use this mating system. In still other species, males and females both have multiple mates during any one period of time. Scientists believe that these different mating systems evolved over time to best meet the needs of each particular species.

Model It

The terms defined below are used to describe the different mating systems that are observed in animal species.

monogamy: one female mates with one male
polygyny: one male mates with multiple females
polyandry: one female mates with multiple males
polygynandry: females mate with multiple males and males mate with multiple females

SEP Develop Models ✏ Use the information above and the symbols for male and female, which are shown to the right, to model the four types of mating systems in the space provided. Monogamy has been completed for you.

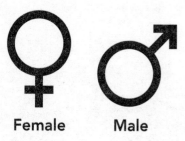

Female   **Male**

Monogamy

Locking Horns

Figure 2 Bighorn sheep are found in the mountains and deserts of southeastern California. These male bighorns display aggression as they compete for mates.

Explain Phenomena What is the goal of this competitive behavior?

....

....

....

....

....

Imagine a male walrus swimming in the icy water making a series of whistling and clacking sounds. A group of females looks on from the floating ice pack. One joins the male in the water and they dive together in a dance-like ritual. This courtship behavior is an activity that prepares males and females of the same species for mating. These behaviors are ways for animals to attract the attention of potential mates.

Communication Animals communicate in many ways, using sounds, scents, and body movements. Often, the goal of communication is reproduction.

One way animals communicate is with sound. You have probably heard birds singing outside. Birds communicate with sound for many reasons, but mainly they sing to attract mates. Many animals also use chemical scents to send messages. A chemical released by one animal that affects the behavior of another animal of the same species is called a **pheromone** (fehr uh mohn). In many species of moths, for example, females release a pheromone into the air that is a signal to males that she is ready to mate.

Competition Animals compete for resources, such as food and water. They also compete for access to mates, which may involve displays of aggression (**Figure 2**). Aggression is a threatening behavior that one animal uses to intimidate or dominate another animal. Another competitive behavior that is often observed in animals is establishing and maintaining a territory. A territory is an area that is occupied and defended by an animal or group of animals. An animal that is defending its territory will drive away other animals that may compete with it for mates.

Reflect As you learn about animal behaviors related to reproduction, spend some time observing animals in the area around your neighborhood and school. Record notes and observations in your science notebook. Explain what type of behavior you think you were observing and why.

Reproductive Strategies

Different animal species have different ways of caring for their young. Some species have no contact with their offspring, while others spend many years caring for them. For example, most amphibian larvae, or tadpoles, develop into adults without parental help. Similarly, the offspring of most reptiles, such as snakes, are independent from the time they hatch. Offspring that do not receive parental care must be able to care for themselves from the time of birth. Generally, animals that provide no parental care release many eggs at a time. Although many will not survive, the sheer number of potential offspring ensures that at least some will make it.

Parental Investment The offspring of most birds and all mammals **typically** spend weeks to years under the care and protection of a parent. Most bird species lay eggs in nests that one or both parents build. Then one or both parents sit on the eggs, keeping them warm until they hatch. After hatching, one or both parents will feed and protect their young until they are able to care for themselves. Young mammals, such as the infant chimpanzee in **Figure 3**, are usually quite helpless for a long time after they are born. After birth, mammals are fed with milk from the mother's body. One or both parents may continue caring for their offspring until the young animals are independent. Typically, animals that provide parental care have only a few offspring at a time. Many only have one. Scientists believe that these animals work harder to care for their young because they have fewer or no other offspring to take their place.

Academic Vocabulary
What are some synonyms, or words and phrases that have a similar meaning, for the term *typically*?

....

....

....

Parenting Behavior
Figure 3 This female chimpanzee carries her infant on her back until it is old enough to better care for itself.

CCC Cause and Effect
What are the benefits and drawbacks of this behavior for the mother chimpanzee?

....

....

....

....

....

....

....

Math Toolbox

Survivorship Curves

To show how the probability of death changes with age for different species, scientists use graphs called survivorship curves. In a Type I survivorship curve, individuals are most likely to live a full life. In a Type III survivorship curve, individuals are most likely to die when they are young. In a Type II survivorship curve, an individual's chance of dying remains constant.

Draw Comparative Inferences What can you infer about the role of parental care for the three species represented in the graph?

....

....

....

....

....

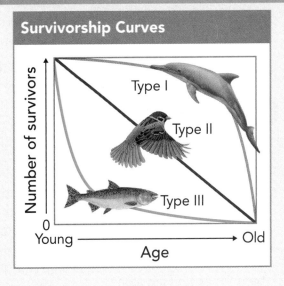

Survivorship Curves

Fertilization Strategies

For animals that reproduce sexually, a new organism begins when a sperm cell and an egg cell are joined in the process of fertilization. Fertilization may occur in one of two ways: externally or internally. **External fertilization** occurs when eggs are fertilized outside of a female's body, and **internal fertilization** occurs when eggs are fertilized inside a female's body.

The male fish in **Figure 4** are fertilizing the females' eggs by releasing a cloud of sperm over eggs the female just released. The fertilized eggs will develop outside the female's body. Not all the eggs will become fertilized but the huge number of potential offspring means that many will.

When fertilization occurs internally, a male animal releases sperm directly into a female's body where the eggs are located. The fertilized eggs may develop inside or outside the mother's body. Many animals, such as reptiles and birds, lay eggs in which offspring develop until they hatch. For others, including most mammals, offspring develop inside the mother's body until they are ready to be born.

✓ CHECK POINT **Determine Central Ideas** How are internal and external fertilization alike and different?

....

....

....

External Fertilization
Figure 4 Male fish release sperm in a cloud over the eggs.

Make Observations What makes the image an example of external fertilization?

....

....

339

INTERACTIVITY

Consider the impact of light pollution on an animals' mating behaviors.

Student Discourse

With a partner, debate the benefits of working alone vs. working on a team. Each take one side, listing the benefits of your side and an argument for each. Take turns sharing your arguments. Then, each partner will refute (argue against) any arguments or to add a benefit your partner did not think of.

Working Together

Figure 5 Orcas live in a group called a pod. All adults in the pod help parent any offspring. Likewise, some spiders live in a nest and work together to raise all young.

CCC Cause and Effect What are the benefits of shared responsibility when raising young? Explain.

....
....
....
....
....

Cooperative Behaviors In some cases, animals increase their chances for surviving and reproducing when they live and work together. For example, some fish form schools, and some insects live in large groups. Hoofed mammals, such as bison and wild horses, often form herds. Living in a group helps these animals stay alive.

One benefit of living in a large group is that it is an effective way to protect young animals from predators. Elephants protect the offspring of the group by forming a defensive circle around them. By working together, each adult female helps to protect the offspring of the other females. In turn, the other members of the group protect her offspring as well.

Other species of animals that live in groups may take on parenting responsibilities of animals that are not their offspring (**Figure 5**). For example, there are worker bees in a hive whose sole job is providing food and protection for the bee larvae. They may not be the parents of the offspring, but they still work hard to care for the hive's young.

☑ **CHECK POINT** **Summarize Text** How can cooperative behaviors help animals that are raising offspring?

....
....
....
....
....

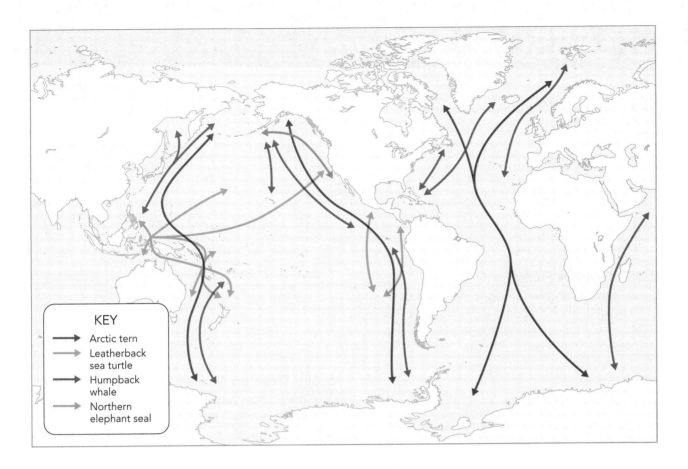

KEY
- Arctic tern
- Leatherback sea turtle
- Humpback whale
- Northern elephant seal

Migratory Behaviors Many animals spend their entire lives in a relatively small area. But there are many others that migrate. **Migration** is the regular, seasonal journey of an animal from one place to another and back again. Animals have different reasons for migration. Some migrate to an area that provides plenty of food or a more comfortable climate during a harsh season. Others, such as the animals whose migratory routes are shown in **Figure 6**, migrate to a better environment for reproduction. In some cases, large groups of animals of the same species gather together in the same place at the same time so they can mate. They may also stay there to begin the process of raising their young. By migrating every year, these animals increase their chances of finding a mate and producing offspring in conditions that will be favorable to their survival.

Animal behaviors related to mating and raising offspring are often tied to Earth's cycles. Polar bears, for example, mate in the spring and give birth in the winter. Other animals reproduce with more or less frequency, but almost all follow some kind of predictable cycle. Following these patterns ensures that offspring are born when they have the best chances of survival.

Migratory Routes

Figure 6 Many animals travel thousands of miles every year to mate and raise their young.

SEP Use Models ✏ A friend took a road trip across the United States from the west coast to the east coast. Draw an arrow on the map showing the trip. How does your friend's trip compare to the animal trips represented in the map?

....

....

....

....

☑ LESSON 3 Check

1. **Determine Differences** What is the difference between learned behaviors and instincts?

....

....

....

....

2. **SEP Evaluate Evidence** Male birds of paradise are known for having bright markings that they flash while making complex movements when females are nearby. What is this behavior an example of and what is its purpose?

....

....

....

....

3. **SEP Construct Explanations** Describe how animals use pheromones to attract potential mates.

....

....

....

....

....

4. **Compare and Contrast** Describe two different parenting strategies that animals use and explain why they are both effective.

....

....

....

....

....

....

....

....

5. **SEP Develop Models** ✏ Draw a picture showing how animals that use cooperative behaviors might be able to protect offspring from predators.

Quest CHECK-IN

In this lesson, you learned how animal behaviors can help individuals find mates. You also learned how animal parenting behaviors can affect how likely their offspring are to survive.

Explain Phenomena Consider various ways a male bird might attract a female mate. Suppose the male bird is of a species that does not display colorful feathers. What sort of behaviors could the male birds use to attract female birds?

....

....

....

INTERACTIVITY

The Mating Game

Go online to explore different techniques and behaviors that animals use to increase their odds of reproductive success.

 MS-LS1-4

Avian Artists

As male birds go, the Vogelkop bowerbird is rather plain. It doesn't have the bright feathers of a cardinal or the fancy plumage of a peacock. But what the bowerbird lacks in color, it makes up for in engineering and decorating skills.

The Vogelkop bowerbird displays some of the most complex courtship behavior observed in birds. To attract a mate, the male builds an elaborate structure out of twigs, called a bower. After completing the bower, the male bowerbird collects brightly colored flowers and berries to decorate the bower. Males compete to build the most magnificent bowers and amass the most beautiful collections in the hopes of impressing female bowerbirds.

When a female comes by to inspect the bower and collection, the male will strut and sing inside the bower. If the female likes the male's decorating expertise, then they will mate. The female will leave to build a nest and raise the young on her own.

MY DISCOVERY

What other animal species display extraordinary behavior when it comes to courtship? Do some research to find out more.

Male Vogelkop bowerbirds spend years making their bowers.

The Vogelkop bowerbird lives on the island of New Guinea in the Pacific Ocean.

343

Factors Influencing Growth

Guiding Questions

- How do environmental and genetic factors influence an organism's growth?
- What stimulates plant growth?
- Which factors control plant and animal growth?

Connections

Literacy Analyze Text Structure

Math Represent Quantitative Relationships

 MS-LS1-5 Construct a scientific explanation based on evidence for how environmental and genetic factors influence the growth of organisms.

HANDS-ON LAB

иInvestigate Observe how environmental factors such as pollution affect plant growth.

Vocabulary

hormone
auxin
tropism
photoperiodism
dormancy
metamorphosis

Academic Vocabulary

stimuli
essential

Connect It !

🖊 **These palm trees grow in the desert. Circle a part of the palm tree that helps it survive in the dry conditions of the desert.**

SEP Construct Explanations How do you think this part of the tree helps it to stay alive in the desert?

....

....

Growth and Development of Organisms

Living things on Earth grow and develop from the beginning of their lives. But the way organisms grow and develop, and the size they reach, varies from species to species.

Several factors influence how organisms grow. Some of these factors are determined by their genetic characteristics and are part of their normal life cycle. Other factors occur outside of the organism and can be related to their access to needed resources, the conditions in their environment, and their responses to other **stimuli**.

Plants and animals have changed over time. These changes are a result of adapting to the stimuli of environmental factors. These adaptations have increased their odds for survival. The palm trees in **Figure 1**, for example, have evolved to survive dry desert conditions. Dried leaves create thick fronds that shade the tree's trunk to prevent it from losing moisture.

INTERACTIVITY

Explore the conditions required for living things to grow and thrive.

Academic Vocabulary

Often, a dog barks when someone rings the doorbell and knocks on the door. What are the stimuli in this situation?

....

....

....

Plant Growth

Figure 1 These California fan palms are adapted to the dry conditions of Indian Gorge in San Diego County.

345

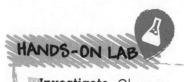

HANDS-ON LAB

Investigate Observe how environmental factors such as pollution affect plant growth.

Plant Responses and Growth

If you've ever grown a garden, you've probably witnessed how plants grow over time. As with all living things, plant growth is controlled by responses to the stimuli of local environmental factors. For plants, these responses are controlled by **hormones**, chemicals that affect growth and development. One important plant hormone is called **auxin** (AWK sin). It speeds up the rate at which plant cells grow and controls a plant's response to light.

Tropisms

In animals, a typical response to a stimulus is to move toward or away from it. But plants cannot move in the same way that animals do, so they often respond by growing either toward or away from a stimulus. A plant's growth response toward or away from a stimulus is called a **tropism** (TROH piz um). Touch, gravity, and light are three stimuli that trigger tropisms in plants.

The stems of some plants, such as the vines, show a response to touch called thigmotropism. As a vine grows, it coils around any object it touches. This is an example of positive thigmotropism, because the vine grows toward the stimulus. Plants also know which direction to grow, because they respond to gravity. This response is called gravitropism. Roots show positive gravitropism if they grow downward. Stems, on the other hand, show negative gravitropism (**Figure 2**). Plants' response to light is called phototropism. The leaves, stems, and flowers of plants grow toward light.

How Plants Respond

Figure 2 Plants respond to local environmental factors in a variety of ways.

Negative Gravitropism The stems of plants respond to the stimulus of gravity by growing upward, away from gravity.

CCC Cause and Effect How does gravitropism affect the growth of a plant?

....

....

Positive Phototropism When stems and leaves grow toward sources of light, they show positive phototropism.

CCC Patterns ✏ Place an arrow pointing to where the sun would be in the picture above.

Seasonal Change Depending on where you live, you may have noticed flowers blooming in the spring and the leaves of trees changing color in autumn. These changes are caused by changing conditions brought on by the seasons.

In many plants, the amount of darkness they experience determines when they bloom. A plant's response to seasonal changes in the length of night and day is called **photoperiodism**. As shown in **Figure 2**, plants respond differently to night length. Other plants are not affected at all by the lengths of days and nights.

Have you ever wondered why some trees lose their leaves in the fall? As winter draws near, many plants prepare to go into a state of **dormancy**. Dormancy is a period when an organism's growth or activity stops. Dormancy helps plants survive freezing temperatures and the lack of liquid water. With many trees, the first visible change is that the leaves begin to turn color. Cooler weather and shorter days cause the leaves to stop making chlorophyll. As chlorophyll breaks down, yellow and orange pigments become visible. This causes the brilliant colors of autumn leaves like the ones shown in **Figure 2**. Over the next few weeks, sugar and water are transported out of the tree's leaves. When the leaves fall to the ground, the tree is ready for winter.

Photoperiodism Irises, left, bloom when days are getting longer and nights are getting shorter. Chrysanthemums, above, bloom when the lengths of the day and night reach a certain ratio.

Dormancy Some species of trees go into a state or dormancy every winter.

Analyze Benefits Why do you think some trees evolved to go into a state of dormancy during the winter months?

....

....

....

Plant Diseases

Figure 3 Insects, worms, and other pests can cause disease in plants and have an impact on their growth.

Make Observations ✏️ Circle the diseased parts of the plant.

📖 **Write About It** Locate two plants in or around your home, school, or neighborhood: one that appears healthy and one that does not. Explain which factors you think are helping the healthy plant grow and which factors are keeping the unhealthy one from growing to its full size.

Environmental Conditions

In ideal conditions, a plant will reach a certain maximum size that is normal for its species. However, in some cases, plants do not get enough of the resources they need, so they do not grow as large as they normally would. A lack of sunlight, for instance, may keep a plant from growing to full size or weaken its structure.

In addition to sunlight, plants need nutrient-rich soil and water to grow. Soil contains the nutrients a plant needs to carry out its life processes. Nutrient-poor soil may result from an area being overly crowded with plants. Competition for the nutrients in the soil may mean that few plants get the nutrients they need. Similarly, if a plant does not receive enough water, it will not grow to a healthy size. Diseases like the one shown in **Figure 3** can impact plant growth as well.

Plan It

Water Needs and Plant Growth

SEP Plan Your Investigation You want to find out how the amount of water you give plants affects their growth. In the space below, describe a plan for an investigation that can help you answer this question.

....

....

....

....

....

....

Animal Growth

Like plants, animals grow and develop. Also like plants, their growth is affected by both internal and external stimuli to which they are constantly responding.

Embryo Development After fertilization, the offspring of animals develop in different ways. The growing offspring, or embryo, may develop outside or inside the mother's body.

One way animal embryos develop is inside an egg that is laid outside the parent's body. Most invertebrates lay eggs. Many fish, reptiles, all birds, and a few mammals do, too. The contents of the egg provide the nutrients a developing embryo needs. The eggs of egg-laying land vertebrates are called amniotic eggs. Amniotic eggs are covered with membranes and a shell.

In other cases, an embryo develops inside an egg that is kept, or retained, within the parent's body. The developing embryo gets its nutrients from the egg's yolk, just like the offspring of egg-laying animals. The egg hatches either before or after being released from the parent's body. This type of development is found in some species of fish, amphibians, and reptiles. Marsupial mammals, such as kangaroos, release partly developed young from a yolk-type sac into a protective pocket where they continue to develop.

In placental mammals, which include elephants, wolves, and humans, the embryo develops inside the mother's body. The mother provides the embryo with everything it needs during development. As is shown in **Figure 4**, **essential** nutrients and gases are exchanged between the embryo and the mother through an organ called the placenta. The embryo develops inside its mother's body until its body systems can function on their own.

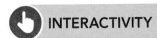

INTERACTIVITY

Observe how animals grow and develop over time.

INTERACTIVITY

Find out how cows are being bred to be bigger and bigger.

Academic Vocabulary

What does it mean when someone describes something as being essential? Use *essential* in a sentence.

....

....

....

....

....

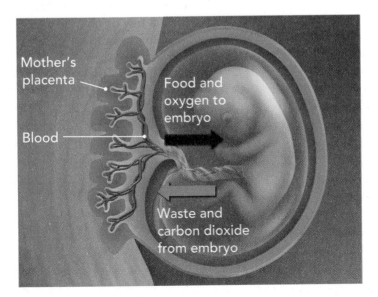

Mother's placenta

Food and oxygen to embryo

Blood

Waste and carbon dioxide from embryo

Placental Mammal Development

Figure 4 The embryos of placental mammals develop inside their mothers' bodies.

Draw Conclusions What would be some of the advantages of this type of embryo development compared to an amniotic egg laid outside the mother's body?

....

....

....

....

....

Life Cycles

Figure 5 Different animals go through different life cycles. Unlike you, both of these animals go through metamorphosis.

Sequence ✎ Add arrows to the diagram to show the order in which these stages occur.

Crayfish and other crustaceans, such as crabs and shrimp, begin their lives as tiny, swimming larvae. The bodies of these larvae do not resemble those of adults. Eventually, crustacean larvae develop into adults.

Egg

Adult

Larval stages

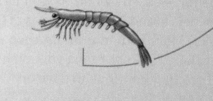

Postlarval stage

Adult frogs reproduce sexually.

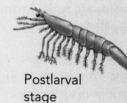

Eggs are fertilized outside the female's body.

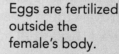

Frogs begin their life cycle as fertilized eggs in water. After a few days, tadpoles wriggle out of the eggs and begin swimming. Over time, tadpoles develop into adult frogs.

Front legs develop and the tail is absorbed.

A tadpole hatches from an egg.

Hind legs develop.

Comparing Life Cycles Many young animals, including most vertebrates, look like small versions of adults from the time they are born. Other animals go through the process of **metamorphosis**, or major body changes, as they grow and develop into adults (**Figure 5**).

External and Internal Factors Animal growth and development are affected by both internal and external factors. Internal factors include genetic and hormonal characteristics that are part of an organism's life processes. External factors, on the other hand, are the environmental conditions that an animal may or may not have any control over.

Environmental Conditions Access to resources and exposure to diseases and parasites can also affect the growth and development of animals. If animals do not receive the nutrition they need during development or if they become sick, they may not reach their full adult size. Space is another resource that can affect animal growth. For example, the growth of some species of fish, such as goldfish like the one in **Figure 6**, is affected by how large a body of water they live in. If its living space is not large enough, it will not reach its full adult size.

✓ CHECK POINT **Determine Meaning** How is your life cycle different from animals that undergo metamorphosis?

....

....

....

👆 **INTERACTIVITY**

Construct an explanation with evidence for how environmental and genetic factors influence the growth of organisms.

Figure 6 If a goldfish's tank is too small, its growth may be restricted.

Draw Conclusions In ideal conditions, a goldfish will grow to be about 10 to 20 cm long. But most people think of goldfish as very small fish that only grow to be a few centimeters long. What conclusion can you draw from this information?

....

....

....

....

....

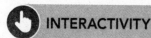

Observe the effects that water and food have on the growth and production of crop plants.

Genes The genes an offspring inherits from its parents are a major factor in how it develops and grows. In your own classroom, you can probably observe how students' heights vary. Part of these differences is due to the genes your classmates inherited from their parents. Children usually grow up to be about the same height as their parents.

Hormones Another internal factor that influences growth and development are the hormones that are naturally produced by animals' bodies. For instance, male animals produce greater amounts of testosterone than female animals. In many animal species, the production of testosterone in male animals results in males growing to be larger than females.

Math Toolbox

Human Malnutrition and Height

In 1945, after World War II, the Korean Peninsula was divided into two nations: North Korea and South Korea. The two countries had different forms of government and economic systems. The data table shows the average heights in the two countries from 1930 to 1996.

1. **Represent Quantitative Relationships** Use the data in the table to make a bar graph in the space below.

2. **Synthesize Information** Are the height differences in these two countries likely the result of genetics, hormones, or environmental conditions? Explain why.

....
....
....
....
....
....
....
....
....

Years	Average height of North Koreans (cm)	Average height of South Koreans (cm)
1930–1939	159.4	158.9
1940–1949	160.6	161.1
1950–1959	161.8	163.1
1960–1969	162.7	165
1970–1979	163.5	166.7
1980–1989	164.5	167.8
1990–1996	165.2	168.4

Source: NCD Risk Factor Collaboration, 2017

Heights of North and South Koreans (1950–1996)

Legend:
/// North Koreans
■ South Koreans

Y-axis: Height (cm) — 0, 158, 160, 162, 164, 166, 168, 170

X-axis: Decade — 1930s, 1950s, 1970s, 1990s

MS-LS1-5

1. Distinguish Relationships Describe three types of stimuli that cause plants to exhibit tropism.

....
....
....
....
....
....

2. CCC Cause and Effect What causes plants to bloom in different seasons?

....
....
....
....
....

3. SEP Construct Explanations Why might soil have an effect on plant growth?

....
....
....

4. Distinguish Differences How does offspring development in egg-laying animals and placental mammals differ?

....
....
....
....
....
....

5. SEP Develop Models ✏ Draw diagrams showing three different ways that animal embryos develop. Include labels.

Quest CHECK-IN

In this lesson, you learned about some of the factors that affect the growth and development of plants and animals. You also learned about some of the different stages that animals go through as they develop.

SEP Design Solutions Consider the environmental impact of new construction near a wildlife habitat. At what point during the year do you think construction would have the least impact? Explain.

....
....
....
....

👆 INTERACTIVITY

Make Your Construction Case

Go online to consider the criteria and constraints involved in your construction project.

☑ TOPIC 6 Review and Assess

1 Patterns of Reproduction

🕐 MS-LS3-2

1. Asexual reproduction is different from sexual reproduction in that the offspring of asexual reproduction
   A. are identical to the parent.
   B. contain half the chromosomes of the parent.
   C. have no genetic material.
   D. have more variety in their traits.

2. Different forms of a gene are called
   A. alleles.
   B. offspring.
   C. recessive.
   D. traits.

3. Which example best describes incomplete dominance?
   A. humans with blood type AB
   B. flowers with red petals
   C. horses with roan color pattern
   D. sheep with gray fleece

4. .... inheritance refers to any trait that is controlled by more than one gene.

5. **CCC Patterns** Explain why sexual reproduction results in offspring with more genetic variation than asexual reproduction.

   ....
   ....
   ....
   ....
   ....
   ....
   ....
   ....

2 Plant Structures for Reproduction

🕐 MS-LS1-4

6. A maple tree produces male and female flowers. Which term best describes the maple?
   A. gymnosperm   B. angiosperm
   C. sporophyte   D. non-vascular

7. Both ferns and cedar trees rely on .... for successful fertilization.

8. **CCC Relate Structure and Function** What are two specialized structures of an apple tree that increase the chances that it will reproduce and have offspring that survive? Explain.

   ....
   ....
   ....
   ....
   ....
   ....

9. **Construct Arguments** Coconut palms are tropical trees usually found growing on shorelines. The tree produces fruit in a hard shell that can float on water. How does this help ensure the tree's successful reproduction?

   ....
   ....
   ....
   ....
   ....
   ....

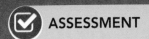
3 Animal Behaviors for Reproduction

 MS-LS1-4

10. What are mating systems?
   A. threatening behaviors that animals use to gain control over other animals
   B. behavior patterns that are related to how animals reproduce
   C. chemicals released by one animal that affect the behavior of another animal of the same species
   D. behaviors related to the movement of animals from one place to another and back again

11. Which statement about fertilization strategies is true?
   A. Internal fertilization mostly occurs in fish and amphibians.
   B. Internal fertilization results in eggs that develop outside the female's body.
   C. External fertilization is common for animals that live in water.
   D. External fertilization occurs in all land animals.

12. Cooperative behaviors can .... (increase/decrease) an animal's chances of surviving to reproduce.

13. Apply Scientific Reasoning In general, how is the number of offspring produced by an animal related to the amount of time and energy it invests in caring for its young?

....

....

....

....

....

....

....

4 Factors Influencing Growth

 MS-LS1-5

14. Which is *not* a stimulus that can trigger tropisms in plants?
   A. light
   B. gravity
   C. touch
   D. temperature

15. An insect such as the butterfly goes through the process of .... as it grows and develops into an adult.

16. CCC Cause and Effect Oak trees go into a state of dormancy during the winter. Suppose that a forest of oaks grows in an area that begins to experience warmer winters due to climate change. What effect do you think this will have on the oak trees? Explain.

....

....

....

....

....

....

17. SEP Construct Explanations How do environmental conditions affect the growth of an animal?

....

....

....

....

....

....

....

....

MS-LS1-4, MS-LS1-5

Evidence-Based Assessment

A team of researchers investigated how climate change and warming temperatures affected animals in the Rocky Mountains. One of the animals they studied was the yellow-bellied marmot. This large rodent lives in small colonies and survives the harsh winters by hibernating for eight months. The marmots forage for grasses and seeds, which only grow once the winter snow has melted.

Because the ground is bare of snow for such a brief time each year, the marmots have a very short breeding season. It begins as soon as they come out of hibernation. Not long after, the snow melts and more food becomes available to the marmots.

However, the researchers discovered that warming temperatures were disrupting marmot hibernation patterns. They compiled data about the first marmot sighted coming out of hibernation each year for over 20 years. The data are summarized in the graph.

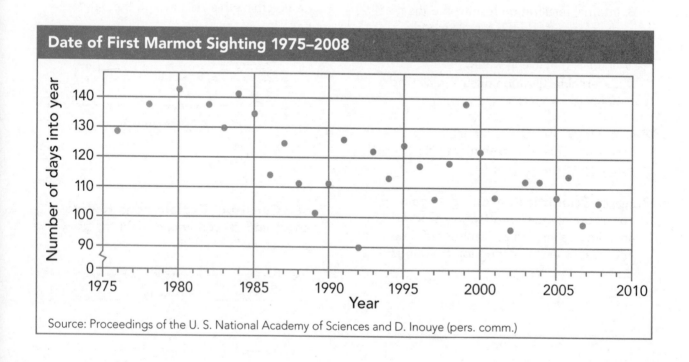

Date of First Marmot Sighting 1975–2008

Source: Proceedings of the U. S. National Academy of Sciences and D. Inouye (pers. comm.)

1. **SEP Analyze Data** What trend is shown by the data in the graph?
   A. The first marmot coming out of hibernation tends to be sighted earlier and earlier.
   B. The first marmot coming out of hibernation was sighted later each year.
   C. The date the first marmot came out of hibernation fluctuated randomly.
   D. There was little or no change in the date the first marmot was sighted each year.

2. **SEP Engage in Argument** What environmental factor do you think influences when marmots wake from hibernation? Provide support.

   ....
   ....
   ....
   ....
   ....
   ....

3. **CCC Cause and Effect** How does the marmot's behavior after coming out of hibernation increase the probability that it will successfully reproduce?

   ....
   ....
   ....
   ....
   ....
   ....

4. **Construct Arguments** What effect might an earlier breeding season have on the growth of young marmots? Select all that apply.
   ☐ Food will be abundant for young marmots.
   ☐ Fewer young marmots will be able to reproduce later.
   ☐ It will be too cold for young marmots to survive.
   ☐ Some young marmots may not grow properly.
   ☐ Some young marmots might starve.

5. **SEP Construct Explanations** The researchers found that while the air temperature is tending to increase earlier, the snow is not melting earlier. The marmots were waking up but struggling to find food. Why aren't the marmots waking up when the snow melts, instead of when the temperature warms?

   ....
   ....
   ....
   ....
   ....
   ....
   ....

Quest FINDINGS

Complete the Quest!

Phenomenon Finalize and present your construction plan using the information you have gathered as evidence to support your recommendations.

Apply Concepts Is there a way your town or city could ensure that the wild plants and animals that live there have the resources they need to grow and reproduce?

....
....
....
....
....

👆 **INTERACTIVITY**

Reflect on Your Basketball Court Plans

Clean and Green

> How can you evaluate **claims** about laundry **detergents** that are marketed as **safe** for the environment?

Background

Phenomenon Many businesses promote products, such as soaps and detergents, that are environmentally friendly. *Greenwashing*, which is a combination of the terms *green* and *whitewashing*, is the practice of claiming that a product is more environmentally safe than it really is. You are a budding botanist working with an environmental watchdog group. You must evaluate the biological effects of "natural" detergents that claim to be safer for the environment than regular detergents.

In this investigation, you will design and conduct an experiment to determine the effects of "eco-friendly" laundry detergents on plant growth. It will probably take several days for the seeds to germinate. Keep in mind that the factors for healthy plant growth include height, color, and general appearance.

Materials

(per group)

- 3 plastic petri dishes with lids
- potting soil
- graduated cylinder
- 30 radish seeds
- masking tape
- day-old tap water
- metric ruler
- wax pencil
- "regular" detergent solution
- "eco-friendly" detergent solution
- scale or balance

Safety

Be sure to follow all safety guidelines provided by your teacher. The Safety Appendix of your textbook provides more details about the safety icons.

Design Your Investigation

1. With your group, discuss how you will investigate the effects of the detergents on plant growth. Also, discuss the types of data you will need to collect in order to determine how environmental factors affect plant growth.

2. Work together to identify the factors you will control and the variables you will change. Think about what a plant normally needs from its environment in order to live and grow. Decide what measurements and observations you will need to make and how often you will need to make them. To make these decisions, consider the following questions:

   • How many different groups of seeds will you use?
   • How will you determine the number of seeds that germinate in each group?
   • How will you determine the health of the shoots in each group of seeds?
   • What qualitative observations will you make?

3. Write a detailed procedure for your experiment in the space provided. Make sure you describe the setup for your investigation, the variables you will measure, a description of the data you will collect, and how you will collect the data. Before proceeding, obtain your teacher's approval.

4. In the space provided, construct a data table to organize the data you will collect. When constructing your data table, consider the following questions:

   • How many seeds will you put in each petri dish?
   • How many times will you collect data?
   • Will you collect data at the same time each day, or at different times?
   • What qualitative observations will you record?

5. Carry out your procedure for investigating the effect of your pollutant on plant growth. You will need to make observations once a day over several days. Make your measurements each day and record the data you collect.

Procedure

....
....
....
....
....
....
....
....
....
....
....
....

Data Table and Observations

Analyze and Interpret Data

1. **SEP Use Mathematics** Identify the dependent variables you measured in this investigation. Calculate the percentage of seeds that had germinated each day in each dish. Then, calculate the mean length of the shoots for each day you collected data. Make this calculation for the seeds in each dish.

....

....

....

....

2. **CCC Cause and Effect** Describe any patterns you see in the data for the seedlings grown under the three conditions in the petri dishes. Summarize the data by writing a cause-and-effect statement about the effects of the detergents on the growth of the plants.

....

....

....

....

....

3. **Make Generalizations** Based on the results of your experiment, do you think the manufacturer's claim is valid? Is the product safe for the long-term health of the environment? Explain.

....

....

....

....

....

4. **Compare Data** Share your results among the groups that tested the other "natural" detergents. Look for similarities and differences in the data. What do you think might account for any differences?

....

....

....

....

....

HANDS-ON LAB

uConnect Explore the effects of different methods of reproduction.

MS-LS3-1 Develop and use a model to describe why structural changes to genes (mutations) located on chromosomes may affect proteins and may result in harmful, beneficial, or neutral effects to the structure and function of the organism.

MS-LS3-2 Develop and use a model to describe why asexual reproduction results in offspring with identical genetic information and sexual reproduction results in offspring

MS-LS4-4 Construct an explanation based on evidence that describes how genetic variations of traits in a population increase some individuals' probability of surviving and reproducing in a specific environment.

MS-LS4-5 Gather and synthesize information about the technologies that have changed the way humans influence the inheritance of desired traits in organisms.

EP&CIIa Students should be developing an understanding that direct and indirect changes to natural systems due to the growth of human populations and their consumption rates influence the geographic.

EP&CIIc Students should be developing an understanding that the expansion and operation of human communities influences the geographic extent, composition, biological diversity, and viability of natural systems.

How can a black bear family have different colored bears?

GO ONLINE
to access your digital course

▶ VIDEO

👆 INTERACTIVITY

🧪 VIRTUAL LAB

☑ ASSESSMENT

📖 eTEXT

⚗ HANDS-ON LABS

The Essential Question

How do offspring receive traits from their parents?

CCC Cause and Effect Scientists estimate that there are about 30,000 black bears in California. You probably thought all black bears are black. But any black bear parents can have black, brown, blonde, gray, or even white cubs! How do you think that happens?

....

....

....

Quest KICKOFF

How can you sell a new fruit?

Phenomenon Consumers are often open to new ideas—especially tasty new ideas. But it may take some convincing. What new fruit sensation can you develop, and how will you get growers and consumers to buy in? In this Quest activity, you will explore reproduction, heredity, and genetics as you choose desirable traits and figure out how to ensure their consistent appearance in your product. Once your new fruit is characterized, you will create a brochure to help growers understand your product, why it is desirable, and how they can grow it successfully.

 **INTERACTIVITY**

 MS-LS3-1, MS-LS3-2, MS-LS4-4, MS-LS4-5, EP&CIIa, EP&CIIc

Funky Fruits

 **NBC LEARN** ▶ VIDEO

After watching the Quest Kickoff video about different kinds of fruit hybrids, think about the qualities you desire in your fruit. In the table below, identify the characteristics you want your new fruit to have.

Color	
Taste	
Size	
Shape	
Texture	

Quest CHECK-IN

IN LESSON 1

How can you use both sexual and asexual reproduction to develop your new fruit? Explore how farmers benefit from using both types of reproduction to establish and maintain a consistent product.

 INTERACTIVITY

An Apple Lesson

Quest CHECK-IN

IN LESSON 2

What role do chromosomes and genes play in fruit reproduction? Make a chromosome map and locate genes that carry desirable traits.

 INTERACTIVITY

About Those Chromosomes

IN LESSON 3

What do DNA and protein synthesis have to do with the traits exhibited by an organism? Consider how genes will affect the characteristics of your fruit.

These white strawberries, called pineberries, taste somewhat like pineapples.

Quest CHECK-IN

IN LESSON 4

How are dominant and recessive traits inherited? Examine data tables for trait inheritance and complete Punnett squares to determine the probable outcomes of crosses.

HANDS-ON LAB

All in the Numbers

IN LESSON 5

How do growers ensure consistency in their product? Consider how you might use genetic technologies to develop your new fruit.

Quest FINDINGS

Complete the Quest!

Create a brochure for prospective growers of your new fruit. Convince readers that your fruit will be a delicious success!

 INTERACTIVITY

Reflect on Funky Fruits

Patterns of Inheritance

Guiding Questions

- How did Gregor Mendel advance the fields of genetics and inheritance?
- How are inherited alleles related to an organism's traits?
- How is probability related to inheritance?

Connections

Literacy Determine Conclusions

Math Use a Probability Model

MS-LS3-2 Develop and use a model to describe why asexual reproduction results in offspring with identical genetic information and sexual reproduction results in offspring with genetic variation.

HANDS-ON LAB

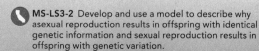

Investigate Explore cross-pollination by examining the parts of a flower

Vocabulary

heredity
dominant allele
recessive allele
probability
genotype
phenotype

Academic Vocabulary

quantify
factor

Connect It!

✎ **Male house finches express the trait for red feather color. Circle the male house finch in the photo.**

Predict ✎ List four more visible characteristics that these birds will pass on to their offspring. Then list the inherited trait that their offspring will possess.

Visible Characteristics	Inherited Traits
grayish bill color	bill color

Apply Concepts Will their offspring look exactly like the parents? Explain.

....

....

Mendel's Observations

Like all other organisms, the finches in **Figure 1** pass their traits to their offspring. To better understand **heredity**, the passing of traits from parents to offspring, it is important to learn about the history behind the science. In the 1800s, a European monk named Gregor Mendel studied heredity. Mendel's job at the monastery was to tend the garden. After several years of growing pea plants, he became very familiar with the traits pea plants could have. Some plants grew tall, while others were short. Some produced green seeds, while others produced yellow.

Mendel's Experiments

Mendel's studies became some of the most important in biology because he was one of the first to **quantify** his results. He collected, recorded, and analyzed data from the thousands of tests that he ran.

The experiments Mendel performed involved transferring the male flower part of a pea plant to the female flower part to get a desired trait. Mendel wanted to see what would happen with pea plants when he crossed different traits: short and tall, yellow seeds and green seeds, and so on. Because of his detailed work with heredity, Mendel is often referred to as the "father of modern genetics."

HANDS-ON LAB

Explore how human height is inherited.

Academic Vocabulary

In Latin, *quantus* means "how much." Have you heard the word quantify used before? Does it remind you of any other words?

....

....

....

....

Passing on Traits
Figure 1 House finches are common yard and feeder birds in California. Male and female house finches share many traits, but also have several that make them unique.

367

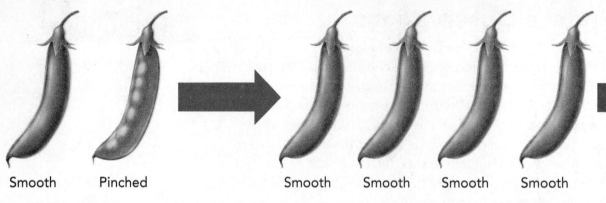

Smooth   Pinched   Smooth   Smooth   Smooth   Smooth

P generation   **F₁ generation**

Pea Pod Shape

Figure 2 ✏️ Circle the pod shape in the P generation that has the dominant trait.

Parents and Offspring When Mendel cross-pollinated, or crossed, a tall plant with a short one, all of the offspring were tall. The tall plant and short plant that were crossed are called the parent plants, or P generation. The offspring are called the F₁, or first filial generation. The term *filial* originates from the Latin terms *filius* and *filia*, which mean "son" and "daughter," respectively.

Mendel examined several traits of pea plants. Through his experimentation, he discovered that certain patterns formed. When a plant with green peas was crossed with one with yellow peas, all of the F₁ offspring were yellow. However, when he crossed these offspring, creating what is called the second filial generation, or F₂, the resulting offspring were not all yellow. For every four offspring, three were yellow and one was green. This pattern of inheritance appeared repeatedly when Mendel tested other traits, such as pea pod shape shown in **Figure 2**. Mendel concluded that while only one form of the trait is visible in F₁, in F₂ the missing trait sometimes shows itself.

Plan It !

SEP Plan Investigations
Consider five other traits that Mendel investigated. Explain how you could repeat Mendel's procedure for one of these traits and what the likely results would be of your investigation.

Trait	Dominant	Recessive
seed shape	round	wrinkled
seed color	yellow	green
pod color	green	yellow
flower color	purple	white
pod position on stem	side of stem	top of stem

....

....

....

....

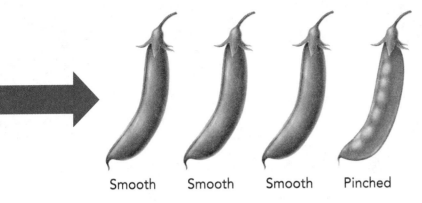

Smooth   Smooth   Smooth   Pinched

F₂ generation

INTERACTIVITY

Examine different methods of passing on genes to offspring.

HANDS-ON LAB

Explore cross-pollination by examining the parts of a flower.

Alleles Affect Inheritance

In Mendel's time, people had no knowledge of genetic material or its ability to carry the code for an organism's traits. However, Mendel was still able to formulate several ideas about heredity from his experiments. He called the information that carried the traits **factors**, because they determined what was expressed. He also determined that for every trait, organisms receive one factor from their mother and one factor from their father. He concluded that one factor can mask the expression of the other even if both are present at the same time.

Genes and Alleles Today, the term *factor* has been replaced with *gene* or *allele*. Alleles are the different forms of a gene. Pea plants have one gene that controls the color of the seeds. This gene may be expressed as either yellow or green through a combination of yellow alleles and green alleles. When crossed, each parent donates one of its alleles for seed color to the offspring. The allele that each parent donates is random. An offspring's seed color is determined by the combination of both alleles.

An organism's traits are controlled by the alleles it inherits. A **dominant allele** is one whose trait always shows up in the organism when the allele is present. A **recessive allele**, on the other hand, is hidden whenever the dominant allele is present. If one parent donates a dominant allele and the other donates a recessive allele, only the dominant trait will be expressed.

☑ **CHECK POINT** **Determine Meaning** What conditions would have to occur for offspring to express the recessive trait?

....

....

Academic Vocabulary

How is *factor* used differently in math and science?

....

....

....

....

....

....

Student Discourse

Think about a time when you saw a baby animal, such as a puppy or kitten. Think about the traits it inherited from its parents. How could you determine which traits were dominant and which were recessive? Discuss the question with a classmate and record your ideas in your science notebook.

Dominant Color

Figure 3 ✏ Mendel discovered that yellow is the dominant pea seed color, while the recessive pea seed color is green. Complete the statements. Use the letters *G* and *g* as needed.

Apply Concepts What are the alleles for the green pea seed? Would it be a purebred or a hybrid?

....

....

The alleles for a purebred yellow seed would be ....

The alleles for a hybrid yellow seed would be ....

Literacy Connection

Determine Conclusions
How did Mendel come to the conclusion that an organism's traits were carried on different alleles? Underline the sentence that answers this question.

Writing Alleles The traits we see are present because of the combination of alleles. For example, the peas in **Figure 3** show two different colors. Pea color is the gene, while the combinations of alleles determines how the gene will be expressed. To represent this, scientists who study patterns of inheritance, called geneticists, use letters to represent the alleles. A dominant allele is represented with a capital letter (*G*) and a recessive allele with a lowercase letter (*g*).

When an organism has two of the same alleles for a trait, it is called a purebred for that trait. This would be represented as *GG* or *gg*. When the organism has one dominant allele and one recessive allele, it is called a hybrid for that trait. This would be represented as *Gg*. Remember that each trait is represented by two alleles, one from each parent. Depending upon which alleles are inherited, the offspring may be a purebred or a hybrid.

Mendel's work was quite revolutionary. Prior to his work, many people assumed that all traits in offspring were a mixture of each parent's traits. Mendel's experiments, where traits appeared in the F_2 generation that were not in the F_1 generation, disproved this idea.

Probability and Heredity

When you flip a coin, what are the chances it will come up heads? Because there are two options (heads or tails), the probability of getting heads is 1 out of 2. The coin has an equal chance of coming up heads or tails. Each toss has no effect on the outcome of the next toss. **Probability** is a number that describes how likely it is that an event will occur. The laws of probability predict what is likely to happen and what is not likely to happen.

Probability and Genetics When dealing with genetics and inheritance, it is important to know the laws of probability. Every time two parents produce offspring, the probability of certain traits getting passed on is the same. For example, do you know any families that have multiple children, but all of them are the same sex? Picture a family where all the children are girls. According to the laws of probability, a boy should have been born already, but there is no guarantee of that happening. Every time these parents have a child, the probability of having a boy remains the same as the probability of having a girl.

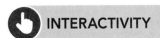

INTERACTIVITY

Collect data to determine whether a trait is genetic or acquired.

Math Toolbox

Determining Probability

Probability is an important part of the science of genetics. Answer the questions on probability below.

1. Predict The probability of a specific allele from one parent being passed on to an offspring is 1 in 2, or ½. This is the same probability as predicting a coin toss correctly. How often would you expect a coin to show tails if you flip it 100 times?

....

2. CCC Identify Patterns A die is a six-sided cube with dots representing the numbers 1 through 6. What is the probability of rolling a 3?

....

3. Use a Probability Model You and a friend both roll a die at the same time. On the first roll, the dots on the two dice add up to 7. On the second roll, they add up to 2. Which do you think was more likely, rolling a total of 2 or a total of 7? Explain your answer.

....

....

....

....

....

Making a Punnett Square

To determine the probability of inheriting alleles, geneticists use a model called a Punnett square. To construct a Punnett square, it is important to know what trait is being considered and whether the parents are pure-bred or hybrid.

The following steps demonstrate how to use a Punnett square to calculate the probability of offspring having different combinations of alleles. The example describes the procedure for a cross between two hybrid parents; however, this procedure will work for any cross.

Using a Punnett Square

Mendel's experiments involved crossing two hybrid pea plants in the F_1 generation. Most plants in the F_2 generation showed the dominant trait, but some showed the recessive trait. A Punnett square uses the laws of probability to demonstrate why those results occurred. Consider the question of what the offspring of two hybrid pea plants with yellow seed color will likely be.

1 **Draw a square box** divided into four square parts.

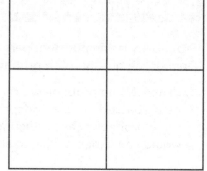

One parent's alleles go on top and the other parent's alleles go on the left.

2 **Determine the alleles** of each of the parents. You know that they are both hybrids, so they have one dominant allele (represented as a capital letter) and one recessive allele (represented as a lowercase letter). Place one set of alleles on top of the columns of the box, and one set of alleles next to the rows of the box, as shown.

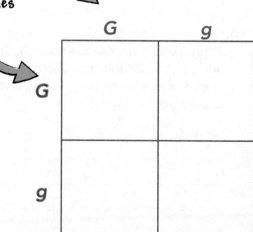

3 Do the cross! Inside each box, combine the letter at the top of the column with the letter to the left of the row the box is in. Always write a dominant allele before a recessive allele.

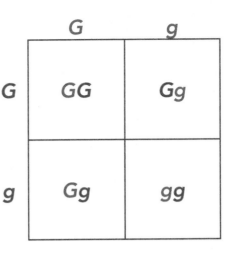

	G	g
G	GG	Gg
g	Gg	gg

4 Determine the likelihood of different combinations of alleles. As you can see from the Punnett square, the combination *GG* occurs ¼ of the time, the combination *Gg* occurs ²/₄, or ½ of the time, and the combination *gg* occurs ¼ of the time.

5 Determine which trait is expressed for each combination of alleles. In this example, the combination *GG* and *Gg* result in the dominant yellow seed color, while the combination *gg* results in the green seed color. Therefore, the dominant allele will be expressed ¾ of the time. This matches the results of Mendel's experiments.

SEP Use Models ✏ You cross a pea plant that is hybrid for yellow seed color (*Gg*) with a purebred green seed color (*gg*) plant. Draw a Punnett square to describe the results of the cross. What is the probability that the offspring will have green seed color?

....

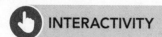

INTERACTIVITY

Use models to describe how sexual reproduction leads to genetic variation.

Genotype

You are already familiar with the terms *purebred* and *hybrid*. These terms refer to a **genotype**, an organism's genetic makeup or combination of alleles. As shown in **Figure 4**, the genotype of a purebred green seed pea plant would be *gg*. Both alleles are the same (purebred) and they are recessive because green is the recessive trait in terms of seed color. The hybrid genotype for this trait would be *Gg*.

The expression of an organism's genes is called its **phenotype**, the organism's physical appearance or visible traits. The height, the shape, the color, the size, the texture—whatever trait is being expressed, is referred to as the phenotype. So, a pea plant with the phenotype of yellow seed color could have two possible genotypes, *GG* or *Gg*.

Genotypes and Phenotypes for Seed Color

Figure 4 The phenotype of an organism is explained as physical characteristics we see, while the genotype describes the combination of alleles that are inherited.

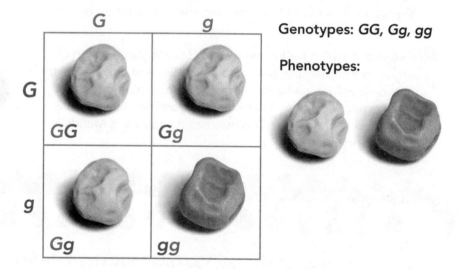

Genotypes: *GG*, *Gg*, *gg*

Phenotypes:

There are two other terms geneticists use to describe genotypes. Instead of saying *purebred*, they refer to an organism with two identical alleles as *homozygous* (*homo-* means "the same"). When the alleles are both dominant, as in the yellow seed plant (*GG*), the genotype is called homozygous dominant. However, when the alleles are both recessive, as in the green seed color (*gg*), the genotype is called homozygous recessive. When an organism is a hybrid, as in yellow seed color (*Gg*), the genotype is called the heterozygous condition (*hetero-* means "different").

☑ CHECK POINT **Cite Textual Evidence** Explain how genotypes and phenotypes are different.

....

....

MS-LS3-2

1. Apply Concepts The dominant allele for dimples is *D* and the recessive allele is *d*. How would a geneticist describe the genotype of an individual with the alleles *dd*?

....

Use the information you calculated in the Punnett square activity to answer questions 2 and 3.

2. SEP Interpret Data How did the probabilities of yellow seeds and green seeds compare with each other?

....
....
....
....

3. CCC Cause and Effect What would happen to the probabilities of yellow and green seeds if one parent were homozygous recessive and the other were homozygous dominant? Explain.

....
....
....
....
....

4. SEP Construct an Explanation Why were Mendel's experiments with pea plants so important toward advancing current knowledge of genetics and inheritance?

....
....
....
....
....
....

5. Predict For plant stem height, the dominant allele for height is *T*, and the recessive allele is *t*. What would be the genotypes, phenotypes, and offspring probabilities of a cross between a heterozygous parent for tall stem height and one that was homozygous recessive for short stem height?

....
....
....
....
....
....
....

Quest CHECK-IN

In this lesson, you learned how inherited alleles determine traits and how probability is related to inheritance. You also explored the factors that determine an organism's genotype and phenotype.

SEP Design Solutions How can you increase the likelihood that the desired trait will be inherited in your fruit?

....
....
....
....

INTERACTIVITY

An Apple Lesson

Go online to explore how you can utilize both sexual and asexual reproduction to develop your new fruit.

② Chromosomes and Inheritance

Guiding Questions

- What is the relationship among genes, chromosomes, and inheritance?
- How is a pedigree used to track inheritance?
- How does the formation of sex cells during meiosis differ from the process of cell division?

Connections

Literacy Determine Meaning

Math Model With Mathematics

MS-LS3-2 Develop and use a model to describe why asexual reproduction results in offspring with identical genetic information and sexual reproduction results in offspring with genetic variation.

HANDS-ON LAB

µInvestigate Investigate genetic crosses in imaginary creatures.

Vocabulary

chromosome
cell cycle
pedigree
meiosis
chromatids
mitosis

Academic Vocabulary

structure
function

Connect It !

✏ **Circle the traits that are similar between the parents and the offspring.**

Apply Concepts How were the traits transferred from the parents to the ducklings during reproduction? Where were those traits found?

....

....

....

SEP Construct Explanations Each duckling came from these parents. They look similar, but they are not exactly the same. Why are they not identical? Explain.

....

....

Chromosomes and Genes

Gregor Mendel's ideas about inheritance and probability can be applied to all living things. Mendel determined that traits are inherited using pieces of information that he called factors and we call genes. He observed and experimented with genes in pea plants. He discovered how genes, such as those in ducks (**Figure 1**), were transferred from parents to offspring and how they made certain traits appear. However, Mendel did not know what genes actually look like.

Today, scientists know that genes are segments of code that appear on structures called **chromosomes**. These thread-like **structures** within a cell's nucleus contain DNA that is passed from one generation to the next. The genetic material of chromosomes is condensed and wrapped around special proteins. These provide support for the chromosome structure.

Chromosomes are made in the beginning of the **cell cycle**, the series of events in which a cell grows, prepares for division, and divides to form daughter cells. During this time, the chromosome gets its characteristic *X* shape.

HANDS-ON LAB

Investigate genetic crosses in imaginary creatures.

Academic Vocabulary

Identify and describe something that has a particular structure.

....

....

....

....

....

Parents Pass Traits to Their Offspring
Figure 1 Each baby mallard duck receives some traits from the mother and some from the father.

Scales of Genetic Material

Figure 2 ✎ Order the structures from smallest to largest by writing the numbers 1 through 5 in the blank circles. Number 1 is the smallest.

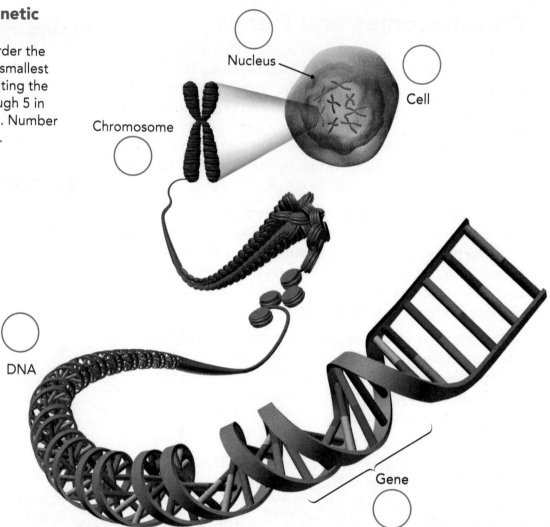

Nucleus

Cell

Chromosome

DNA

Gene

📖 **Make Meaning** Why do sex cells contain only half the number of chromosomes needed for offspring? In your science notebook, explain what would happen if sex cells contained the same number of chromosomes as body cells.

Academic Vocabulary

What is the difference between an object's structure and its function?

....

....

....

Number of Chromosomes Every cell in your body other than the sex cells has the same number of chromosomes. In humans, this number is 46. Other organisms have different numbers of chromosomes, and there is a great variety. For example, mallard ducks have 80 chromosomes. All sexually-reproducing organisms form sex cells, which have half the number of chromosomes that body cells have.

Genes on Chromosomes Every living thing needs instructions to live. Without these instructions, living things would not be able to grow and **function**. These instructions are located on genes. As you can see in **Figure 2,** genes are located on chromosomes.

In humans, between 20,000 and 25,000 genes are found on the 46 chromosomes. Chromosomes are different sizes. Larger chromosomes contain more genes than smaller chromosomes. Each gene contains instructions for coding a particular trait. There are hundreds to thousands of genes coding traits on any given chromosome. For many organisms, these chromosomes come in sets.

Chromosome Pairs During fertilization, you receive 23 chromosomes from your father and 23 chromosomes from your mother. These chromosomes come in pairs, called homologous chromosomes, that contain the same genes. Two alleles—one from the mother and one from the father—represent each trait. However, the alleles for these genes may or may not be the same. Some of the alleles for how the gene is expressed may be dominant or recessive. In **Figure 3**, the offspring that received these chromosomes inherited two different forms of a gene—allele *A* from one parent and allele *a* from the other. The individual will be heterozygous for that gene trait. Because more than one gene is present on the 23 pairs of chromosomes, there is a wide variety of allele combinations.

Gene { (A, b, C, d, E, F, g) (a, b, c, D, E, F, G)

Chromosome pair

A Pair of Chromosomes
Figure 3 🖊 Circle all the pairs of alleles that would be homozygous for a trait.

✅ **CHECK POINT** **Integrate with Visuals** How would geneticists—people who study genes—know whether the organism in **Figure 3** is homozygous or heterozygous for a certain trait by examining the chromosome pair?

....

....

....

....

Math Toolbox

Counting on Chromosomes

1. **SEP Model with Mathematics** 🖊 Fill in the table with the appropriate chromosome number for the missing body cell or sex cell.

2. **Construct Graphs** 🖊 Complete the line plot below. Place an X for each organism whose body cell chromosome number falls within the given range.

Organisms	Number of Chromosomes	
	Body Cells	Sex Cells
House cat	38	
Mallard duck		40
Corn	20	
Peanut	40	
Horse		32
Oak tree		12
Sweet potato	90	
Camel		35
Chicken	78	

Body Cell Chromosome Distribution

0–21   21–40   41–60   61–80   81–100
Number of chromosomes

Tracking Traits

Figure 4 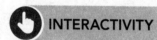 Sickle cell anemia is a recessive genetic disease that changes the structure of red blood cells. In the pedigree, affected members are shaded.

1. **Claim** Circle couples on the pedigree who are both carriers for the trait.

2. **Evidence** What is your proof?

....

....

3. **Reasoning** Explain how your evidence supports your claim.

....

....

....

....

👆 **INTERACTIVITY**

Take a look inside the formation of sex cells through meiosis.

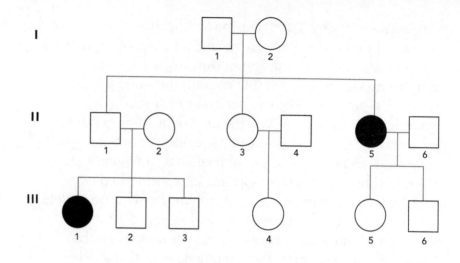

Using a Pedigree

Alelles can sometimes recombine to produce traits that are not favorable, such as a genetic disease. Geneticists study how traits are inherited in order to trace their genetic origin and predict how they may be passed on to future generations.

A **pedigree** is a model that geneticists use to map out the inheritance of traits. The diagram shows the presence or absence of a trait according to the relationships within a family across several generations. It is like a family tree. **Figure 4** shows multiple generations represented by Roman numerals I, II, and III. Most pedigrees show which family members express a particular trait (shaded figures). Some pedigrees show as well as the individuals who carry the trait but do not express it (half-shaded figures). In a pedigree, males are represented with squares and females with circles. One horizontal line connects the parent couple and another line leads down from the parents to their children.

Model It

SEP Develop Models ✏ Think of a trait that you admire. How can that trait get passed through a family? Create a pedigree that outlines the transmission of this trait through a family. Consider who has the trait, who is a carrier for it, and who does not have it.

Forming Sex Cells

In an organism that is reproduced sexually, a body cell has twice as many chromosomes a sex cell. Why is this important? Well, it is through the sex cells that parents pass their genes on to their offspring. When the sperm and egg fuse, they form a zygote, or fertilized egg. The zygote gets two sets of chromosomes—one set from the sperm and one set from the egg. Human eggs, for example, contain 23 total chromosomes in a set and sperm contain 23 total chromosomes in a set. So, each of your body cells contains one set of chromosomes from your mother and another set from your father for a total of 46 chromosomes.

Sex cells (sperm and egg) are formed through a very specialized process called **meiosis**, during which the number of chromosomes is reduced by half. It is through meiosis that homologous chromosomes separate into two different cells. This creates new cells with half as many chromosomes as the parent cell.

Homologous chromosomes have one chromosome from each parent. While the two chromosomes share the same sequence of genes, they may have different alleles. Before the chromosomes separate and move into separate cells, they undergo a process called crossing over. Notice in **Figure 5** that a small segment of one chromosome exchanges places with the corresponding segment on the other chromosome. By exchanging this genetic information, the new cells that form will have a slightly different combination of genes. This allows for minor variations in traits to form, which means there is a higher likelihood that offspring with desirable traits will form within the larger population.

Swapping Genetic Material

Figure 5 ✏ During crossing over, a segment of the gene from the mother changes places with a segment of the same gene from the father. Circle the gene segments that exchanged places.

CCC Cause and Effect
What would happen to offspring if crossing over did not occur during the first part of meiosis?

....

....

....

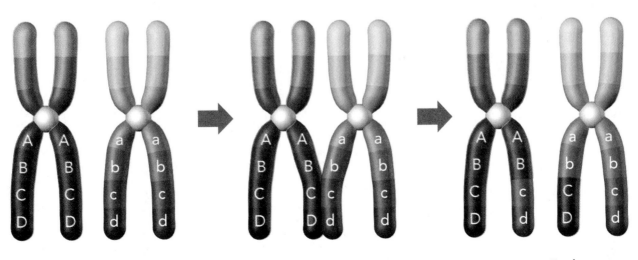

Homologous Chromosomes   **Crossing Over**   **Segments Exchange**

VIDEO

Observe the process of meiosis in action.

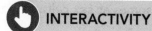

INTERACTIVITY

Trace the path of a particular trait through meiosis.

Meiosis Before a cell can divide, the genetic material condenses into chromosomes. **Figure 6** shows how meiosis starts with the genetic material being copied and condensing into chromosomes. After crossing over, the chromosomes separate, and the cell divides into two cells. Each new cell, now containing half the number of chromosomes, then divides again, making a total of four daughter cells. Meiosis II in **Figure 6** shows how this second division occurs. Each chromosome splits into two rod-like structures called **chromatids**. Each chromatid contains a double helix of DNA. Note that each of the four daughter cells has one distinct chromatid.

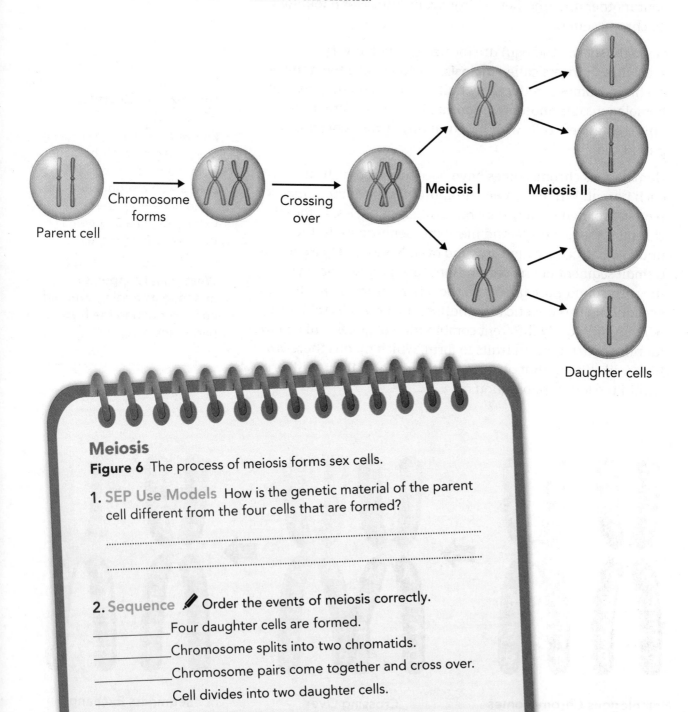

Parent cell → Chromosome forms → Crossing over → Meiosis I → Meiosis II → Daughter cells

Meiosis

Figure 6 The process of meiosis forms sex cells.

1. **SEP Use Models** How is the genetic material of the parent cell different from the four cells that are formed?

....

....

2. **Sequence** 🖊 Order the events of meiosis correctly.

_____ Four daughter cells are formed.

_____ Chromosome splits into two chromatids.

_____ Chromosome pairs come together and cross over.

_____ Cell divides into two daughter cells.

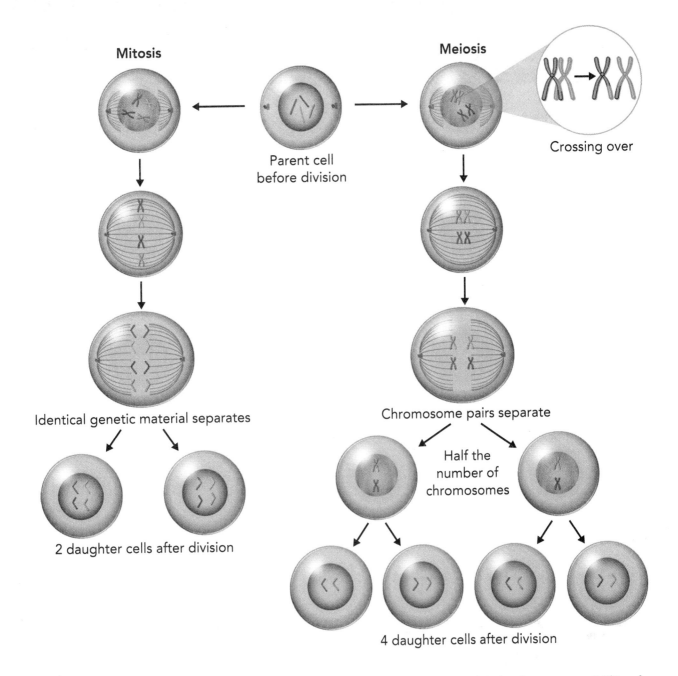

Mitosis

Meiosis

Parent cell
before division

Crossing over

Identical genetic material separates

Chromosome pairs separate

Half the
number of
chromosomes

2 daughter cells after division

4 daughter cells after division

Comparing Meiosis and Mitosis The two main types of cell division are meiosis and mitosis. The majority of our body cells divide to make two genetically identical new cells in a process called **mitosis**: The cell's nucleus divides into two new nuclei, and identical copies of the parent cell's genetic material are distributed into each daughter cell.

Compare the processes of meiosis and mitosis shown in **Figure 7**. Mitosis produces two identical daughter cells with the same DNA as the parent cell. The sex cells produced by meiosis, however, are not genetically identical. There are two reasons for this difference. First, crossing over exchanges genetic material between homologous chromosomes. Secondly, the two cell divisions that occur in meiosis produce four daughter cells and each cell has half its parent cell's DNA. As a result, each sex cell has different genetic information.

Meiosis versus Mitosis
Figure 7 While mitosis forms new body cells, meiosis forms sex cells.

☑LESSON 2 Check

Use the pedigree to answer questions 1 & 2.

In humans, free earlobes are dominant and attached earlobes are recessive. The pedigree shows the transmission of attached earlobes through four generations of a family.

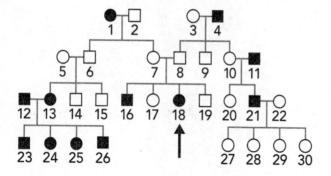

1. SEP Use Models Which male members of the family have attached earlobes?

....

2. Predict If the female marked by the arrow (individual 18) has a child with a male carrier, what is the probability their child will have attached earlobes?

....

3. SEP Provide Evidence Is chromosome number a good predictor of organism complexity? Explain.

....

....

....

....

4. SEP Use Mathematics A male king crab has 104 chromosomes in a sperm cell. How many chromosomes does it have in each of its body cells?

....

5. CCC Cause and Effect How can crossing over lead to the expression of new traits?

....

....

....

....

....

Quest CHECK-IN

In this lesson you learned how chromosomes carry genes and that chromosomes come in pairs—one chromosome you receive from your father, and the other you receive from your mother. You explored how combinations of alleles are passed down in families. You also learned how cells can divide to create genetically similar cells or to create sex cells.

Apply Concepts A domestic cat has 38 chromosomes in its skin cells, while a dog has 78 chromosomes. How does this fact help to explain why dogs and cats cannot interbreed?

....

....

....

INTERACTIVITY

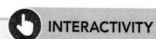

Go online to begin your chromosome map.

CAREERS
Genetic Counselor

Chromosome COUNSELORS

S ometimes it runs in the family, as they say. We get traits such as eye color from genes passed on to us by our parents, but we can inherit diseases, too.

Genetic counselors help people who are at risk for a disease or a genetic disorder. They are experts in genetics, so they know better than anyone how genes work. And they are trained counselors, too. They give emotional support and help families make health decisions.

For example, a genetic counselor might help new parents of a baby with Down syndrome. Or the counselor might meet with a patient whose family has a history of Alzheimer's.

Genetic counselors study a family's health history, order genetic tests, and help people to live with a genetic disease. They even advise doctors. They're the genetic experts, and they share their knowledge to help people.

Genetic counselors complete a four-year bachelor's degree in biology or a healthcare field. After graduating, they work on completing a master's degree. This degree will focus on human genetics and counseling. They also complete extensive research. In addition, excellent communication and decision-making skills are required.

▶ VIDEO
Watch what's involved with being a genetic counselor.

📄 DOCUMENT
Go online to explore more science and engineering careers.

MY CAREER
Want to help people understand their genes? Do an online search for "genetic counselor" to learn more about this career.

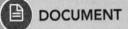

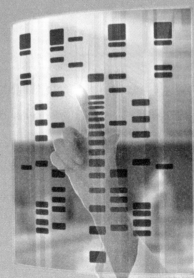

Phenomenon Genetic counselors help others understand the complex world of DNA, genes, and chromosomes.

385

Genetic Coding and Protein Synthesis

Guiding Questions

- Why do cells undergo DNA replication?
- How do cells make proteins?
- Why do cells undergo protein synthesis?

Connection

Literacy Cite Textual Evidence

 MS-LS3-1 Develop and use a model to describe why structural changes to genes (mutations) located on chromosomes may affect proteins and may result in harmful, beneficial, or neutral effects to the structure and function of the organism.

HANDS-ON LAB

ʋInvestigate Make a model of the process of protein synthesis.

Vocabulary

DNA
protein synthesis
messenger RNA
transfer RNA

Academic Vocabulary

sequence

Connect It !

✏ **A blueprint is a plan to build something. Circle the blueprint in the photo.**

Use an Analogy When have you used instructions to build something?

....

....

SEP Construct Explanations How did the instructions help you with building the structure?

....

....

The Genetic Code

Just as the couple in **Figure 1** need a blueprint to renovate a house, your body needs a plan to carry out daily functions. Your "blueprint" is found in the nucleus of each cell in the form of **DNA**. DNA (deoxyribonucleic acid) is the genetic material that carries information about an organism and is passed from parent to offspring.

In 1953, almost 100 years after DNA was discovered, scientists realized that DNA was shaped like a double helix—a twisted ladder. The structure of DNA consists of sugars, phosphates, and nitrogen bases. The sides of the ladder are made of sugar molecules, called deoxyribose, alternating with phosphate molecules. The rungs of the ladder are made of nitrogen bases. DNA has four nitrogen bases: adenine (A), thymine (T), guanine (G), and cytosine (C).

Genes are sections of DNA found on chromosomes. Each gene consists of hundreds or thousands of nitrogen bases arranged in a **sequence**. And it's this order that forms the instructions for building proteins—long chains of amino acids. Genes direct the construction of proteins, which in turn affect the traits that individuals receive from their parent(s). In other words, proteins trigger cellular processes that determine how inherited traits get expressed.

INTERACTIVITY

Explore the role of DNA in cellular processes and reproduction.

Academic Vocabulary

List some other contexts in which you have seen the word sequence.

....

....

....

....

....

Using a Blueprint

Figure 1 A blueprint is a plan for a building. DNA is the blueprint for constructing an organism.

Making Copies

Figure 2 ✏️ In the circles, label the five nitrogen bases that would pair with the bases on the bottom strand that begin and end at the arrows.

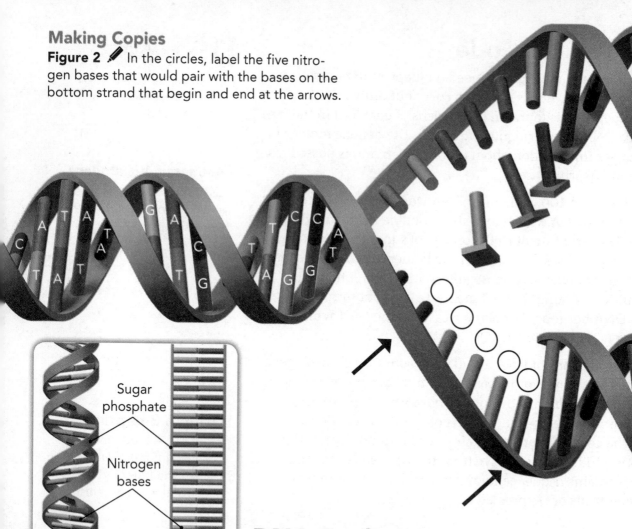

Sugar phosphate

Nitrogen bases

VIDEO

Learn how the simplicity of DNA's four-letter code leads to the complexity of life.

DNA Replication

Scientists estimate that a human body contains approximately 37 trillion cells. As you grow and age, new cells form to build and repair structures or to replace cells that have died. For this to happen, cells need to replicate, and this requires making copies of DNA.

As shown in **Figure 2**, DNA replication begins when the double helix untwists. Then, a protein breaks the DNA strand in half—at the structure's weakest point—between the nitrogen bases. This separation actually looks like a zipper (**Figure 3**), and is often referred to as "unzipping the DNA." Next, nitrogen bases with a sugar and phosphate attached pair up with the bases on each half of the DNA. Because nitrogen bases always pair in the same way, adenine with thymine and guanine with cytosine, the order of the bases on both strands are identical. At the end of replication, a chromosome with two identical DNA strands is formed.

☑️ **CHECK POINT** **Cite Textual Evidence** How is the separation of DNA like a zipper?

....

....

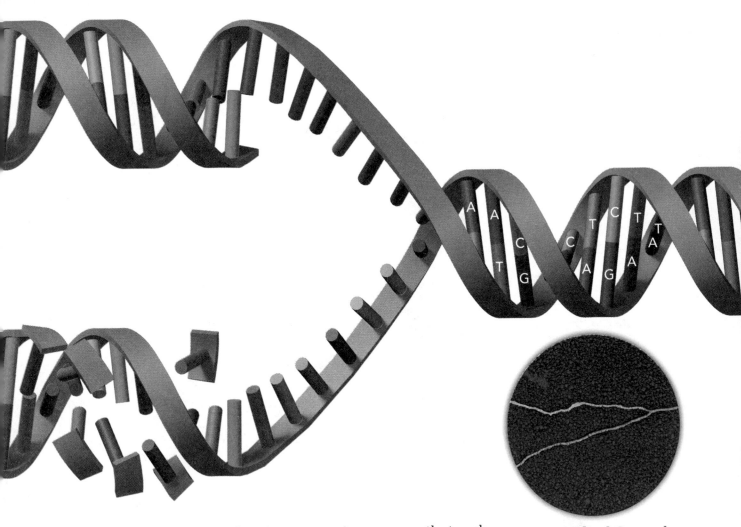

The process of DNA replication, or copying, ensures that each chromatid of a chromosome has identical DNA. During cell division, chromosomes split. During mitosis, the identical chromatids separate, resulting in identical DNA in each daughter cell. During meiosis, crossing over occurs before the chromatids split. No matter the type of cell division, DNA replication ensures that each cell contains the correct amount of DNA to carry out life processes.

Magnified Strand of DNA

Figure 3 This photograph taken by an electron microscope shows DNA replication in action.

Design It

SEP Develop Models ✏ Sketch how you would model DNA replication using household materials such as beads and pipe cleaners. How do the pipe cleaners and beads relate to the structure and function of DNA?

Structure of DNA and RNA

Figure 4 Differences between DNA and RNA are apparent when comparing their structure. Use the diagram to identify two differences between a DNA molecule and an RNA molecule.

....

....

....

....

....

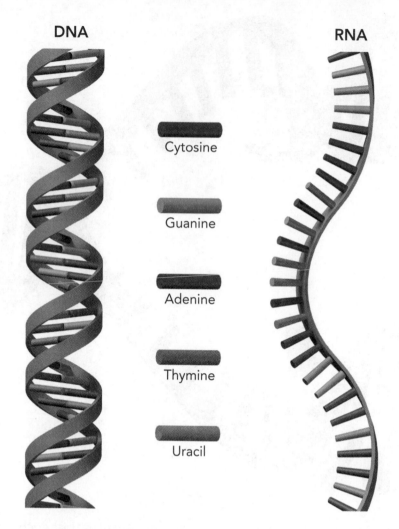

DNA

RNA

Cytosine

Guanine

Adenine

Thymine

Uracil

Literacy Connection

Cite Textual Evidence
Identify locations in both the diagram and the text that describe the similarities and differences between DNA and RNA.

Making Proteins

Proteins are made from building blocks called amino acids. There are only 20 amino acids in the human body, but your body can combine them in thousands of ways to make many different types of proteins needed to carry out cell processes. Inside the cell, amino acids link to form proteins through a process called **protein synthesis**. Once the protein is made, the cell will express the trait or perform a function.

RNA The process of protein synthesis starts in the nucleus, where the DNA contains the code for the protein. However, the actual assembly of the protein occurs at an organelle called the ribosome. Before a ribosome can assemble a protein, it needs to receive the blueprint to assemble the right protein from the nucleus.

The blueprint is transferred from the nucleus to the ribosome by a different nucleic acid called RNA (ribonucleic acid). Even though both RNA and DNA are nucleic acids, they have some differences. One difference is that RNA contains the sugar ribose instead of deoxyribose. **Figure 4** shows two other differences.

How RNA Is Used

There are two main types of RNA involved in protein synthesis: messenger RNA and transfer RNA. **Messenger RNA** (mRNA) carries copies of instructions for the assembly of amino acids into proteins from DNA to ribosomes in the cytoplasm. **Transfer RNA** (tRNA), shown in **Figure 5**, carries amino acids to the ribosome during protein synthesis.

The order of the nitrogen bases on a gene determines the structure of the protein it makes. In the genetic code, a group of three nitrogen bases codes for one specific amino acid. For example, the three-base DNA sequence C-G-T (cytosine-guanine-thymine) always codes for the amino acid alanine. The order of the three-base code units determines the order in which amino acids are put together to form a protein. (**Figure 6**). See **Figure 7** for a summary of the entire process of protein synthesis.

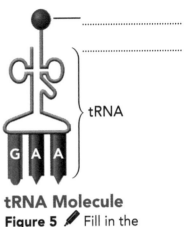

tRNA Molecule

Figure 5 🖉 Fill in the label to identify what tRNA molecules carry.

Knowing the Code

Figure 6 A codon is a sequence of three bases that codes for one amino acid. For the DNA sequence C-T-A, the complementary mRNA codon would be G-A-U. Since RNA does not have thymine, the RNA complement to adenine will always be uracil. Scientists use an mRNA codon table to determine which codons will code for each amino acid. The highlighted parts of the table show you how the codon G-A-U codes for aspartic acid, also known as aspartate.

mRNA Codon Table

First position		Second position				Third position
		U	C	A	G	
U	phenyl-alanine		serine	tyrosine	cysteine	U
						C
	leucine			stop	stop	A
				stop	tryptophan	G
C	leucine		proline	histidine	arginine	U
						C
				glutamine		A
						G
A	isoleucine		threonine	asparagine	serine	U
						C
				lysine	arginine	A
	methionine/start					G
G	valine		alanine	aspartic acid	glycine	U
						C
				glutamic acid		A
						G

1. **Synthesize Information** What is the mRNA sequence for the DNA sequence A-C-C?

....

2. **Use Tables** What amino acid is that mRNA sequence coding for?

....

3. **SEP Engage in Argument** Why would it be incorrect to say that the DNA sequence A-C-G codes for the amino acid threonine?

....

....

....

....

Protein Synthesis

Figure 7 Protein synthesis begins in the nucleus and ends at the ribosome.

👆 **INTERACTIVITY**

Make a protein through protein synthesis.

2 Ribosomes Attach to mRNA

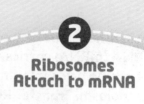

After arriving in the cytoplasm, a ribosome attaches to mRNA. The order of base pairs on mRNA determines which tRNA molecule attaches to the strand.

Each codon on the mRNA strand attaches to a complementary anti-codon on the tRNA strand.

mRNA

cytoplasm

amino acid

tRNA

ribosome

anticodon

U G U

A C A

ribosome movement

Messenger RNA provides the code for protein construction.

codon

1 Formation of messenger RNA

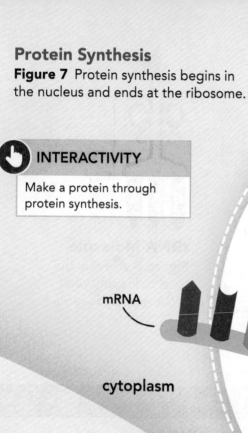

Inside the nucleus, DNA unzips and mRNA is made from the gene.

DNA

mRNA

A U
A U
G C
T A
G C
T A

nucleus

Messenger RNA then leaves the nucleus and enters the cytoplasm.

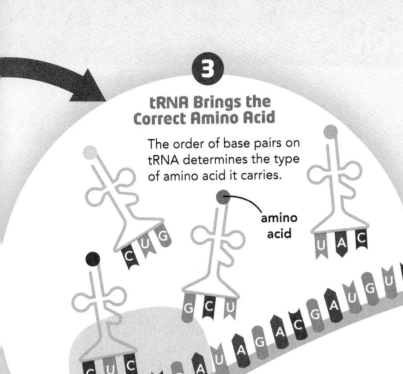

3 tRNA Brings the Correct Amino Acid

The order of base pairs on tRNA determines the type of amino acid it carries.

amino acid

As the ribosome moves along the mRNA strand, molecules of tRNA bring their attached amino acids.

4 Protein Chain Is Formed

protein chain

As tRNA anti-codons line up with mRNA codons, the amino acids bond at the ribosome and form a long protein chain.

Model It!

SEP Use Models ✏ Use the steps in **Figure 7** as a guide to fill in the missing molecules that drive each step of the process. Then complete the flowchart with the complementary nitrogen bases or amino acids (refer to the codon table in **Figure 6**).

Step   Molecules

1 _____   T   G   T   G   A   A

2 _____

3 _____

4 Protein

☑ LESSON 3 Check

MS-LS3-1

1. CCC Identify Patterns List the six nitrogen bases that would pair with the following sequence of bases in a strand of DNA: T C G A C A

....

2. Explain Phenomena Why does the cell complete DNA replication?

....

....

....

....

3. Synthesize Information What will happen to a protein when the DNA codes for a different amino acid?

....

....

4. Support Your Explanation Explain the importance of the sequence of nitrogen bases on a gene to heredity.

....

....

....

....

....

5. CCC Analyze Structure and Function DNA replication begins when the double helix untwists and breaks in half between the nitrogen bases. What are the next two steps in the process of DNA replication?

....

....

....

....

....

....

6. SEP Construct Explanations Explain the relationship of making proteins to inheritance of traits.

....

....

....

7. SEP Develop Models ✏ Sketch and label models of DNA and RNA that show the difference in their shapes, their sugars, and their nitrogen bases.

MS-LS3-1

REINVENTING DNA AS
Data Storage

 VIDEO

Discover how scientists use DNA to solve data storage problems.

How much digital space
do you need for all your texts, emails, photos, and music? Digital information can take up lots of space.

Code	P	l	a	y
Binary data	01010000	01101100	01100001	01111001
DNA nucleotides	GCGAG	ATCGA	AGAGC	TGCTCT

The Challenge: To provide storage solutions for the data storage needs of everyone on Earth.

Phenomenon Some estimates state that the world has 40 trillion gigabytes (GB) of data. Forty trillion GB equals about 40 million petabytes (PB). Ten billion photos on social media sites use about 1.5 PB. So, if every star in our Milky Way galaxy were one byte of data, then we would need 5,000 Milky Ways, each with 200 billion stars, to amass one PB of data. How can we possibly store all of our data?

Science may offer an answer: DNA. Our entire genetic code fits within the nucleus of a single cell. Scientists have figured out how to convert digital data (in 1s and 0s) into DNA's A-C-T-G code. Then they constructed synthetic DNA in a lab. So far, scientists have been able to encode and store images and videos within a single strand of DNA. If current cost constraints are overcome, DNA could be the next microchip. Someday, the data currently stored on computers in enormous buildings may fit in the palm of your hand!

Science may solve the engineering problem of our exploding data storage needs. Scientists can store documents and photos by converting digital code to DNA code and then making synthetic DNA. To retrieve a file, the DNA code gets converted back to digital code.

 **DESIGN CHALLENGE**

Can you design your own code to store information? Go to the Engineering Design Notebook to find out!

Trait Variations

Guiding Questions

- How do genes on sex chromosomes determine different traits?
- How do mutations affect protein synthesis and increase variation?
- How does the environment influence genetic traits?

Connections

Literacy Integrate with Visuals

Math Construct a Scatter Plot

 MS-LS3-1 Develop and use a model to describe why structural changes to genes (mutations) located on chromosomes may affect proteins and may result in harmful, beneficial, or neutral effects to the structure and function of the organism.

MS-LS4-4 Construct an explanation based on evidence that describes how genetic variations of traits in a population increase some individuals' probability of surviving and reproducing in a specific environment. (Also **EP&Cllc**)

HANDS-ON LAB

₩Investigate Observe physical traits found in a group of individuals.

Vocabulary

variation
sex
    chromosomes
autosomal
    chromosomes
mutation
sex-linked genes

Academic Vocabulary

sequence

Connect It !

✏ **Circle a trait that distinguishes the male elephant seal from the female.**

Determine Differences What other differences do you notice between the male and female elephant seals?

....

....

CCC Structure and Function What traits allow the elephant seal to live in water? Explain your reasoning.

....

....

....

Diversity of Life

Organisms that are the same species tend to have many similarities. The Northern elephant seals in **Figure 1**, however, show that very different traits can exist in two individuals. Some differences are visible traits, such as wrinkled skin or brown hair. Others are invisible, such as type I diabetes or sickle-cell anemia. Differences have the potential to be passed on from one generation to the next, and change the population.

The diversity of life on Earth relies in part on the variety of traits within a species. Any difference between individuals of the same species is a **variation**. Two friends with different eye color have a variation (green, brown) of the same trait (eye color). Variations may be due to DNA inherited from the parents, exposure to certain environmental factors, or a combination of both inheritance and environmental factors.

Variations can be helpful, harmful, or neutral. Consider a population of butterflies avoiding predators. Some have the same wing color pattern as a poisonous species. When this variation is passed from one generation to the next, the offspring are more likely to survive and reproduce. A harmful variation, on the other hand, threatens a population's survival. For example, low blood oxygen levels can be found in individuals with sickle-cell anemia. Neutral variations, such as different eye color, do not benefit or harm the population.

INTERACTIVITY

Identify traits found on a dog.

Northern Elephant Seals

Figure 1 These Northern elephant seals relax on a beach near San Simeon. Although these seals are the same species and share most of the same DNA, there are differences in their appearances.

иInvestigate Observe physical traits found in a group of individuals.

INTERACTIVITY

Explore how some genetic disorders are carried on sex chromosomes.

Chromosomes and Variation

You received 23 chromosomes from your mother and 23 chromosomes from your father. The combination of genes found on these chromosomes codes for the proteins that determine your traits.

Types of Chromosomes There are two types of chromosomes found in every one of your cells. Of the 23 pairs of chromosomes, one pair is sex chromosomes, while the other 22 pairs are autosomal chromosomes. **Sex chromosomes** are the pair of chromosomes carrying genes that determine whether a person is biologically male or female.

The combination of sex chromosomes determines the sex of the offspring. A human female inherits one X chromosome from her mother and one X chromosome from her father. A male receives one X chromosome from his mother and one Y chromosome from his father. **Figure 2** compares the X and Y chromosomes.

The 22 pairs of chromosomes that are not sex chromosomes are **autosomal chromosomes**. You inherit half of your autosomal chromosomes from your mother and half from your father. All the pairs of autosomal chromosomes are homologous chromosomes. This means that the genes for a trait are located at the same place on each chromosome in the pair, even though the alleles may be different. Females also have homologous sex chromosomes, while males do not.

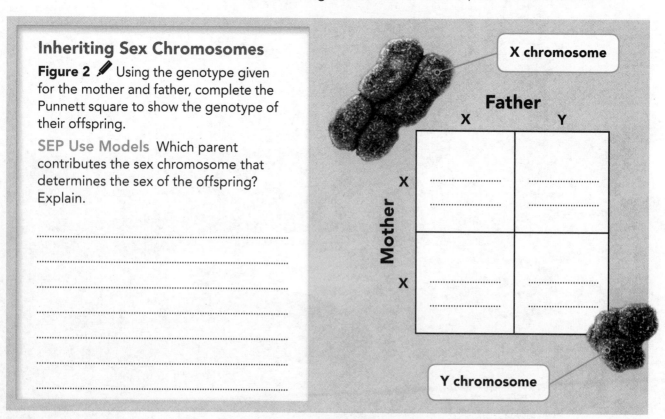

Inheriting Sex Chromosomes

Figure 2 ✎ Using the genotype given for the mother and father, complete the Punnett square to show the genotype of their offspring.

SEP Use Models Which parent contributes the sex chromosome that determines the sex of the offspring? Explain.

....

....

....

....

....

....

....

Chromosome Size Chromosomes contain DNA, and each section of DNA that codes for a protein is a gene. For every trait, there is a gene or group of genes that controls the trait by producing proteins through the process of protein synthesis. Because the number of genes found on each chromosome and the length of each gene varies, chromosomes come in different sizes. For example, the X chromosome is almost three times the size of the Y chromosome and contains close to 16 times as many genes. Thus, it codes for more proteins, and determines more traits.

☑ CHECK POINT **Cite Textual Evidence** Why does the X chromosome express more traits than the Y chromosome?

Math Toolbox

Chromosome and Gene Relationship

This data shows chromosome size as number of base pairs in the millions (Mbp) and estimated number of genes found on each one.

1. Construct a Scatter Plot ✎ Complete the scatter plot. Each dot represents the relationship between the total base pairs and the estimated number of genes for each chromosome.

Human Chromosome Size vs. Number of Genes

Estimated Number of Genes (y-axis: 0, 500, 1,000, 1,500, 2,000)
Millions of Base Pairs (Mbp) (x-axis: 0, 50, 100, 150, 200, 250)

Chromosome	Mbp	Genes
1	248.96	2000
2	242.19	1300
3	198.3	1000
4	190.22	1000
5	181.54	900
6	170.81	1000
7	159.35	900
8	145.14	700
9	138.4	800
10	133.8	700
11	135.09	1300
12	133.28	1100
13	114.36	300
14	107.04	800
15	101.99	600
16	90.34	800
17	83.26	1200
18	80.37	200
19	58.62	1500
20	64.44	500
21	46.71	200
22	50.82	500
X	156.04	800
Y	57.23	50

2. SEP Interpret Data What relationship do you see between chromosome size and number of genes?

Types of Mutations

An organism can develop traits due to changes in their genetic code. A **mutation** is any change in the DNA of a gene or chromosome. Mutations can be inherited from a parent or acquired during an organism's life. Inherited mutations occur when the parent passes on the mutation during reproduction. These mutations are present throughout the life of the organism, and are in every cell of the body. Acquired mutations occur at some point during an organism's lifetime. Acquired mutations can only be passed on from parent to offspring if the mutations occur in sex cells.

Genetic Mutations Many mutations are the result of small changes in the organism's DNA. Just one small change to a base pair is a mutation and may cause an incorrect protein to be made during protein synthesis. For example, the DNA **sequence** ATG is complementary to the mRNA sequence UAC and codes for the amino acid tyrosine. If the second base were replaced, making the DNA sequence AGG (mRNA complement UCC), it would code for the wrong amino acid, serine. As a result, the trait may be different from what was expressed before. Genetic mutations can occur between one base pair or several base pairs. **Figure 4** shows genetic mutations that can result when a base pair is deleted, added, or exchanged for different base pairs. **Figure 5** shows an example of a substitution mutation.

Academic Vocabulary

Explain a situation where you restated a sequence of events.

....

....

....

....

Literacy Connection

Integrate with Visuals

🖊 Find the three examples of mutation. Draw an arrow to show where a base pair was deleted. Circle where a base pair was added. Draw an X on the base pair that was substituted.

Genetic Mutations

Figure 4 The diagram shows three types of single base pair mutations.

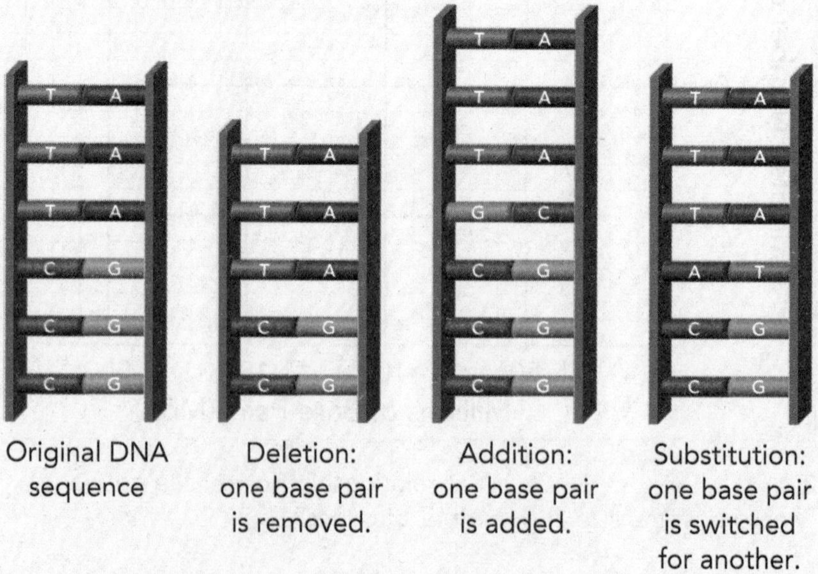

Original DNA sequence

Deletion: one base pair is removed.

Addition: one base pair is added.

Substitution: one base pair is switched for another.

Sex-Linked Mutations A mutation can occur on any chromosome. Some mutations occur on **sex-linked genes**, which are genes carried on a sex chromosome. Because the X chromosome has more genes than the Y chromosome, most sex-linked mutations occur on the X chromosome. In addition, many sex-linked mutations are recessive. Hemophilia is a recessive sex-linked mutation, where the individual's ability to clot blood is reduced. Males are more likely to exhibit hemophilia because they have only one X chromosome.

Model It!

Mutations and Protein Construction

Figure 5 Sickle cell anemia results from a substitution mutation. The mutation alters the shape of red blood cells. Sickled cells can get stuck in blood vessels, blocking the flow of oxygenated blood cells.

SEP Develop Models ✏ Not all mutations result in new traits. Fill in the normal and mutated amino acid in the diagram below. Then, using the normal red blood cell DNA sequence, create a model that has one mutation, but will still make a normal protein. Refer to the mRNA Codon Table in Lesson 3, Genetic Coding and Protein Synthesis.

DNA sequence

| C A C | G T G | G A C | T G A | G G A | C T C | C T C |
| G T G | C A C | C T G | A C T | C C T | G A G | G A G |

| Valine | Histidine | Leucine | Threonine | Proline | | Glutamic acid |

Amino acid sequence

normal

normal red blood cell

DNA sequence

| C A C | G T G | G A C | T G A | G G A | C A C | C T C |
| G T G | C A C | C T G | A C T | C C T | G T G | G A G |

| Valine | Histidine | Leucine | Threonine | Proline | | Glutamic acid |

Amino acid sequence

mutation

sickled red blood cell

DNA sequence

| | | | | | |
| | | | | | |

| | | | | | |

Amino acid sequence

VIDEO

Investigate how mutations can affect organisms.

Environmental Factors

Interactions with our surroundings and the conditions in which we live have the potential to change the way genes are normally expressed. First, environment factors can change nucleotides, the building blocks of nucleic acids—DNA and RNA. Secondly, the chemicals found on DNA can be changed.

Organisms encounter with harmful chemicals and radiation on a regular basis. These agents are called mutagens because they can damage DNA in such way that it causes mutations. Some mutagens naturally occur, while others are synthetic. For example, radiation in the form of ultraviolet (UV) or X-rays are naturally occurring mutagens. Synthetic mutagens can be found in pesticides, asbestos, and food additives introduced by expanding human communities. Human introduced mutagens have the potential to negatively influence biological diversity.

Gene Expression Changes in the way genes are expressed may occur naturally or because of the environment. An example of natural change is when a caterpillar transitions to a butterfly. As the organism develops, the DNA does not change, but the genes are read and expressed differently.

The environment can change the way genes are expressed. Identical twins have the same DNA, but can acquire different traits when they grow up in different environments. Activities such as smoking and unhealthy eating habits can also alter the way genes are expressed, which changes a person's traits. **Figure 6** shows another way genes can be expressed differently.

Damage from Sun Exposure

Figure 6 ✎ UV radiation from the sun harms skin cells. UVA radiation penetrates into the deep layers of the skin. UVB radiation penetrates only the top layer of the skin. Draw arrows in the first diagram to show how deep UVA and UVB penetrate into the skin. Then, identify the radiation type—UVA or UVB—in the box next to the picture that shows a possible effect of the radiation.

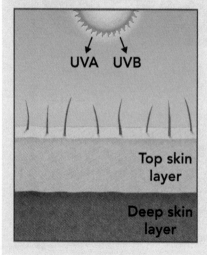

UVA UVB

Top skin layer

Deep skin layer

Camouflage
Figure 7 ✏ Sometimes mutations benefit to survival of a species. Predators will likely not see this animal, passing it as they swim. Circle the leopard flounder fish that is camouflaged.

Mutation Effects Mutations may be harmful, helpful, or neutral. Helpful mutations are those that benefit the survival of the species and are often passed on to offspring. Harmful mutations do not benefit the species and often decrease the likelihood of survival. Neutral mutations are those that do not affect an organism's chance of survival.

Helpful Mutations Some mutations can help an organism survive in their environment. One example of a helpful mutation is camouflage, which is the ability to blend in with the environment. In **Figure 7**, camouflage protects an organism from predators that may be looking for a meal. In humans, a mutation in a gene controlling fast-twitch muscles produces sprinters who are world-class athletes.

Harmful Mutations Genetic disorders and cancer are both the result of harmful mutations. A genetic disorder is an abnormal condition that a person inherits through genes or chromosomes. Cystic fibrosis is a genetic disorder that causes the body to make thick mucus in the lungs and digestive system. The mucus builds up in the lungs and blocks air flow. Cancer is a disease in which some body cells grow and divide uncontrollably, damaging the parts of the body around them. Few cancers are inherited. Most cancers are caused by acquired mutations that occur from damage to genes during the life of an organism.

Neutral Mutations Not all mutations are helpful or harmful. Some mutations, such as human hair color, may be neutral and have no impact on the survival of an organism. There may also be mutations that still code for the same protein. Even though the DNA sequence has changed, the amino acid that is produced remains the same.

✓ CHECK POINT **Distinguish Facts** In what ways can the environment impact the traits of an organism?

....

....

....

Mutations in Reproduction

Not all mutations are the result of small changes in an organism's DNA. Some mutations occur when chromosomes do not separate correctly during the formation of sex cells. When this happens, a sex cell can end up with too many or too few chromosomes. When a chromosomal mutation occurs, either additional proteins are created or fewer proteins are created.

During meiosis, sometimes DNA does not separate normally, instead staying together as the cell divides. This abnormal distribution of DNA is called a nondisjunction, shown in **Figure 8**.

Nondisjunction

Figure 8 DNA can separate abnormally during Meiosis I or Meiosis II.

1. **SEP Use Mathematics** Normal human sex cells have 23 chromosomes. Use the art to determine the number of chromosomes a sex cell has if nondisjuction occurs during Meiosis I. Include all possible chromosome totals.

....

....

2. **SEP Use Models** What is the difference between the sex cells of a nondisjunction that occurred during meiosis I and the sex cells of a nondisjunction that occurred during meiosis II?

....

....

....

....

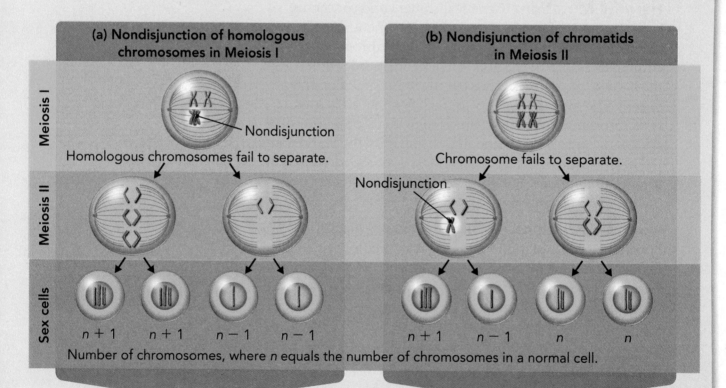

(a) Nondisjunction of homologous chromosomes in Meiosis I

Nondisjunction

Homologous chromosomes fail to separate.

$n + 1$ $n + 1$ $n - 1$ $n - 1$

Resulting sex cells either have additional DNA or not enough DNA.

(b) Nondisjunction of chromatids in Meiosis II

Nondisjunction

Chromosome fails to separate.

$n + 1$ $n - 1$ n n

Resulting sex cells could have one additional chromosome, one less chromosome, or the normal number of chromosomes.

Meiosis I

Meiosis II

Sex cells

Number of chromosomes, where n equals the number of chromosomes in a normal cell.

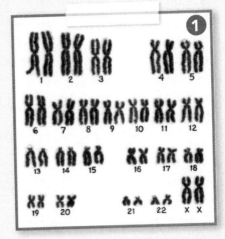

1

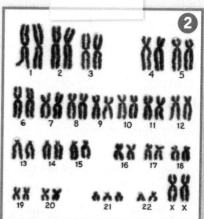

2

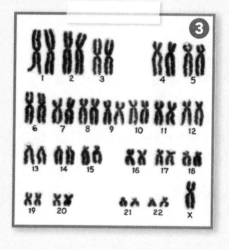

3

4

Comparing Karyotypes

Figure 9 ✏ Karyotype 1 shows what chromosomes would look like without a nondisjunction. Circle the chromosomes in the second, third, and fourth karyotypes that indicate a nondisjunction occurred.

1. **SEP Use Models** What is the sex of the individual found represented in the first karyotype?

   ....

2. **Apply Concepts** How would a scientist name the disorder represented by the third karyotype?

   ....

Karyotypes Sometimes, doctors suspect that an individual has a genetic disorder based on observable traits. To accurately determine if an individual has a chromosomal mutation, a scientist will create a karotype (**Figure 9**), which is a picture of all the chromosomes in a person's cell and then arrange the chromosomes by size and matching chromosome patterns. Homologous chromosomes are paired to provide a quick overview. The karyotypes on this page compare a normal individual and three individuals with genetic disorders. If there is an additional chromosome, the grouping is called a trisomy (*tri-* means "three" and *somy*, from Greek *soma* for *body*, indicates a chromosome). If one chromosome is missing, it is a monosomy (*mono-* means "one"). In addition, scientists include the homologous number and often assign a common name to the disorder. For example, trisomy 18 is Edward's Syndrome, while trisomy 21 is Down Syndrome.

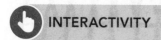

Protein Changes Amino acids are the building blocks
of proteins, which can be considered the architects of cell
function. A change in the amino acid sequence can alter
the directions for protein synthesis. The result is a mutation,
which may or may not be detectable. Some mutations arise
due to protein changes caused when genes move to a different
location on the genome. There are also a few species that can
alter their RNA to synthesize different proteins. Scientists are
studying these types of protein changes to understand any
benefits they might bring to an organism.

Some genes move to a new location on the genome. When
this occurs, it produces the protein at that point on the
genome. Scientists are trying to understand the purpose of
these 'jumping genes'. Sometimes they jump to a location
that disrupts a functioning gene. When this occurs, the gene
is not able to express itself, which can cause traits to change.
Scientists speculate that jumping genes may cause a species to
change.

Scientists recently discovered that some species of octopus
and squid, such as the one shown in **Figure 10**, are able to
change their RNA. Since RNA is needed for the construction
of proteins, they are able make different proteins. Scientists
believe that these organisms are able to create specific proteins
in response to a changing environment.

☑ CHECK POINT **Determine Central Ideas** When a gene jumps,
what might happen to the organism's traits?

....

....

....

Changing RNA

Figure 10 Organisms, like
this squid, are able to change
their RNA, thus changing the
proteins that are constructed.

**Synthesize
Information** Why is it
beneficial for scientists
to understand how other
organisms are able to edit
their RNA?

....

....

....

....

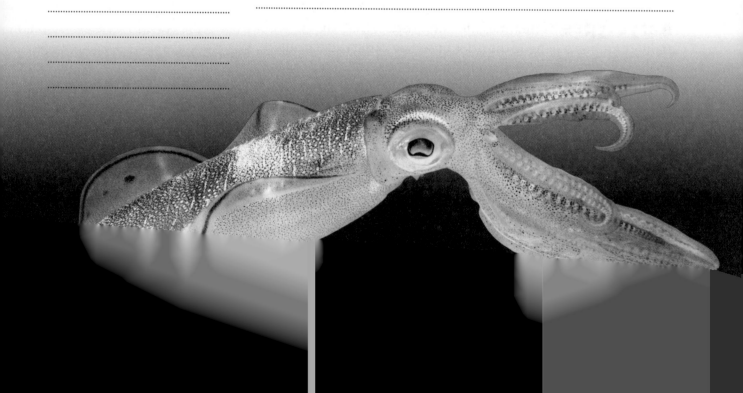

MS-LS3-1, MS-LS4-4, (EP&CIIc)

1. **Communicate** How many and what types of chromosomes are found in every one of your cells?

....

....

2. **SEP Construct Explanations** How is an organism's ability to produce offspring affected by changes to a chromosome?

....

....

....

....

....

3. **Evaluate Claims** A student states that only a male human offspring can express a recessive sex-linked X chromosome mutation. Is this statement accurate? Explain.

....

....

....

....

....

4. **Connect to the Environment** A scientist observes that members of a fish species near a popular beach had more acquired mutations than the same species in a river. Form a hypothesis stating how this difference could affect the future of the species.

....

....

....

5. **SEP Develop Models** ✏ Red-green color blindness is a sex-linked recessive condition. Its gene is located on the X chromosome. Most people with red-green color blindness cannot see the difference in shades of red and green. Suppose a heterozygous female ($X^N X^n$) has offspring with a male who is color blind ($X^n Y$). Draw a Punnett square. Label each offspring as applicable: normal vision, carrier, or color blind. (X^N indicates normal vision; X^n indicates color blindness.)

Quest CHECK-IN

In this lesson, you learned that organisms can inherit traits, acquire traits, and some organisms can change their traits.

Support Your Explanation Why are the desired traits you selected for your fruit not always a guarantee that your fruit will have those traits? Provide support.

....

....

....

....

....

HANDS-ON LAB

All in the Numbers

Do the Hands-On Lab to complete the investigation and discover how experimental results may vary from probability. You will make observations and test the crossing of traits.

Genetic Technologies

Guiding Questions

- How do humans use artificial selection to produce organisms with desired traits?
- How do scientists engineer new genes?
- How can genetic information be used?

Connection

Literacy Corroborate

 MS-LS4-5 Gather and synthesize information about the technologies that have changed the way humans influence the inheritance of desired traits in organisms.

HANDS-ON LAB

uInvestigate Extract DNA from a strawberry.

Vocabulary

artificial selection
genetic engineering
gene therapy
clone
genome

Academic Vocabulary

manipulation

Connect It!

✏️ **Dogs come in many different shapes, sizes, and colors. Which of the ones shown here would you prefer as a pet? Circle your choice.**

CCC Cause and Effect Many purebred dogs have problems later in life, such as joint or eye diseases. Why are purebred dogs more likely to develop problems later in life?

....

....

Make Inferences What can be done to decrease the likelihood of these problems appearing?

....

....

Artificial Selection

When consumers make choices, they are often attracted to products with the highest quality. We want the healthiest and best-tasting fruits and vegetables. We want the right amount of fat and flavor in our meats. We even want the best traits in our pets, such as the dogs you see in **Figure 1**. These high-quality products do not appear only in nature. Scientists and breeders have influenced the traits that other organisms inherit through the process of selective breeding.

Selective Breeding In the natural world, individuals with beneficial traits are more likely to survive and successfully reproduce than individuals without those traits. This is called natural selection. **Artificial selection** is also known as selective breeding. It occurs when humans breed only those organisms with desired traits to produce the next generation. It's important to note that desired traits are not necessarily the traits that benefit the organism's chances for survival. Instead, they are traits that humans desire.

Dogs, cats, and livestock animals have all been selectively bred. Cows, chickens, and pigs have been bred to be larger so that they produce more milk or meat. Breeding and caring for farm animals that have certain genetic traits that humans desire is called animal husbandry. The many different breeds of dogs shown in **Figure 1** have also been bred over time for very specific functions.

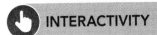

INTERACTIVITY

Consider how artificial selection affects the traits of dogs.

Literacy Connection

Corroborate Find statements in the text that support the claim that artificial selection is not a natural process and does not necessarily help the organism's survival.

Purebred Dogs

Figure 1 Each type of purebred dog shown here is the result of selective breeding over the course of many generations.

Genetic Engineering

With the discovery of DNA and its relationship to genes, scientists have developed more methods to produce desired traits. Through a process called **genetic engineering**, modern geneticists can transfer a gene from the DNA of one organism into another. Genetic engineering is used to give organisms genes they could not acquire through breeding.

Scientists use genetic engineering techniques to insert specific desired genes into animals. By **manipulating** a gene, scientists have created a fish that glows when under a black light **(Figure 2)**. A jellyfish gene for fluorescence was inserted into a fertilized fish egg to produce the glowing fish. Scientists are hoping that further research on this gene will lead to a method that helps track toxic chemicals in the body.

Genetic engineering is also used to synthesize materials. A protein called insulin helps control blood-sugar levels after eating. People who have diabetes cannot effectively control their blood-sugar levels, and many must take insulin injections. Prior to 1980, some diabetics were injecting themselves with insulin from other animals without getting the desired results. To help diabetics, scientists genetically engineered bacteria to produce the first human protein—insulin. The process they used, and still use today, is shown in **Figure 3**. Furthermore, bacteria can reproduce quickly, so large amounts of human insulin are produced in a short time.

Glowing Fish

Figure 2 Genetic engineering made glowing fish possible.

Academic Vocabulary

Explain the difference between manipulating a tool and manipulating another person.

....

....

....

....

....

....

....

Plan It

Synthesize a New Trait

✎ Create a trait that has never been seen before in an animal. Identify a trait you would like an animal to have. Then, sketch the animal and describe a process by which you could achieve your desired result.

....

....

....

....

....

....

....

Bacteria Make Human Insulin

Figure 3 🖊 Bacteria can be used to produce insulin in humans. Complete the diagram by showing the process for Step 5.

HANDS-ON LAB

Investigate Extract DNA from a strawberry.

❶ Small rings of DNA, or plasmids, are found in some bacteria cells.

❷ Scientists remove the plasmid and cut it open with an enzyme. They then insert an insulin gene that has been removed from human DNA.

❸ The human insulin gene attaches to the open ends of the plasmid to form a closed ring.

❹ Some bacteria cells take up the plasmids that have the insulin gene.

❺ When the cells reproduce, the new cells contain copies of the "engineered" plasmid. The foreign gene directs the cells to produce human insulin.

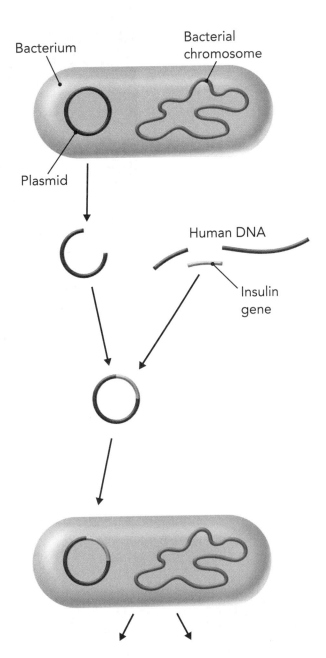

Bacterium

Bacterial chromosome

Plasmid

Human DNA

Insulin gene

T-cell Destroys Cancer Cell

Figure 4 T-cells are a type of white blood cell that help to fight disease in your body. Scientists have genetically engineered a T-cell that can attack and destroy up to 1,000 cancer cells.

Predict How might doctors use this new T-cell?

....

....

....

....

....

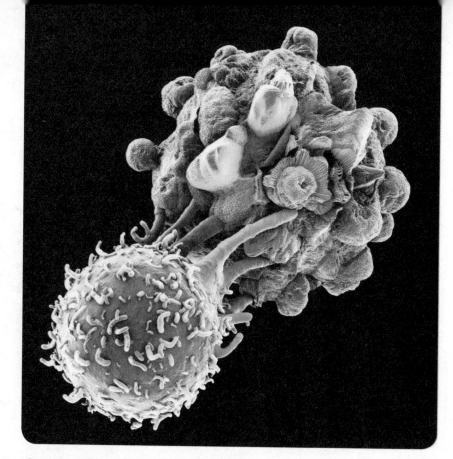

Sickle-cell Disease

Figure 5 Sickle-shaped red blood cells cannot carry as much oxygen as normal cells and can also clog blood vessels.

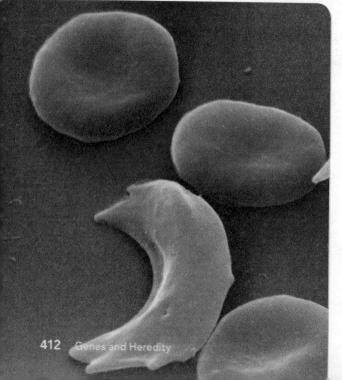

Gene Therapy in Humans Genetic diseases are caused by mutations, or changes in the DNA code. Some mutated genes pass from parent to child; others occur spontaneously. Soon, it may be possible to use genetic engineering to correct some genetic disorders in humans. This process, called **gene therapy**, involves changing a gene to treat a medical disease or disorder. A normal working gene replaces an absent or faulty gene. One promising therapy involves genetically engineering immune-system cells and injecting them into a person's body.

Millions of people worldwide suffer from sickle cell disease. This painful genetic disorder is caused by a single mutation that affects hemoglobin, a protein in red blood cells. Hemoglobin carries oxygen. The mutation causes the blood cells to be shaped like a sickle, or crescent, as shown in **Figure 5.**

CRISPR is a gene-editing tool that can help people with sickle cell disease. CRISPR uses a "guide RNA" and an enzyme to cut out the DNA sequence causing the dangerous mutation. The "guide RNA" takes the enzyme to the DNA sequence with the sickle cell mutation, and the enzyme then removes that sequence. Then another tool pastes a copy of the normal sequence into the DNA.

Cloning Organisms A **clone** is an organism that has the same genes as the organism from which it was produced. The process of cloning involves removing an unfertilized egg and replacing its nucleus with the nucleus of a body cell from the same species. Because this body cell has a full set of chromosomes, the offspring will have the same DNA as the individual that donated the body cell. The egg is then implanted into a female so it can develop. If the process is successful, the clone is born.

Cloning is used to develop many of the foods we eat. Many plants are cloned simply by taking a small piece of the original and putting it in suitable conditions to grow. For example, the Cavendish banana (see **Figure 6**) is the most common banana for eating. All these bananas are clones of the original plant. Cloning helps to produce crops of consistent quality. But a population with little genetic diversity has drawbacks, both for farmers and for people who rely on the crop for food.

☑ CHECK POINT **Summarize Text** List the steps in creating a clone.

....

....

....

....

▶ **VIDEO**

Learn how selective breeding and cloning can lead to populations with desired traits.

🖊 **Write About It**
Cloning food crops has many advantages. Every commercial banana crop, worldwide, is cloned. Write about how a disease that destroyed the Cavendish banana could affect society. Consider farmers, fruit companies, grocery stores, everyday people, and others who would be affected.

Cloned Bananas
Figure 6 A fungus that causes bananas to rot is spreading across the globe. The Cavendish banana is particularly vulnerable.

SEP Construct Explanations
Why is a disease more damaging to cloned crops?

....

....

....

....

....

....

Genetic Cousins

Figure 7 Humans and modern-day chimpanzees share about 99 percent of their DNA.

Infer How does knowing we are close genetically to chimpanzees help humans?

....

....

....

....

....

INTERACTIVITY

Gather fingerprints and identify who committed a crime.

Practical Uses for DNA

Due to new technologies, geneticists now study and use genes in ways that weren't possible before. Modern geneticists can now determine the exact sequence of nitrogen bases in an organism's DNA. This process is called DNA sequencing.

Sequencing the Human Genome Breaking a code with six billion letters may seem like an impossible task to undertake. But scientists working on the Human Genome Project did just that. The complete set of genetic information that an organism carries in its DNA is called a **genome**. The main goal of the Human Genome Project was to identify the DNA sequence of the entire human genome. Since sequencing the human genome, scientists now research the functions of tens of thousands of human genes. Some of these genes also allow scientists to better understand certain diseases.

Our genome can also help us understand how humans evolved on Earth. All life on Earth evolved from simple, single-celled organisms that lived billions of years ago, and we still have evidence of this in our DNA. For example, there are some genes that exist in the cells of almost every organism on Earth, which suggests we all evolved from a common ancestor. Some organisms share a closer relationship than others. By comparing genomes of organisms, scientists continue to piece together a history of how life on Earth evolved.

DNA Technologies Before the Human Genome Project, scientists such as Gregor Mendel used experimentation to understand heredity. Since the project's completion in 2003, the use of technologies to understand heredity and how DNA guides life processes has increased greatly. For example, DNA technologies help diagnose genetic diseases.

Genetic disorders typically result from one or more changed genes, called mutations. Medical specialists can carry out a DNA screening to detect the presence of a mutation. To complete a DNA screen, samples of DNA are analyzed for the presence of one or more mutated genes. This information is then used to help those individuals whose DNA includes mutated genes.

DNA comparisons determine how closely related you are to another person. To do this, DNA from a person's cell is broken down into small pieces, or fragments. These fragments are put into a machine that separates them by size. When this happens, a pattern is produced creating a DNA fingerprint, like the one shown in **Figure 8**. Similarities between patterns determine who contributed the DNA. Genetic fingerprints can be used to tie a person to a crime scene, prevent the wrong person from going to jail, identify remains, or identify the father of a child.

INTERACTIVITY

Consider using technology to solve the world's food problem.

DNA Fingerprint
Figure 8 ✏ Circle the suspect that left his or her DNA at the crime scene.

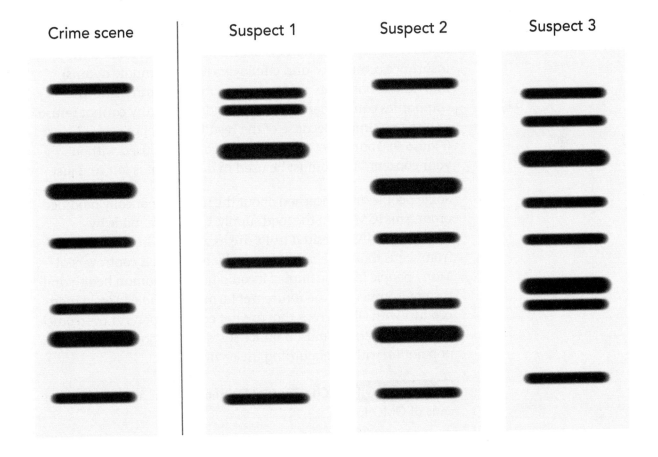

Crime scene | Suspect 1 | Suspect 2 | Suspect 3

Using Genetic Information

Figure 9 Some people fear that medical insurance companies will not cover their medical expenses if they have been genetically tested and results show a genetic disorder.

Evaluate Reasoning Why is this a fear of many people? What can we do to protect our privacy?

....

....

....

....

....

....

....

....

....

Controversies of DNA Use

As genetic research advances, some people are concerned about how genetic information will be used or altered. Some people are concerned about who can access their DNA information, and how this information will be used.

Your genetic information is the only truly unique part of your identity, and many people want to keep it as private as possible. The Genetic Information Nondiscrimination Act (GINA) was signed into law in 2008. This act makes it illegal for health insurance companies and employers to discriminate against individuals based on genetic information. Health insurance companies cannot deny you care, and a company cannot refuse to hire you simply because of the results of a genetic test (**Figure 9**). Your genetic information cannot be used without your consent, and it must be used in a way that is fair and just.

Some people are concerned about the use of genetically modified organisms (GMOs) in the food supply. GMOs are made by changing DNA so desired traits are expressed. Growing our food from seeds that have been genetically modified is controversial. Many people fear the impact it could have on human health and the environment in the future. Yet farmers are able to yield more product with GMO crops that are not eaten by pests or overcome by weeds. Scientists must balance sustaining a growing human population with safeguarding the environment.

✅ **CHECK POINT** **Cite Textual Evidence** What are the pros and cons of GMO foods?

....

....

☑ LESSON 5 Check

MS-LS4-5

1. **Identify** Shortly after World War II, chickens were bred to grow much more quickly and to produce much more meat. Which process is this an example of?

....

2. **Compare and Contrast** What are some positive and negative ways that genetic information may be used?

....

....

....

3. **CCC Cause and Effect** Some genetically engineered organisms can mate with wild members of their species. Farmed fish are often genetically modified. What can happen to wild fish of their species if mating occurs?

....

....

....

4. **SEP Construct Explanations** Gorillas and humans evolved from a common ancestor. Geneticists found that they may be more closely related than previously thought. How can DNA sequencing of the gorilla and human genomes determine this?

....

....

....

....

5. **SEP Evaluate Information** A classmate states that animals that result from artificial selection are "lucky," since they have better traits than naturally bred animals. Given your study of this topic, do you agree? Explain.

....

....

....

....

6. **CCC Relate Structure and Function** How can changes to the structure of DNA lead to the development of new traits in a species?

....

....

....

....

....

....

....

....

....

....

7. **SEP Design Solutions** The procedure used to make insulin in bacteria can also be used to synthesize other biological materials. Think of a chemical or material inside the human body that might be synthesized within bacteria. What would be the potential benefits of this process? What would be the potential drawbacks?

....

....

....

....

....

....

....

....

....

....

....

....

....

1 Patterns of Inheritance

🕐 MS-LS3-2

1. Genes are carried from parents to offspring on structures called
   A. alleles.
   B. chromosomes.
   C. phenotypes.
   D. genotypes.

2. Which combination of alleles represents a heterozygous genotype?
   A. GG
   B. gg
   C. Gg
   D. none of the above

3. An organism's phenotype is the way its
   .... is expressed.

4. SEP Use a Model ✏️ Fill in the Punnett Square to show a cross between two guinea pigs who are heterozygous for coat color. *B* is for black coat color and *b* is for white coat color.

5. Interpret Tables What is the probability that an offspring from the cross in Question 4 has the genotype *bb*?

   ....

2 Chromosomes and Inheritance

🕐 MS-LS3-2

6. Chromosomes are long, thread-like structures of
   A. cells.
   B. proteins.
   C. genes.
   D. DNA.

7. Which process results in the formation of sex cells?
   A. crossing over
   B. meiosis
   C. separation
   D. transfer

8. Geneticists use a ....
   to map the inheritance of particular traits.

9. Apply Concepts Each body cell in a black bear has 74 chromosomes. How many chromosomes are in the black bear's sex cells? Explain your answer.

   ....

   ....

   ....

10. SEP Construct Explanations In sexual reproduction, if each chromosome in a pair has the same genes, how is genetic variety possible?

    ....

    ....

    ....

    ....

    ....

    ....

    ....

    ....

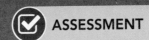

3 **Genetic Coding and Protein Synthesis**

🕐 MS-LS3-1

11. A gene is a section of DNA within a chromosome that codes for a(n)
  A. amino acid.
  B. specific protein.
  C. ribosome.
  D. double helix.

12. Proteins are long-chain molecules made of
  A. nitrogen bases.
  B. chromosomes.
  C. amino acids.
  D. organisms.

13. **Draw Conclusions** How does the pairing of nitrogen bases in a DNA molecule make sure that a replicated strand is exactly the same as the original strand?

....
....
....
....

4 **Trait Variations**

🕐 MS-LS3-1, MS-LS4-4, EP&CIIc

14. **SEP Engage in Argument** A friend says that all genetic mutations are harmful. Do you agree or disagree with this statement? Why?

....
....
....

15. **Connect to the Environment** Your neighbor recently sprayed his yard for wasps. It worked. Since then, you've noticed fewer bees and ants in your yard, but also fewer robins and woodpeckers. Why?

....
....
....
....

5 **Genetic Technologies**

🕐 MS-LS3-5

16. Genetic diseases are caused by
  A. X chromosomes.
  B. modified cells.
  C. plasmids.
  D. mutations.

17. Which is the best example of a possible future technology that could be used to eliminate sickle cell disease in humans?
  A. a genetically engineered virus which can eliminate sickle-shaped cells in human blood
  B. genetic screening which matches sickle cell carriers to non-carriers
  C. the ability to replace all sickle-cell alleles in human red blood cells
  D. the ability to replace all sickle-cell alleles in fertilized eggs

18. Scientists created a new variety of rice. They modified a common strain of rice by inserting the carotene gene from carrots. The addition of this gene resulted in a rice enriched with vitamin-A, a crucial vitamin for humans. What technology does this example represent?
  A. meiosis
  B. genetic engineering
  C. artificial selection
  D. cloning

19. **Support Your Explanation** The technology of genetic engineering holds great promise, yet it frightens some people. What are the advantages and disadvantages of genetic engineering?

....
....
....
....
....
....

MS-LS3-1, MS-LS4-4,
MS-LS4-5

Evidence-Based Assessment

Scientists have figured out a way to insert the genes of one organism into another. A genetically modified organism, GMO, expresses desired traits that prove to be beneficial to many farmers. Reliance on GMO crops has been increasing in the United States for many years.

The graph shows three genetically modified crops—corn, soybeans, and cotton. In each crop, the DNA has been engineered for a desired trait. New DNA sequences that code for specific proteins are inserted into a crop's DNA.

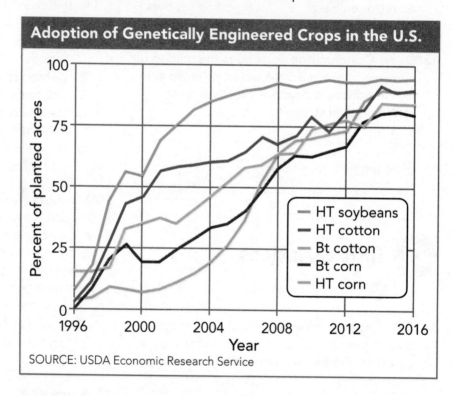

Adoption of Genetically Engineered Crops in the U.S.

- HT soybeans
- HT cotton
- Bt cotton
- Bt corn
- HT corn

SOURCE: USDA Economic Research Service

For example, some crops have been engineerd to resist droughts. The gene for drought resistance is spliced from the DNA of a desert-dwelling species and then inserted into the crop species. The resistance-to-drought trait will be expressed when these genetically engineered crop plants reproduce. Another desirable trait that has been produced through genetic engineering is improved herbicide tolerance (HT). This trait protects the GMO crop when herbicides are sprayed on the fields to kill weeds. In the case of the Bt crops, the desired gene comes from the *Bacillus thuringiensis* bacterium. The gene produces a protein that destroys the corn borer larvae. Farmers can grow Bt crops instead of spraying insecticides that could also kill helpful insects, such as bees.

1. **SEP Analyze Data** Which genetically engineered crop has shown the greatest increase in usage from 2006 to 2016?
   A. HT Corn   B. Bt Corn
   C. HT Cotton   D. HT Soybeans

2. **CCC Patterns** What patterns do you observe in the line graphs for the crops that are herbicide tolerant, HT? Support your claim.

....
....
....
....
....
....
....
....
....
....

3. **Connect to the Environment** Which statements are true regarding the advantages and disadvantages to increased reliance on GMO crops? Select all that apply.
   ☐ GMOs reduce the amount of water needed.

   ☐ GMOs reduce the need for chemical pesticides.

   ☐ Years of research confirm that GMOs are safe for human consumption.

   ☐ GMOs increase the need for chemical pesticides.

   ☐ GMOs could potentially be unsafe for human consumption.

4. **CCC Stability and Change** Each box below contains an idea about why genetically engineered crops will be used in the future. Sequence the boxes to demonstrate how the ideas would be used in a flowchart.

   | GMO crops now account for most acres of farm land. | _____ |

   | Use of GMOs has been increasing for ten years. | _____ |

   | This trend will continue because it saves time and money. | _____ |

Quest FINDINGS

Complete the Quest!

Phenomenon Create a brochure for prospective growers of your new fruit. Convince readers that your fruit will be a delicious success!

SEP Construct Explanations How will you know which traits are most beneficial to the general public so you can use them to create your fruit?

....
....
....
....

👆 **INTERACTIVITY**

Reflect on Funky Fruits

MS-LS3-2

Make the Right Call!

How can you design and use a **model** to make **predictions** about the possible results of **genetic crosses**?

Background

Phenomenon Suppose your neighbors tell you that their cat is going to have kittens. They can't stop talking about what color they think the kittens will be and whether their hair will be long or short. Using the suggested materials and your knowledge of genetic crosses, how can you make a model to show your neighbors the probabilities of the possible color and hair length combinations for the kittens?

Your neighbors got both the mother and father cat from a respected breeder. The index card shows background information about the two cats.

Materials

(per group)

- 4 small paper bags
- 12 red marbles
- 12 blue marbles
- 12 green marbles
- 12 yellow marbles
- marking pen

Max, male cat, short hair, homozygous black hair.

Willa, female cat, heterozygous short hair, heterozygous black hair.

Design Your Investigation

Demonstrate Go online for a downloadable worksheet of this lab.

☐ **1.** In the space below, use Punnett squares to determine the possible outcomes from a cross between the male and female cats. **TIP: First identify each parent's alleles, noting that not all of them are known.**

Homozygous — parent or offspring has either two dominant or two recessive alleles.

Heterozygous — parent or offspring has one of each allele (one dominant and one recessive)

Dominant Trait	Recessive Trait
Short Hair	Long Hair
Black Hair	Brown Hair

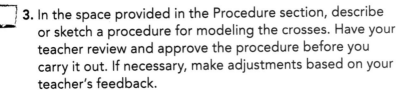

☐ **2.** Design a way to model these crosses using the marbles and bags. The bags should contain the alleles of the male and female parent cats—two bags for each parent (one bag for hair color, the other bag for hair length). **TIP: Use four marbles for each allele in each cat.**

☐ **3.** In the space provided in the Procedure section, describe or sketch a procedure for modeling the crosses. Have your teacher review and approve the procedure before you carry it out. If necessary, make adjustments based on your teacher's feedback.

☐ **4.** Use your model. Record your observations in the data tables.

Procedure

....

....

....

....

....

....

....

....

....

....

Observations

Data Table 1 Hair Length			
Trial Cross	Allele from Bag 1 (Max)	Allele from Bag 2 (Willa)	Offspring's Alleles
1			
2			
3			
4			
5			
6			
7			
8			
9			
10			
11			
12			

Data Table 2 Hair Color			
Trial Cross	Allele from Bag 3 (Max)	Allele from Bag 4 (Willa)	Offspring's Alleles
1			
2			
3			
4			
5			
6			
7			
8			
9			
10			
11			
12			

Analyze and Interpret Data

1. **SEP Develop a Model** How did you use the materials? What did the different parts of the model represent?

....

....

....

2. **SEP Analyze Data** Refer to your Punnett squares. What percentages of black kittens (BB or Bb) and brown kittens (bb) did you predict? What percentages of shorthair kittens (SS or Ss) and longhair (ss) kittens did you predict?

....

....

....

3. **SEP Use a Model to Evaluate** Refer to your data table. Did the percentages of offspring with a given genotype match the percentages that you obtained by completing the Punnett squares? Explain.

....

....

....

....

4. **Compare Data** How did using a Punnett square differ from using your model? Which did you prefer?

....

....

....

....

....

5. **Form an Opinion** Was your model effective at showing the neighbors all of the possible combinations of hair color and length to expect in their kittens? Explain.

....

....

....

....

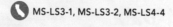
CEPHALOPODS
SPECIAL EDITION

squid

Octopuses, squids, and cuttlefish are a type of mollusk called cephalopods. These soft-bodied invertebrates reproduce sexually. They are fast swimmers and aggressive predators. With prominent heads and multiple tentacles, cephalopods are known for their complex behaviors and for being extremely intelligent.

Cephalopods also have a remarkably large genome—it's even larger than the human genome! Their genome stands out because it has many genes related to neuron connectivity, which might explain their unusually large brains and intelligence. Cephalopods are so smart that they can solve puzzles, use tools, and even open jars.

Adding Variation

Sexual reproduction is not the only process that contributes to making offspring different from their parents. Squids and octopuses, for example, have developed a clever mechanism that increases variation in traits without really having to make changes to their genetic information.

octopus

Some genetic information becomes traits by means of a messenger molecule called RNA. RNA is the molecule that allows the expression of genetic information.

In a process called RNA editing, squids and octopuses can make changes to RNA, the messenger molecule. RNA editing leads to a change in traits that are expressed, regardless of the information coded in the genome. The highest rate of RNA-editing takes place in nervous system cells.

RNA editing in cephalopods is triggered by environmental factors. It could be turned on when the cephalopod travels from the tropics from the arctic. Or it will turn off the RNA editing when the cephalopod remains in one location.

cuttlefish

One fascinating feature of RNA editing is that not all of the messenger molecules are edited the same way. As a result, many different RNA messenger molecules can come out of one single gene.

Scientists think that this increase in variation may also explain cephalopods' complex brains and high intelligence. They also wonder whether there could be a trade off. By relying on RNA editing to adapt to such influences in the environment as temperature changes and experiences, could these special cephalopods be losing something else? After all, these specific changes are not passed down to their offspring.

Read the case study and answer the following questions.

1. SEP Analyze Data Suppose the ability to edit RNA is a dominant trait. A male squid with two dominant alleles for RNA editing sexually reproduces with a female squid that has two recessive alleles for RNA editing. Will their offspring be able to edit their RNA? Explain.

   ....

2. SEP Evaluate Information If there is a change in a squid's messenger RNA, will this change appear in its genetic material? Will it be inherited by its offspring?

   ....

   ....

3. SEP Construct Explanations How can changes in RNA be beneficial for squids?

   ....

   ....

4. CCC Structure and Function What do you think could happen if humans had the same RNA-editing ability as cephalopods? What might be the result?

   ....

   ....

   ....

California Spotlight

Instructional Segment 4

🕐 MS-LS4-1, MS-LS4-2, MS-LS4-4, MS-LS4-6, EP&CIIa, EP&CIIc

Guiding Questions

- How do specific traits help organisms access or utilize resources more efficiently?
- How does a population benefit from having diversity within it?
- What does it mean to have "survival of the fittest?"
- In what ways are humans similar to dinosaurs?
- How do rocks tell us about the history of life?

Topics

8 Natural Selection and Change Over Time

During the Cambrian Period, the land that now makes up California was not yet part of North America. The area that now makes up the White-Inyo mountain range along the border of California and Nevada near Bishop was once covered by a shallow sea.

Identify the Problem

California's Changes Over Time

Phenomenon Californians are always on the move. And so is the ground beneath their feet. Over millions of years, the land that makes up California has changed both its position on Earth and its location relative to the rest of what is now North America.

The oldest rock in the state dates from about 1.7 billion years ago. Life started to appear in what is now California about 570 million years ago, during the Cambrian Period.

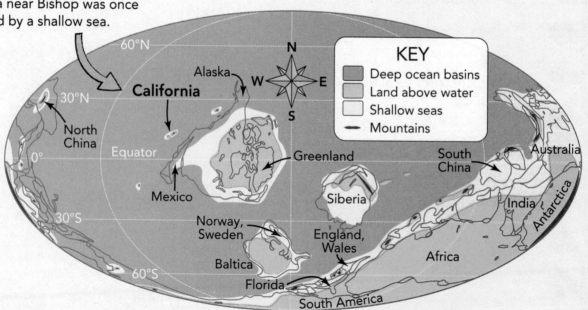

Changes in Rocks

Earth's surface is always changing. Land is constantly forged and destroyed by forces in the rock cycle, shifting tectonic plates, and other system processes. The fossil record indicates that California's present location and composition are the result of geological changes to the Earth's surface. While California's oldest rocks do not contain fossils, some younger rocks contain fossils from marine organisms. The fossils found in these rocks provide evidence to scientists that parts of California could have once been parts of former oceanic plates that collided into a continental plate. Rock record evidence reveals that volcanic activity and continental sediments formed much of California's land.

Today, many different types of rock make up the land that is California. Each rock type was made during a different period in Earth's history. Recent research finds that the rock cycle, particularly changes in the Earth's crust, played a key role in the start of life on the planet. Without these changes, complex life forms could not have developed on Earth.

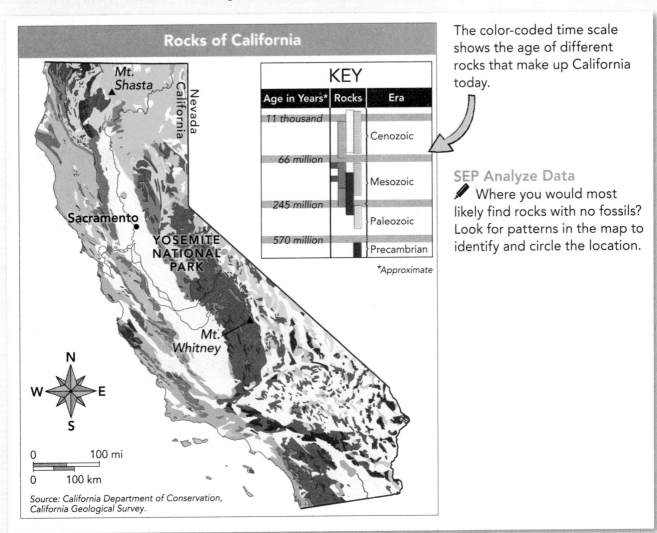

Rocks of California

KEY

Age in Years*	Rocks	Era
11 thousand		
		Cenozoic
66 million		
		Mesozoic
245 million		
		Paleozoic
570 million		
		Precambrian

*Approximate

Source: California Department of Conservation, California Geological Survey.

The color-coded time scale shows the age of different rocks that make up California today.

SEP Analyze Data

Where you would most likely find rocks with no fossils? Look for patterns in the map to identify and circle the location.

429

The Great Oxidation Event

In order for life to develop on Earth, oxygen was needed in Earth's atmosphere. It took geological and biological changes to kick-start a process (around 2.3 billion years ago) that increased levels of oxygen in the atmosphere. This dramatic rise in atmospheric oxygen is known as "the great oxidation event." The increased supply of atmospheric oxygen led to an explosion in the number and diversity of species. It also made it possible for organisms to adapt to life on land.

Some of the oldest known fossils are around 3.5 billion years old and show the presence of cyanobacteria. These bacteria were unicellular organisms that produced oxygen as a by-product of photosynthesis. Until recently, scientists could not explain why oxygen levels did not increase for another billion years. Research, reveals that a rock-forming mineral, olivine, could have been the reason.

Olivine is one of Earth's most abundant minerals. Olivine traps oxygen when it reacts with water. So some scientists have speculated that olivine in the land covered by shallow seas would have absorbed the oxygen that cyanobacteria would have produced. As the composition of Earth's continental surface rocks changed, however, olivine was replaced by other rocks. With less olivine present, oxygen built up in the oceans and atmosphere.

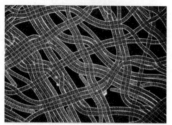

Meet the kick-starters of Earth's atmosphere—olivine (top) and cyanobacteria, better known as blue-green algae (bottom). Rocks with olivine are mined in the Klamath Mountains that run from northern California into Orgeon. Fossils of cyanobacteria can be found in the White-Inyo Mountain range.

Archaeocyatha, a type of ancient sponge, appeared around 530 million years ago. Before going extinct, they evolved into hundreds of different species, many of which were Earth's first reef-builders.

1. **Identify** 🖊 Circle the fossil of an Archaeocyatha.
2. **SEP Construct Explanations** Why would reef-building be important for life on Earth and in the ancient land mass that would become California?

....

....

....

Changes in Life Forms

California is rich in fossils. They reveal the amazing variety of species that once lived in California. The fossils reveal how different species have adapted over time as conditions changed. Many animals that once roamed through California now exist only in the form of fossils. The Mojave Desert, for example, contains fossils of ancient horses, ancient elephants, and camels. While many species that once lived in California disappeared from the land mass that become North America, some animals managed to migrate and thrive on other continents.

California's state fossil, the saber-toothed cat (*Smilodon*), was common in California around 2.5 million years ago but went extinct, disappearing around 10,000 years ago. The excavation site at the La Brea Tar Pits in Los Angeles contains many of their fossils, evidence that there was once a sizable population of these ancient cats in California.

All sorts of animals that lived in California during the last Ice Age met their demise in the La Brea Tar Pits: ancient horses, camels, ground sloths, jaguars, mammoths, and saber-toothed cats.

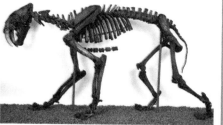

Saber-toothed cats were predators weighing up to 350 kg (770 lbs).

Explain Phenomena What are some environmental conditions that the saber-toothed cat may have not been adapted for that could have caused its extinction?

....

....

....

....

Adapting to Climate Change

Throughout this segment, you will learn about how organisms adapt to their surroundings and how species change over time. You will also explore how humans have influenced the evolution of some species on the planet. Understanding these processes helps scientists see how the interrelationships between Earth's systems and processes can affect evolution and the diversity of life. In the topics in this segment, you will investigate the factors that drive evolutionary changes in animals and plants.

A team of scientists, including researchers from the University of California at Riverside, recently discovered a relationship between climate change and evolution. They found that an extreme climate event in the past drastically increased oxygen levels in Earth's ocean-atmosphere system. That event was the thawing of "Snowball Earth." Analyzing trace elements in rocks provided the team with strong evidence for an oxygen spike after a period of thawing. The fossil record further provided evidence of a sudden increase in biodiversity. Because of the thawing, there was an explosion of algae and then small animal life forms.

Snowball Earth refers to a few brief periods 650–900 million years ago when ice covered most of the planet's surface.

Leatherback sea turtles lay their eggs in Indonesia and then swim thousands of miles to their feeding grounds along California's coast. Jellyfish, their main food source, thrive in the upwelling of cooler waters around California.

CCC Stability and Change Consider how a severe climate event that causes water temperatures to increase might affect the leatherback sea turtle.

....

....

....

....

Evidence **Now that you have completed the topic in this segment, do the following task.**

Impacts on Evolution in California

Case Study You have learned about the evidence that helps scientists to explain how changes in Earth system processes and human activities can bring about changes in life forms. Now you can take a closer look at what drives change in a particular species. Consider the impact of climate change due to human activities and how global warming could alter various ecosystems in California. Identify a specific species for your research. It must be a species found in California or along its coasts. The species could be a plant, mammal, bird, reptile, amphibian, or fish. The species may live in California or migrate through it.

Research your chosen species to learn more about it. Find out how long it has inhabited a California ecosystem and if it appears in the fossil record. Determine how your species has changed over time, if at all. Consider what factors might have caused the organism to change. List ways in which your chosen species could adapt to an extreme climate event. What sort of traits would have to be passed from parent to offspring? Also list any steps that could be taken now to protect it from the effects of climate change.

Describe any instance where human activities, either directly or indirectly, might be causing rapid environmental change. Explain how your species could adapt to that change and what might happen if it cannot adapt.

Extreme climate change in California could impact both of these species.

Bull Trout

American Pika

Communicate a Solution

Based on your research, answer the following questions.

1. **SEP Communicate Information** Describe the species you researched, its habitat in California, and how climate change is affecting it. Also explain how human activities have directly or indirectly impacted the species.

....

....

....

....

....

....

....

....

....

....

....

2. **SEP Construct Explanations** If the species you researched goes extinct, how would the species be reflected in the fossil record? Would the species be fossilized? Explain.

....

....

....

....

....

3. **SEP Explain Phenomena** How could an extreme climate change, such as global warming, affect the evolution of the species you researched? Explain.

....

....

....

....

....

....

4. CCC Stability and Change What sort of adaptations would the organism need in order to survive the effects of sudden climate change, such as global warming? Can these adaptations be passed on from one generation to the next? How does this relate to evolution?

....
....
....
....
....
....
....
....
....

5. Connect to the Environment What can humans do to protect your species? Present one way to protect the species with a solution that could be easily implemented.

....
....
....

6. CCC Cause and Effect Earlier in this segment, you drew a conclusion about the impact of extreme climate change on leatherback sea turtles in California. Consider what you learned researching your species. How might the human impact of climate change affect the two different species?

....
....
....
....
....
....
....

Natural Selection and Change Over Time

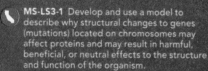
MS-LS3-1 Develop and use a model to describe why structural changes to genes (mutations) located on chromosomes may affect proteins and may result in harmful, beneficial, or neutral effects to the structure and function of the organism.

MS-LS4-1 Analyze and interpret data for patterns in the fossil record that document the existence, diversity, extinction, and change of life forms throughout the history of life on Earth under the assumption that natural laws operate today as in the past.

MS-LS4-2 Apply scientific ideas to construct an explanation for the anatomical similarities and differences among modern organisms and between modern and fossil organisms to infer evolutionary relationships.

MS-LS4-3 Analyze displays of pictorial data to compare patterns of similarities in the embryological development across multiple species to identify relationships not evident in the fully formed anatomy.

MS-LS4-4 Construct an explanation based on evidence that describes how genetic variations of traits in a population increase some individuals' probability of surviving and reproducing in a specific environment.

MS-LS4-5 Gather and synthesize information about the technologies that have changed the way humans influence the inheritance of desired traits in organisms.

MS-LS4-6 Use mathematical representations to support explanations of how natural selection may lead to increases and decreases of specific traits in populations over time.

EP&CIIa Students should be developing an understanding that the direct and indirect changes to natural systems due to the growth of human populations and their consumption rates influence the geographic extent, composition, biological diversity, and viability of natural systems.

EP&CIIc Students should be developing an understanding that the expansion and operation of human communities influences the geographic extent, composition, biological diversity, and viability of natural systems.

Has this dragonfly changed from its fossilized ancestor?

GO ONLINE
to access your
digital course

 VIDEO

 INTERACTIVITY

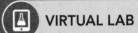 VIRTUAL LAB

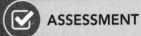 ASSESSMENT

 eTEXT

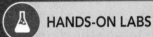 HANDS-ON LABS

HANDS-ON LAB

иConnect Analyze evidence that whales may have walked on land.

The Essential Question

How do characteristics change over time?

CCC Structure and Function At first glance, this modern-day dragonfly and its fossilized ancestor probably don't look very different. Both seem to have long, slender bodies, two sets of wings, and large eyes. Would it surprise you to know that the dragonfly ancestor, *Meganeura*, lived about 300 million years ago and had a wingspan of 75 cm? It's the largest known flying insect! In comparison, the largest modern dragonfly has a wingspan of only 16 cm. Think about why we don't see such large insects anymore. List your ideas below.

....

....

....

Quest KICKOFF

Why is the migration pattern changing for some European bird populations?

Phenomenon To understand how bird populations change over time in response to environmental conditions, ornithologists (scientists who study birds) analyze long-term data. In this problem-based Quest activity, you will investigate factors that may be influencing changes in two populations of European blackcaps. By applying what you learn from each lesson, digital activity, and hands-on lab, you will determine what is causing the changes to the bird populations. Then in the Findings activity, you will prepare a multimedia report to communicate what you have learned and to explain the changes in the blackcap populations.

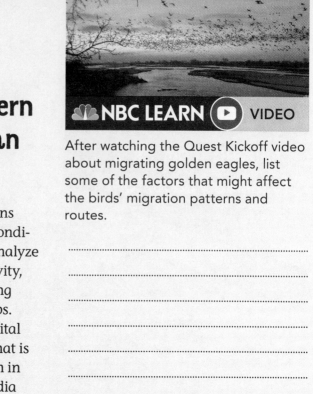

NBC LEARN ▶ VIDEO

After watching the Quest Kickoff video about migrating golden eagles, list some of the factors that might affect the birds' migration patterns and routes.

....

....

....

....

....

....

....

....

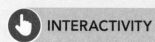 **INTERACTIVITY**

A Migration Puzzle

MS-LS3-1, MS-LS4-1, MS-LS4-2, MS-LS4-4, MS-LS4-5, MS-LS4-6, EP&CIIa, EP&CIIc

---

Quest CHECK-IN

IN LESSON 1
What differences exist between the UK and Spanish blackcaps? Determine evidence for variations in the European blackcap populations.

 INTERACTIVITY

Meet the Blackcaps

IN LESSON 2
What are the roles of genes and mutations in natural selection? Think about how you can include these factors in your report.

Quest CHECK-IN

IN LESSON 3
How can natural selection and inherited variations influence a population? Investigate factors that may have caused the variations in the European blackcaps.

 INTERACTIVITY

Evolution of the Blackcaps

In the 1960s, some European blackcaps started migrating to the United Kingdom from Central Europe during the winter. Over time, they have formed a distinct population of blackcaps.

IN LESSON 4

What can you learn from the fossil record? Think about how the fossil record of the European blackcap might provide information on how the bird has adapted over time.

Quest CHECK-IN

IN LESSON 5

What else would be helpful to know about European blackcaps? Research your questions and gather information to include in your report.

👆 **INTERACTIVITY**

Prepare Your Report

Quest FINDINGS

Complete the Quest!

Create a multimedia report about the two populations of European blackcaps and what caused them to be so different from each other.

👆 **INTERACTIVITY**

Reflect on Blackcap Migration

439

Early Study of Evolution

Guiding Questions

- What processes explain how organisms can change over time?
- What observations and evidence support the theory of evolution?

Connection

Literacy Determine Central Ideas

 MS-LS4-4 Construct an explanation based on evidence that describes how genetic variations of traits in a population increase some individuals' probability of surviving and reproducing in a specific environment.

HANDS-ON LAB

uInvestigate Model how species change over time.

Vocabulary

species
evolution
fossil
adaptation
scientific theory

Academic Vocabulary

hypothesize

Connect It!

✎ **Draw an arrow pointing to the squirrel that you think is better suited for the environment.**

SEP Construct Explanations Why do you think that squirrel is better suited for the environment? Explain your reasoning.

....

....

....

....

Observing Changes

Suppose you put a birdfeeder outside your kitchen or classroom window. You enjoy watching birds and gray squirrels come to get a free meal. The squirrels seem to be perfectly skilled at climbing the feeder and breaking open seeds. One day, you are surprised to see a white squirrel, like the squirrel in **Figure 1**, visiting the feeder. This new white squirrel and the gray squirrel appear to be the same **species**—a group of similar organisms that can mate with each other and produce offspring that can also mate and reproduce. You would probably have a few questions about where this squirrel came from and why it is white!

Curiosity About How Life Changes

Scientists such as Charles Darwin were also curious about the differences they observed in natural populations. A variation is any difference between individuals of the same species. Some scientists asked how life on Earth got started and how it has changed over time throughout the planet's history. The scientists wondered what dinosaurs were like and why they disappeared. Darwin and others worked to develop a theory of **evolution**—the process by which modern organisms have descended from ancient organisms.

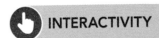

INTERACTIVITY

Explore feeding adaptations of animals in a coral reef ecosystem.

Surprise at the Birdfeeder!

Figure 1 In Brevard, North Carolina, about one-third of the Eastern gray squirrel population is white. In 1949, a resident received a pair of white squirrels as a gift. When one squirrel escaped, the other was released to join its friend. Soon after, people began to spot more white squirrels in town.

Organizing Life

Figure 2 Linnaeus classified life based on the structures of each organism.

Classify ✎ Identify three characteristics that you can observe in the image and list them below. Assign each characteristic a shape: a circle, square, or triangle. Using the characteristics you have identified, organize the organisms in the image into three groups by drawing the appropriate shapes around them.

....

....

....

....

....

....

....

....

....

📖 **Make Meaning** What problem or question have you had that required you to make observations and gather evidence to figure it out?

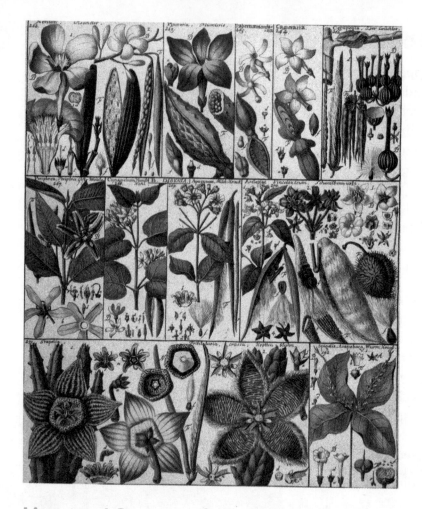

Linnaeus' System of Classification

Carolus Linnaeus (1707–1778) developed the first scientific system for classifying and naming living things. Linnaeus collected samples of organisms from around the world. When classifying the organisms according to shared characteristics like those shown in **Figure 2**, he observed that there were variations of traits within a species. He was able to describe the variations and diversity of life, but not explain what caused that variation and diversity. No one was yet exploring how organisms came to be the way they are. In fact, many people still believed that organisms could appear out of the air as if by magic.

Lamarck's Idea

The first serious attempts to explain evolution began in the late 1700s. A French scientist, Jean-Baptiste Lamarck (1744–1829), was put in charge of a museum department of "Insects and Worms," which also included all the invertebrates, or animals without backbones. Lamarck devoted himself to learning everything he could about invertebrates. Unlike Linnaeus, Lamarck wasn't satisfied with describing what the animals looked like. Instead, Lamarck attempted to figure out how the organisms came to be. After much study, Lamarck developed the first attempt at a scientific hypothesis explaining how species change over time.

Lamarck's Hypothesis of Transformation Lamarck mistakenly believed that organisms could change their traits by selectively using or not using various parts of their bodies. For example, moles could develop long, strong claws by digging through dirt. Lamarck **hypothesized** that if two adult moles with long claws mated, their offspring would inherit those claws, as shown in **Figure 3**. In the next generation, the individuals who used their claws more would pass even longer claws on to their offspring. In this way, the whole population of moles would gradually grow bigger, stronger claws, until they reached the form we see today.

Lamarck's transformation hypothesis doesn't support a consistent pattern for other traits when investigated further. It doesn't explain how features such as eyes could have developed. The hypothesis also does not work when tested with experiments. For example, you can force a plant to grow sideways. However, the offspring of the plant grow straight up toward the light. While his hypothesis was not supported, Lamarck did contribute some important new ideas. First, he suggested that a change in a species takes place by small, gradual steps. Second, he proposed that simple organisms could develop over many generations into more complex organisms.

Academic Vocabulary
Hypothesize comes from the Greek word for *foundation*. To hypothesize means to propose a hypothesis—a possible explanation to a question that can be investigated. A hypothesis can be based on limited evidence. Why is it helpful to hypothesize in subjects like history and science?

....

....

....

....

Lamarck's Transformation Hypothesis
Figure 3 ✐ In the open space, draw what you think the offspring of the mole that did not dig for food will look like, based on Lamarck's hypothesis.

☑ **CHECK POINT** **Determine Conclusions** Why was Lamarck's hypothesis not accepted

....

....

....

443

Reading the Past

Figure 4 Charles Lyell discovered how to read Earth's history from layers of rock. Meanwhile, Mary Anning used fossils to reconstruct ancient animals.

1. **Interpret Photos** Examine the fossil. List the parts of the animal that you recognize. What kind of animal do you think this was?

....

....

....

2. **CCC Identify Patterns** Would you expect to find older or newer fossils in rock layers closer to the surface? Why?

....

....

....

....

....

Charles Lyell's Rocks Not long after Lamarck proposed his ideas, a young lawyer named Charles Lyell (1797–1875) began studying naturally-formed layers of rocks and fossils, like those in **Figure 4**. A **fossil** is the preserved remains or traces of an organism that lived in the past. Lyell concluded that the features of Earth had changed a great deal over time. He also stated that the processes that created land features in the past were still active. Before Lyell, some people estimated that the world was less than 6,000 years old. Lyell and other scientists pushed that estimate back more than 300 million years. Lyell's discoveries set the stage for a theory of gradual evolution, or evolution over long periods of time.

Mary Anning's Fossils Mary Anning (1799–1847) lived a much different life than Linnaeus, Lamarck, or Lyell. Coming from a poor family that made money by collecting fossils, Mary Anning would roam up and down the beach while searching for fossils in the steep cliffs along the English Channel. Anning taught herself how to reconstruct the bodies of fossilized animals. Many of these animals had never before been seen. Because of Anning's work, scientists began to realize that some animals had lived in the ancient past but no longer existed. While Anning had no formal training as a scientist, her observations and discoveries made her a key contributor in the study of both fossils and geology.

CHECK POINT **Summarize Text** How did the scientists show that organisms and Earth changed over time?

....

....

Darwin's Journey

In 1831, 22-year-old Charles Darwin set out on a five-year trip around the world aboard a British navy ship, the HMS *Beagle*. Darwin was a naturalist—a person who observes and studies the natural world. The captain of the *Beagle* wanted someone aboard who could make and record observations as the crew explored South America. One of Darwin's professors suggested inviting Darwin. And thus was launched a brilliant career!

Darwin was surprised to see the diversity of living things he encountered during the voyage. He saw insects that looked like flowers. He also saw armadillos digging insects from the ground. These mammals with a leathery shell that looks like a small suit of armor would have been very strange creatures to see. Today, scientists know that organisms are even more diverse than Darwin thought. Scientists have calculated that there are millions of species on Earth—and new ones are being identified all the time. Scientists have no way to estimate how many undiscovered species exist, but they believe the numbers are very high.

Fossils On his journey aboard the *Beagle*, Darwin also saw fossils of animals that had died long ago. Some of the fossils he observed confused him. **Figure 5** shows fossils Darwin found that resembled the bones of living armadillos but were much larger in size. Darwin wondered what had happened to the ancient, giant armadillos. Over long periods of time, could the giant armadillos have evolved into the smaller species we see today?

Armored Animals

Figure 5 Darwin thought that the fossil bones of giant Glyptodons (right) resembled the bones of modern armadillos (left).

1. **Determine Similarities** List two common features that the animals share.

....

....

2. **Infer** Why might these features be important to both ancient and modern armadillos?

....

....

....

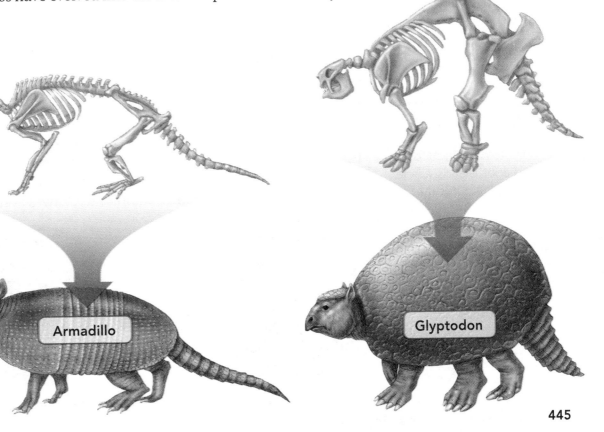

Armadillo

Glyptodon

445

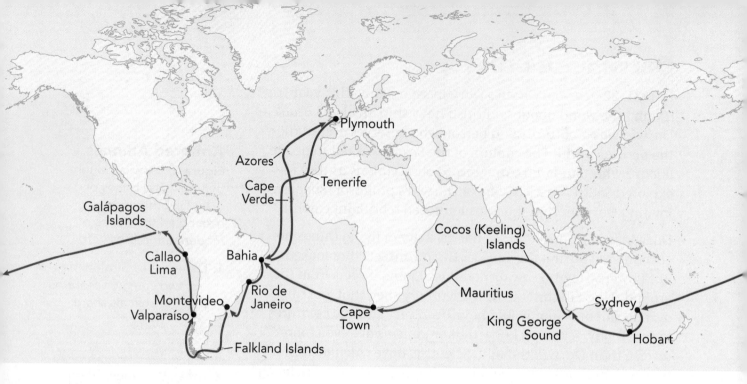

Voyage of the HMS Beagle, 1831–1836

Figure 6 Darwin sailed 40,000 miles around the world during his five-year voyage.

👆 **INTERACTIVITY**

Observe organisms that Darwin encountered in the Galápagos Islands.

Long-Lost Relatives?

Figure 7 ✏️ Mockingbirds on the South American mainland are similar to mockingbirds on the Galápagos Islands. Circle and label the features that are not similar.

CCC Relate Structure and Function Why do you think these birds have different traits?

....
....
....
....

Galápagos Organisms
The *Beagle* sailed to many different locations, as shown in **Figure 6**, and made several stops along the coast of South America. From what is now Peru on the Pacific coast, the ship traveled west to the Galápagos Islands. Darwin observed many different life forms there. He compared organisms from the Galápagos Islands to organisms that lived elsewhere. He also compared organisms living on the different islands.

Comparisons to the Mainland
Darwin discovered similarities between Galápagos organisms and those found in South America. Some of the birds and plants on the islands resembled those on the mainland. However, Darwin also noted important differences between the organisms. You can see differences between island and mainland mockingbirds in **Figure 7**. Darwin became convinced that species do not always stay the same. Instead, he thought species could change and even produce new species over time. Darwin began to think that the island species might be related to South American species. After much reflection, Darwin realized that the island species had become different from their mainland relatives over time.

Galápagos mockingbird　　　**South American mockingbird**

Comparisons Among the Islands Darwin collected birds from several of the Galápagos Islands. The birds were a little different from one island to the next. Darwin would learn that the birds were all types of finches. He concluded that the finch species were all related to a single common ancestor species that came from the mainland. Over time, different finches developed different beak shapes and sizes that were well suited to the food they ate. Beak shape is an example of an **adaptation**—an inherited behavior or physical characteristic that helps an organism survive and reproduce in its environment. Look at **Figure 8**. Birds with narrow, prying beaks can grasp insects. Those with long, pointed, sharp beaks can pick at cacti. Short, hooked beaks tear open fruit, while short, wide beaks crush seeds.

✓ CHECK POINT **Determine Central Ideas** What convinced Darwin that species can change over time?

....

....

Question It

We Got the Beak!
SEP Construct Explanations The finches in **Figure 8** show variations due to adaptation. Suppose someone asks what could cause a species' beak to change. How would you answer the person?

....

....

....

....

....

Galápagos Finches
Figure 8 Darwin observed beak adaptations.

1. Claim Why is it necessary for finches to have different beaks?

....

....

....

....

....

2. Evidence ✏ Draw an arrow from each finch matching it to the type of food you think it eats.

3. Reasoning Explain why your evidence supports your claim.

....

....

....

....

....

....

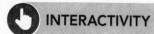

Literacy Connection

Determine Central Ideas
As you read, underline the elements that are needed to develop a scientific theory.

HANDS-ON LAB

☑**Investigate** Model how species change over time.

Darwin's Hypothesis Darwin thought about what he had observed during his voyage on the *Beagle*. By this time, while Darwin was convinced that organisms change over time, he wanted to know how the organisms changed. Darwin consulted other scientists and gathered more information. Based on his observations, Darwin reasoned that plants or animals that arrived on the Galápagos Islands faced conditions different from those on the nearby mainland. Darwin hypothesized that species change over many generations and become better adapted to new conditions. Darwin's hypothesis was an idea that contributed important new knowledge. Later, he and other scientists used it to test and develop a scientific theory.

Developing a Theory In science, a theory explains why and how things happen in nature. A **scientific theory** is a well-tested explanation for a wide range of observations and experimental results. Based on a body of facts, scientific theory is confirmed repeatedly through observation and experimentation. Darwin's ideas are often referred to as the theory of evolution. From the evidence he collected, and from all the discoveries of the scientists who had come before him, Darwin concluded that organisms on the Galápagos Islands had changed over time, or evolved.

☑ CHECK POINT **Cite Textual Evidence** Why do you think theories, like Darwin's theory of evolution, are important to science?

....

....

....

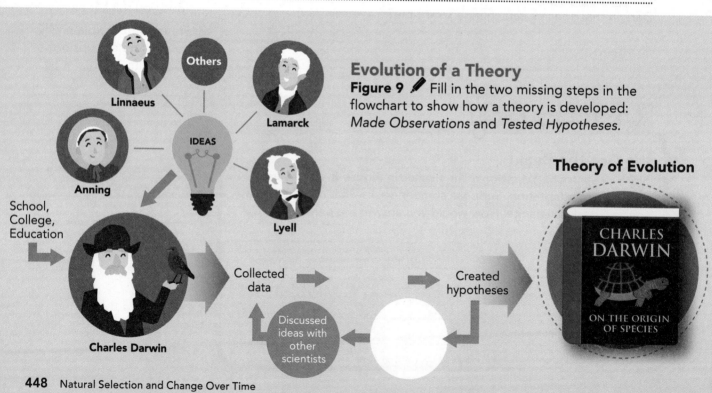

Evolution of a Theory
Figure 9 🖉 Fill in the two missing steps in the flowchart to show how a theory is developed: *Made Observations* and *Tested Hypotheses.*

☑ LESSON 1 Check

1. **Identify** Name four people, other than Darwin, whose work contributed to the study of evolution.

....

....

2. **Apply Scientific Reasoning** Why are fossils important to developing a theory of evolution?

....

....

....

....

3. **Compare and Contrast** How are variations and adaptations similar? How are they different?

....

....

....

....

....

....

4. **Integrate Information** Which two ideas of Lamarck contributed the most to Darwin's theory of evolution?

....

....

....

....

....

5. **SEP Construct Explanations** If the finches on the Galápagos Islands had such different beaks, how could Darwin think they shared a common ancestor from the mainland?

....

....

....

....

....

....

Quest CHECK-IN

In this lesson, you learned about adaptations and variations as well as the people whose ideas and activities contributed to understanding how organisms change over time. You also learned how Darwin developed his theory of evolution.

CCC Stability and Change Consider what you learned about variation and how species change over time. Why is it important to understand how a different migration route might be affecting the blackcaps' physical traits?

....

....

....

....

👆 INTERACTIVITY

Meet the Blackcaps

Go online to draw conclusions about the variations between the two groups, based on what you've learned about where the birds migrate in winter.

449

Guiding Questions

- How does natural selection lead to change over time in organisms?
- What are the roles of genes, mutations, and the environment in natural selection?

Connections

Literacy Cite Textual Evidence

Math Graph Proportional Relationships

MS-LS4-4 Construct an explanation based on evidence that describes how genetic variations of traits in a population increase some individuals' probability of surviving and reproducing in a specific environment.

MS-LS4-5 Gather and synthesize information about the technologies that have changed the way humans influence the inheritance of desired traits in organisms.

MS-LS4-6 Use mathematical representations to support explanations of how natural selection may lead to increases and decreases of specific traits in populations over time.

HANDS-ON LAB

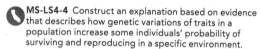

uInvestigate Measure variation in plant and animal populations.

Vocabulary

mechanism
natural selection
competition

Academic Vocabulary

expression

Connect It!

✏️ **Estimate how many dead fish are shown here. Write your estimation on the photograph.**

Explain Phenomena Some fish survived this event, known as a fish kill. What might be different about the fish that survived?

....

....

Apply Scientific Reasoning If low oxygen levels occur every year and cause fish kills, how might the population of fish change over time?

....

Evolution by Natural Selection

Living in a small body of water can be dangerous for fish. If water conditions become unhealthy, there is nowhere for the fish to go. Too little rain, too many fish, and an overgrowth of algae can work together to reduce oxygen levels in water. **Figure 1** shows what happened when oxygen levels fell too low. A "fish kill" can wipe out most of the local population of a species of fish. Some individuals, however, usually survive the disaster. These fish will live to reproduce, thus ensuring the species survives.

Darwin's Search for a Mechanism
After his return to England, Darwin was not satisfied with his theory of evolution. He struggled to determine evolution's mechanism. A **mechanism** is the natural process by which something takes place. Darwin asked himself how organisms could change over time. And how could a species become better adapted to new conditions? To solve this mystery, Darwin performed experiments and read the works of other naturalists and scientists.

INTERACTIVITY

Investigate how a species of butterflyfish adapts to changes in its environment.

Fish Kill
Figure 1 Fish can survive only in water with dissolved oxygen. When oxygen levels fall too low, thousands of fish can perish at once.

Rock pigeon
(*Columba livia*)

Fantail pigeon

Silky fantail pigeon

Fancy Pigeons

Figure 2 Through artificial selection, Darwin helped to create the fantail pigeon (center) from the wild rock pigeon (left). Silky fantails (right) were then bred from the fantail pigeon.

Make Observations List the differences you see between the three different pigeon types.

Write About It
Farmers often selectively breed farm animals. When farmers breed and care for farm animals with certain genetic traits that humans desire, it is called animal husbandry. Write about how animal husbandry affects society. Consider farmers, restaurants, grocery stores, consumers, and the use of land resources.

Literacy Connection

Cite Textual Evidence As you read about natural selection, underline sentences or parts of sentences that you can refer to later to help you support your explanations about this process.

Artificial Selection Darwin studied farm and pet animals produced by artificial selection. In artificial selection, humans have the capacity to influence certain characteristics of organisms by breeding them selectively. Organisms with a desired parental trait, such as color, are bred by humans who calculate the probability of offspring inheriting the trait. Darwin himself bred pigeons with large, fan-shaped tails (**Figure 2**). He repeatedly allowed only those pigeons with many tail feathers to mate. In this way, Darwin produced pigeons with two or three times the usual number of tail feathers. Darwin thought that a process similar to artificial selection might happen in nature. But he wondered what natural process resulted in the selection.

Natural Selection Darwin understood how evolution could work when he read an essay by Thomas Malthus. Malthus noted that both animals and humans can produce many offspring. If all the offspring survived, the world would quickly become overpopulated. There would not be enough food for everyone, and part of the population would starve. Darwin realized that some individuals have traits that help them to survive and reproduce. If these traits are hereditary, they can be passed on to the next generation. Gradually, over many generations, more and more individuals will have the helpful traits.

The Origin of Species Darwin waited a long time to publish his ideas. He thought they might be too revolutionary for the public to accept. Then, in 1858, Alfred Russel Wallace sent Darwin a letter. Wallace had also read Malthus' work and discovered the same mechanism for evolution! The next year, Darwin published his theory in *The Origin of Species*. In his book, Darwin proposed that evolution occurs by means of **natural selection**, a process by which individuals that are better adapted to their environment are more likely to survive and reproduce than other members of the same species.

How Natural Selection Works

Darwin identified three factors that affect the process of natural selection: overproduction, variation, and competition. First, there must be overproduction, shown in **Figure 3** below. Darwin knew that most species produce more offspring than can possibly survive. Secondly, there must be variation. Members of a population differ from one another in many of their traits. For example, sea turtles may differ in color, size, the ability to crawl quickly on sand, and shell hardness. Such variations are hereditary, passed from parents to offspring through genetic material. Finally, there must be **competition**—the struggle among living things to get the necessary amount of food, water, and shelter. In many species, so many offspring are produced that there are not enough resources—food, water, and living space—for all of them.

✔CHECK POINT **Summarize** What are the factors that affect the process of natural selection?

....

HANDS-ON LAB

Investigate Measure variation in plant and animal populations.

Overproduction

Figure 3 Brown rats can give birth up to 12 times each year with about 6 to 11 pups in each litter. The young rats are ready to breed when they are 12 weeks old.

1. SEP Analyze Data About how many pups can each female rat produce every year?

....

2. Draw Conclusions Why can't every rat survive and reproduce at its maximum rate?

....

....

....

....

....

....

....

....

Adaptations and Selection

Figure 4 Once sea turtles hatch from a nest, they must be fast and strong enough to reach the ocean before predators arrive.

Selection Darwin observed that some traits make individuals better adapted to their environment. Those individuals were more likely to survive and reproduce, and their offspring would inherit the helpful trait. The offspring, in turn, would be more likely to survive and reproduce and pass the trait to their offspring. After many generations, the proportion of this helpful trait increases in the population. This is called *predominance* of that trait. The proportion of less helpful traits tends to decrease, a process called *suppression*. **Figure 4** shows how conditions in the environment select sea turtles with helpful traits to become parents of the next generation. Darwin proposed that, over a long time, natural selection can lead to change.

☑ CHECK POINT **Cite Textual Evidence** How is Darwin's proposal that natural selection can lead to change in a species supported in nature?

....

....

....

Math Toolbox

Hatching for Success

Sea turtles play an important role in maintaining Florida's coastal ecosystem.

1. **Graph Proportional Relationships** ✎ Complete the graph to compare the total number of sea turtle nests at each beach to the number of nests that hatched sea turtles. Create a key next to the graph.

2. **SEP Construct an Explanation** On which beach(es) would you create a turtle refuge? Cite evidence to support your response.

....

....

....

Beach	Total Nests	Hatched Nests
Barefoot Beach	174	50
City of Naples	148	14
Delnor Wiggins	46	6
Marco Island	52	15
10,000 Islands	87	13

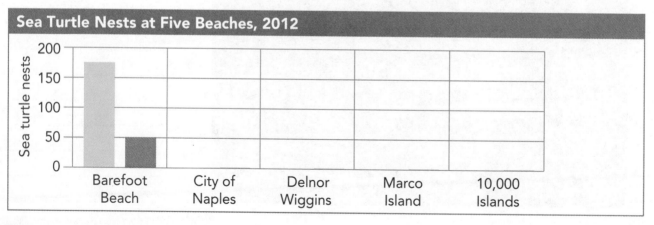

Sea Turtle Nests at Five Beaches, 2012

Environmental Change A change in the environment can affect an organism's ability to survive and may therefore lead to natural selection. For example, a storm can topple many trees in a forest. Trees that are better able to withstand strong winds have a survival advantage. In **Figure 5** you can see how natural selection might result in a shift in the population toward storm-resistant trees.

Natural Selection in Action
Figure 5 Natural events can lead to selection for favorable traits in a population. Read each image caption and use evidence to answer each question.

SEP Use Models List your observations related to the variation, competition, and over-production of this tree population.

....

....

....

Explain Phenomena What helpful trait did most of the surviving trees have?

....

....

....

2017: Another windstorm hits.

Make Observations How is the population different now compared to 1990?

....

....

Develop Models ✏ In the space provided, draw the effect of the storm on the forest.

SEP Construct Explanations How will natural selection have changed the forest from 1990 to 2030?

....

....

INTERACTIVITY

Analyze data on how a mouse population changes.

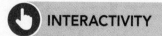

Genes and Natural Selection Darwin did a brilliant job of explaining natural selection, but he was never able to figure out where variations come from. He also did not understand how traits were passed from parents to offspring. Darwin hypothesized that tiny particles from around the parents' bodies passed into the developing offspring. Even at the time, Darwin realized that this explanation was flawed. Yet he did not have enough information to formulate a better explanation. Recall Gregor Mendel and his study of heredity and genetics. Mendel's experiments in plant breeding took place during Darwin's life. His work showed that parents pass genes to their offspring. Genes are units of genetic material that provide instructions for a specific protein or function. Inherited variations result from individuals having different combinations of genes, as shown in **Figure 6**. Your hair color, eye color—and dimples, if you have them—are all determined by the genes your parents passed to you. Only traits controlled by genes can be acted upon by natural selection. Genetic variations contribute to the diversity of organisms.

Inherited Traits

Figure 6 Variations in traits depend on the traits that parents pass on to their offspring.

1. Make Observations List several inherited variations you can observe in this group of students.

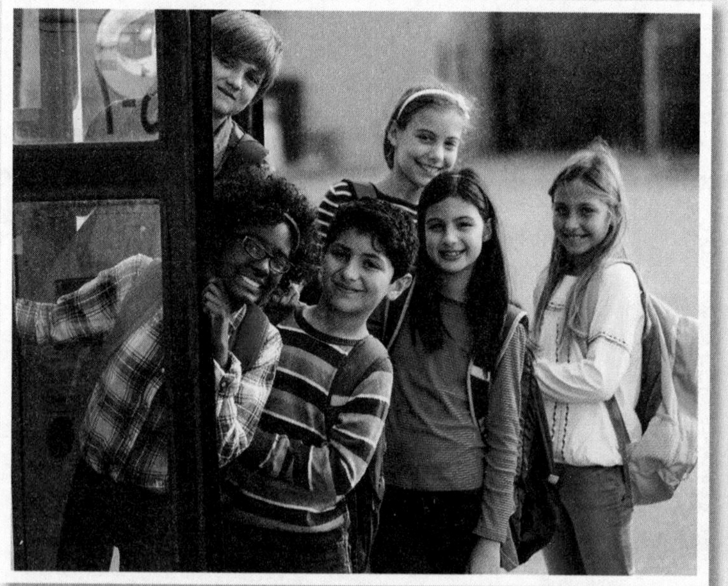

2. CCC Cause and Effect How did the students in **Figure 6** get such variations in traits?

Figure 7 A mutation caused the flower on the right to grow in an unusual way.

Explain Phenomena Describe how the mutation changed the flower.

....

....

....

....

Mutations Sexual reproduction causes existing gene variations to be recombined in each member of a population. To get a new variation, there must be a gene mutation. A mutation is any change to the genetic material. **Figure 7** shows a flower with an obvious mutation. Only mutations to sex chromosomes can be passed on to offspring. In humans, new genetic variations are introduced by mutations to egg or sperm cells. A mutation to a body cell, such as a heart or brain cell, only affects the individual and is not passed on to offspring. If offspring are born with a mutation, natural selection will determine whether that mutation gets passed on to the next generation.

INTERACTIVITY

Explore how a lack of genetic variations can impact crops.

Epigenetic Changes Epigenetics is the study of small changes to DNA that turn genes on or off but do not change the genetic code itself. All the cells in your body have identical DNA, but functions vary greatly. Gene **expression** determines how a cell acts—whether it will function as a bone cell or a skin cell. In your lifetime, there will be small chemical changes to your DNA affecting how genes get expressed. Your offspring can inherit these changes.

Inherited changes can affect multiple generations. For example, smoking makes small changes to DNA. Due to epigenetics, a grandmother who smokes is more likely to have a grandchild with asthma. The grandchild will inherit the same epigenetic changes that smoking caused in his or her grandmother. Epigenetics is challenging the idea that natural selection acts on genetic variation alone. Scientists are working to understand how a gene that gets turned on or off in a body cell could show up two generations later.

Academic Vocabulary

Your friends may be able to tell what you are thinking based on your expression. How is a facial expression similar to gene expression?

....

....

....

....

....

CHECK POINT **Distinguish Facts** A mutation can be inherited only if it occurs in which type of cell?

....

MS-LS4-4, MS-LS4-5, MS-LS4-6

1. Identify Darwin identified three factors affecting the process of natural selection. What are they?

2. Determine Differences The terms *mechanism* and *natural selection* both refer to natural processes. What makes them different?

3. Evaluate Claims A classmate claims that all mutations are harmful and can be passed on. Is this true? Explain.

4. Apply Scientific Reasoning How does natural selection help a species to evolve?

5. SEP Construct Explanations How does the genetic variation of traits within a population affect its probability for survival? Explain.

6. CCC Cause and Effect Sea turtles can lay 50 to 200 eggs in a nest. Some eggs get destroyed or eaten by other animals. The young turtles that hatch face many challenges as they head to the ocean. They may have to crawl over steep slopes, through seaweed, or around obstacles. Raccoons, foxes, crabs, birds, fish, and sharks may eat them. Given the challenges and the data in the Math Toolbox, write an expression and use it to calculate the percent hatched. Use the percent to roughly estimate the number of sea turtles from a nest of 100 in Naples that reach the ocean safely. Express your answer as a percentage.

7. SEP Develop Models ✏ Draw a young turtle and the variations you think could make it more successful. Label the variations and explain how they would benefit the turtle.

MS-LS4-4, MS-LS4-5, MS-LS4-6

Fossils from Bedrock

▶ **VIDEO**

Explore the techniques and technologies that scientists use to extract fossils.

Do you know how to get a fossil out of a rock? You engineer it! Scientists use several methods to extract these remains of the past.

The Challenge: To remove fossils from bedrock without damaging them or the surrounding area.

Phenomenon Fossils stay trapped under layers of rock for millions of years. When the geology of an area changes, these layers are sometimes exposed. This offers a great opportunity to search for evidence of how adaptation by natural selection contributes to the evolution of a species.

Removing a fragile fossil from rock takes skill, time, and special tools. Sometimes fossil collectors have to dig out the larger section of rock holding a fossil. Until recently, extracting a fossil meant slowly and carefully chipping away at the rock with a small chisel and hammer, then sweeping away rock dust with a small brush. The latest technology is the pneumatic drill pen. Vibrating at 30,000 times each minute, the drill pen carves out a fossil more quickly and with greater control. Another method is the acid wash. While it takes much longer than the mechanical methods, and can only be used on fossils found in limestone and chalk, an acid wash is the safest way to remove a fossil.

Scientists carefully brush away dirt and debris from bones discovered in dig sites to gather fossil evidence of how organisms have changed over time.

DESIGN CHALLENGE

How would you modify the process for removing fossils from bedrock? Go to the Engineering Design Notebook to find out!

3 The Process of Evolution

Guiding Questions

- How do natural selection and inherited variations influence a population?
- How does sexual selection influence a population's genetic variation?
- How is species interaction a factor in evolution?

Connection

Literacy Determine Conclusions

MS-LS3-1 Develop and use a model to describe why structural changes to genes (mutations) located on chromosomes may affect proteins and may result in harmful, beneficial, or neutral effects to the structure and function of the organism.

MS-LS4-4 Construct an explanation based on evidence that describes how genetic variations of traits in a population increase some individuals' probability of surviving and reproducing in a specific environment.

MS-LS4-6 Use mathematical representations to support explanations of how natural selection may lead to increases and decreases of specific traits in populations over time.

HANDS-ON LAB

иInvestigate Explore how different birds' feet help them survive in their environments.

Vocabulary

fitness
sexual selection
coevolution

Academic Vocabulary

randomly
interactions

Connect It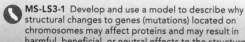

✏️ **Label each duck as either male or female.**

SEP Construct Explanations Do you think that both ducks' appearance could be a result of natural selection? Explain your reasoning.

....

....

....

Processes of Evolution

Charles Darwin's theory of natural selection is straightforward. Any population of living things has inherited variations. In addition, the population produces more young than can survive. According to natural selection, only the individuals that are well-adapted to their environments will survive and reproduce. An organism's **fitness** describes how well it can survive and reproduce in its environment. According to Darwin's theory, the fittest individuals survive to reproduce and pass their traits to the next generation. Organisms with low fitness are not as well-adapted to their environment and may die without reproducing or may not have as many offspring. Over time, as individual organisms successfully respond to changing conditions in the environment, the population evolves and its fitness increases.

Beyond Natural Selection Observe the male and female mandarin ducks in **Figure 1**. Both ducks have many adaptations that help them survive and reproduce in their watery habitat. Oily feathers keep the ducks dry. Webbed feet propel the ducks quickly through the water. Nesting in trees keeps ducklings safe from predators. Dull colors help the female duck blend in with her background. Now, look at the male duck. He seems to be calling for attention! His brightly colored face and the bold black and white stripes on his sides surely attract predators. How could natural selection result in traits that hurt the male duck's chance of survival? Answer: There is more to evolution than "survival of the fittest."

HANDS-ON LAB

☑**Investigate** Explore how different birds' feet help them survive in their environments.

Opposites Attract
Figure 1 Believe it or not, these ducks are both from the same species. Male and female mandarin ducks have evolved to look very different!

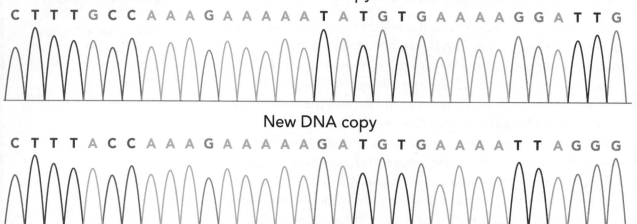

Old DNA copy

C T T T G C C A A A G A A A A A T A T G T G A A A A G G A T T G

New DNA copy

C T T T A C C A A A G A A A A A G A T G T G A A A A T T A G G G

Spellcheck, Please!

Figure 2 ✎ A mutation is like a spelling error in a gene's DNA sequence of nucleotides—A, C, G, and T. Any change in the sequence results in a mutation. Here, each nucleotide has its own color. Observe how the sequence of nucleotides changes. Compare the sequences of the two DNA copies. Circle any differences you observe in the new DNA copy.

Explain Phenomena What do you think may have caused the differences between the two DNA copies?

....

....

Literacy Connection

Determine Conclusions
Why is it that mutations to body cells do not affect offspring?

....

....

....

....

....

....

INTERACTIVITY

Analyze mutations and how they can impact evolution.

Mutations One reason for Darwin's oversimplification of evolution was that he did not yet know about mutations. You've already learned that a mutation is any change to an organism's genetic material. Mutations can create multiple alleles, or forms of a gene. Different alleles cause variations in traits such as eye color, ear shape, and blood type.

How Mutations Happen Mutations are created in two ways. First, a dividing cell can make an error while copying its DNA (**Figure 2**). There are approximately six billion units in one copy of human DNA. Imagine copying by hand a book that had six billion letters. Think how easy it would be to make a mistake! Researchers estimate that each human child inherits an average of 60 new mutations from his or her parents. That sounds like a lot, doesn't it? But it means that the body makes only one mistake out of every 100 million units of DNA copied. Secondly, mutations also occur when an organism is exposed to environmental factors such as radiation or certain chemicals that damage the cell's DNA. While the cell has mechanisms to repair damaged DNA, that repair is not always perfect. Any mistake while fixing the DNA results in a mutation.

Effects of Mutations Most mutations are neutral—they have no effect on the individual's function. The mutation may be in a part of the DNA that is inactive. Out of the mutations that do affect function, most are harmful to the individual. **Randomly** changing a process in the body typically results in decreased function. Only mutations on sex chromosomes can get passed on and affect the fitness of offspring. A beneficial mutation that increases fitness tends to grow more common in a population. A mutation that decreases fitness tends to disappear because the individuals with that mutation die or reproduce less successfully.

Need for Mutations People often think of mutations as harmful. It's true that mutations can lead to cancer and genetic defects. At the same time, however, mutations are necessary for evolution to occur. Mutations create all the variations among members of a species and account for the diversity of organisms on Earth. **Figure 3** shows how mutations can change plant leaf shapes. Imagine if the first single-celled organisms had never experienced mutation! That first species would have been the only life that ever existed on the planet.

✓ CHECK POINT **Summarize Text** How are mutations both harmful and beneficial?

....

....

Academic Vocabulary

List where you may have heard the word *random* used before. What does *randomly* mean as it's used here?

....

....

....

....

....

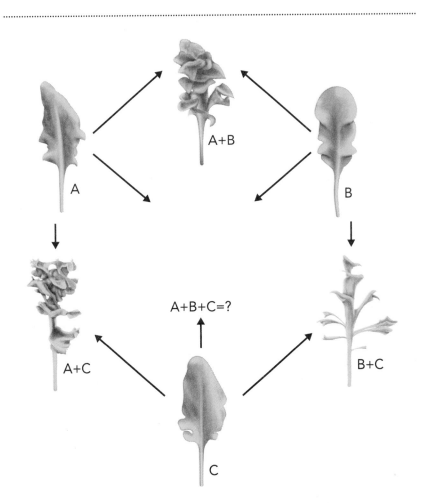

Variations from Mutations

Figure 3 Scientists studied how three mutations in mustard plant DNA (labeled A, B, and C in the image) affect leaf shape.

SEP Use a Model to Predict 🖊 Examine the effects of the mutations on leaf shape. In the center of the image, draw what you think the leaves would look like if a plant had all three mutations.

Gene Flow

Mutations are not the only source of new alleles in a population. Alleles also enter a population through gene flow. As you know, a gene is a unit of genetic material that acts as instructions for a specific protein or function. Gene flow occurs when individuals with new alleles physically move from one population to another. Gene flow can increase the genetic variation of a population.

How do individuals move between populations? Sometimes birds and insects are blown to a new continent by a storm. Plant seeds and pollen can stick to animal fur and travel long distances, too. Humans are often accidentally responsible for gene flow. Animals, seeds, and microorganisms can hitch a ride on trucks or in the water in the bottom of ships.

Genetic Drift

The last mechanism of evolution is a random, directionless process. Just by chance, some alleles may be lost to a population. Think of a small population of birds living on an island. The only bird that carries an allele for light-colored feathers could be hit by lightning and die. It will pass no genes on to the next generation. Through random chance, the genetic variation of the population shrinks over time. This process is called genetic drift. **Figure 4** shows how gene flow and genetic drift affect the level of variation in a population of snakes.

✓CHECK POINT **Determine Central Ideas** How do gene flow and genetic drift play a role in evolution?

....

....

....

Gene Flow and Genetic Drift

Figure 4 ✐ Examine how snakes enter or leave the snake population in each of the images and label the process taking place as either *genetic drift* or *gene flow*.

Original Snake Population

Process: ....

Process: ....

1. Identify 🖊 Circle the feature of the beetles that has grown due to male competition.

2. CCC Structure and Function Do you think that female stag beetles also have the same large feature?

....
....
....
....
....
....

Sexual Selection

The measure of an individual's fitness is its ability to survive and reproduce. An organism that reproduces asexually can reproduce all on its own. An organism that reproduces sexually, however, must blend its genes with those of a mate. **Sexual selection** is natural selection that acts on an organism's ability to get the best possible mate. The fitness of the offspring depends on the fitness of both the parents. Therefore, sexually-reproducing organisms try to choose mates with specific traits that have higher fitness.

Female Choice In some species, females choose which males will father their offspring. Natural selection favors traits that help females choose mates with high fitness. Consider the ducks in **Figure 1**. Suppose that male ducks with bright feathers have better fitness. Females may evolve a trait that causes them to choose males with bright feathers. Over time, male ducks will grow brighter and fancier feathers. Even after the bright colors start to hurt the males' survival, the females may continue to select males with ever-brighter feathers.

Male Competition In other species, males compete to control a territory with access to females. Any trait that gives males an advantage in the competition will be favored by natural selection. Male competition can lead to exaggerated horns, pincers, or body size, as shown in **Figure 5**. The need to reproduce can cause males to evolve characteristics that make them less likely to survive!

✅ CHECK POINT **Determine Conclusions** Why do you think bright feathers make a male duck a desirable mate?

....
....
....

📓 **Reflect** What is a difference that you have observed between male and female members of the same species in a zoo, aquarium, or in your local community? Record your observations in your science notebook.

465

Coevolution and Cooperation

Figure 6 The acacia tree and ants both evolved features that help them work together.

Infer What features do you think the acacia tree and the ants might have that would help one another?

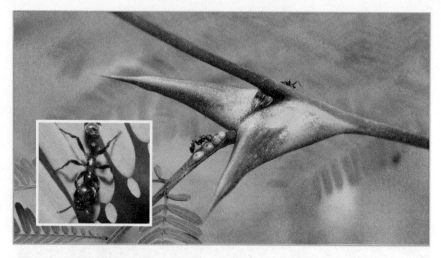

Coevolution

Two or more species with close **interactions** can affect each other's evolution. **Coevolution** is the process by which two species evolve in response to changes in each other over time. Coevolution can happen when species cooperate with each other, as shown in **Figure 6**. Several acacia trees in Central America have coevolved with select species of ants. The acacias trees evolved hollow thorns and nectar pores because of their close interactions with the ants. Likewise, the ants evolved defense behaviors to protect "their" trees. A queen ant lays her eggs in the hollow thorns of an acacia tree. In return for the shelter and food from the tree, the ants protect the tree. They attack when other insects or animals try to devour the acacia leaves. Other examples of interactions that can lead to coevolution include species that compete for resources and species that may be prey to a predator.

Academic Vocabulary

If you break down the word *interactions*, it means "the actions between." How would you define interactions between two species?

Model It!

Mimicry in Coevolution

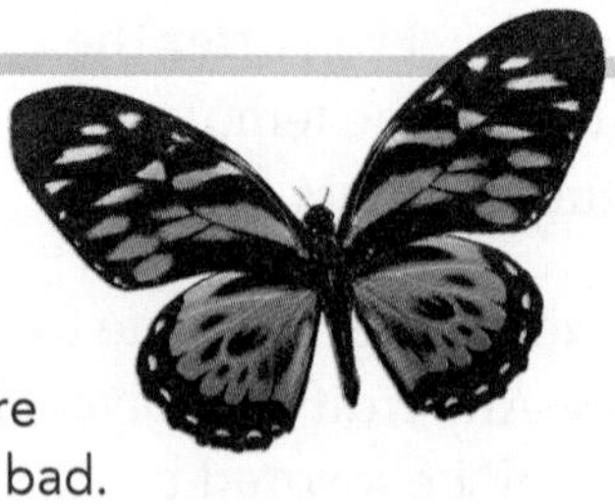

Figure 7 Tiger-wing butterflies evolved to absorb and store toxins from plants they ate when they were caterpillars. This makes them taste bad. Birds avoid eating tiger-wing butterflies and other butterflies that mimic, or closely resemble, them.

SEP Develop Models Sketch the progression of how a butterfly's wing patterns may have changed over time to mimic that of the tiger-wing butterfly.

1. SEP Communicate Information What does fitness mean in terms of evolution?

....

....

2. SEP Cite Evidence How does gene flow affect a population's genetic variation?

....

....

3. Apply Concepts Is sexual selection a form of natural selection? Explain.

....

....

....

....

4. Apply Scientific Reasoning What are the two ways in which mutations are created? Give at least one example of an environmental factor.

....

....

....

....

5. SEP Construct Explanations Explain the role of mutations in genetic variation and in the diversity of living things. Support your explanation with evidence.

....

....

....

....

....

....

....

....

....

6. Explain Phenomena How is species interaction a factor in evolution? Use the ant and the acacia tree as an example.

....

....

....

....

....

Quest CHECK-IN

In this lesson, you learned how a population can be influenced by natural selection, species interactions, and genetic variations due to mutations, gene flow, genetic drift, and sexual selection.

CCC Cause and Effect Why is it important to consider the role of genetic variations when trying to determine what caused the changes to the European blackcaps?

....

....

....

....

....

☝ INTERACTIVITY

Evolution of the Blackcaps

Go online to investigate factors that may have caused the variations in the European blackcaps.

Evidence in the Fossil Record

Guiding Questions

- What supports evidence for the scientific theory of evolution?
- How do fossils show change over time?
- What does the early development of different organisms tell us about evolution?
- How does failure to adapt to a changing environment lead to a species' extinction?

Connections

Literacy Summarize Text

Math Analyze Proportional Relationships

MS-LS4-1 Analyze and interpret data for patterns in the fossil record that document the existence, diversity, extinction, and change of life forms throughout the history of life on Earth under the assumption that natural laws operate today as in the past.

MS-LS4-2 Apply scientific ideas to construct an explanation for the anatomical similarities and differences among modern organisms and between modern and fossil organisms to infer evolutionary relationships.

MS-LS4-3 Analyze displays of pictorial data to compare patterns of similarities in the embryological development across multiple species to identify relationships not evident in the fully formed anatomy.

MS-LS4-6 Use mathematical representations to support explanations of how natural selection may lead to increases and decreases of specific traits in populations over time. (Also **EP&CIIa and EP&CIIc**)

HANDS-ON LAB

⚗ **uInvestigate** Model how different fossils form.

Vocabulary

fossil record
embryo
homologous
    structures
extinct

Academic Vocabulary

evidence

Connect It!

✏ **Draw arrows to connect similar features between the fossil and the modern animal.**

Interpret Photos Which parts of the crinoid's tentacles are best preserved in the fossils? Which parts were not preserved?

....

....

....

The Fossil Record

Fossils are preserved remains or traces of living things. **Figure 1** shows fossils of crinoids, relatives of modern-day starfish. All the fossils that have been discovered and what we have learned from them make up the **fossil record**. It is called a record because the fossils form data patterns that scientists can understand through measurement and observation. The fossil record documents the diversity of the life forms, many now extinct, and shows how life forms existed and changed throughout Earth's history. The fossil record is a treasure trove of **evidence** about how organisms of the past evolved into the forms we see today.

Microevolution and Macroevolution

Scientists can observe evolution taking place within populations of organisms. Small, gradual changes in the color or size of a certain population is called microevolution. *Micro-* means very small, and *evolution* means change through time. One example of microevolution is the northern population of house sparrows. They adapted to a colder climate by growing larger bodies than the southern population. This small change took less than 100 years. Usually, for multicellular organisms, it takes years to thousands of years for a new species to develop. Scientists turn to the fossil record to learn about macroevolution, or major evolutionary change.

A Glimpse of the Past

Figure 1 Crinoids are relatives of starfish. We can learn a lot about the evolution of crinoids by looking at fossils of their extinct relatives. Some ancient crinoids grew more than 40 meters long!

469

A. **As rock erodes, the fossil is exposed on the surface.**

B. **An organism dies and sinks to the bottom of a lake.**

Forming a Fossil

Figure 2 A fossil may form when sediment quickly covers a dead organism.

Relate Text to Visuals
✎ Are the images matched with the correct captions? Or are there some mistakes? Match up each image with the right caption by writing the correct letters in the blank circles.

How Fossils Form

A fossil is the impression that an organism or part of an organism leaves in rock. That impression comes about in one of two ways. A mold creates a hollow area in the rock that is the shape of an organism or part of an organism. Or, a cast makes a solid copy of an organism's shape, sometimes containing some of the original organism.

Most fossils form when living things die and sediment buries them. Sediment is the small, solid pieces of material that come from rocks or the remains of organisms and settle to the bottom of a body of water. Over time, the sediment slowly hardens into rock and preserves the shapes of the organisms. Fossils can form from any kind of living thing, from bacteria to dinosaurs.

Many fossils come from organisms that once lived in or near still water. Swamps, lakes, and shallow seas build up sediment quickly and bury remains of living things. In **Figure 2**, you can see how a fossil might form. When an organism dies, its soft parts usually decay quickly or are eaten by other organisms. Only hard parts of an organism typically leave fossils. These hard parts include bones, shells, teeth, seeds, and woody stems. It is rare for the soft parts of an organism to become a fossil. People often see fossils after erosion exposes them. Erosion is the wearing away of Earth's surface by natural processes such as water and wind.

Many Kinds of Fossils

Figure 3 A fossil may be the preserved remains of an organism's body, or the trace of an organism—something it leaves behind.

1. **Classify** ✎ Label each image as either a body fossil or a trace fossil.

2. **SEP Evaluate Evidence** Why did you classify them that way?

....

....

....

....

....

....

Snail shells

Turtle dropping

C. Over millions of years, the sediment hardens into rock, preserving the remains.

D. Over time, sediment covers the organism.

Kinds of Fossils There are two types of fossils: body fossils and trace fossils. Each one gives us different information about the ancient organism it represents.

Body Fossils Body fossils preserve the shape and structure of an organism. We can learn about what a plant or animal looked like from a body fossil. Body fossils of trees are called petrified wood. The term *petrified* means "turned into stone." Petrified fossils are fossils in which minerals replace all or part of an organism. In petrified wood, the remains are so well preserved that scientists can often count the rings to tell how old a tree was when it died millions of years ago. Ancient mammoths frozen into ice, petrified dinosaur bones, and insects trapped in amber are other examples of body fossils.

Trace Fossils We can learn what an animal did from trace fossils. Footprints, nests, and animal droppings preserved in stone are all trace fossils, as shown in **Figure 3**.

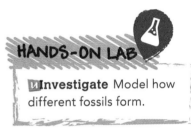

HANDS-ON LAB

◻️**Investigate** Model how different fossils form.

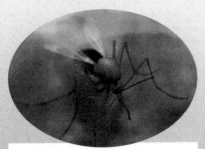

Mosquito in amber

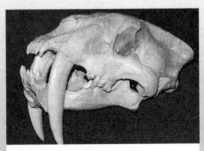

Smilodon, cat skull

Dinosaur tracks

471

Literacy Connection

Summarize Text At the end of each two-page spread, stop and summarize what you just read to a classmate.

Fossil Evidence of Evolution

Most of what we know about ancient organisms comes from the fossil record. The fossil record provides evidence about the history of life and past environments on Earth. The fossil record also shows how different groups of organisms have changed over time. Each new discovery helps to fill holes in our understanding of evolution.

Early Earth When Earth first formed, more than 4.5 billion years ago, it was extremely hot. Earth was likely mostly melted. As Earth cooled, solid rocks became stable at Earth's surface. The oldest known fossils are from rocks that formed about a billion years after Earth formed. **Figure 4** shows a rock made of these fossils. Scientists think that all other forms of life on Earth arose from these simple organisms.

Scientists cannot yet pinpoint when or where life first evolved. Scientists hypothesize that life first evolved in Earth's ocean. The early ocean contained reactive chemicals. Under the right conditions, sunlight and lightning can change those chemicals into molecules similar to those found in living cells. More research will help scientists to settle the question of the origin of life on Earth.

Fossils Reveal Early Life

Figure 4 Stromatolites are rock-like structures formed by layers of fossilized bacteria. Dating as far back as 3.4 billion years ago, they are the oldest evidence of life forms on Earth. Ancient bacteria in water produced thin sheets of film that trapped mud. Over time, these thin sheets formed microfossils—fossils too small to see without a microscope. Eventually, the sheets built up into the layers you see here.

Interpret Photos Using evidence in the picture, determine the oldest and youngest layers. Then, draw a scale next to the stromatolite to show which are the oldest layers and which are the youngest.

Gomphotherium
24–5 mya

Moeritherium
36 mya

Platybelodon
23–5.3 mya

Mammut americanum
(American mastodon)
4 mya–11,500 ya

Mammuthus
(Woolly Mammoth)
Pliocene, from
750,000–11,500 ya

Loxodonta
(African elephant)
1.8 mya–present

ya = years ago; mya = millions of years ago

Fossils and Evolution Through Time The fossil record shows that life on Earth has evolved. Rock forms in layers, with newer layers on top of older layers. When we dig deeper, we see older rocks with fossils from earlier time periods. The oldest rocks contain fossils of only very simple organisms. Younger rocks include fossils of both simple organisms and also more complex organisms. Scientists also place fossils in chronological order using radioactive dating, which uses radioactive isotopes of elements to assign an age range to a fossil. Looking at fossils in rocks from different time periods, scientists can reconstruct the history of evolution. **Figure 5** shows the evolution of the elephant, reconstructed from the fossil record.

The fossil record also shows how Earth's climate has changed. Some plant fossils reveal surprises, such as palm trees in Wyoming and giant tropical ferns in Antarctica. Fossils and preserved remains are also evidence of how climate change influences evolution.

Evolution of the Modern Elephant
Figure 5 Scientists have reconstructed the evolutionary history of the elephant with evidence from the fossil record.

☑ CHECK POINT **Cite Textual Evidence** Would you expect to find fossils related to the evolution of the elephant in the oldest rocks in the fossil record? Explain.

....
....
....
....

Question It !

Kyle has very limited vision and needs someone to explain the evolution of elephants to him. Suppose you are going to work with Kyle to help him understand the changes elephants have undergone.

Interpret Diagrams Using **Figure 5**, what features of the animals have stayed the same? What features have changed?

....
....
....
....
....

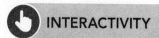

Comparisons of Anatomy

The structure of an organism's body is called its anatomy. Similarities in anatomy between organisms from the fossil record and organisms living today are clues they evolved from a common ancestor. They help us to reconstruct evolutionary history.

Embryological Development An **embryo** is a young organism that develops from a fertilized egg (called a zygote). The growing embryo may develop inside or outside the parent's body. The early development of different organisms in an embryo shows some striking similarities. For example, chickens, fish, turtles, and pigs all resemble each other during the early stages of development. Anatomical similarities in early development suggest that organisms are related and share a common ancestor.

Scientists can also analyze fossilized eggs to infer lines of descent. **Figure 6** shows the model of a duck-billed dinosaur embryo, known as a Hadrosaur, compared to an x-ray of a chicken embryo. You can see many anatomical similarities in their early development.

Homologous Structures Similar structures that related species have inherited from a common ancestor are known as **homologous structures** (hoh MAHL uh gus). Bats, dogs, dolphins, and even flying reptiles have homologous structures in their limbs. Although the structures look very different now, the Math Toolbox shows you the bones that these animals all have in common.

☑ CHECK POINT **Determine Conclusions** If two organisms have homologous structures and similar early development, what can you infer about them?

....

....

Birds and Dinosaurs

Figure 6 ✏ Draw lines and label the features that look similar in both the Hadrosaur and chicken embryos.

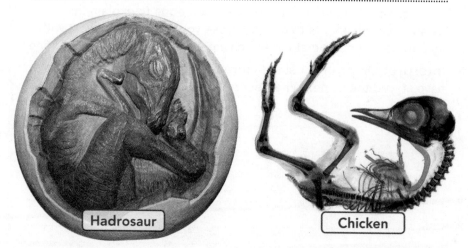

Hadrosaur

Chicken

Homologous Anatomical Structures

The wings, flipper, and leg of these organisms all have similar anatomical (body) structures. Note that the structures are not drawn to scale.

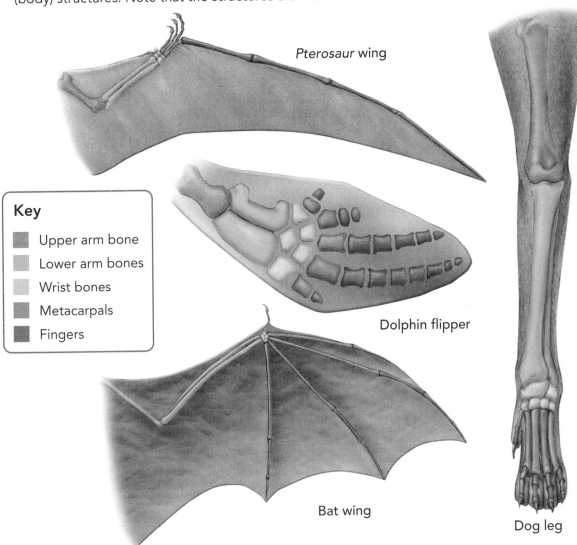

Pterosaur wing

Dolphin flipper

Key
- Upper arm bone
- Lower arm bones
- Wrist bones
- Metacarpals
- Fingers

Bat wing

Dog leg

1. **Construct Tables** 🖊 Choose two of the animals shown above to examine closely. Using a metric ruler, measure the upper arm bone, the lower arm bone, and the fingers. Create a data table to the right and record the measurements in millimeters.

2. **CCC Analyze Proportional Relationships** In each species, compare the upper arm to lower arm, or compare fingers to metacarpals. Can you find any equivalent ratios?

....

....

....

....

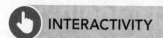

INTERACTIVITY

Interpret data from the fossil record that supports species extinction.

Beginning and End of a Species

Natural selection explains how variations can lead to changes in a species. A new species forms when one population remains isolated from the rest of its species long enough to evolve such different traits that members of the two populations can no longer mate and produce offspring capable of reproduction. **Figure 7** shows an example of a turtle species that has evolved seven different subspecies. Over time, the subspecies could form separate species.

Gradual Change Some species in the fossil record seem to change gradually over time, such as the elephants in **Figure 5**. The time scale of the fossil record involves thousands or millions of years. There is plenty of time for gradual changes to produce new species. The fossil record contains many examples of species that are halfway between two others.

Rapid Change At times, new, related species suddenly appear in the fossil record. Rapid evolution can follow a major change in environmental conditions. A cooling climate, for example, can put a lot of stress on a population. Only the individuals adapted to cooler conditions will survive. Through natural selection, the population may rapidly evolve to a new species.

Extinction A species is **extinct** if it no longer exists and will never again live on Earth. A rapid environmental change is more likely to cause a species to become extinct than to bring about a new species. The fossil record shows that most of the species that ever lived on Earth are now extinct.

New predators, climate change, disease, and competition with other species are a few factors that can lead to extinction. According to natural selection, if a species fails to develop the adaptations necessary to survive the changing conditions in an environment, that species will not survive and reproduce. Small populations that breed slowly and cannot relocate are more likely to become extinct. The fossil record shows that volcanic eruptions, asteroids striking Earth, and sudden climate change can kill off many species in a short time.

☑ CHECK POINT **Translate Information** How do you know that the animals whose limbs are depicted in the Math Toolbox had a common ancestor at one point? What question could you ask to find out more and why would you ask it?

....

....

....

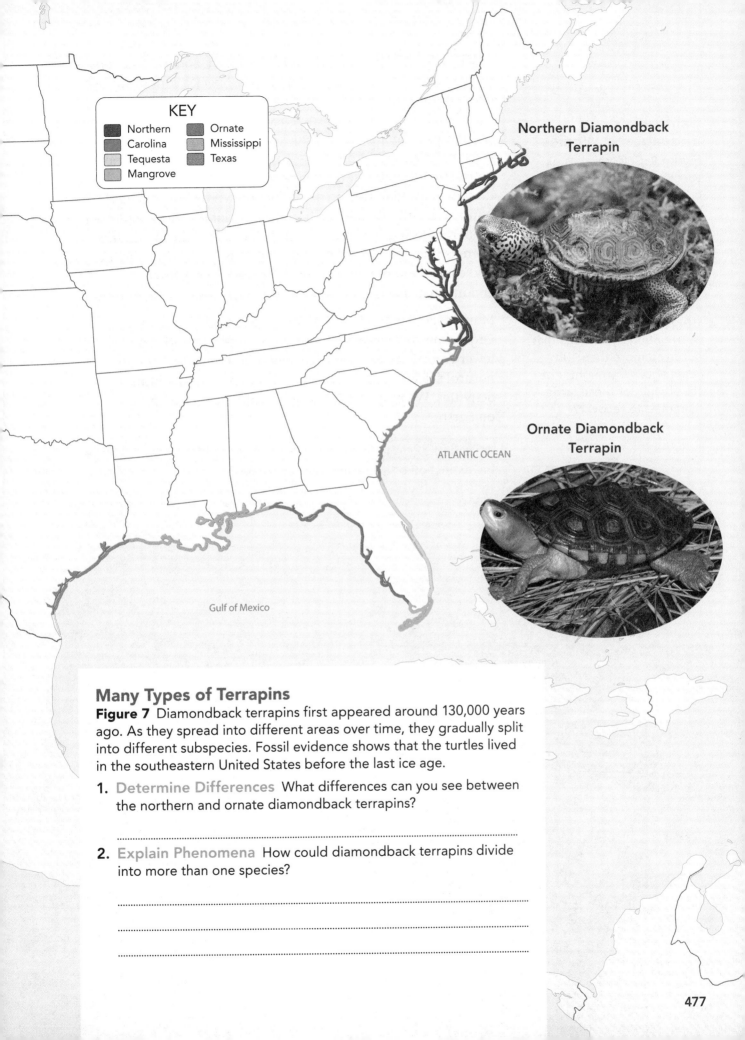

KEY
- Northern
- Carolina
- Tequesta
- Mangrove
- Ornate
- Mississippi
- Texas

Northern Diamondback Terrapin

Ornate Diamondback Terrapin

ATLANTIC OCEAN

Gulf of Mexico

Many Types of Terrapins

Figure 7 Diamondback terrapins first appeared around 130,000 years ago. As they spread into different areas over time, they gradually split into different subspecies. Fossil evidence shows that the turtles lived in the southeastern United States before the last ice age.

1. **Determine Differences** What differences can you see between the northern and ornate diamondback terrapins?

....

2. **Explain Phenomena** How could diamondback terrapins divide into more than one species?

....

....

....

California's Endangered Whales

Figure 8 California has six species of whales on the endangered species list: the north Pacific right, blue, sei, fin, humpback, and the sperm whale.

SEP Cite Textual Evidence

Some species of whale have struggled to overcome overhunting by humans that occurred more than 100 years ago. Why might it be so difficult for these large mammals to recover?

....

....

....

....

Human Influence on Extinction Some extinctions are the direct result of human activities. Species cannot survive over hunting, sudden climate change, and indirect changes to their habitat caused by the actions of human communities. The six species of endangered whales on North America's Pacific coast have suffered from these kinds of changes. As they move within their habitat, some whales are hunted, injured by ships, and are injured in fishing gear. Though whale hunting has been banned since 1949, the northern Pacific right whale population is not recovering. The recovery plan includes reducing injuries from fishing gear, reducing ship collisions, protecting habitats, and continuing the hunting ban. **Figure 8** shows three endangered species of whales living in the waters off California.

Many scientists think extinctions are rapidly increasing. Organisms like whales, who reproduce slowly and produce fewer variations over time, cannot adapt quickly through natural selection to recover from sudden, extreme human activities. We may lose the largest animals ever to live on Earth.

☑ **CHECK POINT** **Summarize Text** How might humans influence the extinction of a species, such as whales?

....

....

humpback whale

sperm whale

blue whale

☑ LESSON 4 Check

🕐 MS-LS4-1, MS-LS4-2, MS-LS4-6, EP&CIIa

1. Determine Differences What sort of information can you get from a body fossil that you can't get from a trace fossil?

....

....

2. SEP Analyze Data According to the fossil record, which level in the rock layers shown in the diagram will have the oldest organisms? Explain.

....

....

....

....

....

....

....

3. SEP Construct Explanations How do you account for differences between the bat's wing and the dolphin's flipper?

....

....

....

....

Dolphin flipper

Bat wing

4. SEP Engage in Argument What can you say to back the claim that the fossil record supports the theory of evolution?

....

....

....

....

5. CCC Describe Patterns If you were a scientist trying to determine if an organism evolved gradually or rapidly, how would patterns in the fossil record help you? Explain how the pattern would provide evidence to support the rate of evolution for that organism.

....

....

....

....

....

....

....

....

....

6. Apply Scientific Reasoning Why is a sudden change in the environment more likely to cause a species to go extinct rather than to cause a new species to develop?

....

....

....

....

....

....

Other Evidence of Evolution

Guiding Questions

- How does modern technology provide evidence that all organisms have a common ancestor?
- What new discoveries about evolution has modern technology made possible?

Connections

Literacy Read and Comprehend

Math Use Algebraic Expressions

 MS-LS4-2 Apply scientific ideas to construct an explanation for the anatomical similarities and differences among modern organisms and between modern and fossil organisms to infer evolutionary relationships.

MS-LS4-6 Use mathematical representations to support explanations of how natural selection may lead to increases and decreases of specific traits in populations over time.

HANDS-ON LAB

иInvestigate Explore how DNA provides evidence for evolution.

Vocabulary

protein
endosymbiosis

Academic Vocabulary

transfer

Connect It!

✏️ **Count the number of different kinds of organisms you see and write your number in the white circle on the photograph.**

SEP Evaluate Evidence What do all the organisms in the photo have in common?

....

....

....

Using Technology to Study Evolution

Advances in technology have led to new knowledge about evolution. Darwin and scientists of his time used their eyes, hand tools, and simple microscopes to study evolution. Darwin's microscope had less than 200x magnification. Modern scientists have much better tools. We now have such powerful microscopes and imaging devices that computers can show us the shapes of individual molecules. Future advances may further our understanding of evolution.

Genetic Material and Evolution The coral reef in **Figure 1** contains an amazing variety of living things. The diverse shapes, body structures, and lifestyles are all due to differences in genetic material, the set of chemical instructions that guide the function and growth of an organism. Evolution results from changes in genetic material. Small changes in genetic material lead to microevolution within species. An accumulation of small changes causes macroevolution, or the creation of new species.

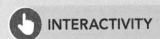

INTERACTIVITY

Discuss how a device or object you use every day has changed over time.

Literacy Connection

Read and Comprehend
As you work your way through this lesson, stop frequently to see if you understand what you just read. Each paragraph has key information. Try to restate it in your own words.

Rainbow of Life on a Reef
Figure 1 All of the differences among the organisms in this coral reef at Anacapa Island, California result from evolutionary changes in genetic material.

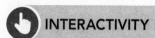

INTERACTIVITY

Explore how technological advances have helped to determine ancestral relationships.

Genetic Evidence for a Common Ancestor

Every living thing uses DNA for genetic material. Mosquitoes, humans, plants, and bacteria all have cells with the same system of genetic material. The shared use of DNA is one piece of evidence that every organism on Earth has a common ancestor. This common ancestor, called LUCA for Last Universal Common Ancestor, was most likely a single-celled organism similar to modern bacteria or archaea.

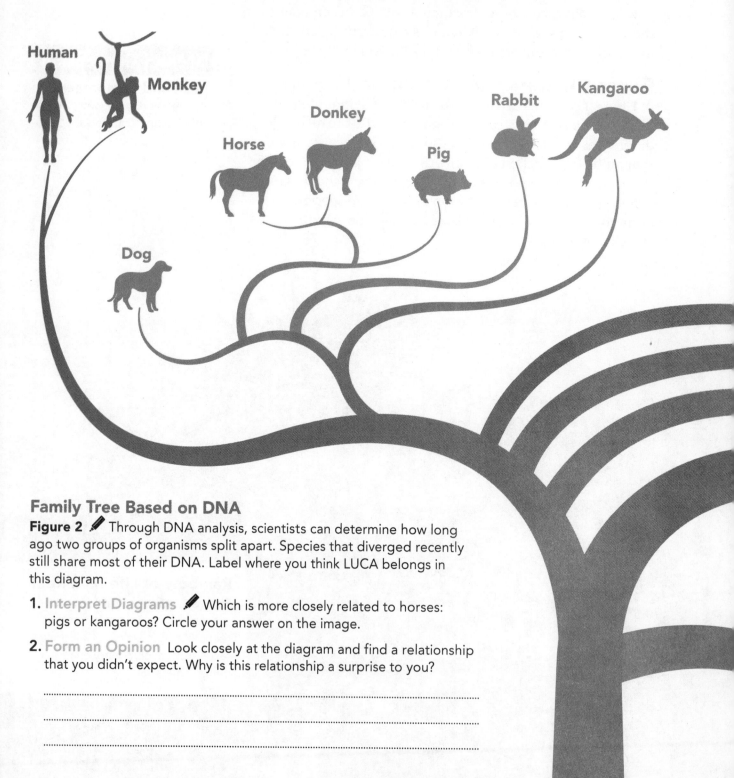

Family Tree Based on DNA

Figure 2 Through DNA analysis, scientists can determine how long ago two groups of organisms split apart. Species that diverged recently still share most of their DNA. Label where you think LUCA belongs in this diagram.

1. Interpret Diagrams Which is more closely related to horses: pigs or kangaroos? Circle your answer on the image.

2. Form an Opinion Look closely at the diagram and find a relationship that you didn't expect. Why is this relationship a surprise to you?

....

....

....

Dawn of Evolution DNA is a complex molecule, difficult to copy without making any mistakes. LUCA started to change as it accumulated mutations, or changes to its DNA. Natural selection and other processes shaped LUCA's evolution. The original population of LUCA split and diverged, evolving into all the species that live or have ever lived on Earth. The traces of this evolution are recorded in the DNA of every organism. Shared DNA between species provides evidence of the evolutionary past. The more similar the DNA between two species, the more closely related they are. **Figure 2** shows a family tree based on differences in one stretch of DNA.

HANDS-ON LAB

Investigate Explore how DNA provides evidence for evolution.

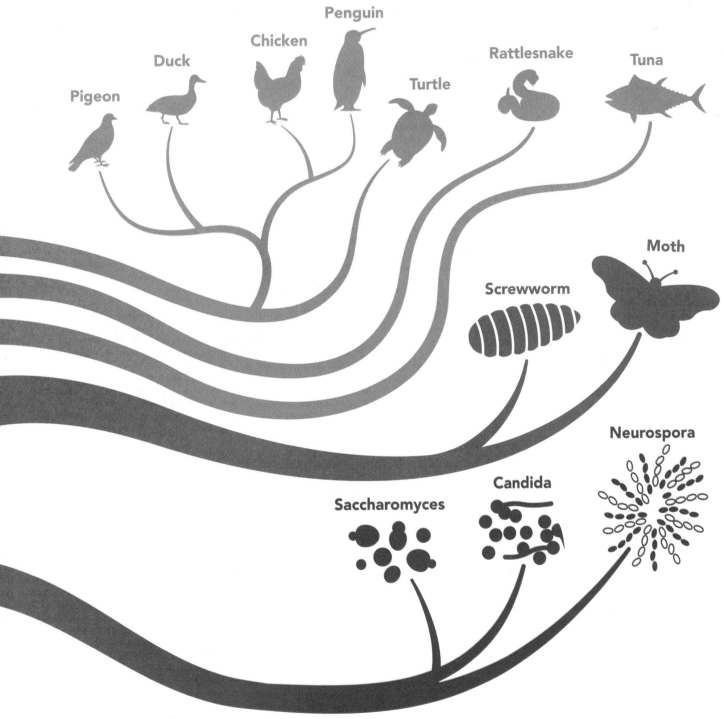

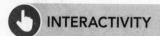

INTERACTIVITY

Explore how different types of evidence help to establish evolutionary relationships.

Proteins Recall that genes code for different **proteins**, which are complicated molecules that carry out important cellular functions. Proteins can act as the building blocks for cell materials and carry out important cellular functions. For example, some muscle fibers are made of chains of the protein actin. Other proteins act as messengers, fight diseases, carry out chemical reactions, or carry materials around the body.

Proteins and Evolution Consider what could happen to the function of a protein if the gene for it contains a mutation. The mutant genetic material may code for a different form of the protein, as shown in **Figure 3**. The new version of the protein may increase the individual's fitness. More likely, the mutation will lower the individual's fitness or leave it unchanged. Changes in proteins lead to variations within a population. Natural selection acts on those variations, causing evolution.

✓CHECK POINT **Determine Central Ideas** What are the possible effects of a mutation on the function of a protein?

....

....

Mutations and Proteins

Figure 3 The Mre11-Rad50 protein group helps cells to repair breaks in DNA molecules. There is only a small mutation in the genetic code for the bottom form.

Determine Differences How are the two forms of the protein group different?

....

....

....

....

....

....

....

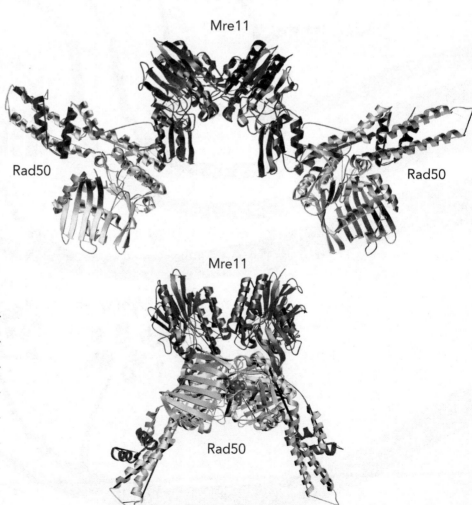

Mre11

Rad50

Rad50

Mre11

Rad50

Protein Analysis and Evolution Scientists compare proteins to see how closely two species are related. In most cases, evidence from DNA and protein structure confirms conclusions based on fossils, embryos, and body structure. For example, DNA comparisons show that dogs are more similar to wolves than to coyotes. This confirms an earlier conclusion based on similarities in the structure and development of the three species.

Student Discourse On your own, consider the data in the Math Toolbox table. Then use mathematical expressions to decide which two primate groups likely have the least traits in common with each other. Then in a small group, compare and discuss your answers and the supporting math.

Math Toolbox

All in the Family

Humans, apes, and monkeys are all members of the order Primates. Bonobos, chimpanzees, gorillas, and orangutans are all considered apes, but monkeys are not. Humans and monkeys share about 93 percent of their DNA.

Primate	Genetic Difference with Humans
Bonobo	1.2%
Chimpanzee	1.3%
Gorilla	1.6%
Orangutan	3.1%
Monkey	7.0%

1. **SEP Use Algebraic Expressions** Write an expression representing the percentage of DNA that gorillas share with humans. Let g = gorilla.

....

....

2. **Draw Comparative Inferences** What can you say about the evolutionary relationship between the apes and monkeys compared to humans?

....

....

An Evolutionary Leap

Figure 4 Normally, a new trait evolves over thousands of generations. In this case, bacteria species 2 gets a fully formed gene from a different species.

1. **Identify** Label the transferred gene in Species 2.

2. **Predict** Will the transferred gene be passed on to the next generation? Explain.

....

....

....

....

Academic Vocabulary

How does the everyday meaning of *transfer* help you understand what gene transfer is?

....

....

....

....

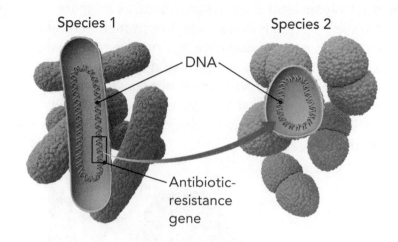

Species 1   Species 2

DNA

Antibiotic-resistance gene

Gene Transfer Between Species

Individuals usually inherit DNA from their parent or parents. Surprisingly, scientists have discovered that genes can also pass between individuals from different species! The **transfer** of genes can happen when one cell engulfs another or when bacteria share their DNA with other cells. The transferred DNA is almost always destroyed. But occasionally, a cell adds the new genes to its DNA.

Bacteria use gene transfer to pass on adaptive traits. **Figure 4** shows how one bacterium can pass the trait of antibiotic resistance to a different species of bacteria. Being immune to antibiotics could provide a big boost in fitness for the bacterium. DNA analysis shows scientists which genes have passed from one species to another.

Design It!

Designer Genes

By transferring helpful genes from one species directly into cells of another species, scientists can produce desired traits in an organism. This creates genetically modified organisms, or GMOs. Scientists have modified eggplant genes to produce an insect-resistant plant. Insects attacked the plants on the left, but not those that were modified on the right.

SEP Design a Solution Draw an organism that you think could benefit from gene transfer and modification to become the next GMO. Label its features and describe the benefits.

Symbiosis Two organisms of different species that have a close relationship that involves living with each other is called symbiosis. In endosymbiosis, shown in **Figure 5**, one organism actually moves inside the other organism's cell. Scientists have theorized that endosymbiosis may be the mechanism that allowed life to generate on Earth. Mitochondria (the cell's powerhouse) and chloroplasts (they capture the sun's energy and store it as food) are both organelles. Just as a bacterium cell contains its own DNA and ribosomes, so do mitochondria and chloroplasts. Bacteria, mitochondria, and chloroplasts are also similar in size. Over millions of years of evolution, one type of bacteria became mitochondria and another type of bacteria became chloroplasts. At first, many scientists rejected the idea that mitochondria and chloroplasts had evolved from bacteria. Finally, advances in technology led to DNA sequencing that gave evidence supporting the hypothesis.

☑ CHECK POINT **Read and Comprehend** What are two ways that genetic material can move from one species to another?

....

....

Endosymbiosis

Figure 5 Evidence supports the idea that both mitochondria and chloroplasts evolved through endosymbiosis.

1. **Integrate with Visuals** 🖍 Label what happens in the two missing steps.

2. **CCC Structure and Function** Chloroplasts are parts of plant cells that turn sunlight into chemical energy for food. Consider how bacteria became chloroplasts. How might the bacteria have benefited from the arrangement?

....

....

....

❶ There are two different bacteria cells.

❷ ....
....

❸ Now the larger cell has the smaller one living inside it.

❹ Both bacteria cells benefit.

❺ ....
....

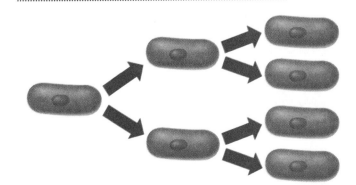

MS-LS4-2, MS-LS4-6

1. SEP Provide Evidence What evidence is there that every organism on Earth once had a common ancestor?

....

....

2. Compare and Contrast What do microevolution and macroevolution have in common? How do they differ?

....

....

....

....

....

3. Synthesize Information How have advances in technology supported the theory of evolution?

....

....

....

....

....

....

4. SEP Use Mathematics Refer to the data table in the Math Toolbox. Given that natural selection acts on variations and influences evolution, which two primate groups would you expect to have the most traits in common? Support your answer with a mathematical expression.

....

....

....

....

....

5. Support Your Explanation What does LUCA stand for and how did it evolve into all the life forms we see today?

....

....

....

....

....

....

....

....

....

....

Quest CHECK-IN

In this lesson, you learned more about how genetics drives evolution and how mutations to proteins lead to variations within a population.

CCC Cause and Effect What caused changes to the blackcap populations? How was natural selection at work here?

....

....

....

....

....

☞ INTERACTIVITY

Prepare Your Report

Go online to investigate the European blackcaps. Look for new information to add to your report. Brainstorm ideas for different ways to represent information.

MS-LS4-2, MS-LS4-4, MS-LS4-5

DNA, Fossils, and Evolution

All living things contain DNA. This blueprint carries the codes for every trait an organism expresses. We now have the technology to extract DNA from living things, as well as fossils, and then map out the locations of all the genes. By comparing modern DNA with that of fossils, it is possible to determine which traits similar species have in common.

Scientists are able to remove and analyze DNA from fossils using a process called an assay. DNA is removed from the center of a fossil and then prepared using an assortment of different chemicals. The DNA sample is then amplified and run through a process called gel electrophoresis. This separates different pieces of the DNA. The results are then compared to known DNA to see how similar they are.

One of the interesting things DNA research has discovered is that the domestication of dogs has changed their diet. While ancestral wolves ate mostly meat, modern dogs have more genes to help them digest starch and other carbohydrates. This suggests that the early dogs who could handle the starches in the human diet had an advantage.

MY DISCOVERY

With a classmate, research how dogs were domesticated from wolves. Engage in a classroom debate about the evidence that supports and refutes the descent of dogs from wolves.

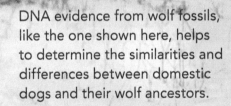

DNA evidence from wolf fossils, like the one shown here, helps to determine the similarities and differences between domestic dogs and their wolf ancestors.

☑TOPIC 8 Review and Assess

1 Early Study of Evolution

🕐 MS-LS4-4

1. Adaptations and variations show evidence of past
   A. evolution.
   B. offspring.
   C. diversity.
   D. fossils.

2. Who made the first attempt at developing a hypothesis of change over time?
   A. Anning
   B. Darwin
   C. Lamarck
   D. Lyell

3. On his five-year journey sailing around the world, Darwin was amazed by the .... of living things that he saw.

4. A species is a group of similar ....that can mate with each other and produce offspring capable of ....

5. **SEP Construct Explanations** Consider what caused the variation in finch beaks on the Galápagos Islands. How did it bring about new species of birds?

....

....

....

....

....

....

....

....

2 Natural Selection

🕐 MS-LS4-4, MS-LS4-5, MS-LS4-6

6. Darwin was able to create the fantail pigeon from the wild rock pigeon by using
   A. artificial selection.
   B. mechanisms.
   C. natural selection.
   D. overproduction.

7. Darwin observed that some variations make individuals better adapted
   A. to accumulate traits.
   B. to their environment.
   C. for population change.
   D. for more mutations.

8. Helpful variations may .... in a population leading to predominance, while unfavorable ones may decrease, leading to suppression.

9. Natural selection is affected by three factors: ...., variations among members of the population, and

   ....

10. **Explain Phenomena** How do environmental factors contribute to evolution by natural selection?

....

....

....

....

....

....

....

....

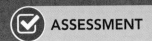
3 The Process of Evolution

MS-LS3-1, MS-LS4-4, MS-LS4-6

11. Unlike an organism with low fitness, an organism with high fitness has the ability to survive and
   A. mutate.
   B. coevolve.
   C. reproduce.
   D. interact.

12. Because they create multiple alleles, mutations can cause
   A. cell division.
   B. damaged DNA to repair itself.
   C. overproduction of offspring.
   D. variations in traits.

13. ...., a mechanism of evolution, is a random, directionless process.

14. Mutations can occur when an organism is exposed to .... or certain chemicals that damage the cell's ....

15. Distinguish Relationships Consider two species that compete for the same resources. Could their interactions affect each other's evolution? Explain.

   ....
   ....
   ....
   ....
   ....
   ....
   ....
   ....

4 Evidence in the Fossil Record

MS-LS4-1, MS-LS4-2, MS-LS4-3, MS-LS4-6

16. Evidence supporting biological evolution is found in the fossil record and in
   A. adaptations to changing environments.
   B. similar anatomies and embryos.
   C. offspring with various traits.
   D. layers of sediment.

17. Support Your Explanations
What can you infer about this fossilized organism and its environment?

   ....
   ....
   ....
   ....
   ....
   ....
   ....

5 Other Evidence of Evolution

MS-LS4-2, MS-LS4-6

18. Evolution results from changes in
   A. genetic material.   B. migration patterns.
   C. habitats and climate.   D. the fossil record.

19. Apply Scientific Reasoning DNA comparisons show that dogs are more similar to wolves than to coyotes. How else could scientists confirm their close relationship?

   ....
   ....
   ....

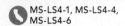
MS-LS4-1, MS-LS4-4,
MS-LS4-6

Evidence-Based Assessment

A group of scientists was researching evolutionary relationships. They decided to investigate a particular protein called cytochrome-c. They compared the amino acid sequence that codes for the protein among several species. They made a surprising discovery. In moths, whales, and Baker's yeast—organisms that do not look at all related—almost half of the positions in the cytochrome-c amino acid sequence were identical.

Cytochrome-c is a very important protein when it comes to releasing energy from food. Like other proteins, cytochrome-c is made of a sequence of amino acids that may or may not vary among organisms. The analysis of cytochrome-c in different organisms provides strong evidence for determining which organisms are closely related. Scientists can predict evolutionary relationships by looking at the amino acid sequences in cytochrome-c that different organisms have in common.

The data table shows ten positions where there are different amino acids in the sequence that codes for the cytochrome-c protein from five different species. In all other positions, the amino acids are the same.

Species	Amino Acid, Position Number in Sequence									
	20	23	52	55	66	68	70	91	97	100
human	M	S	P	S	I	G	D	V	E	A
horse	Q	A	P	S	T	L	E	A	T	E
kangaroo	Q	A	P	T	I	G	D	A	G	A
pig	Q	A	P	S	T	G	E	A	G	E
whale	Q	A	V	S	T	G	E	A	G	A

SOURCE: National Center for Biotechnology Information

Amino Acid Symbols

A = Alanine   M = Methionine

D = Aspartic Acid   P = Proline

E = Glutamic Acid   Q = Glutamine

G = Glycine   S = Serine

I = Isoleucine   T = Threonine

L = Lysine   V = Valine

1. **SEP Analyze Data** According to cytochrome-c analysis, to which other species is the horse most closely related?

A. human   **B**. pig

C. kangaroo   **D**. whale

2. **Support Your Explanation** How did you determine the horse's closest relation among the four species? Use evidence from the data table to support your claim.

....

....

....

....

....

....

....

....

....

....

....

....

....

....

3. **SEP Cite Evidence** Complete the table below to compare the number of different amino acids among the five organisms. Based on the table, circle the organism that is least like the human. Underline the organism that is most like the human.

Organism	Number of Shared Amino Acids with Humans
horse	
kangaroo	
pig	
whale	

4. **SEP Construct Explanations** Cows and sheep have the same sequence of amino acids in their cytochrome-c protein. How is it possible that they can be different species? Select all that apply.

☐ This is the result of convergent evolution.

☐ These two species share a recent common ancestor.

☐ They evolved under different environmental pressures.

☐ They are not closely related.

☐ Similar sequences of cytochrome-c protein do not indicate relatedness.

Quest FINDINGS

Complete the Quest!

Phenomenon Create a multimedia report about the two populations of European blackcaps and what caused them to be so different from each other.

Draw Conclusions If evolution of the blackcaps continues at the current rate, what can be said about similarities of the populations of European blackcaps to their common ancestor and to one another?

....

....

....

....

INTERACTIVITY

Reflect on Blackcap Migration

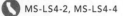
MS-LS4-2, MS-LS4-4

A Bony Puzzle

How can you analyze **patterns** in structures to **show** evolutionary **relationships?**

Materials

(per group)
- Activity Sheets 1, 2, and 3
- ruler

Background

Phenomenon A new museum of natural history is opening in your community. The director of the museum has asked your class to help with an exhibit about evolutionary history. The director hopes you can show how patterns in skeletons provide clues about common ancestors.

In this investigation, you will analyze and compare the internal and external structures of a pigeon, a bat, and a rabbit. Then you will use the similarities and differences you observe to describe a possible common ancestor and infer evolutionary relationships among these organisms.

Rock pigeon
(*Columba livia*)

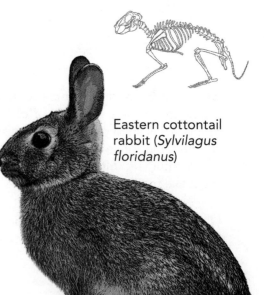

Eastern cottontail rabbit (*Sylvilagus floridanus*)

Indian flying fox (*Pteropus giganteus*)

Plan Your Investigation

☐ **1.** Using the photographs and the diagrams, you will compare the features and structures of the pigeon, bat, and rabbit. You will look for patterns in the skeletons and note similarities and differences among the three animals.

☐ **2.** Work with your group to plan a procedure for comparing the skeletons of the three animals. Write out your plan in the space provided. Consider the following questions as a guide for planning your procedure:

- Should we compare all the bones shown in the diagrams or select a few important features that they all have in common to compare?

- Do we also want to include our observations from the photographs of the animals?

- What's the best way to record and organize our observations so we can analyze them more easily? Should we write notes summarizing what we see? Or should we use only data tables to organize the data?

☐ **3.** After receiving your teacher's approval, follow the procedure your group developed. Remember that you may need to revise the plan as you carry it out. Record your observations about the three skeletons in the data tables.

HANDS-ON LAB

☑**Demonstrate** Go online for a downloadable worksheet of this lab.

Procedure

Observations

Skeleton	Similarities	Differences
Spine		
Skull		
Limbs		

Photos	Similarities	Differences
covering		
faces		
other		

Analyze and Interpret Data

1. **CCC Identify Patterns** What evidence did you find that will help you describe how these three skeletons are alike?

....

....

....

....

2. **SEP Evaluate Evidence** How does the skeleton pattern that you identified provide evidence for a common ancestor among the pigeon, bat, and rabbit?

....

....

....

3. **Explain Phenomena** Which bones of the common ancestor do you think might have changed the most in its descendants? Which bones remained about the same? Cite evidence from the skeleton diagrams to support your answer.

....

....

....

....

4. **CCC Structure and Function** How are the wings of the bat and the bird, and the rabbit's front legs, all examples of homologous structures? Use evidence from your investigation to support your answer.

....

....

....

....

5. **SEP Construct Explanations** The museum exhibit will include information to explain evolutionary relationships. What evidence can you use to show that bats share a more recent common ancestor with rabbits than they do with birds?

....

....

....

Vegavis is not the direct ancestor of modern-day ducks or chickens, but it is closely related to waterfowl such as geese.

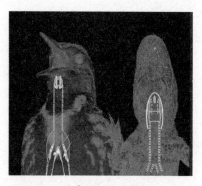

Location of syrinx in living songbird compared to larynx in an alligator

The presence of a syrinx in the *Vegavis iaai* fossil strongly suggests that the bird was capable of producing sounds. In the songbird, as in *Vegavis*, the syrinx is located in the chest. In the alligator, the larynx is located in the throat.

Photo Credit: Dr. Julia Clarke, University of Texas at Austin

Could DINOSAURS Roar?

So many movies have dinosaurs roaring as they roam across the landscape shredding trees and devouring prey the size of SUVs. Fossil evidence, however, supports a more silent world. In fact, it wasn't until about 65 to 68 million years ago that a very important piece of anatomy developed—the syrinx. Think of it as a voice box.

In 1992, on an Antarctic island, scientists found a fossil of *Vegavis iaai*, a bird that lived between 68 and 65 million years ago. At that time in Earth's history, Antarctica had a tropical climate. It wasn't until recently that technology revealed the most important find in the fossil: a syrinx.

Connections to Modern-Day Birds

The presence of a syrinx helps us to understand the ancestry of modern birds. Because of the asymmetrical structure of the syrinx, scientists speculate that the bird may have honked like a goose. Scientists analyzed the same structures in 12 living birds and compared them to the next oldest fossilized syrinx that was available. They found similarities in structure across the samples. Their findings supported the claim that *Vegavis iaai* was related to modern birds, but not an ancestor of modern reptiles, who are also able to vocalize through the larynx.

It would take a large brain to produce a selection of noises that meant something. If dinosaurs were able to vocalize or utter any sounds at all, then the sounds they made would have been a far cry from what you hear in the movies.

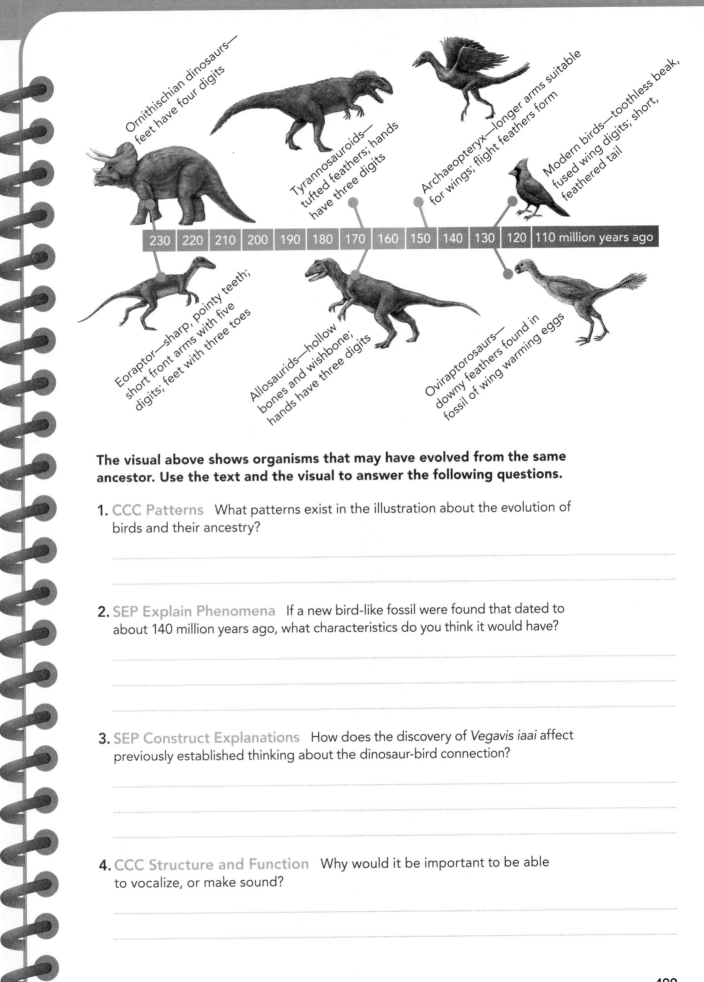

Ornithischian dinosaurs—feet have four digits

Tyrannosauroids—tufted feathers; hands have three digits

Archaeopteryx—longer arms suitable for wings; flight feathers form

Modern birds—toothless beak, fused wing digits; short, feathered tail

| 230 | 220 | 210 | 200 | 190 | 180 | 170 | 160 | 150 | 140 | 130 | 120 | 110 million years ago |

Eoraptor—sharp, pointy teeth; short front arms with five digits; feet with three toes

Allosaurids—hollow bones and wishbone; hands have three digits

Oviraptorosaurs—downy feathers found in fossil of wing warming eggs

The visual above shows organisms that may have evolved from the same ancestor. Use the text and the visual to answer the following questions.

1. CCC Patterns   What patterns exist in the illustration about the evolution of birds and their ancestry?

....

....

2. SEP Explain Phenomena   If a new bird-like fossil were found that dated to about 140 million years ago, what characteristics do you think it would have?

....

....

....

3. SEP Construct Explanations   How does the discovery of *Vegavis iaai* affect previously established thinking about the dinosaur-bird connection?

....

....

....

4. CCC Structure and Function   Why would it be important to be able to vocalize, or make sound?

....

....

SEP.1, SEP.8

The Meaning of Science

Science Skills

Science is a way of learning about the natural world. It involves asking questions, making predictions, and collecting information to see if the answer is right or wrong.

The table lists some of the skills that scientists use. You use some of these skills every day. For example, you may observe and evaluate your lunch options before choosing what to eat.

Reflect Think about a time you misplaced something and could not find it. Write a sentence defining the problem. What science skills could you use to solve the problem? Explain how you would use at least three of the skills in the table.

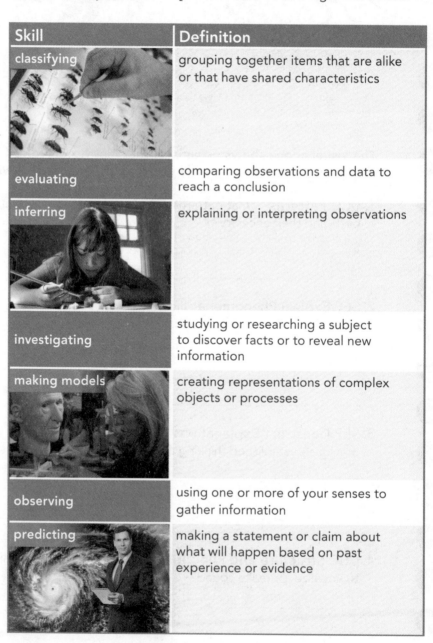

Skill	Definition
classifying	grouping together items that are alike or that have shared characteristics
evaluating	comparing observations and data to reach a conclusion
inferring	explaining or interpreting observations
investigating	studying or researching a subject to discover facts or to reveal new information
making models	creating representations of complex objects or processes
observing	using one or more of your senses to gather information
predicting	making a statement or claim about what will happen based on past experience or evidence

Scientific Attitudes

Curiosity often drives scientists to learn about the world around them. Creativity is useful for coming up with inventive ways to solve problems. Such qualities and attitudes, and the ability to keep an open mind, are essential for scientists.

When sharing results or findings, honesty and ethics are also essential. Ethics refers to rules for knowing right from wrong.

Being skeptical is also important. This means having doubts about things based on past experiences and evidence. Skepticism helps to prevent accepting data and results that may not be true.

Scientists must also avoid bias—likes or dislikes of people, ideas, or things. They must avoid experimental bias, which is a mistake that may make an experiment's preferred outcome more likely.

Scientific Reasoning

Scientific reasoning depends on being logical and objective. When you are objective, you use evidence and apply logic to draw conclusions. Being subjective means basing conclusions on personal feelings, biases, or opinions. Subjective reasoning can interfere with science and skew results. Objective reasoning helps scientists use observations to reach conclusions about the natural world.

Scientists use two types of objective reasoning: deductive and inductive. Deductive reasoning involves starting with a general idea or theory and applying it to a situation. For example, the theory of plate tectonics indicates that earthquakes happen mostly where tectonic plates meet. You could then draw the conclusion, or deduce, that California has many earthquakes because tectonic plates meet there.

In inductive reasoning, you make a generalization from a specific observation. When scientists collect data in an experiment and draw a conclusion based on that data, they use inductive reasoning. For example, if fertilizer causes one set of plants to grow faster than another, you might infer that the fertilizer promotes plant growth.

Make Meaning

Think about a bias the marine biologist in the photo could show that results in paying more or less attention to one kind of organism over others. Make a prediction about how that bias could affect the biologist's survey of the coral reef.

Write About It

Suppose it is raining when you go to sleep one night. When you wake up the next morning, you observe frozen puddles on the ground and icicles on tree branches. Use scientific reasoning to draw a conclusion about the air temperature outside. Support your conclusion using deductive or inductive reasoning.

SEP.1, SEP.2, SEP.3, SEP.4, CCC.4

Science Processes

Scientific Inquiry

Write About It
Describe a question that you posed, formally or informally, about an event in your life that you needed to investigate or resolve. Write the hypothesis you developed to answer your question, and describe how you tested the hypothesis.

Scientists contribute to scientific knowledge by conducting investigations and drawing conclusions. The process often begins with an observation that leads to a question, which is then followed by the development of a hypothesis. This is known as scientific inquiry.

One of the first steps in scientific inquiry is asking questions. However, it's important to make a question specific with a narrow focus so the investigation will not be too broad. A biologist may want to know all there is to know about wolves, for example. But a good, focused question for a specific inquiry might be "How many offspring does the average female wolf produce in her lifetime?"

A hypothesis is a possible answer to a scientific question. A hypothesis must be testable. For something to be testable, researchers must be able to carry out an investigation and gather evidence that will either support or disprove the hypothesis.

Scientific Models

Models are tools that scientists use to study phenomena indirectly. A model is any representation of an object or process. Illustrations, dioramas, globes, diagrams, computer programs, and mathematical equations are all examples of scientific models. For example, a diagram of Earth's crust and mantle can help you to picture layers deep below the surface and understand events such as volcanic eruptions.

Models also allow scientists to represent objects that are either very large, such as our solar system, or very small, such as a molecule of DNA. Models can also represent processes that occur over a long period of time, such as the changes that have occurred throughout Earth's history.

Models are helpful, but they have limitations. Physical models are not made of the same materials as the objects they represent. Most models of complex objects or processes show only major parts, stages, or relationships. Many details are left out. Therefore, you may not be able to learn as much from models as you would through direct observation.

Reflect Identify the benefits and limitations of using a plastic model of DNA, as shown here.

Science Experiments

An experiment or investigation must be well planned to produce valid results. In planning an experiment, you must identify the independent and dependent variables. You must also do as much as possible to remove the effects of other variables. A controlled experiment is one in which you test only one variable at a time.

For example, suppose you plan a controlled experiment to learn how the type of material affects the speed at which sound waves travel through it. The only variable that should change is the type of material. This way, if the speed of sound changes, you know that it is a result of a change in the material, not another variable such as the thickness of the material or the type of sound used.

You should also remove bias from any investigation. You may inadvertently introduce bias by selecting subjects you like and avoiding those you don't like. Scientists often conduct investigations by taking random samples to avoid ending up with biased results.

Once you plan your investigation and begin to collect data, it's important to record and organize the data. You may wish to use a graph to display and help you to interpret the data.

Communicating is the sharing of ideas and results with others through writing and speaking. Communicating data and conclusions is a central part of science.

Scientists share knowledge, including new findings, theories, and techniques for collecting data. Conferences, journals, and websites help scientists to communicate with each other. Popular media, including newspapers, magazines, and social media sites, help scientists to share their knowledge with nonscientists. However, before the results of investigations are shared and published, other scientists should review the experiment for possible sources of error, such as bias and unsupported conclusions.

Write About It

List four ways you could communicate the results of a scientific study about the health of sea turtles in the Pacific Ocean.

SEP.1, SEP.6, SEP.7, SEP.8

Scientific Knowledge

Scientific Explanations

Suppose you learn that adult flamingos are pink because of the food they eat. This statement is a scientific explanation— it describes how something in nature works or explains why it happens. Scientists from different fields use methods such as researching information, designing experiments, and making models to form scientific explanations. Scientific explanations often result from many years of work and multiple investigations conducted by many scientists.

Scientific Theories and Laws

A scientific law is a statement that describes what you can expect to occur every time under a particular set of conditions. A scientific law describes an observed pattern in nature, but it does not attempt to explain it. For example, the law of superposition describes what you can expect to find in terms of the ages of layers of rock. Geologists use this observed pattern to determine the relative ages of sedimentary rock layers. But the law does not explain why the pattern occurs.

By contrast, a scientific theory is a well-tested explanation for a wide range of observations or experimental results. It provides details and describes causes of observed patterns. Something is elevated to a theory only when there is a large body of evidence that supports it. However, a scientific theory can be changed or overturned when new evidence is found.

Write About It

Choose two fields of science that interest you. Describe a method used to develop scientific explanations in each field.

SEP Construct Explanations Complete the table to compare and contrast a scientific theory and a scientific law.

	Scientific Theory	Scientific Law
Definition		
Does it attempt to explain a pattern observed in nature?		

Analyzing Scientific Explanations

To analyze scientific explanations that you hear on the news or read in a book such as this one, you need scientific literacy. Scientific literacy means understanding scientific terms and principles well enough to ask questions, evaluate information, and make decisions. Scientific reasoning gives you a process to apply. This includes looking for bias and errors in the research, evaluating data, and identifying faulty reasoning. For example, by evaluating how a survey was conducted, you may find a serious flaw in the researchers' methods.

Evidence and Opinions

The basis for scientific explanations is empirical evidence. Empirical evidence includes the data and observations that have been collected through scientific processes. Satellite images, photos, and maps of mountains and volcanoes are all examples of empirical evidence that support a scientific explanation about Earth's tectonic plates. Scientists look for patterns when they analyze this evidence. For example, they might see a pattern that mountains and volcanoes often occur near tectonic plate boundaries.

To evaluate scientific information, you must first distinguish between evidence and opinion. In science, evidence includes objective observations and conclusions that have been repeated. Evidence may or may not support a scientific claim. An opinion is a subjective idea that is formed from evidence, but it cannot be confirmed by evidence.

Write About It

Suppose the conservation committee of a town wants to gauge residents' opinions about a proposal to stock the local ponds with fish every spring. The committee pays for a survey to appear on a web site that is popular with people who like to fish. The results of the survey show 78 people in favor of the proposal and two against it. Do you think the survey's results are valid? Explain.

Make Meaning

Explain what empirical evidence the photograph reveals.

SEP.3, SEP.4

Tools of Science

Measurement

Making measurements using standard units is important in all fields of science. This allows scientists to repeat and reproduce other experiments, as well as to understand the precise meaning of the results of others. Scientists use a measurement system called the International System of Units, or SI.

For each type of measurement, there is a series of units that are greater or less than each other. The unit a scientist uses depends on what is being measured. For example, a geophysicist tracking the movements of tectonic plates may use centimeters, as plates tend to move small amounts each year. Meanwhile, a marine biologist might measure the movement of migrating bluefin tuna on the scale of kilometers.

Units for length, mass, volume, and density are based on powers of ten—a meter is equal to 100 centimeters or 1000 millimeters. Units of time do not follow that pattern. There are 60 seconds in a minute, 60 minutes in an hour, and 24 hours in a day. These units are based on patterns that humans perceived in nature. Units of temperature are based on scales that are set according to observations of nature. For example, 0°C is the temperature at which pure water freezes, and 100°C is the temperature at which it boils.

Write About It
Suppose you are planning an investigation in which you must measure the dimensions of several small mineral samples that fit in your hand. Which metric unit or units will you most likely use? Explain your answer.

Measurement	Metric units
Length or distance	meter (m), kilometer (km), centimeter (cm), millimeter (mm) 1 km = 1,000 m 1 cm = 10 mm 1 m = 100 cm
Mass	kilogram (kg), gram (g), milligram (mg) 1 kg = 1,000 g 1 g = 1,000 mg
Volume	cubic meter (m³), cubic centimeter (cm³) $1\ m^3 = 1{,}000{,}000\ cm^3$
Density	kilogram per cubic meter (kg/m³), gram per cubic centimeter (g/cm³) $1{,}000\ kg/m^3 = 1\ g/cm^3$
Temperature	degrees Celsius (°C), kelvin (K) 1°C = 273 K
Time	hour (h), minute (m), second (s)

Math Skills

Using numbers to collect and interpret data involves math skills that are essential in science. For example, you use math skills when you estimate the number of birds in an entire forest after counting the actual number of birds in ten trees.

Scientists evaluate measurements and estimates for their precision and accuracy. In science, an accurate measurement is very close to the actual value. Precise measurements are very close, or nearly equal, to each other. Reliable measurements are both accurate and precise. An imprecise value may be a sign of an error in data collection. This kind of anomalous data may be excluded to avoid skewing the data and harming the investigation.

Other math skills include performing specific calculations, such as finding the mean, or average, value in a data set. The mean can be calculated by adding up all of the values in the data set and then dividing that sum by the number of values.

Hour	Number of Ducks Observed at a Pond
1	12
2	10
3	2
4	14
5	13
6	10
7	11

SEP Use Mathematics The data table shows how many ducks were seen at a pond every hour over the course of seven hours. Is there a data point that seems anomalous? If so, cross out that data point. Then, calculate the mean number of ducks on the pond. Round the mean to the nearest whole number.

Graphs

Graphs help scientists to interpret data by helping them to find trends or patterns in the data. A line graph displays data that show how one variable (the dependent or outcome variable) changes in response to another (the independent or test variable). The slope and shape of a graph line can reveal patterns and help scientists to make predictions. For example, line graphs can help you to spot patterns of change over time.

Scientists use bar graphs to compare data across categories or subjects that may not affect each other. The heights of the bars make it easy to compare those quantities. A circle graph, also known as a pie chart, shows the proportions of different parts of a whole.

Write About It
You and a friend record the distance you travel every 15 minutes on a one-hour bike trip. Your friend wants to display the data as a circle graph. Explain whether or not this is the best type of graph to display your data. If not, suggest another graph to use.

 SEP.1, SEP.2, SEP.3, SEP.6

The Engineering and Design Process

Engineers are builders and problem solvers. Chemical engineers experiment with new fuels made from algae. Civil engineers design roadways and bridges. Bioengineers develop medical devices and prosthetics. The common trait among engineers is an ability to identify problems and design solutions to solve them. Engineers use a creative process that relies on scientific methods to help guide them from a concept or idea all the way to the final product.

Define the Problem

To identify or define a problem, different questions need to be asked: *What are the effects of the problem? What are the likely causes? What other factors could be involved?* Sometimes the obvious, immediate cause of a problem may be the result of another problem that may not be immediately apparent. For example, climate change results in different weather patterns, which in turn can affect organisms that live in certain habitats. So engineers must be aware of all the possible effects of potential solutions. Engineers must also take into account how well different solutions deal with the different causes of the problem.

Reflect Write about a problem that you encountered in your life that had both immediate, obvious causes as well as less-obvious and less-immediate ones.

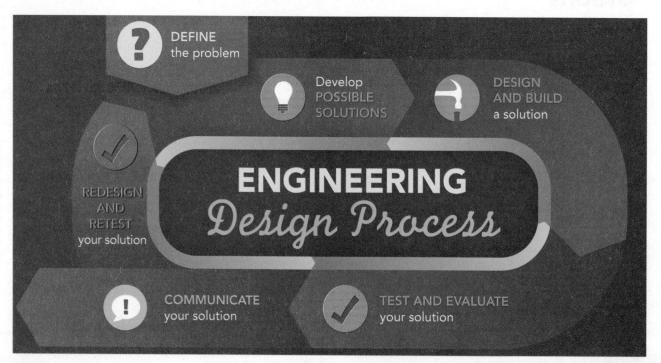

As engineers consider problems and design solutions, they must identify and categorize the criteria and constraints of the project.

Criteria are the factors that must be met or accomplished by the solution. For example, a gardener who wants to protect outdoor plants from deer and rabbits may say that the criteria for the solution are "plants are no longer eaten" and "plant growth is not inhibited in any way." The gardener then knows the plants cannot simply be sealed off from the environment, because the plants will not receive sunlight and water.

The same gardener will likely have constraints on his solution, such as budget for materials and time that is available for working on the project. By setting constraints, a solution can be designed that will be successful without introducing a new set of problems. No one wants to spend $500 on materials to protect $100 worth of tomatoes and cucumbers.

Develop Possible Solutions

After the problem has been identified, and the criteria and constraints identified, an engineer will consider possible solutions. This often involves working in teams with other engineers and designers to brainstorm ideas and research materials that can be used in the design.

It's important for engineers to think creatively and explore all potential solutions. If you wanted to design a bicycle that was safer and easier to ride than a traditional bicycle, then you would want more than just one or two solutions. Having multiple ideas to choose from increases the likelihood that you will develop a solution that meets the criteria and constraints. In addition, different ideas that result from brainstorming can often lead to new and better solutions to an existing problem.

Make Meaning
Using the example of a garden that is vulnerable to wild animals such as deer, make a list of likely constraints on an engineering solution to the problem you identified before. Determine if there are common traits among the constraints, and identify categories for them.

Design a Solution

Engineers then develop the idea that they feel best solves the problem. Once a solution has been chosen, engineers and designers get to work building a model or prototype of the solution. A model may involve sketching on paper or using computer software to construct a model of the solution. A prototype is a working model of the solution.

Building a model or prototype helps an engineer determine whether a solution meets the criteria and stays within the constraints. During this stage of the process, engineers must often deal with new problems and make any necessary adjustments to the model or prototype.

Test and Evaluate a Solution

Whether testing a model or a prototype, engineers use scientific processes to evaluate their solutions. Multiple experiments, tests, or trials are conducted, data are evaluated, and results and analyses are communicated. New criteria or constraints may emerge as a result of testing. In most cases, a solution will require some refinement or revision, even if it has been through successful testing. Refining a solution is necessary if there are new constraints, such as less money or available materials. Additional testing may be done to ensure that a solution satisfies local, state, or federal laws or standards.

Make Meaning Think about an aluminum beverage can. What would happen if the price or availability of aluminum changed so much that cans needed to be made of a new material? What would the criteria and constraints be on the development of a new can?

A naval architect sets up a model to test how the the hull's design responds to waves.

Communicate the Solution

Engineers need to communicate the final design to the people who will manufacture the product. This may include sketches, detailed drawings, computer simulations, and written text. Engineers often provide evidence that was collected during the testing stage. This evidence may include graphs and data tables that support the decisions made for the final design.

If there is feedback about the solution, then the engineers and designers must further refine the solution. This might involve making minor adjustments to the design, or it might mean bigger modifications to the design based on new criteria or constraints. Any changes in the design will require additional testing to make sure that the changes work as intended.

Redesign and Retest the Solution

At different steps in the engineering and design process, a solution usually must be revised and retested. Many designs fail to work perfectly, even after models and prototypes are built, tested, and evaluated. Engineers must be ready to analyze new results and deal with any new problems that arise. Troubleshooting, or fixing design problems, allows engineers to adjust the design to improve on how well the solution meets the need.

SEP Design Solutions Suppose you are an engineer at an aerospace company. Your team is designing a rover to be used on a future NASA space mission. A family member doesn't understand why so much of your team's time is taken up with testing and retesting the rover design. What are three things you would tell your relative to explain why testing and retesting are so important to the engineering and design process?

....
....
....
....
....
....
....
....

APPENDIX A

Safety Symbols

These symbols warn of possible dangers in the laboratory and remind you to work carefully.

 Safety Goggles Wear safety goggles to protect your eyes in any activity involving chemicals, flames or heating, or glassware.

 Lab Apron Wear a laboratory apron to protect your skin and clothing from damage.

 Breakage Handle breakable materials, such as glassware, with care. Do not touch broken glassware.

 Heat-Resistant Gloves Use an oven mitt or other hand protection when handling hot materials, such as hot plates or hot glassware.

 Plastic Gloves Wear disposable plastic gloves when working with harmful chemicals and organisms. Keep your hands away from your face, and dispose of the gloves according to your teacher's instructions.

 Heating Use a clamp or tongs to pick up hot glassware. Do not touch hot objects with your bare hands.

 Flames Before you work with flames, tie back loose hair and clothing. Follow your teacher's instructions about lighting and extinguishing flames.

 No Flames When using flammable materials, make sure there are no flames, sparks, or other exposed heat sources present.

 Corrosive Chemical Avoid getting acid or other corrosive chemicals on your skin or clothing or in your eyes. Do not inhale the vapors. Wash your hands after the activity.

 Poison Do not let any poisonous chemical come into contact with your skin, and do not inhale its vapors. Wash your hands when you are finished with the activity.

 Fumes Work in a well-ventilated area when harmful vapors may be involved. Avoid inhaling vapors directly. Test an odor only when directed to do so by your teacher, and use a wafting motion to direct the vapor toward your nose.

 Sharp Object Scissors, scalpels, knives, needles, pins, and tacks can cut your skin. Always direct a sharp edge or point away from yourself and others.

 Animal Safety Treat live or preserved animals or animal parts with care to avoid harming the animals or yourself. Wash your hands when you are finished with the activity.

 Plant Safety Handle plants only as directed by your teacher. If you are allergic to certain plants, tell your teacher; do not do an activity involving those plants. Avoid touching harmful plants such as poison ivy. Wash your hands when you are finished with the activity.

 Electric Shock To avoid electric shock, never use electrical equipment around water, when the equipment is wet, or when your hands are wet. Be sure cords are untangled and cannot trip anyone. Unplug equipment not in use.

 Physical Safety When an experiment involves physical activity, avoid injuring yourself or others. Alert your teacher if there is any reason you should not participate.

 Disposal Dispose of chemicals and other laboratory materials safely. Follow the instructions from your teacher.

 Hand Washing Wash your hands thoroughly when finished with an activity. Use soap and warm water. Rinse well.

 General Safety Awareness When this symbol appears, follow the instructions provided. When you are asked to develop your own procedure in a lab, have your teacher approve your plan.

Using a Laboratory Balance

The laboratory balance is an important tool in scientific investigations. Different kinds of balances are used in the laboratory to determine the masses and weights of objects. You can use a triple-beam balance to determine the masses of materials that you study or experiment with in the laboratory. An electronic balance, unlike a triple-beam balance, is used to measure the weights of materials.

The triple-beam balance that you may use in your science class is probably similar to the balance depicted in this Appendix. To use the balance properly, you should learn the name, location, and function of each part of the balance.

Triple-Beam Balance

The triple-beam balance is a single-pan balance with three beams calibrated in grams. The back, or 100-gram, beam is divided into ten units of 10 grams each. The middle, or 500-gram, beam is divided into five units of 100 grams each. The front, or 10-gram, beam is divided into ten units of 1 gram each. Each gram on the front beam is further divided into units of 0.1 gram.

Apply Concepts What is the greatest mass you could find with the triple-beam balance in the picture?

....

Calculate What is the mass of the apple in the picture?

....

The following procedure can be used to find the mass of an object with a triple-beam balance:

1. Place the object on the pan.

2. Move the rider on the middle beam notch by notch until the horizontal pointer on the right drops below zero. Move the rider back one notch.

3. Move the rider on the back beam notch by notch until the pointer again drops below zero. Move the rider back one notch.

4. Slowly slide the rider along the front beam until the pointer stops at the zero point.

5. The mass of the object is equal to the sum of the readings on the three beams.

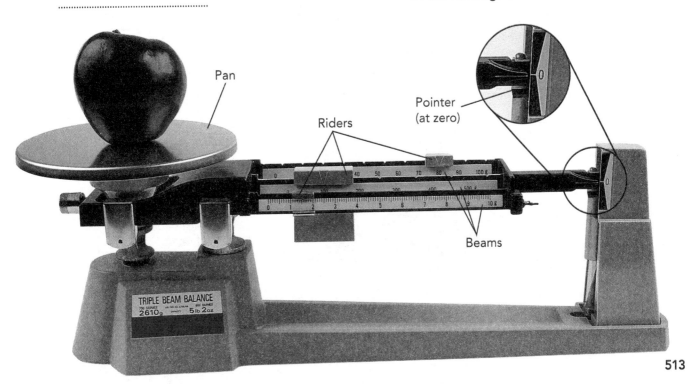

Pan

Riders

Pointer (at zero)

Beams

TRIPLE BEAM BALANCE
700 SERIES
2610g   CAPACITY 5 lb 2 oz

Using a Microscope

The microscope is an essential tool in the study of life science. It allows you to see things that are too small to be seen with the unaided eye.

You will probably use a compound microscope like the one you see here. The compound microscope has more than one lens that magnifies the object you view.

Typically, a compound microscope has one lens in the eyepiece (the part you look through). The eyepiece lens usually magnifies 10×. Any object you view through this lens will appear 10 times larger than it is.

A compound microscope may contain two or three other lenses called objective lenses. They are called the low-power and high-power objective lenses. The low-power objective lens usually magnifies 10×. The high-power objective lenses usually magnify 40× and 100×.

To calculate the total magnification with which you are viewing an object, multiply the magnification of the eyepiece lens by the magnification of the objective lens you are using. For example, the eyepiece's magnification of 10× multiplied by the low-power objective's magnification of 10× equals a total magnification of 100×.

Use the photo of the compound microscope to become familiar with the parts of the microscope and their functions.

The Parts of a Microscope

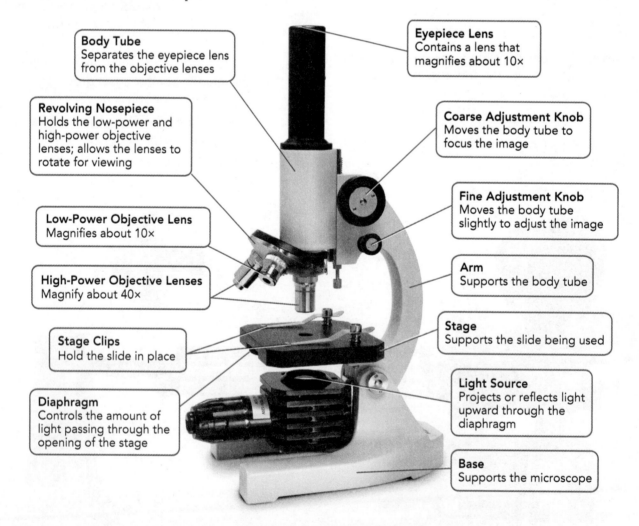

Body Tube
Separates the eyepiece lens from the objective lenses

Revolving Nosepiece
Holds the low-power and high-power objective lenses; allows the lenses to rotate for viewing

Low-Power Objective Lens
Magnifies about 10×

High-Power Objective Lenses
Magnify about 40×

Stage Clips
Hold the slide in place

Diaphragm
Controls the amount of light passing through the opening of the stage

Eyepiece Lens
Contains a lens that magnifies about 10×

Coarse Adjustment Knob
Moves the body tube to focus the image

Fine Adjustment Knob
Moves the body tube slightly to adjust the image

Arm
Supports the body tube

Stage
Supports the slide being used

Light Source
Projects or reflects light upward through the diaphragm

Base
Supports the microscope

Using the Microscope
Use the following procedures when you are working with a microscope.

1. To carry the microscope, grasp the microscope's arm with one hand. Place your other hand under the base.

2. Place the microscope on a table with the arm toward you.

3. Turn the coarse adjustment knob to raise the body tube.

4. Revolve the nosepiece until the low-power objective lens clicks into place.

5. Adjust the diaphragm. While looking through the eyepiece, adjust the mirror until you see a bright white circle of light. **CAUTION:** Never use direct sunlight as a light source.

6. Place a slide on the stage. Center the specimen over the opening on the stage. Use the stage clips to hold the slide in place. **CAUTION:** Glass slides are fragile.

7. Look at the stage from the side. Carefully turn the coarse adjustment knob to lower the body tube until the low-power objective almost touches the slide.

8. Looking through the eyepiece, very slowly turn the coarse adjustment knob until the specimen comes into focus.

9. To switch to the high-power objective lens, look at the microscope from the side. Carefully revolve the nosepiece until the high-power objective lens clicks into place. Make sure the lens does not hit the slide.

10. Looking through the eyepiece, turn the fine adjustment knob until the specimen comes into focus.

Making a Wet-Mount Slide
Use the following procedures to make a wet-mount slide of a specimen.

1. Obtain a clean microscope slide and a coverslip. **CAUTION:** Glass slides and coverslips are fragile.

2. Place the specimen on the center of the slide. The specimen must be thin enough for light to pass through it.

3. Using a plastic dropper, place a drop of water on the specimen.

4. Gently place one edge of the coverslip against the slide so that it touches the edge of the water drop at a 45° angle. Slowly lower the coverslip over the specimen. If you see air bubbles trapped beneath the coverslip, tap the coverslip gently with the eraser end of a pencil.

5. Remove any excess water at the edge of the coverslip with a paper towel.

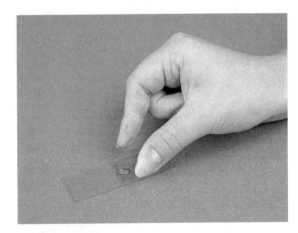

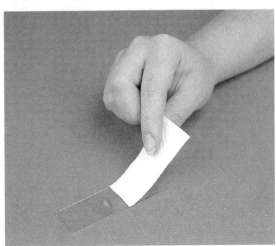

Periodic Table of Elements

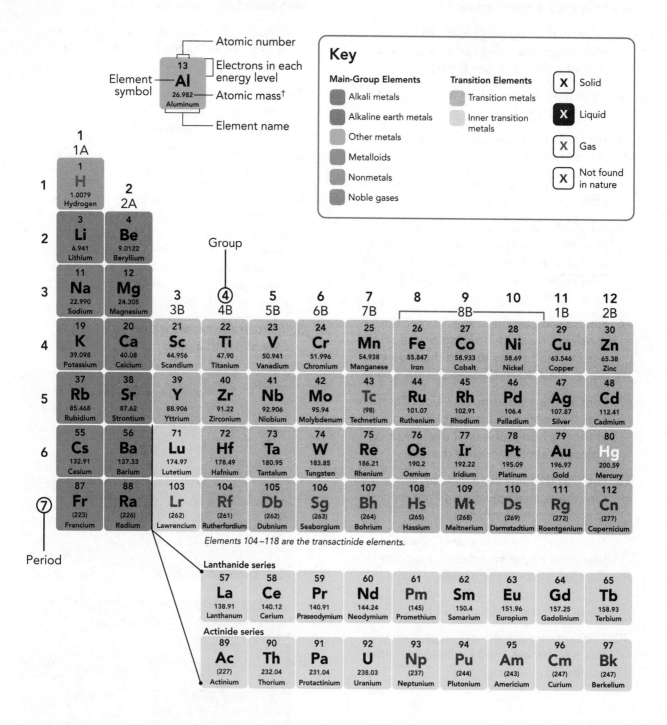

Atomic number

13

Al — Element symbol

26.982 — Atomic mass†

Aluminum — Element name

Electrons in each energy level

Key

Main-Group Elements
- Alkali metals
- Alkaline earth metals
- Other metals
- Metalloids
- Nonmetals
- Noble gases

Transition Elements
- Transition metals
- Inner transition metals

- X Solid
- X Liquid
- X Gas
- X Not found in nature

1 1A											
1 **H** 1.0079 Hydrogen	2 2A										
3 **Li** 6.941 Lithium	4 **Be** 9.0122 Beryllium										
11 **Na** 22.990 Sodium	12 **Mg** 24.305 Magnesium	3 3B	4 4B	5 5B	6 6B	7 7B	8	9 8B	10	11 1B	12 2B
19 **K** 39.098 Potassium	20 **Ca** 40.08 Calcium	21 **Sc** 44.956 Scandium	22 **Ti** 47.90 Titanium	23 **V** 50.941 Vanadium	24 **Cr** 51.996 Chromium	25 **Mn** 54.938 Manganese	26 **Fe** 55.847 Iron	27 **Co** 58.933 Cobalt	28 **Ni** 58.69 Nickel	29 **Cu** 63.546 Copper	30 **Zn** 65.38 Zinc
37 **Rb** 85.468 Rubidium	38 **Sr** 87.62 Strontium	39 **Y** 88.906 Yttrium	40 **Zr** 91.22 Zirconium	41 **Nb** 92.906 Niobium	42 **Mo** 95.94 Molybdenum	43 **Tc** (98) Technetium	44 **Ru** 101.07 Ruthenium	45 **Rh** 102.91 Rhodium	46 **Pd** 106.4 Palladium	47 **Ag** 107.87 Silver	48 **Cd** 112.41 Cadmium
55 **Cs** 132.91 Cesium	56 **Ba** 137.33 Barium	71 **Lu** 174.97 Lutetium	72 **Hf** 178.49 Hafnium	73 **Ta** 180.95 Tantalum	74 **W** 183.85 Tungsten	75 **Re** 186.21 Rhenium	76 **Os** 190.2 Osmium	77 **Ir** 192.22 Iridium	78 **Pt** 195.09 Platinum	79 **Au** 196.97 Gold	80 **Hg** 200.59 Mercury
87 **Fr** (223) Francium	88 **Ra** (226) Radium	103 **Lr** (262) Lawrencium	104 **Rf** (261) Rutherfordium	105 **Db** (262) Dubnium	106 **Sg** (263) Seaborgium	107 **Bh** (264) Bohrium	108 **Hs** (265) Hassium	109 **Mt** (268) Meitnerium	110 **Ds** (269) Darmstadtium	111 **Rg** (272) Roentgenium	112 **Cn** (277) Copernicium

Elements 104–118 are the transactinide elements.

Lanthanide series

57 **La** 138.91 Lanthanum	58 **Ce** 140.12 Cerium	59 **Pr** 140.91 Praseodymium	60 **Nd** 144.24 Neodymium	61 **Pm** (145) Promethium	62 **Sm** 150.4 Samarium	63 **Eu** 151.96 Europium	64 **Gd** 157.25 Gadolinium	65 **Tb** 158.93 Terbium

Actinide series

89 **Ac** (227) Actinium	90 **Th** 232.04 Thorium	91 **Pa** 231.04 Protactinium	92 **U** 238.03 Uranium	93 **Np** (237) Neptunium	94 **Pu** (244) Plutonium	95 **Am** (243) Americium	96 **Cm** (247) Curium	97 **Bk** (247) Berkelium

Group

Period

†The atomic masses in parentheses are the mass numbers of the longest-lived isotope of elements for which a standard atomic mass cannot be defined.

18 8A
2 **He** 4.0026 Helium

13 3A	14 4A	15 5A	16 6A	17 7A	
5 **B** 10.81 Boron	6 **C** 12.011 Carbon	7 **N** 14.007 Nitrogen	8 **O** 15.999 Oxygen	9 **F** 18.998 Fluorine	10 **Ne** 20.179 Neon
13 **Al** 26.982 Aluminum	14 **Si** 28.086 Silicon	15 **P** 30.974 Phosphorus	16 **S** 32.06 Sulfur	17 **Cl** 35.453 Chlorine	18 **Ar** 39.948 Argon
31 **Ga** 69.72 Gallium	32 **Ge** 72.59 Germanium	33 **As** 74.922 Arsenic	34 **Se** 78.96 Selenium	35 **Br** 79.904 Bromine	36 **Kr** 83.80 Krypton
49 **In** 114.82 Indium	50 **Sn** 118.69 Tin	51 **Sb** 121.75 Antimony	52 **Te** 127.60 Tellurium	53 **I** 126.90 Iodine	54 **Xe** 131.30 Xenon
81 **Tl** 204.37 Thallium	82 **Pb** 207.2 Lead	83 **Bi** 208.98 Bismuth	84 **Po** (209) Polonium	85 **At** (210) Astatine	86 **Rn** (222) Radon
113 **Nh** (284) Nihonium	114 **Fl** (289) Flerovium	115 **Mc** (288) Moscovium	116 **Lv** (292) Livermorium	117 **Ts** (294) Tennessine	118 **Og** (294) Oganesson

66 **Dy** 162.50 Dysprosium	67 **Ho** 164.93 Holmium	68 **Er** 167.26 Erbium	69 **Tm** 168.93 Thulium	70 **Yb** 173.04 Ytterbium
98 **Cf** (251) Californium	99 **Es** (252) Einsteinium	100 **Fm** (257) Fermium	101 **Md** (258) Mendelevium	102 **No** (259) Nobelium

GLOSSARY

A

abiotic factor A nonliving part of an organism's habitat. (70)

adaptation An inherited behavior or physical characteristic that helps an organism survive and reproduce in its environment. (447)

allele A different form of a gene. (318)

alveoli Tiny sacs of lung tissue specialized for the movement of gases between air and blood. (276)

artery A blood vessel that carries blood away from the heart. (273)

artificial selection The process by which humans breed only those organisms with desired traits to produce the next generation; selective breeding. (409)

asexual reproduction A reproductive process that involves only one parent and produces offspring that are genetically identical to the parent. (315)

autosomal chromosomes The 22 pairs of chromosomes that are not sex chromosomes. (398)

autotroph An organism that is able to capture energy from sunlight or chemicals and use it to produce its own food. (211)

auxin A hormone that controls a plant's growth and response to light. (346)

B

bacteria Single-celled organisms that lack a nucleus; prokaryotes. (36)

behavior The way an organism reacts to changes in its internal conditions or external environment. (335)

binomial nomenclature The classification system in which each organism is given a unique, two-part scientific name indicating its genus and species. (23)

biodiversity The number and variety of different species in an area. (127)

biotic factor A living or once living part of an organism's habitat. (70)

brain The part of the central nervous system that is located in the skull and controls most functions in the body. (285)

bronchi The passages that direct air into the lungs. (276)

C

capillary A tiny blood vessel where substances are exchanged between the blood and the body cells. (273)

carbohydrate An energy-rich organic compound, such as a sugar or a starch, that is made of the elements of carbon, hydrogen, and oxygen. (260)

cell The basic unit of structure and function in living things. (14, 173)

cell cycle The series of events in which a cell grows, prepares for division, and divides to form two daughter cells. (204, 377)

cell membrane A thin, flexible barrier that surrounds a cell and controls which substances pass into and out of a cell. (185)

cell theory A widely accepted explanation of the relationship between cells and living things. (176)

cell wall A rigid supporting layer that surrounds the cells of plants and some other organisms. (184)

cellular respiration The process in which oxygen and glucose undergo a complex series of chemical reactions inside cells, releasing energy. (219)

chlorophyll A green photosynthetic pigment found in the chloroplasts of plants, algae, and some bacteria. (212)

chloroplast An organelle in the cells of plants and some other organisms that captures energy from sunlight and changes it to an energy form that cells can use in making food. (187)

chromatid The structure formed when a chromosome divides during meiosis (382)

chromosome A threadlike structure within a cell's nucleus that contains DNA that is passed from one generation to the next. (377)

circulatory system An organ system that taransports needed materials to cells and removes wastes. (271)

classification The process of grouping things based on their similarities. (23)

clone An organism that is genetically identical to the organism from which it was produced. (413)

coevolution The process by which two species evolve in response to changes in each other over time. (466)

commensalism A type of symbiosis between two species in which one species benefits and the other species is neither helped nor harmed. (114)

community All the different populations that live together in a certain area. (71)

competition The struggle between organisms to survive as they attempt to use the same limited resources in the same place at the same time. (111, 453)

condensation The change in state from a gas to a liquid. (89)

cones The reproductive structures of gymnosperms. (329)

conservation The practice of using less of a resource so that it can last longer. (145)

consumer An organism that obtains energy by feeding on other organisms. (78)

convergent evolution The process by which unrelated organisms evolve similar characteristics. (29)

cytokinesis The final stage of the cell cycle, in which the cell's cytoplasm divides, distributing the organelles into each of the two new daughter cells. (208)

cytoplasm The thick fluid region of a cell located inside the cell membrane (in prokaryotes) or between the cell membrane and nucleus (in eukaryotes). (186)

D

decomposer An organism that gets energy by breaking down biotic wastes and dead organisms and returns raw materials to the soil and water. (79)

diffusion The process by which molecules move from an area of higher concentration to an area of lower concentration. (195)

digestion The process that breaks complex molecules of food into smaller nutrient molecules. (259)

DNA Deoxyribonucleic acid; the genetic material that carries information about an organism and is passed from parent to offspring. (387)

domain The most basic level of organization in the classification of organisms. (24)

dominant allele An allele whose trait always shows up in the organism when the allele is present. (369)

dormancy A period of time when an organism's growth or activity stops. (347)

E

ecological restoration The practice of helping a degraded or destroyed ecosystem recover from damage. (145)

ecology The study of how organisms interact with each other and their environment. (139)

ecosystem The community of organisms that live in a particular area, along with their nonliving environment. (71)

ecosystem services The benefits that humans derive from ecosystems. (139)

embryo The young organism that develops from a zygote. (474)

endocytosis The process by which the cell membrane takes particles into the cell by changing shape and engulfing the particles. (198)

endosymbiosis A relationship in which one organism lives inside another organism's cells. (487)

energy pyramid A diagram that shows the amount of energy that moves from one feeding level to another in a food web. (82)

enzyme A type of protein that speeds up chemical reactions in the body. (263)

evaporation The process by which molecules at the surface of a liquid absorb enough energy to change to a gas. (88)

evolution Change over time; the process by which modern organisms have descended from ancient organisms. (28, 441)

excretion The process by which wastes are removed from the body. (278)

exocytosis The process by which the vacuole surrounding particles fuses with the cell membrane, forcing the contents out of the cell. (198)

external fertilization When eggs are fertilized outside a female's body. (339)

extinct Term used to refer to a group of related organisms that has died out and has no living members. (476)

extinction The disappearance of all members of a species from Earth. (131)

GLOSSARY

F

fermentation The process by which cells release energy by breaking down food molecules without using oxygen. (223)

fertilization The process in sexual reproduction in which an egg cell and a sperm cell join to form a new cell. (316)

fitness How well an organism can survive and reproduce in its environment. (461)

food chain A series of events in an ecosystem in which organisms transfer energy by eating and by being eaten. (80)

food web The pattern of overlapping feeding relationships or food chains among the various organisms in an ecosystem. (80)

fossil The preserved remains or traces of an organism that lived in the past. (444)

fossil record All the fossils that have been discovered and what scientists have learned from them. (469)

fruit The ripened ovary and other structures of an angiosperm that enclose one or more seeds. (330)

G

gene A sequence of DNA that determines a trait and is passed from parent to offspring. (316)

gene therapy The process of replacing an absent or faulty gene with a normal working gene to treat a disease or medical disorder. (412)

genetic engineering The transfer of a gene from the DNA of one organism into another organism, in order to produce an organism with desired traits. (410)

genome The complete set of genetic information that an organism carries in its DNA. (414)

genotype An organism's genetic makeup, or allele combinations. (374)

genus A taxonomic category that names a group of similar, closely-related organisms. (23)

germination The sprouting of the embryo out of a seed; occurs when the embryo resumes its growth following dormancy. (331)

gland An organ that produces and releases chemicals either through ducts or into the bloodstream. (252, 288)

H

habitat An environment that provides the things a specific organism needs to live, grow, and reproduce. (69)

heredity The passing of traits from parents to offspring. (367)

heterotroph An organism that cannot make its own food and gets food by consuming other living things. (211)

homeostasis The condition in which an organism's internal environment is kept stable in spite of changes in the external environment. (20)

homologous structures Structures that are similar in different species and that have been inherited from a common ancestor. (474)

hormone The chemical produced by an endocrine gland. (252, 346)

host An organism that provides a source of energy or a suitable environment for a parasite to live with, in, or on. (34)

I

inheritance The process by which an offspring receives genes from its parents. (318)

instinct A response to a stimulus that is inborn. (335)

internal fertilization When eggs are fertilized inside a female's body. (339)

interphase The first stage of the cell cycle that takes place before cell division occurs, during which a cell grows and makes a copy of its DNA. (206)

invasive species Species that are not native to a habitat and can out-compete native species in an ecosystem. (134)

invertebrate An animal without a backbone. (50)

K

keystone species A species that influences the survival of many other species in an ecosystem. (129)

L

law of conservation of energy The rule that energy cannot be created or destroyed. (87)

law of conservation of mass The principle that the total amount of matter is neither created nor destroyed during any chemical or physical change. (87)

limiting factor An environmental factor that causes a population to decrease in size. (74)

lymph Fluid that travels through the lymphatic system consisting of water, white blood cells, and dissolved materials. (275)

M

mammal A vertebrate whose body temperature is regulated by its internal heat, and that has skin covered with hair or fur and glands that produce milk to feed its young. (52)

mating system Behavior patterns related to how animals mate. (336)

mechanism The natural process by which something takes place. (451)

meiosis The process that occurs in the formation of sex cells (sperm and egg) by which the number of chromosomes is reduced by half. (381)

messenger RNA Type of RNA that carries copies of instructions for the assembly of amino acids into proteins from DNA to ribosomes in the cytoplasm. (391)

metamorphosis A process in which an animal's body undergoes major changes in shape and form during its life cycle. (351)

microscope An instrument that makes small objects look larger. (174)

migration The regular, seasonal journey of an animal from one place to another and back again. (341)

mitochondria Rod-shaped organelles that convert energy in food molecules to energy the cell can use to carry out its functions. (187)

mitosis The second stage of the cell cycle during which the cell's nucleus divides into two new nuclei and one set of DNA is distributed into each daughter cell. (207, 383)

multicellular Consisting of many cells. (14)

mutation Any change in the DNA of a gene or a chromosome. (400)

mutualism A type of symbiosis in which both species benefit from living together. (114)

N

natural resource Anything naturally occuring in the environment that humans use. (140)

natural selection The process by which organisms that are best adapted to their environment are most likely to survive and reproduce. (453)

negative feedback A process in which a system is turned off by the condition it produces. (290)

nephron Small filtering structure found in the kidneys that removes wastes from blood and produces urine. (279)

neuron A cell that carries information through the nervous system. (283)

niche How an organism makes its living and interacts with the biotic and abiotic factors in its habitat. (110)

nonvascular plants A low-growing plant that lacks true vascular tissue for transporting materials. (49)

nucleus In cells, a large oval organelle that contains the cell's genetic material in the form of DNA and controls many of the cell's activities. (186)

nutrients Substances in food that provide the raw materials and energy needed for an organism to carry out its essential processes. (259)

O

organ A body structure that is composed of different kinds of tissues that work together. (50, 241)

organ system A group of organs that work together to perform a major function. (241)

organelle A tiny cell structure that carries out a specific function within the cell. (183)

organism A living thing. (13, 69)

osmosis The diffusion of water molecules across a selectively permeable membrane. (196)

ovule A plant structure in seed plants that produces the female gametophyte; contains an egg cell. (329)

GLOSSARY

P

parasite An organism that benefits by living with, on, or in a host in a parasitism interaction. (39)

parasitism A type of symbiosis in which one organism lives with, on, or in a host and harms it. (116)

pedigree A tool that geneticists use to map out the inheritance of traits. (380)

peristalsis Waves of smooth muscle contractions that move food through the esophagus toward the stomach. (262)

phenotype An organism's physical appearance, or visible traits. (374)

pheromone A chemical released by one animal that affects the behavior of another animal of the same species. (337)

photoperiodism A plant's response to seasonal changes in the length of night and day. (347)

photosynthesis The process by which plants and other autotrophs capture and use light energy to make food from carbon dioxide and water. (210)

pioneer species The first species to populate an area during succession. (119)

pollination The transfer of pollen from male reproductive structures to female reproductive structures in plants. (327)

population All the members of one species living in the same area. (71)

precipitation Any form of water that falls from clouds and reaches Earth's surface as rain, snow, sleet, or hail. (89)

predation An interaction in which one organism kills another for food or nutrients. (112)

probability A number that describes how likely it is that a particular event will occur. (371)

producer An organism that can make its own food. (77)

protein Large organic molecule made of carbon, hydrogen, oxygen, nitrogen, and sometimes sulfur. (484)

protein synthesis The process by which amino acids link together to form proteins. (390)

protist A eukaryotic organism that cannot be classified as an animal, plant, or fungus. (39)

R

recessive allele An allele that is hidden whenever the dominant allele is present. (369)

reflex An automatic response that occurs rapidly and without conscious control. (287)

replication The process by which a cell makes a copy of the DNA in its nucleus before cell division. (206)

response An action or change in behavior that occurs as a result of a stimulus. (15, 251)

S

saliva A fluid produced in the mouth that aids in mechanical and chemical digestion. (263)

scientific theory A well-tested explanation for a wide range of observations or experimental results. (448)

selectively permeable A property of cell membranes that allows some substances to pass across it, while others cannot. (194)

sex chromosomes The pair of chromosomes carrying genes that determine whether a person is biologically male or female. (398)

sex-linked gene A gene carried on a sex chromosome. (401)

sexual reproduction A reproductive process that involves two parents that combine their genetic material to produce a new organism which differs from both parents. (316)

sexual selection A type of natural selection that acts on an organism's ability to get the best possible mate. (465)

species A group of similar organisms that can mate with each other and produce offspring that can also mate and reproduce. (23, 441)

spinal cord A thick column of nervous tissue that links the brain to nerves in the body. (285)

spontaneous generation The mistaken idea that living things arise from nonliving sources. (16)

stimulus Any change or signal in the environment that can make an organism react in some way. (15, 251)

stress The reaction of a person's body to potentially threatening, challenging, or disturbing events. (256)

succession The series of predictable changes that occur in a community over time. (119)

sustainability The ability of an ecosystem to maintain bioversity and production indefinitely. (145)

symbiosis Any relationship in which two species live closely together and that benefits at least one of the species. (114)

synapse The junction where one neuron can transfer an impulse to the next structure. (284)

T

taxonomy The scientific study of how living things are classified. (24)

tissue A group of similar cells that perform a specific function. (48, 240)

trait A specific characteristic that an organism can pass to its offspring through its genes. (316)

transfer RNA Type of RNA in the cytoplasm that carries an amino acid to the ribosome during protein synthesis. (391)

tropism A plant's growth response toward or away from a stimulus. (346)

U

unicellular Made of a single cell. (14)

V

vaccine A substance used in a vaccination that consists of pathogens that have been weakened or killed but can still trigger the body to produce chemicals that destroy the pathogens. (34)

vacuole A sac-like organelle that stores water, food, and other materials. (188)

variation Any difference between individuals of the same species. (397)

vascular plants A plant that has true vascular tissue for transporting materials. (48)

vein A blood vessel that carries blood back to the heart. (273)

vertebrate An animal with a backbone. (50)

virus A tiny, nonliving particle that enters and then reproduces inside a living cell. (34)

Z

zygote A fertilized egg, produced by the joining of a sperm and an egg. (326)

INDEX
Page numbers for key terms are printed in boldface type.

INDEX

W

Z

CREDITS

Text Acknowledgments

The following selections appear in this grade level of Elevate Science. Some selections may appear online only.

Pearson Education

"Call of the Deep Wilds" by Helen Strahinich/Pearson Education.

Public Domain

"On the Origin of Species" by Charles Darwin (1859); "A Bird Came Down the Walk", from Poems by Emily Dickinson: Second Series (1891); "The Tell Tale Heart" by Edgar Allen Poe (1843); "Winter Trees" by William Carlos Williams from Sour Grapes: A Book of Poems (Boston: The Four Seas Company, 1921).

Society for Science & the Public

"Wolf Species Shake-Up" by Laurel Hamers, "U.S. Army Developing High-Tech Underwear" by Kathiann Kowalski. Reprinted with Permission of Science News for Students.

Photographs

Covers:

Front Cover: Don Johnston/All Canada Photos/Getty Images
Back Cover: Marinello/DigitalVision Vectors/Getty Images

Front Matter

iv: Nick Lundgren/Shutterstock; vi: Michael Nichols/National Geographic/Getty Images; vii: Brian J. Skerry/National Geographic/Getty Images; viii: Kong Act/Shutterstock; ix: NIBSC/Science Photo Library/Getty Images; x: Stefan Schurr/Getty Images; xi: Kelly vanDellen/Alamy Stock Photo; xii: Dr P. Marazzi/Science Source; xiii: Tonyz20/Shutterstock

Instructional Segment 1

xvi: Westend61/Getty Images; 002 BR: Sarah Fields Photography/Shutterstock; 002 CL: Ronnie Gregory/EyeEm/Getty Images; 002 CR: Peter Essick/Aurora Photos/Alamy Stock Photo; 003: Mike Flippo/Shutterstock; 004 BL: David Courtenay/Getty Images; 004 BR: MARK RALSTON/AFP/Getty Images; 006 BL: Suzanne L and Joseph T. Collins/Getty Images; 006 BR: Kevin Schafer/Nature Picture Library.

Topic 1

008: Michael Nichols/National Geographic/Getty Images; 010: Jutta Klee/Getty Images; 012: Wonderful-Earth.Net/Alamy Stock Photo; 014 B: Edo Schmidt/Alamy Stock Photo; 014 CR: Cdascher/Getty Images; 014 TL: Ed Reschke/Getty Images; 015 B: Edo Schmidt/Alamy Stock Photo; 015 CL: SCIENCE PICTURES LIMITED/SCIENCE PHOTO LIBRARY/Getty Images; 015 TR: Tom Grill/Corbis/Glow Images; 020: Roberta Olenick/All Canada Photos/Alamy Stock Photo; 023: Antonio Camacho/Getty Images; 024: Holly Kuchera/Shutterstock; 026 C: Robert Wyatt/Alamy Stock Photo; 026 CL: JohnatAPW/Fotolia; 026 CR: Arco Images GmbH/Alamy Stock Photo; 027: Wayne Lynch/All Canada Photos/Getty Images; 029 C: Kirsanov Valeriy Vladimirovich/Shutterstock; 029 CL: Christopher Mills/Alamy Stock Photo; 029 T: Steve

Bloom Images/Alamy Stock Photo; 031 B: Prisma by Dukas Presseagentur GmbH/Alamy Stock Photo; 031 T: Critterbiz/Shutterstock; 032: M. I. Walker/Science Source; 034 BCL: Lee D. Simon/Science Source; 034 CL: Cultura RM/Alamy Stock Photo; 034 TL: James Cavallini/Science Source; 036 BCL: Sebastian Kaulitzki/Shutterstock; 036 TCL: Chris Bjornberg/Science Source; 036 TL: VEM/Science Source; 037: B. Murton/Southampton Oceanography Centre/Science Source; 038: Andrew Syre/Science Source; 039 BC: Moment Open/Getty Images; 039 BL: Royaltystockphoto/123RF; 039 BR: Paul Glendell/Alamy Stock Photo; 041 BC: Jackan/Fotolia; 041 BR: Steve Gschmeissner/Science Photo Library/Getty Images; 041 CL: Domenico Tondini/Alamy Stock Photo; 041 CR: Unicusx/Fotolia; 041 TR: Eye of Science/Science Source; 044: Matthew Oldfield Underwater Photography/Alamy Stock Photo; 047 TL: Kateko/Shutterstock; 047 TR: Digital Paradise/Shutterstock; 048 T: NigelSpiers/Shutterstock; 048 TC: Valzan/Shutterstock; 048 TL: StudioByTheSea/Shutterstock; 048 TR: Guliveris/Shutterstock; 050 BC: Ashley Cooper/Getty Images; 050 BL: Silvia Iordache/Shutterstock; 050 BR: Andrew Burgess/Shutterstock; 051 BCR: Edgieus/Shutterstock; 051 BR: Stubblefield Photography/Shutterstock; 051 C: Igor Sirbu/Shuterstock; 051 CL: Royaltystockphoto/Shutterstock; 051 TCR: Harmonia101/123RF; 051 TR: 2009fotofriends/Shutterstock; 052 BL: WaterFrame/Alamy Stock Photo; 052 BR: Arto Hakola/Shutterstock; 052 C: Robert W. Ginn/Alamy Stock Photo; 052 CL: Dinda Yulianto/Shutterstock; 052 CR: Kathy Kay/Shutterstock; 053 BC: Audrey Snider-Bell/Shutterstock; 053 BCR: Jay Ondreicka/Shutterstock; 053 BR: Oleg Nekhaev/Shutterstock; 053 CL: Jim Cumming/Shutterstock; 053 TC: BMCL/Shutterstock; 053 TCR: John Downs/redbrickstock/Alamy Stock Photo; 053 TL: Worldswildlifewonders/Shutterstock; 053 TR: Bernd Wolter/Shutterstock; 054 C: Rudmer Zwerver/Shutterstock; 054 CL: Mark Boulton/Alamy Stock Photo; 054 CR: Vladimir Wrangel/Shutterstock; 054 TC: SuperStock/Alamy Stock Photo; 054 TR: Julia Golosiy/Shutterstock; 058 TL: Marek Mis/Science Source; 058 TR: Lebendkulturen.de/Shutterstock; 060: BSIP SA/Alamy Stock Photo; 061 BC: The Natural History Museum/Alamy Stock Photo; 061 BL: Cultura RM/Alamy Stock Photo; 061 BR: Zoonar GmbH/Alamy Stock Photo;

Topic 2

064: Brian J. Skerry/National Geographic/Getty Images; 066: Helen H. Richardson/The Denver Post/Getty Images; 068: Hartrey Media/Shutterstock; 070: David Litman/Shutterstock; 073: Martin Harvey/Alamy Stock Photo; 074: Awie Badenhorst/Alamy Stock Photo; 076: Design Pics/Getty Images; 081 BC: Ken Kistler/Shutterstock; 081 BCR: National Geographic Creative/Alamy Stock Photo; 081 Bkgrd: Moelyn Photos/Getty Images; 081 BL: Ashley Cooper/Alamy Stock Photo; 081 CL: IrinaK/Shutterstock; 081 CR: Anthony Mercieca/Science Source; 081 TC: Davies and Starr/Getty Images; 081 TL: Audrey Snider-Bell/Shutterstock; 081 TR: Jim Cumming/Getty Images; 083: Hal Beral/VWPics/AGE Fotostock; 085 Bkgrd: Christopher Berkey/EPA/Alamy Stock Photo; 085 CR: STILLFX/Shutterstock; 085 TR: Christoph Gertler/Bangor University; 086: Somkiet Poomsiripaiboon/Shutterstock; 088: Paul Lemke/Fotolia; 090 Bkgrd: Jovannig/Fotolia; 090 BL: Cvalle/Shutterstock; 090 BR: Aleksander Bolbot/Getty Images; 091 BC: Danny Frank/Shutterstock; 091 BL: Steven Widoff/

CREDITS

Topic 6

310: Kelly vanDellen/Alamy Stock Photo; 312: Rickyd/Shutterstock; 315 Bkgrd: Draleksun/Fotolia; 315 C: Biosphoto/Superstock; 315 CL: Alan J. S. Weaving/ardea/AGE Fotostock; 316 CL: Laurent Geslin/Nature Picture Library; 316 TL: cbimages/Alamy Stock Photo; 316: Bill & Brigitte Clough/Design Pics Inc/Alamy Stock Photo; 318: Les Gibbon/Alamy Stock Photo; 319 BL: Sujata Jana/EyeEm/Getty Images; 320: Kadmy/Fotolia; 321: Danita Delimont/Alamy Stock Photo; 322: Kali9/Getty Images; 324: Gino Santa Maria/Shutterstock; 326: Blickwinkel/Alamy Stock Photo; 328 B: Inga Spence/Alamy Stock Photo; 328 CR: Barsan ATTILA/Shutterstock; 329 C: WILDLIFE GmbH/Alamy Stock Photo; 329 TR: Krystyna Szulecka/Alamy Stock Photo; 333 CR: NASA Images; 333 TR: NASA; 334: Jaynes Gallery/Danita Delimont/Alamy Stock Photo; 337: Steve Shinn/Alamy Stock Photo; 338: Kitch Bain/Shutterstock; 339: Tony Wu/Nature Picture Library; 340 C: Morley Read/Alamy Stock Photo; 340 B: Tony Wu/Nature Picture Library; 343 B: Tim Laman/Nature Picture Library; 343 CR: Tim Laman/Nature Picture Library; 344: Bill Gorum/Alamy Stock Photo; 346 BC: Cathy Melloan/Alamy Stock Photo; 346 BL: Martin Shields/Alamy Stock Photo; 346 BR: Haru/Shutterstock; 347 BL: Patjo/Shutterstock; 347 BR: Artens/Shutterstock; 348: Panuwat Kanisarn/Shutterstock; 351: Alex Staroseltsev/Shutterstock; 356: Nina B/Shutterstock

Topic 7

362: Dr P. Marazzi/Science Source; 365 Bkgrd: Tim Gainey/Alamy Stock Photo; 365 TR: Luis Abrantes/Shutterstock; 367: Jeff Goulden/Getty Images; 370: Martin Shields/Alamy Stock Photo; 371: James Steidl/Shutterstock; 372: Martin Shields/Alamy Stock Photo; 376: Cuppyuppycake Creative/Getty Images; 385 BR: MixAll Studio Creative/Getty Images; 385 TR: Miodrag Gajic/Getty Images; 387: UpperCut Images/Alamy Stock Photo; 395: Panther Media GmbH/Alamy Stock Photo; 396: Marc Moritsch/National Geographic Creative/Alamy Stock Photo; 398: Power and Syred/Science Source; 401: Eye of Science/Science Source; 402 BC: D. Kucharski & K. Kucharska/Shutterstock; 402 BR: Dragon Images/Shutterstock; 403: Aquapix/Shutterstock; 405: BIOPHOTO ASSOCIATES/Getty Images; 406: Inga Ivanova/Shutterstock; 408: Eriklam/123RF; 410: Reuters/Alamy Stock Photo; 412 BL: Eye of Science/Science Source; 412 TR: Coneyl Jay/Getty Images; 413: Clive Gee/AP Images; 414: M. Watson/Ardea/AGE Fotostock; 422: Sheilaf2002/Fotolia; 423: Eurobanks/Fotolia

Instructional Segment 4

430 B: Science Stock Photography/Science Source; 430 TCL: Sinclair Stammers/Science Source; 430 TL: Sabena Jane Blackbird/Alamy Stock Photo; 431 B: The Natural History Museum/Alamy Stock Photo; 431 T: Georg Gerster/Science Source; 432 B: Brian J. Skerry/Getty Images; 432 T: Mikkel Juul Jensen/Science Source; 433 L: iStock/Getty Images; 433 R: Moose henderson/Shutterstock.

Topic 8

436: Tonyz20/Shutterstock; 437: John Cancalosi/Alamy Stock Photo; 438: Blickwinkel/Alamy Stock Photo; 441 Bkgrd: Jo Crebbin/Shutterstock; 441 CL: Loop Images Ltd/Alamy Stock Photo; 442: Fototeca Gilardi/AKG Images; 444 T: Holmes Garden Photos/Alamy Stock Photo; 444 TCL: Russell Shively/Shutterstock; 446 BC: Westend61/Getty Images; 446 BR: Brian Kushner/Alamy Stock Photo; 450: Visual China Group/Getty Images; 452 TC: Pises Tungittipokai/Shutterstock; 452 TL: Nature Photographers Ltd/Alamy Stock Photo; 452 TR: Oli Scarff/AFP/Getty Images; 453: Nature Photographers Ltd/Alamy Stock Photo; 454: IrinaK/Shutterstock; 456: Kali9/Getty Images; 457 TC: Patricia Isaza; 457 TL: Zeljko Radojko/Shutterstock; 458: IrinaK/Shutterstock; 459 BCR: All Canada Photos/Alamy Stock Photo; 459 TCR: REUTERS/Ulises Rodriguez/Alamy Stock Photo; 460: imageBROKER/Alamy Stock Photo; 465: Blickwinkel/Alamy Stock Photo; 466 BC: Sailorr/Shutterstock; 466 TC: Bazzano Photography/Alamy Stock Photo; 466 TR: Angel DiBilio/Shutterstock; 468: Martin Shields/Alamy Stock Photo; 469: Vodolaz/Fotolia; 470 BC: YAY Media AS/Alamy Stock Photo; 470 BR: Wwing/Getty Images; 471 BC: Scott Camazine/Alamy Stock Photo; 471 BL: The Science Picture Company/Alamy Stock Photo; 471 BR: Fabian von Poser/Getty Images; 472: Bildagentur Zoonar GmbH/Shutterstock; 474 BC: Steve Vidler/Alamy Stock Photo; 474 BR: Pedro Bernardo/Shutterstock; 477 CR: Barry Mansell/Nature Picture Library; 477 TR: Michelle Gilders/Alamy Stock Photo; 478 B: Wolfgang Pölzer/Alamy Stock Photo; 478 BR: Mark Carwardine/Getty Images; 478 CL: Francois Gohier/VWPics/Alamy Stock Photo; 480: WaterFrame/Alamy Stock Photo; 485: Abeselom Zerit/Shutterstock; 486: Pallava Bagla/Getty Images; 489 B: Don Johnston/Getty Images; 489 CR: BGSmith/Shutterstock; 491: John Cancalosi/Science Source; 494 BL: Gallinago_media/Shutterstock; 494 BR: CLS Digital Arts/Shutterstock; 495: J Hindman/Shutterstock

End Matter

500 BCL: Africa Studio/Shutterstock; 500 BL: Jeff Rotman/Alamy Stock Photo; 500 TCL: Nicola Tree/Getty Images; 500 TL: WaterFrame/Alamy Stock Photo; 501: Regan Geeseman/NASA; 502: Grant Faint/Getty Images; 503 BR: Pearson Education Ltd.; 504: Pearson Education Ltd.; 505 CR: Pearson Education Ltd.; 506: Pearson Education Ltd.; 509: Ross Armstrong/Alamy Stock Photo; 510: Geoz/Alamy Stock Photo; 511: Martin Shields/Alamy Stock Photo; 513 BCL: Philippe Plailly & Elisabeth Daynes/Science Source; 514 BL: EHStockphoto/Shutterstock; 515 BR: Javier Larrea/AGE Fotostock; 515 CR: Cyndi Monaghan/Getty Images

Take Notes

Take Notes

Use this space for recording notes and sketching out ideas.

Take Notes

Use this space for recording notes and sketching out ideas.

Take Notes